Get Paid to Play

EVERY STUDENT ATHLETE'S GUIDE TO OVER $1 MILLION IN COLLEGE SCHOLARSHIPS

Nancy Nitardy

KAPLAN)

PUBLISHING

New York

Vice President and Publisher: Maureen McMahon
Editorial Director: Jennifer Farthing
Acquistions Editor: Megan Gilbert
Development Editor: Cynthia Ierardo
Production Editor: Julio Espin
Production Designer: Ivelisse Robles Marrero
Typesetter: the dotted i
Cover Designer: Carly Schnur

Published by Kaplan Publishing, a division of Kaplan, Inc.
1 Liberty Plaza, 24th Floor
New York, NY 10006

August 2007
07 08 09   10 9 8 7 6 5 4 3 2 1

ISBN 13: 978-1-4195-9407-6

contents

Chapter 11 Nonathletic Scholarships

ABOUT THE AUTHOR Nancy Nitardy has 14 years of head coaching experience at NCAA Division I institutions, including Indiana University, Harvard University, and Dartmouth College. She has presented at high schools across the country and at national college counseling annual conferences, including the College Board's 2005 and 2006 National Forums. She was a two-time U.S. Olympic Trial Qualifier and an 18-time Division I College All-American while on a full athletic scholarship at the University of South Carolina. Nancy grew up in Oswego, New York. Currently residing in Austin, TX, she travels across the country presenting on college athletic recruiting and works with families one on one connecting the athlete with college coaches.

Introduction

· ·

Participating in college athletics is a blast! If you like high school sports, you are going to love college sports. Not every high school athlete will get the chance to play at the next level, but for those who really want to, there are colleges out there that will offer you the opportunity to participate.

Get Paid to Play will educate you on the recruiting process, also known as the "recruiting game." Although college athletic recruiting can seem like a challenging game, you the athlete have more control over it than you might think. Earning financial assistance can be a lengthy and often confusing process, so this book will guide you through it and help you "win the game" by explaining how to earn financial assistance for your college education.

Chapters 1, 2, and 3 fill you in on the various athletic associations, the scholarship opportunities, and the various recruiting rules and regulations guiding each association, including academic eligibility requirements. You will learn a tremendous amount of information on scholarships, including who controls the money and what you as an athlete can and cannot do during the recruiting process.

Chapters 4, 5, and 6 will help you determine what level(s) you can compete at, what steps to take during your college search, and what relationships to build along the way. A year-by-year check list of academic and athletic priorities is provided to keep you on track during high school. Starting your college search early will open more doors and will leave you better prepared when making your final decision during senior year.

Chapter 7 provides the basic steps athletes should take to begin and complete the recruiting process. Sample letters and resumes are provided as well as advice on making your athletic video to share with coaches. You will learn about where and how coaches recruit and what you can do to increase your exposure to college coaches. This is a must-read chapter for all athletes.

Chapter 8 provides a wealth of information on making college visits, from how to plan the trip to important people to meet on campus, and essential questions to ask during your visit. It is highly recommended that you make college visits prior to your senior year, especially if you are an athlete. If you want to apply for an athletic scholarship, your number one priority is meeting the coach and touring the athletic facilities. If you are even considering playing college sports, meeting the coach is an absolute must.

Chapters 9 and 10 wrap up your college search process with information on the admissions process, including what to do with your application and how ultimately to choose the best school for you. If you use the tools provided in this book, you will be able to make a well-informed decision about where you will spend the next four or five years of your life.

Chapter 11 gives a brief description of non-athletic fiancial aid available to any student searching for assistance with paying for college. When athletic scholarships are not available these options are. Many of these athletic related scholarships offered by corporations and communities are listed in the scholarship listings at the back of this book.

So in summary, don't sit back and wait for coaches to find you—take the initiative! Research schools, contact coaches, ask lots of questions, and follow your heart. In the end, you *can* win—by getting your college education paid for while playing the sport you love.

Your College Athletic Options

You might be surprised to know that in this country, there are over 1,600 men's and 1,600 women's varsity basketball programs, more than 1,100 men's and women's varsity soccer programs, and 1,400 baseball and softball programs at the college level. About two-thirds of these colleges offer athletic scholarships. Of the over 1,500 American colleges offering varsity women's volleyball programs, more than 1,000 can offer athletic scholarships. Colleges that do not offer athletic scholarships offer institutional scholarships and grants. Opportunities to play sports in college are far-reaching and varied.

You are most likely familiar with NCAA Division I athletics because of the media exposure Division I universities receive, but in most sports, less than 30 percent of athletic scholarships are at the NCAA Division I level. In this chapter, we will go over the various college athletic opportunities available, compare each level, and help you understand who does and does not offer athletic scholarships. Not every high school athlete can earn a scholarship to play college sports, but if you are an athlete and want to find a team to compete for, a scholarship is likely out there for you. Whether you can get paid to play by earning an athletic scholarship or receive other financial assistance and still be able to play is one of the questions we will answer in this book.

ATHLETIC ASSOCIATIONS

There are three different college athletic associations in the United States, and all three are allowed to offer athletic scholarships. The largest and most widely recognized is the National Collegiate Athletic Association (NCAA). Within the NCAA are three divisions: Division I, Division II, and Division III. The NCAA members are four-year colleges where students earn a bachelor's degree. Another association with four-year programs is the National Association of Intercollegiate

Athletics (NAIA). The third athletic association available to athletes is the National Junior College Athletic Association (NJCAA), which consists of two-year colleges where students earn an associate's degree. Like schools in the NCAA, NJCAA schools compete at the Division I, II, or III level.

Colleges and universities join one of these associations and compete against other members in that association. Except for Division III colleges, members of these associations may offer athletic scholarships. Although Division III institutions do not award athletic scholarships, students have access to other money, including grants, merit scholarships, and loans, for which many athletes qualify.

What Level of Winning Matters to You?

Overall, every opportunity to play college sports has a tremendous amount of excitement and competitiveness associated with it. Winning a championship means being the best at that level of play. You need to determine which level of athletics fits best with your future life goals. If just being on a team is okay with you, then you can find plenty of opportunities to do just that. If earning a scholarship and playing on a nationally recognized team is your goal, then that could be a possibility, too. You can make a better decision once you know your options, so read on and find out what might be out there for you. Let's begin by looking at four-year colleges and then at NJCAA two-year degree colleges.

NCAA MEMBERS

The NCAA is divided into three different levels of competition: Division I, II, and III. A school chooses to be a member of a Division by committing to financial sponsorship of a certain number of sports at that level and by agreeing to follow the Division's rules and regulations in areas such as recruiting and academic eligibility.

NCAA Division I Membership Criteria

To be a Division I institution, a college needs to commit to sponsoring seven men's teams and seven women's teams, two of which must be team sports. A minimum number of athletic scholarships must be awarded for the college to stay at the Division I level, and it must commit to a minimum number of competitions and participants in each sport.

The amount of funding the institution commits to athletics programs will affect the number of teams it sponsors, the number of athletic scholarships it offers, and which teams receive more funding. Some teams may not receive more than the minimum number of scholarships required by the NCAA, while others may receive the maximum allowed. Ivy League schools compete at the Division I level, but they do not offer athletic scholarships (yet some offer over 30 different varsity sports).

THE UNIVERSITY PRESIDENT AND THE SCHOOL BOARD (E.G. TRUSTEES, BOARD OF OVERSEERS), NOT THE ATHLETIC DIRECTOR, MAKE THE FINAL DECISION AS TO WHAT LEVEL THE SCHOOL WILL COMPETE. The same holds true for the conference a college joins. The school makes both decisions and then either funds the programs with institutional money (just as it does academic departments) or expects the athletic department to support the teams with the revenue it produces.

Many athletes in the Ivy League do receive need-based financial aid from the institution, which could be more than an athletic scholarship would be. On the other hand, a school like the University of Texas, which offers athletic scholarships in all of their sports, has 16 varsity teams and provides the maximum number of scholarships allowed by the NCAA for each team. Because of this support, the Texas teams compete for a national championship in most of their sponsored sports every year.

NCAA Division II Membership Criteria

To be a member of Division II, a college must sponsor a minimum of four men's and four women's sports, at least two of which must be team sports. It must also follow the association guidelines for membership, including a minimum number of competitions against Division II schools and a minimum number of participants in athletics. The division has its own set of recruiting guidelines and academic eligibility requirements, which are discussed later in this chapter.

NCAA Division III Membership Criteria

To be a member of Division III, a college must sponsor a minimum of five men's and five women's sports, at least two of which must be team sports. The school must compete against a minimum number of Division III schools within their region and maintain a minimum number of participants in athletics. Colleges must follow the division's recruiting rules and regulations, which are minimal for Division III teams and emphasize the educational experience for their athletes.

The major restriction that Division III athletic programs have is that they cannot award athletic scholarships. In fact, coaches are not supposed to have any connection with the financial aid office. Athletes choosing this level of play may not receive athletically related financial aid, but many receive institutional scholarships and grant money based on merit or financial need. The majority of coaches at Division III schools are hired as faculty members and as coaches. They can recruit but have small budgets and rely more on athletes contacting them with interest in the college. The coaches of the top teams in Division III usually spend a lot of their own time and money recruiting.

For example, a former baseball and basketball coach at the State University of New York at Oswego, a Division III member, often traveled to New York City and Long Island to recruit. He would stay at his mother's house in Brooklyn to cut expenses. His teams won the conference championships and made it to the NCAA playoffs with the help of the athletes he found on his recruiting trips. Had his mother not lived in Brooklyn, he might not have been able to afford those recruiting trips, and his teams might not have been as strong.

Competitiveness of the NCAA Divisions

The top Division I teams are usually fully funded, meaning they have the maximum number of scholarships allowed by NCAA rules, but as indicated earlier, some programs are better funded than others. Just because a team is competing at the Division I level does not mean that they are better than a Division II or III team. For example, there are 311 Division I women's volleyball programs in the United States. The top 100 are better funded than the bottom 100; thus, the top teams are more competitive within the division. Of the 269 Division II volleyball programs, the top 50 (or more) are probably better funded than the bottom 100 Division I teams. Thus, these Division II teams can compete against the Division I teams. Of the 410 Division III programs, the top 20 can compete with the bottom Division I teams.

As you can see from Figure 1.1, there are more Division III programs than Division I or II programs in most sports. The Division III level offers tremendous opportunities for athletes to continue to compete in college for the love of the game. If you contact a Division III coach and have a solid academic record, you will probably end up with a great opportunity to join a team and may even receive a wonderful financial aid package. In essence, getting paid to play.

THE NCAA DIVISION I ATHLETIC EXPERIENCE

NCAA Division I athletic programs are considered the highest level of college athletics. These programs tend to have the largest budgets for recruiting, athletic scholarships, facilities, and coaches. Along with all of this comes a great deal of pressure on the coaches, the athletes, and the athletic departments. You will definitely get great competition experience, excellent training facilities, top-level coaches, and academic support, but you will also need to perform, both on the field and in the classroom. If you make a Division I team, you will eat, sleep, walk, and talk your sport.

If you are lucky enough to receive an athletic scholarship from a Division I athletic department, be sure you clearly understand that you are getting paid to play. You will have to practice and compete at a high level to maintain your spot on the team. You will need to stay in shape, maintain academic eligibility, and compete year-round.

There is rarely an off-season. Fall sports have spring training, and spring sports have fall training. Summers are for improving your athletic prowess, not vacationing. Many Division I athletes use

■ Figure 1.1: NCAA Sponsored Sports List (as of August 1, 2006) ■

Sport	Men's			Women's		
	Div I	Div II	Div III	Div I	Div II	Div III
Baseball	286	233	359			
Basketball	326	283	395	324	281	281
Bowling				17	15	5
Cross Country	303	229	349	323	260	374
Equestrian				9	2	25
Fencing	20	3	12	25	1	17
Field Hockey				77	26	154
Football (I-A 117) (I-AA 118)	235	155	231			
Golf	289	210	273	232	125	143
Gymnastics	17	0	2	64	6	15
Ice Hockey	58	7	68	32	2	42
Lacrosse	56	32	132	80	36	157
Rifle (Mixed Teams I-18, II-2, III-7)	7	0	3	10	0	3
Rowing				86	15	42
Skiing	14	8	14	16	9	15
Soccer	199	159	385	301	213	406
Softball				265	257	391
Swimming	139	51	189	189	72	236
Tennis	264	170	311	310	213	360
Track, Indoor	243	107	221	291	113	229
Track, Outdoor	263	152	249	298	161	259
Volleyball	22	15	43	311	269	410
Water Polo	21	9	16	31	10	20
Wrestling	87	42	97			

their college's weight-training facilities for strength building, staying on campus during the summer to work out while employed at the institution's sports camps and taking summer school classes. At the end of the spring semester, coaches will give you a summer training program and expect you to do it. If you don't, you could lose your spot on the team as a starter, or worse yet, get cut from the team altogether—regardless of your scholarship status. Just because you are on scholarship does not make you immune to being cut.

IF YOU ARE PLAYING IN NCAA DIVISON I ATHLETIC, GET READY TO EAT, SLEEP, WALK, AND TALK YOUR SPORT. If on scholarship, you are getting paid to play. You are now working for your college education.

Benefits of Division I Athletics

If you earn the opportunity to play for a Division I program, you will rarely have to buy another practice outfit or piece of equipment. You may get to travel to some exciting places for competition or training camps. You have access to the best training and competition facilities in the country. You will have access to the college's tutoring program, have your own academic advisor, and may have access to an athletic academic center fully outfitted with the latest technology. On your recruiting visit, coaches will be sure to show you these facilities and introduce you to the support staff, if the school has them. If not, you might want to ask about academic support and team funding.

Playing Time

During your freshman year at a Division I college, one of the biggest shocks you (and your parents) will most likely experience will be the amount of playing time you get. In high school, you may have started for the varsity team the last three years, but in college, you may find yourself sitting on the bench. The fact of the matter is that at this level—especially in team sports—freshmen rarely have starting positions. You should be prepared to earn your spot on your team even if you are a scholarship athlete. In team sports, whether or not you play is up to the coaching staff. Starters are selected based on performance at practice and previous playing experience. Returning letter winners know the offense and defense better and thus tend to get starting roles. In individual sports, your level of performance will determine whether or not you compete. If you are fast, you'll compete in the meet. If you have the lowest round in golf, you'll tee off. In tennis, if you win the practice ladder, you'll compete in matches.

Lack of playing time might be hard for you and your parents to understand, especially if you have spent the last few years starring on your high school team and your parents were in the stands

Some athletes do not adjust well to the pressure of playing for a Division I team or the frustration that comes with sitting on the bench, leading them to quit their sport after their freshman year or to transfer to a different division that better fits their level of commitment. Realizing that you're unhappy is okay. Talk to the coach first, then make your decision. If you begin to think about transferring, be sure you know the association's and division's rules so you don't lose your eligibility and end up sitting out another year.

for every game. Be patient, work hard, and when juniors and seniors ahead of you graduate, you may earn the chance to take over their vacated positions. If you are truly unhappy, you can always transfer (you will find more information on transferring later in this chapter), but remember, at the next school, you will have to start all over trying to earn a starting position.

"Redshirting"

During the recruiting process, coaches may mention "redshirting." Redshirting means that, as an incoming freshman, you may be asked just to practice for the first year and sit out competition. Athletes at four-year institutions have five years to complete four seasons of competition. Athletes at junior colleges have three years to complete two seasons of competition. Therefore, redshirting would make you eligible to compete during your fifth year of enrollment at a four-year college or your third year at a two-year college. Some coaches decide that redshirting you for your first year while you learn their system makes the most sense for the team and for your development as an athlete. This is a coach's decision and is often used when young players may fill a team's future needs better than its immediate needs.

An extra year gives you time to adjust to college academics, to develop and learn the team's game philosophy, or recover from an injury. Think of it as substituting a fifth-year senior for a freshman athlete. The fifth year senior is older, wiser, more mature, and better adjusted to the game and college life. Football players are commonly redshirted because coaches know that the real strength of an athlete begins to develop after the baby fat is shed at age 18. A freshman and a fifth-year student are two totally different athletes.

A young swimmer had just qualified for U.S. Swimming's Junior National Championships for the first time during his senior year of high school. Even though the swim coach at the University of Texas could recruit much faster athletes, the coach took a chance on this swimmer and recruited him. The swimmer was a skinny, scrawny kid who redshirted his freshman year, long enough to grow a few inches, get stronger, and develop into one of the world's fastest swimmers. He went on to become an Olympic gold medalist and NCAA champion while competing in college. Being redshirted isn't the worst thing that can happen to you. And if you do get redshirted and perform well academically, you may be able to graduate in four years and use your athletic scholarship to work toward a graduate degree during your fifth year of enrollment.

Little Fish in a Big Pond

What do you want to be, the star of the team as a freshman or fighting for a starting position? How do you want athletics to fit into your college experience, and what are your athletic goals? Some athletes rarely get any playing time in four years but remain on a team out of love for their sport and the camaraderie of being a part of the team. The simple fact is that coaches recruit new and better players every year. In football, as many as 25 new freshmen may be brought in each year—with only 11 players on the field at a time, someone is not going to get to play. A lot of team sports, like baseball, soccer, softball, lacrosse, and volleyball bring in four to six (or more) new players each year.

Even if you are a scholarship athlete, each year, your athletic skills must continue to improve, and you need to be prepared to fight for a starting position. Just as new players join the team, other players leave school, quit the team, or transfer. It's worthwhile to stick with it and fight for an opportunity to play. No matter at what level you'll be playing in college, check out the team's roster to see how many freshmen and how many seniors are on the team. If the senior class is small, ask about the retention of athletes within the program; are athletes quitting, transferring, failing academically, or being cut? If so, then the program may not be functioning very well, and you may want to choose another school.

Two-Sport Athletes

If you are a two-sport athlete, it is very tough to continue with both sports at the Division I or II level, especially if you are a scholarship athlete. Division I and II coaches will want you practicing with the team fall, winter, and spring and taking part in summer training. There is almost always overlap in the seasons of different sports. On the other hand, sports like football and track share athletes well. Training as a running back or receiver is similar to the training of a track runner. The outdoor track season does not conflict with football as much as volleyball would conflict with basketball. Division I two-sport athletes are more common in the Ivy League, because those schools impose additional limits on out-of-season practice time. If you are academically eligible for the Ivy League, you might have a shot at competing in more than one sport.

If you do want to try two sports, you will need to let each coach know that you are interested in both sports and keep in mind that any recruiting rules at the Division I or II level refer to an institution, not individual teams. For example, one rule allows one call per week from an institution during your senior year—you cannot receive a telephone call from the track coach one night and the football coach the next, but you may call a coach any time. Read the NCAA's "Guide for College Bound Student Athletes," located at *www.ncaa.org*, carefully for these rules. (Recruiting rules are covered in Chapter 3.)

Division I Summary

The NCAA Division I experience is intense and requires a huge commitment on your part, but you will have the best of the best in terms of resources, coaching staff, facilities, academic support, and level of competition at most schools. If you want to compete against or with the best athletes in the United States, then consider playing for a Division I program.

THE DIRECTOR'S CUP: DIVISION I

The Director's Cup ranks the overall performance of all Division I members' athletic programs. It takes into account a college's final ranking in 20 varsity sports, 10 women's and 10 men's, and assigns points according to the national ranking in each sport. Figure 1.2 shows the 2006 final results for Division I athletics.

■ Figure 1.2: 2006 Division I Director's Cup Results ■

Overall Place	College or University
1	Stanford University
2	University of California Los Angeles
3	University of Texas
4	University of North Carolina
5	University of Florida
6	University of Notre Dame
7	University of California Berkeley
8	Duke University
9	University of Georgia
10	University of Southern California
11	University of Arizona
12	Ohio State University
13	Arizona State University
14	University of Tennessee
15	Penn State University
16	University of Minnesota
17	Florida State University
18	University of Washington
19	University of Nebraska
20	Louisiana State University
21	University of Alabama
22	University of Wisconsin
23	Texas A & M University
24	University of Michigan
25	Auburn University

To determine whether you will be happy at this level, you'll have to decide how you want athletics to fit into your college experience and whether the commitment matches your expectations of yourself. You will also have to qualify academically, which can be the toughest part for some athletes. (Academic requirements are covered in Chapter 3.) Remember, you must complete an admissions application and be admitted by the admissions committee as well as meet the NCAA academic requirements to be eligible for Division I athletics and an athletic scholarship.

THE NCAA DIVISION II ATHLETIC EXPERIENCE

Division II colleges and universities tend to have smaller student bodies and offer fewer varsity teams. If you are on an athletic scholarship, you are working for your education, just like Division I athletes. On average, the Division II athletic programs do not have state-of-the-art athletic facilities, but the competition is tough. Your team may not travel cross-country to compete, but you will be expected to stay in shape, stay eligible, and improve as an athlete. Some incredible athletes compete at this level, and some Division II teams can beat Division I teams.

If you were to ask the Lindsey Wilson College (Columbia, Kentucky) soccer team or the Carroll College (Helena, Montana) football team about winning the 2005 NCAA Division II championships, they would tell you that they are national champs. Their excitement is just as genuine as the Division I champions'. Coaches can be just as intense about competing as in Division I but feel less stress over keeping alumni happy. Overall, Division II teams compete at a different level and typically offer fewer resources than teams in Division I, but they may offer more perks than Division III teams.

Benefits of Division II Athletics

Because Division II schools typically have smaller student bodies, you have a chance to get a great education with more individual attention than at some of the larger Division I schools. If your goal is to get a scholarship and significant playing time, you might find more of each at this level than at the Division I level. Within the division, there are different levels of competitiveness. As mentioned earlier, the top Division II teams can compete with some Division I teams, and the bottom Division II teams will have a tough match with some of the best Division III teams.

When you graduate from college, who you have become as a person, what you have learned, and the contacts you have made will help you with any career path you take. Being an athlete will help you learn discipline, time management, dedication, commitment, and goal setting, and you can learn these traits at any level.

THE DIRECTOR'S CUP: DIVISION II

The Director's Cup ranks the overall performance of all Division II members' athletic programs. It takes into account a school's final ranking in 14 varsity sports, 7 women's and 7 men's, and assigns points according to the national ranking in each sport. Figure 1.3 shows the 2006 final rankings for Division II athletics.

■ Figure 1.3: 2006 Division II Director's Cup Results ■

Overall Place	College or University
1	Grand Valley State (MI)
2	Abilene Christian University (TX)
3	University of Nebraska at Omaha
4	Southern Illinois University at Edwardsville
5	California State University at Bakersfield
6	University of California San Diego
7	University of Central Missouri State
8	California State University at Chico
9	Minnesota State University at Mankato
10	Lynn University (FL)
11	University of Massachusetts at Lowell
12	Emporia State University (KA)
13	University of Nebraska at Kearney
14	Seattle Pacific University (WA)
15	Florida Southern College
16	Adams State College (CO)
17	Drury University (MO)
18	Barry University (FL)
19	Northwest Missouri State University
20	University of Tampa (FL)
21	University of West Florida
22	Colorado School of Mines
23	North Dakota State University
24	St. Cloud State University (MN)
25	Western State College (CO)

THE NCAA DIVISION III ATHLETIC EXPERIENCE

If you love to play more than one sport, as many high school athletes do, you should consider Division III athletics. It is easier to be a two-sport athlete at this level. The demands on your time may be less, and the competition and training seasons are more limited. The seasons are limited to fall, winter, and spring with minimal out-of-season expectations. Coaches may recommend a summer training program, but students rarely stay on campus during the summer to train, work in camps, or take summer school classes like Division I athletes.

Because coaches do not have huge budgets to travel across the country in search of recruits, teams are typically made up of athletes from within the state or bordering states. Also, due to limited budgets, teams travel within the immediate region. Because Division III colleges consider athletics a valuable part of one's education but not the highest priority, they do not offer athletic scholarships. Any financial assistance you receive will be between you and the financial aid office and any outside scholarship agencies from whom you earn awards.

Benefits of Division III Athletics

As you can see from the NCAA Sports Sponsorship Summary in Figure 1.1, the NCAA Division III level offers the greatest number of opportunities for athletes to play in college. Because there are no scholarships, the athletic departments' budgets are smaller; also, less money is given to coaches to recruit, and less money is spent on facilities and team travel. This means less stress for everyone involved, including the athletes.

At this level, you may have to supply your own workout gear and equipment. Teams may travel by van or bus but rarely by airplane. You might have to help fund raise for your winter training or spring break road trip. If one of your classes conflicts with practice, a Division III coach will be willing to work with you.

Division III athletes enjoy winning their NCAA Division III national championships just as much as anyone else does. In fact, Division III athletic departments compete for the national Director's Cup, just as Division I and II schools do, and they take great pride in having one of the top athletic departments in the country. Just ask Williams College's (Williamstown, Massachusetts) student-athletes how they feel about winning the 2006 Director's Cup, their 10th win in 11 years, and you will see a whole lot of pride.

THE NATIONAL ASSOCIATION OF INTERCOLLEGIATE ATHLETICS (NAIA)

There are about 300 NAIA member schools and 23 national championship events in 13 different sports. The philosophy of the NAIA is that each school has autonomy and can make its own decisions about sport sponsorship; thus there are no minimum requirements. However, the different

THE DIRECTOR'S CUP: DIVISION III

The Director's Cup ranks the overall performance of all Division III athletic programs. It takes into account a school's final ranking in 18 varsity sports, 9 women's and 9 men's, and assigns points according to the national ranking in each sport. Figure 1.4 shows the 2006 final rankings for Division III athletics.

Figure 1.4: 2006 Division III Director's Cup Results

Overall Place	College or University
1	Williams College (MA)
2	College of New Jersey
3	Middlebury College (VT)
4	Emory University (GA)
5	State University College - Cortland (NY)
6	Tufts University (MA)
7	Washington University (MO)
8	Trinity University (TX)
9	Calvin College (MI)
10	Gustavus Adolphus College (MN)
11	Amherst College (MA)
12	Hope College (MI)
13	De Pauw University (IN)
14	University of Wisconsin - La Crosse
15	Messiah College (PA)
16	Denison University (OH)
17	Claremont -Mudd-Scripps Colleges (CA)
18	Warburg College (IA)
19	Rowan University (NJ)
20	University of Redlands (CA)
21	Bowdoin College (ME)
22	University of Wisconsin - Stevens Point
23	Wheaton College (IL)
24	Salisbury University (MD)
25	Nebraska Wesleyan University

Figure 1.5: NCAA Sponsored Sports List (as of August 1, 2006)

Sport	# of Men's Teams	# of Women's Teams
Baseball	212	—
Basketball Division I	97	96
Basketball Division II	151	158
Cross Country	183	192
Football	94	—
Golf	172	128
Soccer	210	218
Softball	—	204
Swimming and Diving	18	24
Tennis	113	133
Track and Field (Indoors)	124	127
Track and Field (Outdoors)	146	146
Volleyball	—	243
Wrestling	29	—

conferences within the NAIA do have minimum sport sponsorship requirements. NAIA members can offer athletic scholarships and have merit money available for strong academic students. In fact, if recruits are in the top 10 percent of their class or maintain a 3.6 GPA, their academic scholarship award will not count against the athletic department's scholarship allotment.

Benefits of NAIA Athletics

NAIA schools tend to have smaller student bodies, so as in NCAA Division III schools, you will receive more personalized academic attention. Their athletic facilities range from very nice to okay; it depends on the school. Coaches may or may not be under pressure to have successful teams year after year, and they may be faculty members as well as coaches. NAIA coaches have fewer recruiting restrictions, making it easier for you to build a relationship with them. Because there are no restrictions on the number of calls made to athletes, the coach will have unlimited access to you during the recruiting process. This open communication should lead to confidence in your final decision.

Transferring between NAIA schools is easy, because they have very few rules about transferring. The top NAIA schools can compete with the lower-ranked NCAA Division I and II teams in some sports and can be very competitive with most of the top Division III teams. Lewis and Clark State's (Lewiston, Idaho) baseball team felt as though they won a college world series when they took home the 2006 NAIA national championship trophy. Similar to athletes in NCAA Division III programs,

THE DIRECTOR'S CUP: NAIA

The Director's Cup ranks the overall performance of all NAIA members' athletic programs. It takes into account a school's final ranking in 12 varsity sports, 6 women's and 6 men's, and assigns points according to the national ranking in each sport. Figure 1.6 shows the 2006 final rankings for NAIA athletics.

■ **Figure 1.6: 2006 NAIA Director's Cup Results** ■

Overall Place	College or University
1	Azusa Pacific University (CA)
2	Lindenwood University (MO)
3	Lindsey Wilson College (KY)
4	Oklahoma Baptist University
5	Simon Fraser University (Canada)
6	Concordia University (CA)
7	Embry Riddle Aeronautical University (FL)
8	Point Loma Nazarene University (CA)
9	Berry College (GA)
10	Oklahoma City University
11	Savannah College of Art and Design (GA)
12	McKendree College (IL)
13	University of British Columbia (Canada)
14	Missouri Baptist University
15	Cedarville University (OH)
16	Lee University (TN)
17	Indiana Wesleyan University
18	University of the Cumberlands (KY)
19	University of Mobile (AL)
20	Malone College (OH)
21	Morningside College (IA)
22	Vanguard University (CA)
23	California Baptist University
24	The Aquinas Institute (NJ)
25	Hastings College (NE)

many NAIA athletes are from within the state and were probably not highly recruited by NCAA Division I schools. You may feel less pressure playing at an NAIA school, even though you are on scholarship.

THE NATIONAL JUNIOR COLLEGE ATHLETIC ASSOCIATION (NJCAA)

The National Junior College Athletic Association, with its 500 members, has gained a great deal of strength in the past few years due to all the high school students involved in sports who are interested in continuing to compete. Members are two-year colleges where a student graduates with an associate's degree and either goes out into the professional world or transfers to a four-year college to get a bachelor's degree. NJCAA programs are excellent programs that offer athletic scholarships.

Students choose junior colleges for a variety of reasons. Many football and basketball players head to junior colleges to play for two years before transferring to four-year colleges. By choosing NJCAA, they know they have a better chance of getting playing time, because only freshmen and sophomores compete for starting spots. Some students must take this route because they are academically ineligible for NCAA Division I or II athletics. Some want to improve their GPA to get admitted to the four-year college of their choice. A lot of students simply want a two-year associate's degree so they can then head off to pursue a full-time career.

NJCAA Divisions

Like the NCAA, NJCAA offers three divisions of athletic opportunities in many sports. However, the divisions are different when it comes to scholarships. An NJCAA Division I program can offer a full scholarship, which includes tuition, room and board, fees, and books. A Division II program can only offer tuition, fees, and books. The Division III program, like the NCAA Division III, cannot offer any athletic aid. The teams compete for national championships within their divisions, and some of the national championships are even broadcast on television.

During college football's bowl-game month (December), a former A.N. McCallum High School (Austin, Texas) athlete, Ben McMahan, led Trinity Valley Junior College (Athens, Texas) to a win in the 2005 Pilgram's Pride Bowl Game televised on ESPN2. Athletes at this level love the experience of playing and can go on to compete at the NCAA or NAIA level. Many former NJCAA players are on professional teams. In 2006, approximately 145 former NJCAA football players were playing in the NFL, and many professional baseball players had competed in the NJCAA as well. The overall athletic budgets are not what a NCAA Division I budget would be—thus the facilities and other benefits don't compare—but the experience of competing is exciting and well worth a look for many high school athletes.

■ Figure 1.7: NJCAA Sponsored Sports List (as of July 2006) ■

Sport	# of Men's teams	# of Women's teams
Baseball Division I	186	—
Baseball Division II	117	—
Baseball Division III	87	—
Basketball Division I	208	180
Basketball Division II	114	121
Basketball Division III	96	86
Bowling (Coed)	19 Total	19 Total
Cross Country Division I	71	74
Cross Country Division III	35	36
Fast-Pitch Softball Division I	—	153
Fast-Pitch Softball Division II	—	118
Fast-Pitch Softball Division III	—	78
Football	68	—
Golf Division I	40	83
Golf Division II	93	—
Golf Division III	79	—
Ice Hockey	8	—
Indoor Track and Field	51	52
Lacrosse	27	13
Outdoor Track and Field Div. I	44	48
Outdoor Track and Field Div. III	26	25
Soccer Division I	116	106
Soccer Division III	73	58
Swimming and Diving	17	19
Tennis Division I	50	59
Tennis Division III	39	38
Volleyball Division I	—	102
Volleyball Division II	—	113
Volleyball Division III	—	80
Wrestling	41	—

THE MAJORITY OF U.S. OLYMPIC TEAM ATHLETES WHO HAVE ATTENDED COLLEGE COMPETED AT THE DIVISION I LEVEL. On occasion, a Division II athlete makes it to this level, but rarely does a Division III athlete compete at the Olympic level. Yet quite a few former NJCAA athletes are in the NFL.

CHAPTER SUMMARY

If your number one goal is to participate in college athletics, you can find a team that will fit your idea of playing in college. Whether you qualify for an athletic scholarship or other institutional financial aid will depend on your skills and academic record and, in the case of need-based aid, your family's ability to pay. The best way to determine your options is to research the various associations, contact the coaches, and take the initiative to maintain contact with those coaches. (The next few chapters can help you with these tasks.)

Know that once you agree to be a scholarship athlete you are working for your education: you are getting paid to play. You will get some great coaching, excellent competition experience, and state-of-the-art facilities in which to improve your athletic talents, but these benefits may come with a price. You must decide how much of your college life you want to commit to athletics. In the end, pick the school at which you feel most comfortable and where you feel that you can best develop as a person. By understanding the differences among the associations and divisions, you should be able to identify a variety of schools that match your academic and athletic goals. Start early and use the tools provided in this book, and you will find your match.

Understanding Scholarships

A wide variety of college athletic opportunities are available to you, and they all offer some form of financial assistance. You can get paid to play college sports through athletic, academic (institutional merit-based), or community scholarships. Athletic scholarships are awarded by the athletic department at each school, and if you earn one, you must continue to play. The financial aid office awards the institution's merit money, usually for good grades, test scores, and interest of study. Community scholarships are awarded by community organizations or foundations and national corporations.

This chapter will provide an in-depth discussion of the athletic scholarship—how it works, who makes decisions, the allotments per sport, and what signing an athletic letter of intent means. Because a larger number of athletes end up on institutional, community, and corporate scholarships and grant awards, Chapter 11 will cover these.

ATHLETIC SCHOLARSHIPS

If you are an athlete looking for financial assistance to attend college, coaches are your resource. If athletic scholarships are allowed at an institution, the coach controls the awarding of the money to athletes. The financial aid department awards grants, merit scholarships, and loans. At the Division III level, coaches cannot get involved with the financial aid application, but they may know whom you can talk to in the financial aid office about your award package.

Full and Partial Funding

A school may be fully funded, meaning it can award the full allotment of scholarships allowed by its athletic association, or it may be partially funded. The college, through the athletic conference it belongs to, decides how to award athletic scholarships. Colleges can choose to not offer athletic aid, to offer scholarships equal to in-state tuition only, or to offer just the minimum required by their association for membership.

Offering scholarships is a huge financial commitment on the college's part, so some conferences do not allow their members to offer scholarships even though they compete at a level in which it is allowed. The Ivy League is a perfect example of this. They can award every athlete institutional merit money, federal grants and scholarships, and low-interest loans, none of which is controlled by the coaches but rather by the financial aid office.

Other schools have chosen to give their programs the full allotment of scholarships but at the in-state tuition price. Many California public universities have allotted their coaches a budget for scholarships equal to the dollar amount of a full in-state tuition scholarship. If coaches recruit an out-of-state athlete, they use an amount that equals two athletes from the state of California.

Other colleges fully fund some of their teams but fund other teams at a reduced level. For example, at one time in the Big Ten, there were 14 full scholarships to award swimmers and divers, which was the NCAA Division I allotted amount. Penn State University, which offers 30 varsity teams, only gave their swimming and diving program 11 full scholarships. (Penn State's women's swimming and diving has since switched to the 14 full scholarships allowed and has won three Big Ten titles.) Keep in mind that although a team may be a member of an association where scholarships are allowed, the team does not automatically have athletic scholarships and a huge recruiting budget. Ask the coach about how well the team is funded and, if you are an out-of-state applicant, how that could affect your scholarship.

Allotments

Each association (NCAA, NAIA, and NJCAA) determines the total number of athletic scholarships allowed for each sport. Each institution decides, of the total scholarships allowed, how much money it wants to provide each sport. (Figure 2.1 shows the number of scholarships allowed per sport within each association.) Each college determines which sports best fit its student body. An institution typically chooses to offer and fund the sports that are played within its state at the high school level, the Olympic sports, and the sports that fit the environment or location of the college. For instance, schools in the state of Florida do not offer skiing but do offer golf.

Headcount and Equivalency

The NCAA has headcount sports and equivalency sports. *Headcount* means that only a certain number of athletes on the team can be on scholarship in any given year. An athletic department may not allow a team to exceed that number of athletes on scholarship. For example, if women's basketball is allowed 15 scholarships, the school can have only 15 athletes on the team on scholarship. If a college

◼ Figure 2.1: Scholarship Allotment by Sport, Association, and Division ◼

Sport	NCAA DI-M	NCAA DI-W	NCAA DII-M	NCAA DII-W	NAIA Men	NAIA Women	NJCAA Men	NJCAA Women
Archery	—	5	—	9	—	—	—	—
Badminton	—	6	—	10	—	—	—	—
Baseball	11.7	—	9	—	12	—	24	
Basketball	13	15	10	10	DI-11 DII-6	DI-11 DII-6	16	16
Bowling	—	5	—	5	—	—	—	—
Cross Country	See Track	See Track	See Track	See Track	5	5	30*	30*
Equestrian	—	15	—	—	—	—	—	—
Fencing	4.5	5	4.5	4.5	—	—	—	—
Field Hockey	—	12		6.3	—	—	—	—
Football	85	—	36	—	24	—	85	—
Football I-AA	63	—	—	—	—	—	—	—
Golf	4.5	6	3.6	5.4	5	5	8	8
Gymnastics	6.3	12	5.4	6	—	—	—	—
Ice Hockey	18	18	13.5	18	—	—	16	16
Lacrosse	12.6	12	10.8	9.9	—	—	20	20
Rifle	3.6	—	3.6	—	—	—	—	—
Rowing	—	20	—	20	—	—	—	—
Skiing	6.3	7	6.3	6.3	—	—	—	—
Soccer	9.9	12	9	9.9	12	12	18	18
Softball	—	12	—	7.2	—	10	—	24
Squash	—	12	—	9	—	—	—	—
Swimming	9.9	14	8.1	8.1	8	8	15	15
Synchronized Swimming	—	5	—	5	—	—	—	—
Team Handball	—	10	—	12	—	—	—	—
Tennis	4.5	8	4.5	6	5	5	8	8
Track & Cross Country	12.6	18	12.6	12.6	12	12	30*	30*
Volleyball	4.5	12	4.5	8	—	8	—	14
Water Polo	4.5	8	4.5	8	4.5	8	4.5	8
Wrestling	9.9	—	9	—	6	—	16	—

* NJCAA Cross Country, Track and Marathon are limited to a combined total of 30 scholarships.
  • NJCAA Division I members may offer full scholarships (tuition, room and board, fees, and books).
  • NJCAA Division II members may offer the allowable scholarships, but are restricted to covering only tuition, fees and/or books.

only funds a team with 10 scholarships, the coach can split up some of the full scholarships to fund a total of 15 athletes.

Equivalency sports have a certain number of scholarships and are not allowed to give out more money than what would equal that allotment at their institution. For example, one college may cost $15,000 to attend (tuition, room and board, and books), while another may cost $30,000. Although the costs are different, the less expensive school may not offer more money than what would equal the allowable allotment for their sport by their association.

With equivalency sports like soccer, a coach can divvy up the scholarships so that, as long as they don't exceed the total money allowed, the team can have 20 or more athletes on scholarship. For example, coaches can offer one athlete 50 percent of a full scholarship, another athlete 30 percent, and a third 20 percent, which equals one full scholarship. Or a coach may offer one athlete a tuition scholarship, another room and board, and a third books. Either way, find out exactly how much you would pay out of your pocket to attend that college.

In equivalency sports, it can be very hard to get a full scholarship. If a coach gives a full scholarship to a player and that athlete gets injured, the scholarship will be tied up with that athlete on the bench. However, if a coach gets three athletes for the price of one, the coach will have a chance to develop the remaining two athletes into solid contributors. Do not expect a full scholarship from equivalency sports; such scholarships are hard to come by.

THE LETTER OF INTENT

When a coach offers you an athletic scholarship, you will get what is called a Letter of Intent. The NCAA Letter of Intent is a legal document issued by the National Collegiate Commissioners Association that states the university's financial commitment to you and your commitment to the NCAA member university. It is a contract that lasts one complete academic year and is renewable each year by each party. The NAIA and NJCAA have their own Letters of Intent that are sent by those institutions.

The different associations do not acknowledge each other's Letters of Intent. This is important to some students who might be considering an NCAA Division I or II athletic scholarship while also looking at NAIA or NJCAA opportunities. For example, two different NCAA Division I or II member schools may *not* sign the same athlete. NJCAA Division I or II schools may not do so, either. But an athlete may sign with both an NJCAA college and an NCAA Division I or II college (double sign), because the colleges are members of two different associations. Some students do this when they are waiting to find out whether they will be academically eligible for NCAA competition.

Read the Letter of Intent very carefully. It is important that you clearly understand what you are signing and what the consequences are for not abiding by the rules of the letter. You must be admitted, complete one full year at that institution, and know what happens if you don't fulfill your side of the contract. You can access the text of the National Letter of Intent at *www.national-letter.org/guidelines/*

■ Figure 2.2: NCAA Division I Headcount and Equivalency Sports ■

Men's Headcount Sports*

Basketball	13	Football	85 (limit 25/year)

Women's Headcount Sports*

Basketball	15	Tennis	8
Gymnastics	12	Volleyball	12

Men's Equivalency Sports**

Baseball	11.7	Rifle	3.6
Cross Country	12.6	Skiing	6.3
Fencing	4.5	Soccer	9.9
Golf	4.5	Swim and Diving	9.9
Gymnastics	6.3	Tennis	4.5
Ice Hockey	18 (30 athletes max)	Volleyball	4.5
Lacrosse	12.6	Water Polo	4.5
		Wrestling	9.9

Women's Equivalency Sports**

Archery	5	Rugby	12
Badminton	6	Skiing	7
Bowling	5	Soccer	14
Cross Country/Track	18	Softball	12
Equestrian	15	Squash	12
Fencing	5	Swim and Diving	14
Field Hockey	12	Synchronize Swimming	5
Golf	6	Team Handball	10
Ice Hockey	18	Water Polo	8
Lacrosse	12		
Rowing	20		

* **Headcount Sports** are allowed only that number of athletes (heads) on athletic financial aid. Athletic financial aid may not exceed the cost of attendance as determined by the institution's financial aid office for students attending that college.

** **Equivalency Sports** are allowed to award financial assistance to a number of athletes as long as the total dollar amount awarded in any one year does not exceed the dollar amount equal to the cost of attendance as determined by the institution's financial aid office and does not exceed the allowable number of full scholarships.

nli_text.php. If you have further questions about the Letter of Intent, contact the NCAA's Initial Eligibility Clearinghouse office at 877-262-1492 or log on to *www.ncaaclearinghouse.net.*

Athletic Letter of Intent Signing Dates

Each association and the different sports have their own signing dates. College teams that compete in the fall typically have an early signing date in February with a second date in April. College sports that compete in the winter or spring have an early signing date in November with a second date in April. Table 2.1 shows the signing dates for the 2007–2008 academic year.

■ Table 2.1: NCAA Signing Dates for the 2007–2008 Academic Year ■

Do not sign prior to 7:00 AM (local time) on the following dates or after the final signing date listed for each sport.

Sport	Initial Signing Date	Final Signing Date
Basketball (Early Period)	November 8, 2006	November 15, 2006
Basketball (Late Period)	April 11, 2007	May 16, 2007
Football (Midyear JC Transfer)	December 20, 2006	January 15, 2007
Football (Regular Period)	February 7, 2007	April 1, 2007
Field Hockey, Soccer, Men's Water Polo*	February 7, 2007	August 1, 2007
All Other Sports (Early Period)	November 8, 2006	November 15, 2006
All Other Sports (Late Period)	April 11, 2007	August 1, 2007

* These sports do not have an early signing period.

The November NCAA early signing date is one week long. For women's volleyball and winter and spring sports, the week begins on the second Wednesday in November at 7:00 AM and ends the following Wednesday at midnight. The second signing date for these sports is in the spring, beginning the second Wednesday of April and ending August 1. The signing date for field hockey, soccer, and men's water polo begins on the first Wednesday of February at 7:00 AM and lasts until August 1. The Letter of Intent has a deadline for when the contract must be signed. *Read* the contract carefully. If the deadline is Tuesday, November 14, at midnight, then the letter needs to be signed and postmarked by that date.

Always read all documents carefully before signing—preferably the day you receive them. The Letter of Intent may be mailed to you or your coach, but it may *not* be hand delivered by the college coach. As mentioned earlier, you do not have to apply or be accepted prior to signing a Letter of Intent, but you do eventually need to be admitted by the college for the Letter of Intent to be valid. If you do not apply or are not admitted, you will lose your scholarship.

The Contract

When you sign a Letter of Intent to attend and compete for a specific college, you will be given responsibilities within that contract that you are obligated to uphold or lose the financial award. Once again, read every word of the Letter of Intent! You will learn what is expected of you and what happens if you do not live up to those expectations. You will also find out exactly what the college's commitment to you will be.

Even if you are given a Letter of Intent to play at the collegiate level, you must apply to the college and be admitted by admissions. Although many coaches will request that you complete the application and send it in by the signing date, you may submit it after the date. Should you fail to apply, you will be ineligible for an athletic scholarship at any other institution within that association. The Letter of Intent becomes null and void if you are not admitted to the university. If you are admitted, you must be academically eligible for the association you are signing with—NCAA, NAIA, or NJCAA—for the scholarship to be applied. (Chapter 3 details on the academic requirements of each association.)

If upon high school graduation, you are not academically eligible to compete for the college you have signed with, you become a *nonqualifier*, and the Letter of Intent becomes null and void. At this point, you become eligible for other associations' scholarships where you are academically eligible. As you will find out in Chapter 3, each association has its own set of academic eligibility standards, so if you do not have the GPA and test scores needed for a Division I program, you might qualify for a Division II school. For example, an athlete who signed a Division I scholarship but was not eligible for Division I upon graduation was notified by the NCAA that she was Division II eligible. Because she is not allowed to sign two NCAA scholarships at two different colleges, she had to wait until after graduation and after she was verified as ineligible for Division I before signing with a Division II school in June.

Null and Void

A Letter of Intent becomes null and void under the following situations: you are not admitted to the university, you are academically ineligible, you do not attend college for a year, you join the U.S. Armed Forces or a church mission, the college discontinues the sport (they may choose to honor their one-year commitment), or it is determined that recruiting rules violations occurred during your recruitment. If any of the above occurs, your Letter of Intent will become null and void, and the institution will notify you of the situation.

You Must Complete One Academic Year

The Letter of Intent states that you must complete one academic year at that university. Should you arrive on campus and find that you are too far from home, or there are three athletes who play your position and you may not get to play, or you simply do not get along with the coach, you must stay on the team and consider transferring the following fall. If you happen to get cut from the team freshman year, you can keep your scholarship, but it will not be renewed a second year. Coaches rarely cut freshmen who have signed a scholarship, because they work hard to recruit athletes who can make their team better. More commonly, freshmen transfer due to lack of playing time. When an athlete transfers, the scholarship can be used for another athlete. If you decide to quit the team, you must return your scholarship money to the institution immediately.

Scholarship Length

The Letter of Intent, and the financial award that accompanies it, is good for one full academic year. The athletic department will notify you on a yearly basis of your athletic aid renewal. Colleges usually renew scholarships without any hassle. A coach can increase aid if an athlete is not on a full scholarship but can also take money back. Though athletes rarely lose a scholarship, if you stop participating or fail to meet academic requirements, you might lose your funding. Also, if you have a discipline problem at the institution or break the law, you might lose the award.

The scholarship can be renewed for up to five years (six, on very rare occasions). The fifth year would occur when an athlete has been redshirted. (See Chapter 1 for information on redshirting.) Because you have five years to play four years, a college is allowed to continue the financial award an additional year.

Signing with a College, Not a Coach

When signing a Letter of Intent, the last line above where you sign basically states that you are signing with an institution, not a coach. College coaches come and go, but once you have signed the letter, you are committed to that institution, regardless of whether the coach is there. For example, an athlete attended college on a scholarship, and after his sophomore year, there was a coaching change. The new coach was very different than the one who had recruited him, and his whole college athletic experience changed. Luckily, he was able to maintain his spot on the team, because he worked hard to meet all of the new coach's expectations and requirements. If a coaching change occurs, be prepared to prove yourself to a new coach to keep playing.

Read the Letter of Intent carefully. Know exactly what you are getting yourself into and know your responsibilities to the university. Remember: You are getting paid to play. The last question you should ask yourself prior to signing the Letter of Intent is "If I could never compete in my sport again, would I choose this school?" The answer should be yes. If it's not, rethink your choice.

PARTIAL QUALIFIERS AND NONQUALIFIERS

A *partial qualifier* is someone who meets some of an association's academic requirements but not all of them. NCAA Division I no longer has this option for incoming freshman; you must meet all the academic standards to be eligible for scholarships and to compete at this level, period. However, Division II and NAIA coaches are allowed to offer athletic scholarships to partial qualifiers, but the athlete cannot compete the first year. NJCAA simply requires an athlete to graduate from high school to be allowed athletic aid. (Information on academic requirements can be found in Chapter 3.)

Nonqualifiers who do not meet the academic eligibility standards for either Division I or Division II may attend that college without athletic aid, earn 24 credits with a GPA of at least 2.0 their freshman year, and become eligible to play and earn athletic aid. If you do meet the academic standards after one full year at the university, you will have used up one year of eligibility because you were a nonqualifier out of high school. But you can gain back one additional year of athletic eligibility by earning your bachelor's degree within four years. You will not be allowed to practice or compete for the university during freshman year, but you can join the team once you become eligible. (This is different from redshirting, because a redshirted athlete was academically eligible; the coach just decided to give the athlete an extra year to grow athletically.)

TRANSFERRING

If you are a nonscholarship athlete, transferring is easy. Because you have not signed a Letter of Intent, you have no obligations to the institution or the athletic program. If you have signed an NCAA Letter of Intent with a Division I or II institution and you have fulfilled your commitment, you will need to get a release from the athletic director before transferring and accepting an athletic scholarship at another Division I or II NCAA member institution. However, if the scholarship offer is from a different association, NAIA or NJCAA, you can transfer without the release. As mentioned earlier, the different associations do not recognize each other's letters. NCAA Division I or II athletes can transfer to an NCAA Division III college without any problem, because Division III institutions do not offer athletic aid.

Before you transfer, you must complete your obligations as stated in the Letter of Intent and finish the academic year in good standing. Once you have secured the written release from the athletic director, you can begin the recruiting process all over again. The rules governing each association must be followed. Be aware that the academic requirements are different for students transferring after completing one year of college—check with each association to determine your eligibility.

CHAPTER SUMMARY

Signing a Letter of Intent to compete for a college is a commitment to work, or get paid to play, for that college and for your education. Read every line of the Letter of Intent so you clearly understand what your obligations are to the college. Make sure you feel certain in your gut the college you are about to sign with is *the* place for you, both academically and athletically.

Ask yourself: "Is this the job I want for the next four years, or more, of my life?" It can be the best job ever—or the worst. The information and recommendations provided throughout this book can help you build confidence in your final decision of where to play college sports. You can find a college to compete at, and you just might get paid to play while there.

Academic Requirements and Recruiting Rules

Once you have begun researching colleges and decided at which level of athletics you want to compete, you need to review the academic requirements and make sure you meet those standards. It will also be important for you to review the rules governing recruiting at each level to keep yourself eligible and to know what coaches can and cannot do during the recruiting process.

Each association and division has its own set of academic standards that you must meet to be eligible to compete in athletics. NCAA Division I has the most complicated requirements. NCAA Division III and NJCAA have very few requirements. The associations' governing bodies will determine the verification of your eligibility. NCAA Division I and II schools use the NCAA Clearinghouse, which charges a registration fee. NAIA and NJCAA use an eligibility form that you can download from their websites. For these associations, you will not have to pay a registration fee, and each institution verifies an athlete's eligibility.

NCAA DIVISION I ACADEMIC REQUIREMENTS

Division I academic requirements allow for some flexibility with regard to standardized test scores. As you can see from Figure 3.1, the SAT and ACT scores are matched up with GPAs on a sliding scale. A student with a low GPA needs higher test scores to be eligible than a student with a high GPA. Your NCAA GPA includes core course grades only. The association's goal is to ensure that a student athlete is prepared to compete in the classroom and in athletics.

If you graduate in 2007, then besides graduating from high school, you will need to have completed 14 courses from your school's NCAA-certified list of core courses and earn a combined Math and Verbal SAT score or a sum of all the ACT scores that matches your core course GPA on the NCAA sliding index for Division I athletic eligibility. If you graduate in 2008 or later, you will need to complete *16* core courses along with the other requirements.

NCAA DIVISION I ACADEMIC REQUIREMENTS

If you plan to enroll for the 2008–2009 academic year, or later, and plan to participate in Division I athletics, you must meet all four of the below requirements to be considered eligible:

1. Graduate from high school
2. Complete the NCAA 16 core courses:
   - Four years of English
   - Three years of math (Algebra I or higher)
   - Two years of natural or physical science (including one year of lab science, if offered by your high school)
   - One extra year of English, math, or natural or physical science
   - Two years of social science
   - Four years of extra core courses (from any category above, or in a foreign language, nondoctrinal religion, or philosophy)
3. Achieve a minimum required grade point average in your core courses
4. Achieve a combined Math and Critical Reading SAT score or sum ACT score (combined Math, Science, Reading, and English scores) that matches your core course grade point average on the sliding scale shown below.

■ **Figure 3.1: Division I Core GPA and Test Score Sliding Scale** ■

Core GPA	SAT	ACT	Core GPA	SAT	ACT	Core GPA	SAT	ACT
3.550 & above	400	37	3.025	610	51	2.500	820	68
3.525	410	38	3.000	620	52	2.475	830	69
3.500	420	39	2.975	630	52	2.450	840–850	70
3.475	430	40	2.950	640	53	2.425	860	70
3.450	440	41	2.925	650	53	2.400	860	71
3.425	450	41	2.900	660	54	2.375	870	72
3.400	460	42	2.875	670	55	2.350	880	73
3.375	470	42	2.850	680	56	2.325	890	74
3.350	480	43	2.825	690	56	2.300	900	75
3.325	490	44	2.800	700	57	2.275	910	76
3.300	500	44	2.775	710	58	2.250	920	77
3.275	510	45	2.750	720	59	2.225	930	78
3.250	520	46	2.725	730	59	2.200	940	79
3.225	530	46	2.700	730	60	2.175	950	80
3.200	540	47	2.675	740–750	61	2.150	960	80
3.175	550	47	2.650	760	62	2.125	960	81
3.150	560	48	2.625	770	63	2.100	970	82
3.125	570	49	2.600	780	64	2.075	980	83
3.100	580	49	2.575	790	65	2.050	990	84
3.075	590	50	2.550	800	66	2.025	1000	85
3.050	600	50	2.525	810	67	2.000	1010	86

Reprinted with permission from the NCAA © 2006

KAPLAN

Grades and GPA

Your grades are as important as your athletic ability. Coaches want athletes who can perform athletically and academically. Usually, coaches recruit three to five athletes for the same position on the team, some strong students and some not-so-strong students. When athletic talent is equal, the stronger students are usually higher on a coach's list. Just as high schools have "pass to play" requirements, the NCAA has strict academic requirements for its student athletes.

On the NCAA Clearinghouse website, under "Administrator," look up your high school's countable course list and find the points (on a scale from 1.0–5.0) that your high school awards for grades earned in countable courses. At most high schools, a 90 in an honors or AP class is usually worth 5.0 points. The highest points you can earn for a course that is not honors or advanced is typically a 4.0.

You are allowed to repeat a class that you have previously passed to earn a higher grade. The NCAA will accept your best grade in a countable course. For example, a student who received a passing grade of 70 in his freshman English course took the class over, because a 70 translates into only a 2.0 according to that high school's point system. The second time around, he received an 87, which counts as a 3.0 and strengthened his GPA and academic eligibility.

Once you arrive on a college campus, a new set of rules will be in place. You must continue to make progress toward graduation to stay eligible to compete. Check with your college coach for these requirements so you know the academic expectations at that college.

Your SAT and ACT Scores

You will need to take one of the standardized college entrance exams (SAT or ACT) to be eligible for NCAA and NAIA athletics. The NCAA will combine your best Math and Critical Reading scores from different SAT test dates, and it will combine all four scores of the ACT (Reading, Math, Science, and English) from a variety of dates. The NAIA combines your scores from one test sitting, or date, and they, like the NCAA, do not use the writing scores at this time to determine eligibility. Once admissions departments begin using the writing scores, then the athletic associations may begin using them as well.

Athletes are encouraged to take the tests during the spring of their junior year and then retake the tests in the fall of their senior year. Because the ACT test is similar to the standardized state tests students take to graduate from high school, many athletes are more successful with taking, and retaking, the ACT. One reason is that on the SAT, you lose points for a

> **IF YOU ARE INTERESTED IN NCAA DIVISION I OR II ATHLETICS,** you should check your high school's core course list on the NCAA Clearinghouse website, *www.ncaaclearinghouse.net* (click on the "Administrator" tab) and calculate your GPA using the worksheet in the NCAA's *Guide for the College-Bound Student-Athlete* located at *www.ncaa.org* (click on "Academics & Athletes").

wrong answer, but on the ACT test points are not taken away for guessing wrong. In fact, students should guess rather than leave an answer blank on the ACT. You are allowed to take the test as many times as you want. After taking the ACT test six different times, an outstanding football player became NCAA Division I eligible in May of his senior year because his test score finally matched his GPA on the sliding scale.

If you are a student on free or reduced lunch or on any federal assistance, you should check with your college counselor for testing fee waivers. The SAT allows one fee waiver per academic year and the ACT allows one fee waiver during your high school career. Once you have used a waiver, and taken an entrance test, you will be eligible for admission application fee waivers and the Clearinghouse fee waiver as well. (Additional information on the Clearinghouse appears later in this chapter.)

■ Table 3.1: SAT Test Dates ■

SAT 2007–08 Test Dates	Test
October 6, 2007	SAT & Subject Tests
November 3, 2007	SAT & Subject Tests
December 1, 2007	SAT & Subject Tests
January 26, 2008	SAT & Subject Tests
March 1, 2008	SAT only
May 3, 2008	SAT & Subject Tests
June 7, 2008	SAT & Subject Tests

■ Table 3.2: ACT Test Dates ■

ACT 2007–2008 Test Dates	Registration Deadline	(Late Fee Required)
September 15, 2007 *	August 10, 2007	August 11–24, 2007
October 27, 2007	September 21, 2007	Sept. 22–Oct. 5, 2007
December 8, 2007	November 2, 2007	November 3–15, 2007
February 9, 2008 **	January 4, 2008	January 5–18, 2008
April 12, 2008	March 7, 2008	March 8–21, 2008
June 14, 2008	May 9, 2008	May 10–23, 2008

* The September 15, 2007, test date is available only in Arizona, California, Florida, Georgia, Illinois, Indiana, Maryland, Michigan, Missouri, Nevada, New York, North Carolina, Oregon, Pennsylvania, South Carolina, Tennessee, Texas, Washington, and West Virginia.
** The February 2008 test is not scheduled in New York.

Just as athletes practice to get better, taking practice tests or attending test prep classes or workshops can help build your confidence and familiarize you with the SAT or ACT exam. At a minimum, you should review the test prep booklet available in your counselor's office. Both the SAT and ACT websites have practice tests and questions. Kaplan (*http://kaplan.com*) has a whole bookstore of test prep materials and online classroom courses. There is likely a test prep center near you for one-on-one tutoring; go to the Kaplan website and find the center nearest to you. Practice can only help a student-athlete.

NCAA Clearinghouse

Who should register for the Clearinghouse? You must register with the NCAA Clearinghouse if you are interested in competing at the NCAA Division I or II level. Division III athletes do not need to register, but if you think you might choose to compete at a Division I or II institution, you should. The Clearinghouse verifies that the courses you have taken are college preparatory courses and that you are academically eligible for Division I or II athletics. You should register with the Clearinghouse in June following your junior year of high school. You should register before making an official visit to a Division I campus in the fall of your senior year. You must provide an NCAA Division I college with a copy of your official transcript and test scores (SAT or ACT) prior to an official visit.

If You Are Ineligible for NCAA Division I or II Athletics

If you find that you are ineligible to play Division I or II sports, you do have options. First, retake the SAT and ACT and earn higher grades in countable courses to change your placement on the sliding scale. If you are still not eligible, you can choose to attend a preparatory school for a post-graduate year. Another choice, one that many athletes choose, is to attend a junior college or opt to go to a Division III or NAIA college. If you are a nonqualifier, you are allowed to attend the Division I college without an athletic scholarship, sit out the whole year (no practicing or competing), earn required academic standards, and become eligible. You are a nonqualifier if you fail to meet one or more of the academic requirements.

IF YOU ARE CONSIDERING NCAA DIVISION I OR II ATHLETICS, you *must* have your SAT or ACT scores sent to the NCAA Clearinghouse by putting its code, 9999, in the section where you designate where College Board should send your scores. Beginning in 2006, the NCAA only accepts scores directly from the testing agencies.

■ Figure 3.2: Division I Academic Worksheet ■

Division I Worksheet

This worksheet is provided to assist you in monitoring your progress in meeting NCAA initial-eligibility standards. The clearinghouse will determine your official status after you graduate. Remember to check your high school's list of approved courses for the classes you have taken. Use the following scale:
A = 4 quality points; B = 3 quality points; C = 2 quality points; D = 1 quality points

English (4 years required)

Course Title	Credit	X	Grade	=	Quality Points (multiply credit by grade)
Example: English 9	.5		A		(.5 x 4) = 2
Total English Units					Total Quality Points

Mathematics (2 years required 2006–2007; 3 years required 2008 and after)

Course Title	Credit	X	Grade	=	Quality Points (multiply credit by grade)
Example: Algebra 1	1.0		B		(1.0 x 3) = 3
Total Mathematics Units					Total Quality Points

Natural/physical science (2 years required)

Course Title	Credit	X	Grade	=	Quality Points (multiply credit by grade)
Total Natural/Physical Science Units					Total Quality Points

Additional year in English, mathematics or natural/physical science (1 year required)

Course Title	Credit	X	Grade	=	Quality Points (multiply credit by grade)
Total Additional Units					Total Quality Points

Social science (2 years required)

Course Title	Credit	X	Grade	=	Quality Points (multiply credit by grade)
Total Social Science Units					Total Quality Points

Additional academic courses (3 years required 2006–2007; 4 years required 2008 and after)

Course Title	Credit	X	Grade	=	Quality Points (multiply credit by grade)
Total Additional Academic Units					Total Quality Points

Core Course GPA (14 credits required 2006–2007; 16 required 2008 and after)

Total Quality Points	Total Number of Credits	Core-Course GPA (Total Quality Points/Total Credits)

Reprinted with permission from the NCAA © 2006

■ Figure 3.3: Division II Academic Worksheet ■

Division II Worksheet

This worksheet is provided to assist you in monitoring your progress in meeting NCAA initial-eligibility standards. The clearinghouse will determine your official status after you graduate. Remember to check your high school's list of approved courses for the classes you have taken. Use the folowing scale:
A = 4 quality points; B = 3 quality points; C = 2 quality points; D = 1 quality points

English (3 years required)

Course Title	Credit	X	Grade	=	Quality Points (multiply credit by grade)
Example: English 9	.5		A		(.5 x 4) = 2
Total English Units					Total Quality Points

Mathematics (2 years required)

Course Title	Credit	X	Grade	=	Quality Points (multiply credit by grade)
Example: Algebra 1	1.0		B		(1.0 x 3) = 3
Total Mathematics Units					Total Quality Points

Natural/physical science (2 years required)

Course Title	Credit	X	Grade	=	Quality Points (multiply credit by grade)
Total Natural/Physical Science Units					Total Quality Points

Additional year in English, mathematics or natural/physical science (2 years required)

Course Title	Credit	X	Grade	=	Quality Points (multiply credit by grade)
Total Additional Units					Total Quality Points

Social science (2 years required)

Course Title	Credit	X	Grade	=	Quality Points (multiply credit by grade)
Total Social Science Units					Total Quality Points

Additional academic courses (3 years required)

Course Title	Credit	X	Grade	=	Quality Points (multiply credit by grade)
Total Additional Academic Units					Total Quality Points

Core Course GPA (14 credits required)

Total Quality Points	Total Number of Credits	Core-Course GPA (Total Quality Points/Total Credits)

Reprinted with permission from the NCAA © 2006

Retake the SAT and ACT and Earn Better Grades

Retake the SAT and ACT if your sum on either test is close; you have until your high school graduation date to become eligible. There are seven test dates for the SAT each academic year and six dates for the ACT. If you begin taking the test during your junior year, you have even more opportunities. Take a test prep course and get some tutoring, as mentioned earlier. The majority of students retaking a test improve one or more scores the second time around. With the tougher academic standards (16 core course requirement), more athletes than before will need to retake the SAT or ACT to become eligible. You can also improve your GPA by earning more 90s in core classes, thus changing where you fall on the sliding scale.

Postgraduate Year

You always have the option of postgraduate work at a prep school prior to attending college. *Postgraduate* refers to attending a preparatory school for one year prior to attending college. If you choose this route, you should take courses that count towards the Division I or II GPA. Check the prep schools course list with the NCAA Clearinghouse. You may have already passed these courses in high school but received low grades. By taking a postgraduate year, you can try to improve these grades, and you will also have an opportunity to retake the SAT and ACT to try for better scores. Some students need this year to build their academic confidence prior to tackling college-level work.

NJCAA

Another option is to attend an NJCAA college. There is a new rule allowing students who are not academically eligible for Division I or II to attend junior college. To be eligible to play Division I or II athletics, these students are required to earn an associate's degree from a junior college prior to transferring. If you are not a strong student and you choose to compete at a junior college, be sure you know the rules and expectations for the next level of competition. The rules continue to change and are updated on a yearly basis. Check the NCAA's rules about attending junior college and transferring to an NCAA Division I or II school. These can be found at *www.ncaa.org* under "Academics & Athletes."

   If you are academically eligible to compete at the Division I or II level but choose to attend a junior college first, you can transfer and be eligible as long as you meet the academic progress requirements for that level. Depending on the number of semesters you have completed, a 2.0 GPA with 24 credits earned towards a degree per academic year is required. There is a limit on countable credits earned during the summer sessions, so check with your institution on eligibility options prior to making any academic decisions.

NCAA Division III

You can also opt to attend a Division III school. This division does not have academic requirements for athlete eligibility, but each institution does have general academic standards for all members of the incoming student body. Check the school's website to see if you meet the general academic requirements. If you are admitted, you can play. If you were academically eligible for Division I or II athletics prior to attending or competing for a Division III college, you may transfer to a Division I school and be eligible as long as you meet the academic progress requirements.

Nonqualifier Status

Even if you are academically ineligible to play a Division I sport, you can still attend a Division I institution and become eligible by completing at least 24 college credits toward a degree with a GPA of at least 2.0. You will not be eligible for an athletic scholarship your first year, and you may not practice with the team, but you will have access to coaches.

If you become academically eligible, you are now eligible to compete and earn a scholarship should the coach choose to offer you one. You will lose one year of athletic eligibility, but can gain it back if you earn a bachelor's degree within your first four years of attendance. Because an athlete has five years to complete four years of competition, you would be eligible to play your fifth year of college and be on scholarship should you earn the degree.

NCAA DIVISION II ACADEMIC REQUIREMENTS

The academic requirements for Division II athletics are simple: graduate from high school, have a 2.0 grade point average in the 14 NCAA core courses, and earn a combined 820 (Math and Critical

---

NCAA DIVISION II ACADEMIC REQUIREMENTS

YOU MUST MEET ALL FOUR OF THE REQUIREMENTS BELOW TO BE ELIGIBLE FOR DIVISION II.

You will be a partial qualifier if you graduate from high school and meet either the GPA or test score requirement.

1. Graduate from high school
2. Complete the NCAA 14 core courses
3. Earn a 2.0 or better in the 14 core courses
4. Achieve a combined Math and Critical Reading SAT score of 820 or a combined ACT score of 68 from the sum of the Math, Science, Reading, and English scores

Reading) SAT score or a combined ACT score of 68 (Reading, English, Math, and Science). Your school's core course list is the same for Division I and II. Division II offers a *partial qualifier status,* which is for athletes who have a high school diploma but do not meet all three of the academic requirements. To be a partial qualifier, you must have a diploma and meet either the GPA *or* the test scores requirement. As a partial qualifier, you will be allowed to sign a scholarship and practice with the team, but you will not be allowed to compete during your freshman year. Because you are allowed five years to play your four years, you will still have four years of eligibility remaining.

NCAA DIVISION III ACADEMIC REQUIREMENTS

Because Division III coaches do not award athletic scholarships, there are no NCAA academic requirements to compete at this level. If you choose to play at a Division III school, check with the institution for their general student body admissions requirements. Each institution admits and verifies each student's eligibility independently.

NAIA ACADEMIC REQUIREMENTS

To be eligible for NAIA athletics, you must have graduated from an accredited high school (earn a high school diploma) and meet at least two of these three criteria:

1. A GPA of 2.0 on a 4.0 scale
2. Either a composite score of 18 on the ACT or an 860 (Math and Critical Reading only) on the SAT
3. Graduate in the top half of your graduating class

One important note: The test scores, from either the SAT or ACT, must be a combined score or sum of scores from *one* testing date (sitting). This differs from the NCAA's policy, which will com-

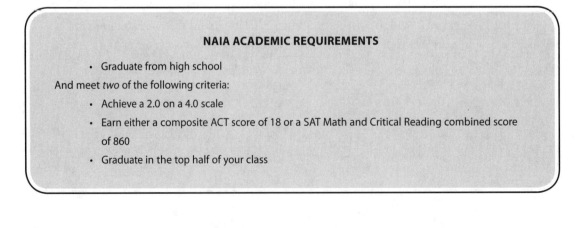

NAIA ACADEMIC REQUIREMENTS

- Graduate from high school

And meet *two* of the following criteria:

- Achieve a 2.0 on a 4.0 scale
- Earn either a composite ACT score of 18 or a SAT Math and Critical Reading combined score of 860
- Graduate in the top half of your class

bine scores from more than one sitting for an overall score. If an athlete earns a high school diploma and meets two of these academic standards, they are eligible for NAIA athletics.

NJCAA ACADEMIC REQUIREMENTS

To be eligible for junior college athletics, an athlete needs to have completed high school requirements. Therefore, the athlete must have graduated from an accredited high school, received a high school equivalency diploma, or passed the General Education Development Test (GED) to be eligible for NJCAA athletics. Each institution can verify your eligibility once they receive your final transcript. NJCAA does *not* require standardized test scores, a minimum GPA, or a set list of courses for athletes to complete. Students do take a placement test, but the score is not used for admission or eligibility, just for placement into classes. Check each college's website for admissions information.

ACADEMIC SUMMARY

Because each athletic association has its own academic eligibility standards, you can begin looking at the criteria for eligibility early (freshman or sophomore year), giving yourself more time to improve your grades and prepare for the SAT and ACT. Academics are important to coaches as well. They do not want to worry about whether you will remain eligible once you arrive on campus. Earn good grades and challenge yourself academically. Remember to take the entrance exams in the spring of your junior year so you will know whether you need to retest. Now that you know the academic eligibility information, we will move on to recruiting rules.

RECRUITING RULES AND REGULATIONS

Each athletic division has its own set of recruiting rules. As you may have guessed, NCAA Division I athletics has stricter and more sport-specific rules than the NCAA Divisions II or III, NAIA, or NJCAA programs. Division II rules are similar to those of Division I but with fewer sport-specific rules; the rules are the same for all sports. Division III and NAIA programs have very few rules and are free to contact you anytime they want, but they also have small recruiting budgets, so these coaches tend to be less active in the pursuit of athletes. In the following paragraphs, we will discuss the rules for Division I and II and indicate any particular rules that have significance for the other associations.

As you can see in the Figure 3.4, each year of high school brings a new set of recruiting rules for college coaches. During the freshman and sophomore year, coaches can have very little contact with you and are limited to sending recruiting materials. However, you are not limited in what you choose to send coaches or in your visits to colleges. Junior year, recruiting begins to pick up a little;

■ Figure 3.4: NCAA's Summary of Recruiting Rules ■

Summary of recruiting rules for each sport—Division I

RECRUITING METHOD	MEN'S BASKETBALL	WOMEN'S BASKETBALL	FOOTBALL	OTHER SPORTS
Recruiting materials	• You may receive brochures for camps and questionnaires. • You may begin receiving recruiting materials June 15 after your sophomore year.	• You may receive brochures for camps and questionnaires.	• You may receive brochures for camps and questionnaires.	• You may receive brochures for camps and questionnaires.
Telephone calls	• You may make calls to coach at your expense. • College may accept collect calls from you at end of year. • College coach cannot call you.	• You may make calls to coach at your expense only. • College coach cannot call you.	• You may make calls to coach at your expense only. • College coach cannot call you.	• You may make calls to coach at your expense only. • College coach cannot call you. • Ice Hockey—if you are an international prospect, a college coach may call you once in July after sophomore year.
Off-campus contact	• None allowed.	• None allowed.	• None allowed.	• None allowed.
Official visit	• None allowed.	• None allowed.	• None allowed.	• None allowed.
Unofficial visit	• You may make an unlimited number of unofficial visits.	• You may make an unlimited number of unofficial visits.	• You may make an unlimited number of unofficial visits.	• You may make an unlimited number of unofficial visits.
RECRUITING METHOD	MEN'S BASKETBALL	WOMEN'S BASKETBALL	FOOTBALL	OTHER SPORTS
Recruiting materials	• Allowed.	• You may begin receiving September 1 of junior year.	• You may begin receiving September 1 of junior year.	• You may begin receiving September 1 of junior year.
Telephone calls **College coaches may call you**	• You may make calls to the coach at your expense. • Once per month beginning June 15, before your junior year, through July 31.	• You may make calls to the coach at your expense. • Once per month in April, May and June 1-20. • Once between June 21 and June 30 after your junior year. • Three times in July after your junior year.	• You may make calls to the coach at your expense. • Once during May of your junior year.	• You may make calls to the coach at your expense. • Once per week starting July 1 after your junior year.
Off-campus contact	None allowed.	None allowed.	None allowed.	• Allowed starting July 1 after your junior year. • For gymnastics—allowed after July 15 after your junior year.
Official visit	• None allowed.	• None allowed.	• None allowed.	• None allowed.
Unofficial visit	• You may make an unlimited number of unofficial visits.	• You may make an unlimited number of unofficial visits.	• You may make an unlimited number of unofficial visits.	• You may make an unlimited number of unofficial visits.

(Left margin labels: SOPHOMORE YEAR for top section; JUNIOR YEAR for bottom section.)

Reprinted with permission from the NCAA © 2006

Figure 3.4: NCAA's Summary of Recruiting Rules, continued

RECRUITING METHOD	MEN'S BASKETBALL	WOMEN'S BASKETBALL	FOOTBALL	OTHER SPORTS
Recruiting materials	• Allowed.	• Allowed.	• Allowed.	• Allowed.
Telephone calls College coaches may call you	• You may make calls to the coach at your expense. • Twice per week beginning August 1.	• You may make calls to the coach at your expense. • Once per week beginning August 1.	• You may make calls to the coach at your expense. • Once per week beginning September 1.	• You may make calls to the coach at your expense. • Once per week.
Off-campus contact	• Allowed beginning September 9.	• Allowed beginning September 16.	• Allowed beginning November 27.	• Allowed.
Official visit	• Allowed beginning opening day of classes your senior year. • You are limited to one official visit per college up to a maximum of five official visits to Divisions I and II colleges.	• Allowed beginning opening day of classes your senior year. • You are limited to one official visit per college up to a maximum of five official visits to Divisions I and II colleges.	• Allowed beginning opening day of classes your senior year. • You are limited to one official visit per college up to a maximum of five official visits to Divisions I and II colleges.	• Allowed beginning opening day of classes your senior year. • You are limited to one official visit per college up to a maximum of five official visits to Divisions I and II colleges.
Unofficial visit	• You may make an unlimited number of unofficial visits.	• You may make an unlimited number of unofficial visits.	• You may make an unlimited number of unofficial visits.	• You may make an unlimited number of unofficial visits.
Evaluation and contacts	• Up to seven times during your senior year.	• Up to five times during your senior year.	• Up to six times during your senior year.	• Up to seven times during your senior year.
How often can a coach see me or talk to me off the college's campus?	• A college coach may contact you or your parents/legal guardians not more than three times during your senior year.	• A college coach may contact you or your parents/legal guardians not more than three times during your senior year.	• A college coach may contact you or your parents/legal guardians (including evaluating you off the college's campus), six times. • One evaluation during September, October and November.	• A college coach may contact you or your parents/legal guardians not more than three times during your senior year.

(Left margin label: SENIOR YEAR)

Summary of recruiting rules—Divisions II and III

	DIVISION II	DIVISION III
Recruiting materials	• A coach may begin sending you printed recruiting materials Sepember 1 of your junior year in high school.	• You may receive printed materials anytime.
Telephone calls	• A college coach may call you once per week beginning June 15 between your junior and senior year. • You may make calls to the coach at your expense.	• No limit on number of calls or when they can be made by the college coach. • You may make calls to the coach at your expense.
Off-campus contact	• A college coach can have contact with you or your parents/legal guardians off the college's campus beginning June 15 after your junior year. • A college coach is limited to three in-person contacts off campus.	• A college coach may begin to have contact with you and your parents/legal guardians off the college's campus after your junior year.
Unofficial visits	• You may make an unlimited number of unofficial visits any time.	• You may make an unlimited number of unofficial visits any time.
Official visits	• You may make official visits starting the opening day of classes your senior year. • You may make only one official visit per college and up to a maximum of five official visits to Divisions I and II colleges.	• You may make official visits starting the opening day of classes your senior year. • You may make only one official visit per college.

Reprinted with permission from the NCAA © 2006

coaches can send recruiting information, but they still may not make calls to you or visit with you off their campus (also known as an off-campus contact). The summer following your junior year (you are officially a senior) is when coaches can recruit more heavily.

Know the recruiting rules for the association(s) in which you are interested so that you understand when a coach can contact you, what they can send you, when you can visit, and what you can do on your visit. In the remainder of this chapter, we will discuss recruiting rules and regulations in chronological order according to your year in high school.

Recruiting Rules for Freshmen and Sophomores

Basically in NCAA Division I and II recruiting, during your freshman or sophomore year, coaches are only allowed to send you a camp brochure and an introductory letter with an athletic recruiting questionnaire. They cannot call you or pay for your visit. You, however, may send a letter with a videotape and make as many unofficial visits (you pay your own expenses) to a college campus as you would like. (Chapter 7 has details on contacting coaches, including writing your initial letter and making a videotape. Later in this chapter and in Chapter 8 are more details on college visits.)

One of the biggest mistakes athletes at this age make is to leave a phone message for a Division I or II coach and ask the coach to call you back to set up an on-campus meeting. Unfortunately, these coaches are not permitted to call you back. If this happens to you, do not assume that the coach is uninterested in you. Instead, find a different way of contacting the coach: email, go through the athletic department (ask for the best time to reach the coach), or have your high school coach call. College coaches are allowed to call high school and club coaches and vice versa.

Although college coaches are not allowed to have face-to-face contact with you off their campus, they can attend a competition to recruit seniors, and if you happen to be competing, they will see you play, especially if you have sent them a letter of interest. The earlier you contact the coach, the more time you will have to develop a relationship. NAIA and NJCAA coaches are allowed to call you any time during your high school career. NCAA Division III coaches have to wait until after your junior year to have off-campus contact.

Recruiting Rules for Juniors

As you can see in Figure 3.4, there are some changes in the rules for college coaches, specifically the date on which mailings are allowed and, for some sports, the date on which telephone contact is allowed. Prior to 2005, the NCAA allowed coaches in all sports to make one phone call to an athlete during the spring of their junior year. Coaches, except for coaches of basketball, ice hockey, and football, are no longer allowed to contact juniors. Because the NCAA can make changes to recruiting rules each year, be sure to review the NCAA's *Guide for the College-Bound Student-Athlete* every year.

During your junior year, NCAA Division I coaches are allowed to begin actively recruiting you. Other than men's basketball coaches, which can begin sending recruiting material on June 15 following your sophomore year, all other coaches may begin mailing you recruiting material on September 1 of your junior year. If they know your address, they can send materials such as team brochures, competition schedules, and academic information.

As mentioned earlier, although most college coaches (basketball and football are the exception) are not allowed to have face-to-face contact with you off their campus until July 1 of your senior year, coaches can watch you compete if high school seniors are also competing at the event. Rarely does a sports competition not include at least juniors and seniors; many include freshman and sophomores as well. If you sent an initial letter with your competition schedule, a coach might come to see you play. Observing you compete in person is the best way for coaches to determine whether you are a potential recruit for their program. (Chapter 7 talks about how coaches recruit and find athletes for their program.)

Remember, you are always allowed to make an unofficial visit to a college campus at your own expense. In fact, it is highly recommend that you do so during your junior year. Lots of coaches offer a recruiting weekend for juniors and try to get their top recruits to visit unofficially as one big group. This is a great opportunity for you to see the campus, meet the team, and scope out your competition or future teammates.

Division II and III coaches have fewer and slightly different rules. You can always visit a campus as much as you want, and you can always call a coach as often as you want, but coaches do have limits on what they can do in terms of recruiting. As you can see from Figure 3.4, Division II coaches can start sending out material September 1 of your junior year and can call you and make off-campus visits to your games or home after June 15 between your junior and senior year.

Division III and NAIA coaches can contact you and send you printed material at any time throughout your high school years. These coaches have very little money to spend on phone calls or mailings, so they do not phone weekly or send out mailings on a regular basis, but they will respond to your letter or call. While Division III coaches can have off-campus contact with you after your junior year, NAIA coaches can have off-campus contact anytime.

WHEN COACHES ATTEND A MAJOR RECRUITING EVENT, THEY HIGHLIGHT THE NAMES OF STUDENTS WHO HAVE SENT THEM LETTERS, AND THEY MAKE SURE TO SEE THEM COMPETE. If you have had contact with coaches (sent a letter or made an unofficial visit) and you know that they attended one of your competitions, follow up with them to see what they think about your chance of playing for them. You will be doing yourself and the coach a favor.

Recruiting Rules for Seniors

Senior year becomes more exciting for NCAA Division I and II recruited athletes. College coaches may now call you on the phone, pay for your visit to their campus, come to your athletic competitions, and offer you a scholarship. No matter what division you want to play in, senior year is decision time for both you and the coach. Senior year is the time to visit or revisit your top colleges. This is probably the biggest decision of your young life, and visiting a campus will help you tremendously with your final choice.

In most sports, July 1 following your junior year will be the first time you receive a call from a Division I coach, and they can now call you once per week. Basketball and football players should review the chart above for the dates college coaches are allowed to start calling. The amount of contact you have with coaches prior to these dates will determine if you get any calls and who calls. Before the calling dates, be sure the coaches at the top of your list have your most up-to-date contact information. You wouldn't want to miss out on a great opportunity to play at your dream school because of an obsolete cell phone number!

If you don't hear from your top choices' coaches, call them and see if they are interested in recruiting you. If it turns out that the coach actually isn't interested, that information will be disappointing, but take heart: you can move on to those coaches who are interested and will most likely end up with some choices that are better suited for you. During the first phone call, you may be invited to visit the campus. Ask whether the coach is inviting you on an official or unofficial visit. There are rules governing both, so be sure you know them.

UNOFFICIAL AND OFFICIAL VISITS

There are two types of visits you can make to prospective colleges: unofficial and official. The difference between the two depends on who pays the bill. Beginning with the first day of classes your senior year, you become eligible for a paid—official—visit at any NCAA institution. A clearer explanation of each type of visit is provided below.

Unofficial Visits

An unofficial visit is any visit you make to a college where you pay all of your own expenses. These can happen at any point during your high school career. You should try to make unofficial visits during your sophomore and junior year. Make sure to set up a meeting with the coach. You may need to get creative in setting up this meeting. Prior to senior year, Division I and II coaches are not allowed to call you back, so you may need to have your club or high school coach help set up the meeting.

During your visit, you will get a sense of the type of students on campus and, hopefully, meet team members. Try to make these visits during the academic year when students are on campus and you can get a better sense of the atmosphere. A coach is allowed to leave three tickets to a home contest at will-call for you and may eat a meal with you. But remember, they are not allowed to pay for the meal. Many admissions offices set up overnight stays for prospective students, so you may be able to stay in a dorm. As long as you go through the admissions office, not the athletic department or the coach, you will be within the rules, and the visit will be counted as unofficial.

We cannot emphasis enough how helpful making unofficial visits to your top schools before senior year will be in your decision making. Senior year is busy enough with college applications and official visits. You will help yourself out tremendously if you make unofficial visits before then.

Official Visits

An official visit, or paid visit, cannot occur until your first day of class senior year. You are allowed to make five paid visits to five different NCAA Division I or Division II colleges, and each visit cannot last more than 48 hours. You may take only one paid visit per college at Division III, NAIA, or NJCAA schools, but there is no limit on the number of different colleges that may pay for your visit. A paid visit occurs when an institution's athletic department pays for your transportation, meals, or housing expenses. It may also pay for entertainment, such as a concert or theater show, but a coach cannot purchase or give you any merchandise.

If you have been making unofficial visits prior to your senior year, you will know which schools you want to visit officially. If you have more than five Division I or II colleges on your list and want to visit a school, but you don't want to use up one of your five allowable official visits, you may make an unofficial visit. Be aware that a coach may think their institution is not in your top five if you don't accept an official visit. If you have more than five favorite colleges at the beginning of your senior year, make unofficial visits to the schools within driving distance to your home. (Chapter 8 has additional information on college visits, including on how official visits are set up, what to see, what to do, and what questions to ask.)

EVALUATIONS AND CONTACT RULES

Depending on the sport, an NCAA member coach is allowed to observe, evaluate, and have face-to-face, off-campus contact with you after you complete your junior year of high school. NAIA and NJCAA coaches may evaluate and observe you anytime during your high school career.

An *evaluation* is when a coach observes you compete or practice or visits your high school to evaluate your academics. Coaches like seeing you perform live and want to impress you by coming to your campus. If they have not been able to see you at a competition, they may come watch a practice. Again, the coach's recruiting budget affects his or her ability to travel. Rarely will a Division III, NAIA, or NJCAA coach get to make an in-person evaluation of you at your high school. These coaches will rely on videotapes to observe you. (Videotapes are discussed in Chapter 7.)

A *contact* is when a coach speaks with you or your parents at a competition, a practice, or home visit off the coach's campus. Division I and II coaches are allowed to talk to seniors and their parents/legal guardian off campus three times (six for football) during the recruiting process. These contacts also count as evaluations. NCAA member coaches are not allowed to talk to juniors or their parents/legal guardians while off campus. They may, however, talk to club and high school coaches as much as they want. NAIA and NJCAA coaches may talk to you and your parents/legal guardian anytime.

RECRUITING SUMMARY

Review the "Summary of Recruiting Rules" in Figure 3.4 for your sport, especially the number of times and dates Division I coaches are allowed to evaluate and contact you. Division II coaches may conduct three in-person, off-campus contacts beginning on June 15 after your junior year. Division III, NAIA, and NJCAA coaches may conduct an unlimited number of evaluations and contacts but rarely have the finances to travel for recruiting.

CHAPTER SUMMARY

Be sure you know exactly what you need to do academically to be eligible for each association in which you are interested. Even if you are an incredible athlete, you may need to eliminate an option based solely on your grades or test scores. Also, know the rules for the association you are pursuing. If a rule is broken by the coach, she may not be able to recruit you anymore. In such a case, you may still attend the college and hope to make the team, but you will not be able to communicate with the coach, and you won't be eligible for an athletic scholarship. Thus, it is important that you know the rules governing the association so the rules are followed and you and the coach are communicating in compliance with them.

Determing Your Level of Play

Determining what level of college athletics matches up with your goals and desires takes a little time. If you haven't received letters from college coaches or had contact with a coach through your club or high school coach, you may not know what your options are. Even if you have received letters, you might want to determine how you would fit into a program and what your chances are of making the team and earning a scholarship. This chapter will help you begin your athletic search, recommend resources, and guide you through them. Give yourself time to explore all of the options. When you start your search, use a chart, like the one in Figure 4.1, to keep track of information. You should also keep a file or notebook of information you receive from colleges and coaches.

BEGINNING YOUR COLLEGE SEARCH

The best way to begin your search is to find schools that offer your area of academic interest and are located where you would like to go to college. Look up the athletics and academics at each school. Excellent sites with career-search and college-match programs are the College Board's *http://collegeboard.com* and ACT's *http://actstudent.org*. You can enter some criteria, and each will provide a list of colleges that match your interests.

After you compile a list, write to the coaches at each school, informing them of your interest in their program. If you are undecided on what you want to study in college, then you can take notes on the majors offered at the colleges you are considering for athletics. Once you have a list of schools, go to each college's website to look up the academic requirements, possible majors you can pursue, and application types and deadlines. A great book that contains all of this information, and more, is Kaplan's *You Are Here: A Guide to Over 350 Colleges and Unlimited Paths to Your Future.*

▓ Figure 4.1: College Search Organizational Chart ▓

Important Items	College 1	College 2	College 3	College 4	College 5
Name of College					
Location					
Admissions (GPA, Class Rank, Test Scores)					
Majors Offered					
Student Population					
Early Application Deadline					
Reg. Application Deadlines					
Scholarship App. Deadline					
Cost of Attendance					
Coach's Name					
Address and Phone Number					
Email Address					
# of Years as Coach					
Assistant Coach's Name					
Association and Division					
Conference					
# Of Athletes Graduating					
Graduating in My Position					
Athlete's Size (Height and Weight)					
Time, Distance, Average Score, or Level of Play of Current Team Members					
Teams Win/Lose					

  KAPLAN

Big Fish versus Little Fish

At some point in your athletic search, you will need to decide whether you will perform your best as a big fish in a little pond or a little fish in a big pond. You must decide where you want to fit into a program. If you want to be the big fish in the little pond, you will be one of the best athletes on the team. The coach probably expresses this to you. If you want to be a little fish in a big pond, you may never get to start a game in your four years on the team, but you will be part of a championship team.

The University of North Carolina's women's soccer team has athletes on it that could easily start for other Division I programs, but they chose to attend UNC and be on a potential national championship team. They are also getting a great education.

On the other hand, a swimmer who was being recruited by many of the top teams in the country decided she wanted to be on a team where she would make a big difference with less pressure to win. She chose a lower-ranked Division I school where she had already beaten the school and conference records. She received a full athletic scholarship and went on to win conference titles, setting records in her best events. Her team is not nationally ranked but is competitive within the conference. She continued to improve and loves her sport. She was a big fish in a little pond, but knew she would have very little competition for her spot on the team.

You have to decide on your commitment to athletics and be realistic about your ability. If you are not starting on your varsity high school team, you will have a hard time finding NCAA Division I or II colleges that will recruit you. The same is true for athletes who do not compete year-round. The majority of scholarship athletes at these levels compete year-round beginning in high school and earlier. Do you think you will perform best as the big fish or little fish?

Athletic Association Links

A great place to find a list of colleges that offer your sport is through the athletic associations' websites. Each association has a link on its website to a list of colleges that offer teams (usually under "Sport" or "Participating Schools"). In Chapter 1, we listed the number of schools in each association that offer your sport, but now we will help you locate the list by college.

- *www.ncaa.org.* You will find the NCAA schools sponsor list if you click on "Academics & Athletes," then "Eligibility & Recruiting." Click on "List of NCAA Schools and Conferences by Division," where you can look up colleges by institution, division, conference, or region of the country. Just choose your sport and division, and the list comes up. You can then click on the college and get an address for the athletic department, and if the team is underlined, you can get the team's competition schedule.
- *http://naia.cstv.com.* To get a list of NAIA schools offering your sport, click on your sport. Look in the "Notes" section and click on "Participating Schools" to get a list of all

of the NAIA members with your sport. You can look up each college's athletic website for further information on specific programs.

- *http://njcaa.org.* To find NJCAA schools that offer your sport, look on the right side of the page under "Find Your College." Click "Colleges by Sport," then click on your sport, and a list of colleges will come up.

If College Coaches Contact You First

For those of you who have already received letters from coaches, you need to decide whether the college and the team are good matches for you. If a coach contacted you, that coach has probably mass-mailed a list of potential athletes and is waiting to see if you respond. Many athletes receive dozens of packets from coaches all over the country and think they are being recruited. When they never receive another piece of recruiting material from a coach, they are surprised. If you are interested in a school or even think you might be, you need to return the athletic questionnaire included with the letter from the coach. Unless you reply and show further interest, the coach may not continue to recruit you.

If you are a junior and you have received only one piece of communication from a coach, you are probably not on that program's radar any longer. Follow up with that coach if you are still interested in the program. If you get information from a school about which you know nothing, follow the steps given in the beginning of this chapter to see if the school is a good match for you.

COLLEGE WEBSITES

Now that you have a list of potential schools, go on each college's athletic website. To find these sites, type the name of the college with "athletics" after the name into a search engine. Keep track of your research using Figure 4.1. You can also add columns to the chart or make up your own. Begin with academic requirements, application deadline, and majors offered. Be sure to write down the coach's name, phone number, and address; the conference and division the team competes in; and some information on the current members. Based on your year in high school and the year of the roster you are looking at, you should be able to tell who will graduate from the team the same year you graduate. This will help you determine the team's needs.

Academic Requirements and Majors Offered

Remember to click on the home page of the college and look up the academic requirements under the admissions tab. The requirements are fairly firm, but certain coaches across the country have excellent relationships with their admissions departments. You need to know what the academic expectations will be for you. If you are concerned about your ability to be admitted to a college, talk to the coach. Coaches will tell you right away if it will be tough for you to get admitted. Coaches don't like to waste their time recruiting on an athlete who can't get in. At the same time, if you get your transcript into the coach's hands early in the recruiting process, he or she might be able to help you through the admissions process. A coach can give you advice on your course selection for your junior and senior years. If a college says their average SAT test score is 1,200 (Math and Verbal combined), then some students with higher scores and some students with lower scores are admitted. Don't stop looking at a school simply because you know your score is below the average SAT score. Go through the coach before you give up on a school.

Coach's Information

Include a coach's information on your chart (address and phone number) so you will have easy access to this information when you prepare your initial letter and are ready to schedule a college visit. Other information you might want to know about the coach would be how long he has been coaching at his school, how long he has been a coach in general, and whether or not he has any assistant coaches. If a coach hasn't been at the school long, where was she before that, and who was the coach that preceded her? All of this information will help you get a clear picture of your options.

There is a trend in women's college athletic departments of hiring young female coaches who recently played in college. If this is the case at a school you are looking at, read the coach's bio to learn more about her background. If a coach has recently graduated from college, she will not be as experienced at recruiting, so you will definitely want to be sure to follow up with her. But don't think this means she cannot coach. Kelley Amonte, the head lacrosse coach at Northwestern University, was hired to resurrect the program from scratch. With only three years' experience as an assistant, Coach Amonte, a celebrated All-American lacrosse player herself, was able to walk onto Northwestern's campus and win two NCAA Division I national women's lacrosse titles within her first four years of running the program.

Team Roster

One of the quickest ways to determine whether you have a shot at making a team is by checking out the team's current roster. Rosters typically include each athlete's year in college, height, weight, and hometown and, possibly, the high school or junior college they attended. Many websites allow you to click on the athlete's name and get a short bio, which might include high school or secondary accomplishments as well as statistics for each college season. Let's look at how each piece of information can be helpful in determining your chances of being recruited.

Year

The athletes who are in the same year of college as you are in high school will be graduating from college at the same time you graduate from high school. Look closely at which position or in which events these athletes are competing.

For example, if you are an outstanding varsity swimmer who specializes in the butterfly, and the college team you're looking at already has two butterfliers (a junior and freshman) swimming the 100 m. butterfly in 55 seconds, the coach won't need another butterflier on the team. If you are a 6′5″ basketball player who plays center or power forward, and one of your top choices is only graduating two guards your senior year and retaining seven juniors (some of whom are forwards), the coach probably doesn't have money for a forward in your recruiting class. While a coach may not have scholarship money available for you as an entering freshman, he may promise to offer you money sophomore year. Be sure to check the roster for the team's needs.

Also, check the number of freshmen versus the number of seniors on the team. If the freshman class is huge and the senior class small, ask the coach if the senior class was a small class to begin with or if athletes are quitting or transferring. A small senior class often means less scholarship money available for incoming freshman. If you follow a team's performance and results beginning your sophomore or junior year of high school, you can see how much the athletes improve and who gets a starting position.

Size

Look at the height and weight of the athletes currently on the team, especially in sports where size matters, like basketball, volleyball, and football, to name a few. If you are a 5′10″ volleyball player and you look at a team's roster and not one player is under 6′, you will have a tough time getting recruited. If you are a 5′10″, 178-pound running back and the team already has six running backs, all over 210 pounds, you either need to beef up, change positions, or find another program. Even in sports like soccer, field hockey, or lacrosse, an athlete's size may indicate the type of athlete a particular coach likes to recruit for that position.

For example, a soccer player who is small but good—an Olympic Development player—found out by looking at team rosters that he would be the smallest player on most of the top teams in the country. He received letters from many of these teams. He contacted those coaches whose programs he was interested in and let the coaches decide whether he fit their program. Some of the coaches contacting him dropped him because of his size, but others didn't care about his size and recruited him for his ability.

Hometown

Look at the hometown of the current athletes. Find out if they are in-state, out-of-state, or international students. This can give you an idea of where the coach recruits and may indicate whether the program has much athletic scholarship money. A private college will probably have more students from across the country than a public college, because the tuition is the same for all students at a private college. Recruiting foreign athletes is common in sports like soccer, tennis, swimming, and golf and is becoming more common in all sports. If you see that the roster has a lot of junior college or community college transfers, you might want to ask the coach about this. Some coaches like junior college transfers who have been competing and can enter the program ready to play at the college level. If you will be heading to junior college first, you should find schools to which you can transfer once you earn your associate's degree.

Athlete Bios

If you can find athletes' bios, read them to find out what type of athletes they were coming out of high school. Were they nationally ranked, a state All-Star, a regional All-American, or on a competitive travel team? What made them special? Bios can give you a good indication of what type of athlete the coach is looking for and where the coach looks. You can also find out how much playing time that athlete is getting in college. Most sites with bios will include stats from the athlete's college years as well as the athlete's high school or secondary performances.

Results and Statistics

If you are an athlete in a sport that uses times, measurements, or individual scores to determine athletic ability (like swimming or track, for example), look up the competition results or top times to determine what it takes to make the team. Look at the conference championship results and find out what it takes to score in the top 8, top 12, and top 16. Most coaches will recruit athletes who can help their team win a conference championship. For golf, look at the team's averages and championships results. Cross country is a little bit different because each course is different, but you can get an idea of the pace per mile you need to be running to make the team.

It is not easy to use college statistics to determine an athlete's ability in team sports, but statistics can give you an indication of who's playing and how well. Statistics will not mean much unless you know an athlete's competition. A baseball player hitting .350 in one conference may only hit .250 in another because the competition is tougher. You can gain insight into a coach's philosophy from looking at statistics. Does the bench get a chance to play, or are only the top players competing? Are the quarterback's passing stats higher than the running backs' stats? Is one ball player scoring all the points in the basketball game, or are the points spread across the team? How many saves is the goalie making compared to the goals being scored by the team? These are a few things you can look for that will give you some ideas for questions to ask a coach once you begin the recruiting process.

Additional Information

While you are on the school's website, you might want to make note of a few other pieces of information that may be valuable to you later. For example, note the conference the team competes in, the team's record and individual athletes' records, team history, coaching staff, and facilities.

Conference

It is very important to note the conference in which the team competes. Then look at other schools in the same conference as possible places for you to play. The only difference between these schools might be in the school's location (urban versus rural) or its size (10,000 versus 4,000 students on campus). Coaches do not want a star recruit competing against them in their conference. Coaches might offer a slightly better scholarship to keep a star athlete in their pool rather than another college's pool. This is true with nonathletic scholarships as well. Find a few more schools in the same conference, and you just might find a financial surprise.

Team Record(s)

Review the team's overall win-lose record as well as individual records to find out how competitive the team is within its conference. Have a conversation with the coach about the team's performance. What are the team records, and how old are they? Is the team continuing to improve? Does the team have a history or tradition of performing at a certain level? How has it done in the conference? And, if it matters to you, is the team going to have a shot at playing for a conference championship?

Coaching Staff

You will find that teams within the same conference have varying numbers of coaches and support staff. How much support does the program get from the college? By NCAA rules, schools are limited to the number of coaches and support staff they are allowed depending on what division they are in; you will see this difference if you look at the composition of a Division I team's coaching staff versus that of a Division III team. Basketball, football, and other team sports might have position coaches. Some sports have graduate assistants or fifth-year seniors helping with the program. If you see some discrepancies within a conference from one program to the next, you might want to ask some questions about the support a particular program receives from the athletic department.

Facilities

There are big differences from one college to the next as to what facilities each offers its teams. You might be able to tell right away which sports are most important to a college by looking at the facilities. Several colleges have built impressive student recreational centers over the past five to ten years that benefit both the general student body and the athletes. If a school has a great facility, photos will most likely be available on its website.

Within a conference, you may find very old to brand-new facilities from school to school. Some schools have built gorgeous academic centers for their athletes; others use the college's academic centers or general student services and career placement centers for all students on campus. Weight rooms are going high tech. Many different kinds of strength-building machines and equipment are available today; look for them on your college visits. Be sure you see all the athletic facilities on each campus you visit. If a coach doesn't show you a facility, ask about it.

ADDITIONAL COLLEGE SEARCH RESOURCES

Several people, including coaches, counselors, teachers, parents, and relatives, might suggest colleges to consider. Start with your current coach. Has he sent athletes off to college to play, and what level did they head off to? Ideally, your high school coach is familiar with college recruiting and can help you. A club coach tends to understand the different levels of college sports a little better than a high school coach and can give you some direction and suggestions about schools to look into. A coach at a college camp might also be very helpful, especially if she is a college coach or a top high school coach. Ask her for some recommendations and advice.

Your high school guidance counselor works with college-bound students all the time. Your counselor may not know a lot about athletics but will know about colleges with good programs of study that match your academic goals. Teachers may be willing to share their college experiences with you, providing you with feedback on their alma mater, but unless they played sports, they probably won't be much help with the athletic part of your college search. Parents and relatives can be good resources as well, because some students end up attending a college that someone in their family has already attended. And most importantly, your family members know you best; it can't hurt to consider their suggestions.

> **IF SOMEONE YOU ENCOUNTER HAS HAD A NEGATIVE EXPERIENCE WITH A PARTICULAR SCHOOL,** don't let that fact be the only reason you take a school off your list. Research the school further and verify information before jumping to conclusions. It's all about your making an informed decision on where to play and being happy for the next four years.

CHAPTER SUMMARY

Whether you initiate contact with a coach or the coach contacts you first, you should do some research on each college. You can find out a great deal of information on the type of athlete a coach likes to recruit, or will be recruiting, from the team's website. Take notes on your findings.

Where you play college athletics should be your choice, so be sure to research options that match your future goals. The final decision should not come down to only the schools that contact you. Begin the search process as if you haven't received any letters from coaches and see what kind of list you come up with on your own. Over and over again, you can find stories in the newspaper about athletes transferring from one college to another. These athletes probably did not do their homework, letting the coaches choose them rather than the other way around. Many of these athletes showed up on campus to find three other athletes already playing their position, and they didn't want to fight for a spot. They didn't ask the right questions during the recruiting process.

Take responsibility for your future. Make your own list of priorities. Get input from people you know and trust. If you do your homework, you will be confident about your final college decision, and you will have very few surprises once you arrive on campus.

chapter 5

Year-by-Year Plan

B esides being fun, if you start early and follow a year-by-year check list, the college and athletic search process will also be smooth. The most important area for you, or any athlete, to pay attention to is your grade point average (GPA). Just about every college application will ask for your class rank and GPA. And many, many institutional and corporate scholarships have GPA requirements.

As far as college admissions officers are concerned, GPA begins the moment you take a course for high school credit, even if you do so in middle school, but for the NCAA Clearinghouse, only classes taken during your high school years count towards your academic eligibility GPA. Credits earned in middle school, or junior high, do not count towards your NCAA academic eligibility GPA. Find out which classes at your school count for higher points (usually honor and advance placement classes) and see if you can attempt any of them. Passing these classes will affect your class rank as well.

Also, your GPA and college entrance exam scores determine athletic eligibility. (See Chapter 3 for more information about academic eligibility and the various college athletic association requirements.) The following pages provide steps you can take each year to help increase your college options and improve your resume for college. The steps presented here all need to happen, so if you are a senior just beginning your search, review the sophomore and junior check lists to be sure you have taken each step.

PRIOR TO JUNIOR YEAR

Prior to junior year, you should begin to research the career and athletic options available to you and determine where you want athletics to fit into your college experience. If you take time to visit college campuses or attend college camps, you will get an idea of what college is all about and what your future might hold.

Grade Point Average

The need to challenge yourself academically early in your high school career cannot be stressed enough. Too many athletes wait until senior year to decide that they want to play college sports and then have to scramble to improve their GPA before graduation. Pay attention to your grades now. Earning a 70 in a core class will not cut it. If you want to get good grades, do your homework and turn it in on time. Homework is like practice. You know you can't improve your athletic ability if you don't go to practice; likewise, you can't bring up your grades without doing your homework. Teachers want you to succeed. If you show them how important good grades are to you, you just might end up with better grades.

Take the challenge and sign up for honors, pre-advanced placement (AP), and AP classes whenever you can. You will impress coaches, and college admissions officers love to see you challenge yourself academically. Passing these classes will greatly improve your GPA and ultimately improve your class rank.

Searching for Scholarships

Your class rank and GPA come into play with nonathletic scholarship opportunities. Most scholarships include a GPA requirement of around a 3.0 and above. The majority of scholarships are for seniors in high school, but there are some for 9th through 12th graders. You can search for them on your school district's scholarship database, at *http://fastweb.com,* and in your local newspaper. Although these scholarships are intended primarily for seniors, they are given away annually to deserving students. A freshman once wrote an essay for a scholarship and, because no seniors applied, she won it. In addition, by searching for scholarships freshman and sophomore year, you can put together a list of those you might want to apply for senior year. By then, you will have had more time to work on your essays and can be one of the first to apply when the scholarship is posted.

Additional Steps

Along with keeping your grades up and searching for scholarships, visiting college campuses and preparing for the PSAT are important steps you should take during your early high school years. Also, meeting with your counselor, researching athletic programs, attending camps, and volunteering will add to your college search process. Most students and their parents wait until the end of junior year or senior year to think about college, but you can open more doors and make a better college decision if you begin your search earlier and follow the check list provided later in this chapter.

Meet with Your High School Counselor

Freshman year is a great time to meet your counselor and discuss your interest in playing college sports. Regardless of whether you ultimately play NCAA Division I or NJCAA, you want to be sure

KAPLAN

you take the right classes to improve your chances of being admitted to your future school. Your counselor will help keep you on target to graduate and may write a recommendation letter to send with your admissions application. Your counselor should be able to help you research colleges and find those that match your career interests. Begin with your interest of study and future career choices and then find colleges with the level of athletic program that interests you. (See Chapter 4 for help with this.) The counselor usually has reference books and college resource guides for you to review and should be able to help you evaluate your academic level as well. Stop by and visit with your counselor freshman year and begin building that relationship.

Research Colleges

Begin your research by using resource books and websites to identify your college options. Check which colleges offer your major or courses in your field of interest and find out at what level of athletics they compete. Or if you have some favorite colleges, check out what you need to do to play for them and what majors they offer. If you don't know exactly what you want to study, look through some of the majors offered and see what they entail.

Both the College Board and ACT have great career exploration tools on their websites. The ACT's eDiscover program can help you find careers that match your interests, values, and abilities. After you have taken the PSAT, College Board has a free site where you can explore career interests, college majors, and colleges. Before you take the PSAT, you can pay a small fee for access to the website.

Also, ask your teachers and your guidance counselor for some career advice. High school elective courses usually are set up to help students explore different areas of interest. Check the course offerings for your school to see if there is something you might want to try. Remember, you can never start your college search too early!

Attend Sports Camps

An excellent way to begin looking at colleges is to attend summer sports camps. Most college coaches, especially at the NCAA Division I level, run summer camps. These are great recruiting opportunities for the coaches and an excellent place for young athletes to begin checking out what it really takes to compete at that school's athletic level. Some Division III coaches may run camps, but usually they are daytime camps rather than overnight ones. Check to see if schools you are interested in offer a camp and consider attending for a week or two. At a camp, you will get to meet the coach and some of the athletes on the team; they usually are the counselors at the camp. If it is an overnight camp, you will eat in the cafeteria and sleep in the dorms, which will expose you to what it might be like to attend that college. When on the campus, plan to stop by the admissions office for an information session and a campus tour. Stop by the financial aid office as well for information on potential aid options.

PARENTS SHOULD TAKE TIME TO VISIT COLLEGE CAMPUSES WHILE TRAVELING ON VACATION OR TAKING ROAD TRIPS. The sooner you get your child onto college campuses, the sooner they will begin thinking about college and start the search process. Try to arrange a meeting with the college coach while on the campus. Just meeting and speaking with a coach can motivate an athlete, and you and your child can find out exactly what it takes to become a recruit for that college. Such visits may also motivate your child academically, because most coaches will ask about grades and encourage the student to do well. Review the "Questions to Ask" section in Chapter 8 with your child before meeting with the coach or an admissions representative.

Volunteer

One of the top five components of your college application is your volunteer work. In fact, many colleges put community service hours high on their evaluation check list for admission. Students who have been involved in their community tend to become involved on college campuses and tend to graduate college at higher rates than those who have not been involved. Athletes lead very busy lives with year-long practice demands, but if you are interested in academically prestigious colleges, you can find a few hours a month to do some volunteer work. It just might help you get admitted.

A good time to fit in volunteer work is during the summer prior to your junior year. Find one or two areas you enjoy and dedicate time to them. You might love animals and volunteer at a shelter; you might enjoy working with children and volunteer at a daycare or recreation center; if you want to go into medicine, volunteering at a hospital would be a rewarding experience. Some students volunteer with eldercare, at road races, cleanup and charity events, or local farmer's markets. Some have initiated their own activities at school, such as coat drives, food drives, or letters for soldiers. Others volunteer for local elementary or middle school after-school or before-school programs.

Look in the yellow pages or online to find nonprofit agencies in your community that could use your help. Colleges are looking for your commitment to your community. Once you have found something you enjoy, try to commit to a regular schedule during your junior and senior years. Volunteering once a week or once a month will make a difference on your college application and in your community.

Take Practice Tests and College Entrance Exams

You should take the PSAT in October of your junior year, but you can take it as a practice test during your sophomore year. The Austin Independent School District in Texas offers the PSAT exam for all sophomores and juniors. Experiencing the exam once may help students perform better the second time as well as helping them earn a higher SAT score junior year. Retaking college entrance exams is recommended.

Some excellent review materials and courses are available for this test and the SAT and ACT. These tests are as much about test-taking strategies as they are about testing your knowledge. Check to see if your school offers a college entrance exam prep class or check with your counselor to locate free programs. You might also pay to take one of the many preparation classes taught by private individuals or companies.

If preparation classes are not your style, or you just want extra practice during your own time, great test-prep books are Kaplan's *SAT 2008 Edition Premier Program* and Kaplan's *ACT 2008 Edition Premier Program*. Both these books include an online companion and CD-ROM with additional practice tests, score analysis, tutorials, and more to provide students the tools needed for success. Go to *www.kaptest.com* for more information on each of these books.

By taking practice tests, you will gain experience with each exam, which in turn can help you become more comfortable with the test, ultimately raising your scores. Along with reviewing test preparation materials, the best way to improve your score is to read more magazines, newspapers, and books on a wide variety of subjects. (You will find more information about these exams later in this chapter.)

If you follow the plan shown in Figure 5.1 and check off each item, you should have a smooth transition into junior year and have a good idea of which colleges you are interested in researching, both academically and athletically.

PRIOR TO JUNIOR YEAR SUMMARY

Prior to your junior year, meet with your counselor, challenge yourself in the classroom by taking honors and AP classes, take the PSAT for practice, and begin searching for scholarships. Attend college sports camps; take time to visit campuses before or after the camp, and do all you can to gain information to aid you in your decision. Find time to volunteer; when you are filling out your college applications, you'll be very glad that you did. You may even end up with a great college essay based on your experience as a volunteer.

JUNIOR YEAR

Junior year is a big year in terms of your college search. This is the year to focus on what you are capable of and what you want to reach for, academically and athletically. You can work to improve your grade point average over the next two years. Athletically, you have an idea of where you fit on your high school team or on your club team. If you haven't already done so, take time to assess your talent, search for colleges that match your ability, and contact those coaches. Continue volunteering, visit as many of your top schools as possible, and attend your top colleges' sports camps if they are

■ **Figure 5.1: Prior to Junior Year: A Check List** ■

Academics

- Meet with your guidance counselor about your high school academic plan
- Review NCAA and NAIA Academic Eligibility Requirements (see Chapter 3)
- Take challenging high school courses; advanced placement and honors courses when offered
- Take the PSAT, SAT II's, and AP if applicable
- Calculate your GPA and find out your class rank (may not be available until after sophomore year)
- Ask your counselor about the college search resources available at your school
- Get to know your teachers (you will need recommendations from them senior year)
- Develop good study habits, time management, and writing skills
- Read books, newspapers, magazines, etc.
- Learn how to use the high school and public library
- Learn how to use the Internet for academics
- Get involved in extracurricular activities (clubs, committees, mentor programs, etc.)
- Create a filing system for any college information you receive or collect
- Talk to teachers, friends, and family about colleges and the college search process
- Begin to think of areas you would be interested in studying
- Begin to write down college goals for your academics
- Volunteer in your community and/or the workplace
- Travel

Athletics

- Assess your athletic abilities
- Talk to your coach about college athletics
- Learn about different levels of competition within college athletics (see Chapter 1)
- Become familiar with the NCAA and NAIA rules and regulations governing athletic recruitment
- Create a file of your achievements, newspaper clippings, awards, etc.
- Develop athletic goals for the next four years
- Send an initial contact letter to college coaches (see Chapter 7)
- Fill in and return any questionnaires you receive from colleges you might be interested in
- Attend camps, clinics, and/or special programs at colleges
- Check for college athletic results in newspapers and on the Internet
- Visit college campuses while traveling to or from competitions (see Chapter 8)
- Meet the coach on your unofficial college visit
- Be aware that coaches are observing and evaluating you at competitions
- Compete at the highest level offered in your sport
- Videotape your competitions for future use (see Chapter 7)
- Attend a college competition in your sport

KAPLAN

offered. If you do stay on top of everything, you should be able to narrow down your choices to your top five to ten schools by the end of your junior year.

Take Challenging Courses

If you haven't yet attempted advanced placement or honors classes, try one or two. Usually by junior year, you have settled into high school life and can step it up academically. Colleges like to see students challenging themselves by taking the hardest courses offered. A "B" in an AP class looks better to an admissions officer than an "A" in a regular class. Also, by taking an AP class, you will be better prepared for college classes. In addition, coaches don't mind having good students to recruit.

Your GPA and class rank at the end of junior year are the figures you will use on your college applications in the fall. Your test scores can change, but your rank and GPA will not change much during your senior year. If you contact coaches early in your junior year, you will have time to make adjustments in your junior and senior course selection should you need to. Also, coaches will have an easier time pulling for you with admissions if you have done so. College coaches also want athletes who show they are up for a challenge academically. Typically, those athletes who have pushed themselves academically will also do so athletically. Academic ability is just as important as athletic ability, especially at the top academic universities.

Taking the PSAT, SAT, and ACT

Taking the PSAT in October will indicate how you might do on the SAT later in the year and what you should work on to improve your SAT score. The PSAT is used to determine recipients of National Merit Scholarships, but more importantly, it is practice for the SAT.

One basic strategy to use on the SAT is "S stands for *skip*." You lose points for answering a question wrong on the SAT, so if you don't know the answer or cannot narrow it down to two choices, skip it. You do not gain or lose points for omitting an answer on the SAT. On the other hand, for the ACT, "*A* stands for *answer*." On this exam, you do not lose points for guessing wrong or skipping a question, and you gain points if you guess correctly. Take both exams and decide which one you feel more comfortable with. Then retake that test as many times as it takes to earn a score that matches the score ranges for your top colleges.

The SAT and ACT should be taken during your junior year, preferably in the spring (March, April, or May) but no later than June. Currently, the writing portion of the test is being phased into the admissions equation; thus, the athletic associations have yet to add this score to their academic eligibility requirements. Because the NCAA will use a combination of ACT scores from any sitting, the ACT may be the better test for you. The ACT tests students in Science, Math, English, and Reading, so each time you improve a score on one of the four sections, your combined score increases. Also, the ACT test seems to match better the type of tests students are accustomed to taking

BOTH THE SAT AND ACT ARE SCHEDULED FOR DIFFERENT WEEKENDS DURING THE TESTING MONTHS, and each test has a registration deadline. If you miss the deadline, there is a late fee. If you miss the late registration, you can show up at the test site, hope there is an open seat, and pay a much higher fee. Refer to SAT and ACT test date charts in Chapter 3 (Table 3.1) for registration deadlines.

in high school. The SAT test has Math, Critical Reading, and Writing sections, but the NCAA only considers the Math and Critical Reading sections, so you will have only two chances to improve your overall score.

Test-Taking Tips

Do not sign up for the test the day after your homecoming football game. Look at your school calendar and plan to take the test on a weekend with the least number of school activities. You need a good night's sleep. You should get up early and be awake, ready to take the test. Bring a photo ID, a watch, a calculator, and a snack.

Send Letters to College Coaches

Fall of your junior year (early spring at the latest) is the time to send letters out to coaches. (Chapter 7 provides advice on contacting coaches and information on possible responses you can expect from them once you send a letter.) Junior year is also the time to collect some videotape of your athletic ability. (Chapter 7 also provides information on how to make a great tape.) By beginning early, you will have more time to get to know the coach, the team, the college, and the academic programs, and you should be able to get a good read on the financial commitment your family will have to make.

Know the Recruiting Rules

Familiarize yourself with the recruiting rules governing your top colleges' association. Some of these rules are discussed in Chapter 3. You can find the *Guide for the College-Bound Student-Athlete* containing recruiting rules at *www.ncaa.org* or *http://naia.cstv.com;* it can be either downloaded or reviewed online. Remember, if for any reason a recruiting rule is broken during your recruitment, the coach will be reprimanded, but more importantly, you will not be allowed to be recruited by that coach.

As you learned in Chapter 3, September 1 of your junior year is the earliest date that NCAA Division I and II coaches can begin sending you recruiting material, while Division III, NAIA, and

NJCAA schools can send you recruiting materials anytime during your high school years. Once you have been in touch with the coach via mail or by attending a camp, you may begin receiving information on the program and university. Remember that the sooner you get this information, the more time you have to do research to make a well-informed decision about your college match.

Visit Your Top Choices

Make as many visits to colleges during your junior year as possible. During your senior year, you can revisit your top choices. (Chapter 8 has more information on planning your visits, important questions to ask, and people to meet.)

Many colleges offer an early admissions application deadline in the fall of your senior year, so knowing as much about your top choices as possible will help you decide if you would like to be considered for early admission. However, making college visits during the fall can be tough for athletes who compete in the fall or winter. High school and club coaches do not like athletes to miss practice. Therefore, the more college visits you can make in the spring or summer before senior year, the better.

The early signing date for athletes playing winter or spring sports (and women's volleyball) is in November of your senior year. If you have narrowed down your choices to your top five by September 1 of your senior year, you should feel less pressure about deciding where to apply early or about signing an athletic scholarship commitment early. If a coach is encouraging you to apply early, you have a good chance of being admitted; there are fewer applicants, so the coach will have an easier time supporting you with the admissions department than when the applicant pool is larger.

College coaches would love to have all their recruiting done in the fall. If they can get commitments and early acceptances from their future athletes, they can focus on coaching their team. If you are prepared to make your college decision in the fall of your senior year, you might improve your options and will likely feel less stressed about your decision. Most college coaches will say they would love to know their incoming class as early as possible. And most seniors would love to know where they are going to college before their December holiday break.

Register with the NCAA Clearinghouse

The very last item you need to do at the end of your junior year, if you have any desire to play NCAA Division I or II athletics, is to register with the NCAA Clearinghouse. The registration form is located at *www.ncaa.org* and can be downloaded or completed online at *www.ncaaclearinghouse. net*. There is a fee, so you will need a credit card to complete the online version. If you had a waiver for the SAT or ACT exam, you can receive a waiver for the registration fee. To receive a fee waiver, you will need to get a hard copy of the Clearinghouse registration form signed by an administrator, verifying that you used a waiver for one of the exams.

Registering with the Clearinghouse allows the NCAA to certify your academic eligibility for Division I or II athletics. You must have an official transcript sent to the Clearinghouse. This does not need to occur until after your junior year. Once you have registered, you will not be officially cleared until after you have graduated from high school with the academic requirements to attend either the Division I or II college. (These requirements are covered in Chapter 3.)

You can determine your own NCAA GPA by using the Division I (or II) Academic Eligiblity worksheet located in the NCAA *Guide for the College-Bound Student-Athlete* (see worksheet in Chapter 3). Your high school counselor may be able to help you if you have trouble understanding the procedure. You do not need to fill in the Clearinghouse form if you are planning on attending an NCAA Division III, NJCAA, or NAIA school, but NJCAA and NAIA each have an academic eligibility form on their websites that you must complete after your junior year.

If you follow the junior-year plan in Figure 5.2 and check off each item, you should have a smooth transition to senior year and have a good idea of which colleges you can compete at, both academically and athletically.

JUNIOR YEAR SUMMARY

This is the year for you to do all your homework, take action, and follow up. Contact coaches; do not sit around waiting for them to call. Study hard, get good grades, research your options, take the SAT and ACT in the spring, and get excited about senior year and your big decision. If you stay on top of your search during your junior year, by the fall of your senior year, you will know exactly which five schools you are most interested in and be able to narrow it down further by November. Follow the steps suggested, and you should have a smooth, less stressful college search process.

■ Figure 5.2: Junior Year: A Check List ■

Academics

- Meet with your guidance counselor and review college search resources (see Chapter 6)
- Check out the college guides at your guidance counselor's office, library, on the Internet, or at the book store
- Take challenging high school courses, advanced placement and honors courses when offered
- Take the SAT, ACT, and SAT II's, have scores sent to top schools on your list
- Take AP exams when offered
- Calculate your GPA and find out your class rank
- Continue to develop a good student-teacher relationship with your teachers
- Begin a list of possible people for recommendations
- Develop good study habits and time management skills; spend time reading and writing
- Get involved in volunteer work and other extracurricular activities (clubs, committees, organizations, etc.)
- Review college academic goals

- Attend college fairs (see Chapter 6)
- Organize and file all information for various colleges (see Chapter 4)
- Solicit input from friends, guidance counselor, coaches, parents, siblings, teachers, and alumni on various college programs and their reputation
- Begin seriously thinking of what type of college setting you may like (see Key Areas of Consideration Check List in Chapter 10)
- Write to colleges in which you are interested, ask for brochures and an application (see Chapter 7)
- Talk to parents about financial needs; YOUR expected contribution
- Obtain information on scholarships, both athletic and public
- Create a scholarship, financial aid, and college application due date
- Apply for financial aid and scholarships; check deadlines on all forms, some may need to be done before your senior year
- Consider applying early decision or early action

Athletics

- Register with the NCAA Clearinghouse at the end of your junior year
- Review the *NCAA Guide for the College-Bound Student-Athlete* from the NCAA and the NAIA *College Bound Student Athlete* on each association's website
- Know the NCAA and NAIA rules and regulations governing athletic recruitment by July 1 before your senior year
- Be aware, coaches may *now* begin sending you correspondence on a regular basis (see Chapter 3)
- Assess your level of athletic ability (NCAA Div. I, II, III, Jr college, NAIA)
- Talk to your coach about colleges at which you are interested in competing
- Evaluate your athletic goals for college
- Add to your achievement file any additional awards, articles, honors you have received, etc.
- Develop a personal resume from your achievement file
- Send a letter and resume to coaches whose program you are interested in and haven't heard back from yet (see Chapter 7)
- Fill in and return any questionnaires you receive from colleges in which you might be interested
- Follow up with a call to coaches
- Collect college team results from correspondence, newspapers, sport magazines, and the Internet
- Plan to visit colleges during school breaks or while traveling to or from competitions (see Chapter 8)
- Schedule meetings with the coach, an admissions officer, a financial aid representative (see Chapter 8)
- Keep a notebook of your impressions of various colleges you visit
- Ask your coach to recommend you to the college coach
- Be aware that coaches are observing and evaluating you at competitions
- Compete at the highest level offered in your sport
- Videotape competitions to be sent to coaches on request (see Chapter 7)
- Attend camps, clinics, and/or special programs at colleges
- Inform college coaches of the camps and clinics you will be attending
- Narrow down your choices to 10 to 12 colleges, or less, by the end of summer prior to your senior year

SENIOR YEAR

If you have done all the proper steps during your junior year, senior year will consist of revisiting colleges, retaking entrance exams, assembling your admission and scholarship application packets, and continuing to take challenging classes. Most importantly, you will be celebrating your acceptances!

Revisit Colleges

If you have done all your research and visited colleges during your junior year, you are now ready to revisit and apply. (If you haven't visited any college campuses, then the fall is the best time to do that.) Some athletes have a hard time missing school or practice to make second college visits during their senior year, but these visits are crucial. This will probably be the most important decision you will have to make up to this point in your life, and it will profoundly affect your future. Remember, if you visited during your junior year and met athletes on the college team, you will have met only some of your future teammates. The seniors you met in the spring are no longer there. The new freshmen on the college team have just now arrived, and they are going to be your closest future teammates; you will compete with them longer than anyone else you have previously met. So return in the fall and meet the team again just to be absolutely sure that this college and this athletic program are right for you.

Retaking the SAT or ACT

You should have taken the SAT or ACT at least once during your junior year, now you can retake either or both. However, if you have not taken either test, do so right away. You may want time to retake them to improve your scores for academic eligibility or academic scholarships. Colleges offer merit scholarships to students with high class ranks and good test scores. Students in the top 10 percent of their class with an SAT Math and Critical Reading combined score of 1,200 or above or an ACT composite score (average of all four section scores) of 31 or greater have an excellent chance of earning financial aid at many colleges. Some colleges will look at GPA and test scores. Ask each college's financial aid representative what that school's standards are so you will know what to reach for.

The NCAA will take the best combination of Math and Critical Reading scores from any test dates. Thus, it can use your Math score from one test date and your Critical Reading score from another. The NCAA will also use your best combination of scores from the ACT. Because the ACT has four different scored areas, you can take the test four times and end up with a Reading score from one test, a Math score from another, a Science score from a third, and a Verbal score from a fourth. For this to happen, you must start taking the test during your junior year. The NAIA colleges will take your best Math score and Critical Reading score from one sitting (test date) of the either the SAT or the ACT.

Some colleges require SAT subject tests for specific majors. Check your top college's admissions requirements to see if you need to take any. This information can be found on the college's website, usually under a heading like "Admissions and Requirements."

Complete College Applications

College applications are usually available around September 1 of your senior year. Most colleges have online applications and would prefer that you complete the online version. Some schools accept—others require—the Common Application (found at *http://commonapp.org*). Once completed, the Common Application can be sent to any number of schools that subscribe to the service. Check the college's admissions website for that school's online application. Let the coach know when you complete and submit the online version.

To begin filling in the application, you will need a list of your senior classes (these are not on your transcript because you have not received grades in these classes yet), a list of any extracurricular and volunteer activities you have been a part of (and the hours spent doing these activities), any awards and honors you have earned, and any work experience you have thus far. If you have all this information available when you sit down to begin the online application, it should not take you long to complete. Have a friend, counselor, teacher, or family member read over your completed application and make sure it's accurate and complete before submitting. A simple typo can affect your admission.

You need to request that your high school send an official transcript. Talk to your guidance counselor about this procedure. Many colleges also require an essay and recommendation letters as part of your application packet. Do your best to have all these items sent together—admissions officers prefer the packet this way, and it helps prevent the loss of any one part of the application. Also, the admission office will not even begin reading your application until it receives your application fee, so if you are applying online, have a credit card ready the day you want to submit your applications.

Continue to Take Challenging Courses

Senior year is no time to slack off academically. You'll need to continue to challenge yourself in the classroom. On your college applications, you will be asked to list your senior class schedule and, in many cases, will be asked for your midyear (December/January) grades. College admissions committees want to see if you are continuing to develop your academic skills by taking a challenging senior class load rather than a fluff schedule. Maintain the academic standards you have achieved through senior year—or do better. Any acceptance letter you receive from a college will clearly state that you must maintain your academic progress and graduate. Students have had their college acceptances withdrawn because of unsatisfactory academic progress or misconduct. Even an athletic

> **PARENTS SHOULD TRY TO HAVE TAX INFORMATION COMPILED AND READY FOR FILING IN JANUARY.** Parents can complete the FAFSA with estimated information and then go back in and make changes if necessary once they receive their W-2 and other tax forms. If your family income has not changed from one year to the next, your Estimated Family Contribution (EFC) towards college may not change.

scholarship you sign will state that you must graduate and earn the academic requirements for the offer to be good.

Submit the Online FAFSA

Every college financial aid applicant requires students complete the Free Application for Federal Student Aid (FAFSA) to be considered for financial aid. Colleges will request a completed FAFSA to go along with their own scholarship applications. Although athletic scholarships are not connected to the FAFSA, most athletic departments will have students complete a FAFSA, especially if you want to be considered for any federal money. An athlete on a full ride can still receive Pell Grant funds, a need-based grant, above the athletic allotment, which can be used for school supplies, clothes, and other miscellaneous needs.

January 1 is the earliest date you can fill in and submit the FAFSA online. This is a very important step in the college application process. By completing the FAFSA you will receive an Estimated Family Contribution (EFC), an estimate of what the government believes your family can pay for your education. Whoever claims you on their tax forms will need to complete the FAFSA and supply their previous year's tax return to the colleges to which you are applying. Colleges will award financial aid on a first-come, first-served basis. The first completed financial applications are looked at and awarded money first. So if your parent or guardian waits until April 15 to complete their taxes, you will be way down on the list for financial assistance. Colleges have an allotment of financial aid to award, and once it is gone, it is gone. Even if your family shows need, if your financial aid application is submitted in April and the money has already been awarded to other students, you will be out of luck.

SENIOR YEAR SUMMARY

Summer and fall of your senior year will be busy, but if you have planned ahead, researched your options, contacted coaches, and visited your top campuses, you will spend most of your time making

■ Figure 5.3: Senior Year: A Check List ■

Academics

- Meet with high school counselor to review NCAA and NAIA Academic Eligibility Requirements and evaluate your academic progress
- Check out the college guides at your guidance counselor's office, library, on the Internet, or at the book store (see College Resources in Chapter 7)
- Continue to challenge yourself academically, take advanced placement and honors courses when offered
- Take the SAT, ACT, Achievement tests and SAT II's; have tests scores sent to your top college choices
- Take AP Exams when applicable
- Calculate your GPA and find out your class rank
- Choose teachers for recommendation letters and ask them in early September especially for early action and early decision applications
- Choose teachers that know you well and will write a positive letter
- Share your transcript and any other relevant information with them
- Continue developing good study habits; time management reading and writing skills
- Volunteer some more! Join a club, organization, committee, etc.
- Make a list of various colleges you may be interested in attending
- Solicit input from friends, guidance counselor, coaches, parents, siblings, teachers, and alumni on various college programs and their reputation
- Review the list of qualities that make a college right for you and compare with your list of colleges (see Chapter 10)
- Write to colleges you have not received information from
- Categorize your college list into reaches, possibles, and safeties
- Talk to parents about financial needs; YOUR expected contribution
- Obtain information on scholarships, both athletic and public
- Create a scholarship and financial aid application due date timetable
- Apply for grants, loans, financial aid and scholarships; check deadlines on all forms—**DO NOT MISS THE DEADLINES**
- Submit recommendations, transcript and test scores requested to your guidance office as early as possible
- Fill out all college applications and aid request forms <u>completely</u> and send in <u>BEFORE deadline</u>
- Be sure to have essays edited, absolutely <u>NO</u> mistakes

Athletics

- Register with the NCAA Clearinghouse, if you have not already done so (go to *ncaaclearinghouse.net*)
- Review the **new** *NCAA Guide for the College-Bound Student-Athlete (www.ncaa.org)*
- Know the rules and regulations governing athletic recruitment by July 1 before your senior year
- Be aware of the date college coaches may contact you by phone

(continued on next page)

- Review your college athletic goals with your coach and solicit your coach's input on your athletic level (Div. I, II, III, etc.) and how competitive each college you're looking at is
- Add to your achievement file and add to your a personal resume from your achievement file
- Send a letter and resume to coaches whose program you are interested in and haven't heard back from yet (see Chapter 7)
- Fill in and return any additional questionnaires you receive from colleges you might be interested in
- Continue to update coaches, with a letter or phone call, on a regular basis when there are changes in your performance; highlights, improvements, championships, injuries, or sicknesses
- Ask coaches about scholarships and what athletic needs they have for the next year
- Ask coaches about a visit to the college (review rules on official and unofficial visits)
- Have your coach call the college coach to recommend you
- Plan visits to your top schools (see Chapter 8)
- Remember to ask LOTS of questions (see Chapter 8)
- Write notes immediately after each visit
- Collect college team results from correspondence, newspapers, sport magazines, and the Internet
- Introduce yourself to college coaches when they are at your athletic competitions
- Be aware that coaches are observing and evaluating you at competitions
- Compete at the highest level offered in your sport
- Videotape your competitions for future use
- View college competition in your sport

final decisions and completing paperwork. If you are just now contacting coaches, you will need to work fast and be aggressive. If you need recommendation letters, ask your teachers and guidance counselor for them soon after Labor Day.

Continue to work hard academically; you don't want to mess up now. If you are on top of things and have your application(s) completed by November 1, you'll get to enjoy your senior year. Complete your FAFSA by early January so you are first in line for financial aid. If you are still researching colleges, try to have your applications submitted by January 1—February 1 at the latest—and make February 15 your deadline for competing your FAFSA. Remember, financial aid is first-come, first-served, so if others have their FAFSA application done by January 15, they are in line for free money ahead of you, no matter how badly your family needs help.

Last bit of advice: Make sure you stay in shape. If the coach sends you a summer training program to be completed prior to showing up at college, you better be following it, or you may not get a spot on the team come fall. Ask the freshmen on your college visit about the first day of training and the coach's expectations.

Building Key Relationships

The college recruiting process is all about interacting and communicating with adults. Whether it is your high school coach or club coach, your counselor or teacher, the college coach, an admissions representative from a college, or a financial aid officer, you can best open doors and find options by building relationships with these very important people. These adults, as well as your parents or guardian, are each an important part of your college search. If you build these relationships, you will be more confident in your final decision of where to compete in college. Don't wait for anyone to come to you. Take the initiative in building these relationships. It is your future, and it should be your choice.

HIGH SCHOOL AND CLUB COACHES

Begin with your high school and/or club coach. Let them know you are interested in competing in college. They may be able to help you locate opportunities and may become another voice for you, besides your own, during the recruiting process. Ask them at what level they think you can compete. Have your coach recommend schools to research. Many college coaches find athletes through high school and club coaches' recommendations. Be aware that most high school coaches do not know everything about college recruiting, so do not rely solely on your coach as your advocate. *You* are your number one advocate. You need to contact college coaches and follow up with them. However, do use your high school and club coaches as a resource and for support during the process.

HIGH SCHOOL COUNSELOR OR COLLEGE ADVISOR

Your high school counselor or college advisor will be very important in helping you stay on the path to graduation and meet all your state graduation requirements as well as college admissions requirements. Your counselor should be able to help determine your academic eligibility for the different levels of NCAA competition, as well as NAIA and NJCAA competition. (See Chapter 3 for more information on the academic eligibility requirements for each association.) Many colleges and nonathletic scholarship applications require at least one counselor's recommendation and one or two teacher recommendations. Get to know your counselor, and find a teacher who can write a strong recommendation for you. College coaches don't need these recommendations, but many college admissions applications and most scholarship applications require recommendation letters. (Additional information regarding recommendation letters is provided in Chapter 9.)

COLLEGE ADMISSIONS REPRESENTATIVES

Other important people to build relationships with are the college admissions representatives from each college you are interested in attending. Just because the coach wants you, has been recruiting you, and says you are on the list does not mean you will be accepted to the university. The admissions department, *not* the coach, ultimately decides on your admittance to the college. Each college assigns an admissions person to different regions of the country. This person is responsible for reading your application and making a recommendation to the admissions committee on your acceptance or denial. At the more competitive academic colleges and universities across the country, the admis-

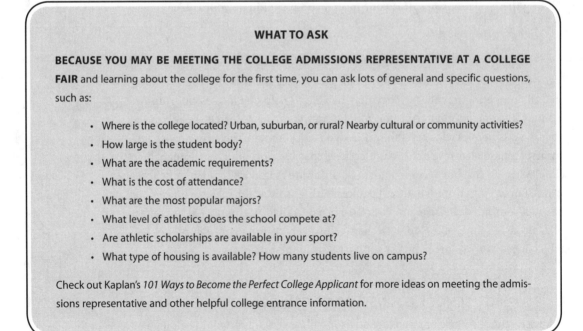

WHAT TO ASK

BECAUSE YOU MAY BE MEETING THE COLLEGE ADMISSIONS REPRESENTATIVE AT A COLLEGE FAIR and learning about the college for the first time, you can ask lots of general and specific questions, such as:

- Where is the college located? Urban, suburban, or rural? Nearby cultural or community activities?
- How large is the student body?
- What are the academic requirements?
- What is the cost of attendance?
- What are the most popular majors?
- What level of athletics does the school compete at?
- Are athletic scholarships are available in your sport?
- What type of housing is available? How many students live on campus?

Check out Kaplan's *101 Ways to Become the Perfect College Applicant* for more ideas on meeting the admissions representative and other helpful college entrance information.

sions representative is the most important person to know. When you visit the college campus, be sure to stop by the admissions office. It keeps track of who has been on campus and may include this information in your admissions review.

Other than on the college campus, the best place to meet the admissions representative is at a college fair. College fairs are held at area high schools and convention centers during the fall and spring in or near your hometown. The larger the fair, the more likely the representative will be there. Your high school counselor will know when these events are scheduled, and local newspapers typically advertise the larger events. While at the fair, be sure to get the representative's business card and sign up to receive information from the college and ask some questions. The representative's job is to recruit you. Share a little information about yourself so you will be memorable. The more effort you put into the admissions process, the stronger your application and the better your chance of admission.

FINANCIAL AID OFFICERS

Like the admissions officer, the financial aid officer is someone with whom you should become familiar if you are applying for financial aid. The financial aid office controls institutional scholarships for which you might be eligible. All colleges have their own financial resources for incoming freshman and typically award the merit-based money on a first-come/first-served basis. Each college also has an allotment of federal money, grants, scholarships, and loans that it is responsible for awarding. This money is also on a first-come/first-served basis. To be considered for aid, turn your financial and scholarship application in before the deadlines and be one of the first to complete the Free Application for Federal Student Aid (FAFSA) in January each year. Regardless of your financial situation, you should complete the FAFSA in January of your senior year and each January during college. The majority of the aid from each college is based on your Student Aid Report (SAR) from your completed FAFSA. Do not miss this important step in the college application process.

When you receive your initial financial aid package or award from the college, you can always ask if there is anything else you can apply for. Or if you have two colleges you like that are similar, and one gives you a better package, you can ask the other to rework your financial aid award. Sometimes, you'll end up with a little bit more than originally offered. You should definitely let the financial aid office know if your family's income has changed or any tragedies have occurred. Most financial aid officers will try to work with you.

Review the list of scholarships in the back of this book. These are corporate and community scholarships that are available to any student who meets the criteria. Apply to as many as you can and see what happens. You may end up with some extra financial support that you will not have to pay back.

Once the academic school year begins, visit your financial aid advisor to see if any more money is available. Sometimes, students who committed to the college do not show up in the fall, or some

IF YOU ARE CONSIDERING NCAA DIVISION III ATHLETICS, THESE COACHES DO NOT HAVE ACCESS TO ATHLETIC SCHOLARSHIPS, but they can recruit and assist athletes in the admissions process. However, it is against NCAA rules for a Division III coach to intervene with the financial aid process. At the same time, many athletes at the Division III level are awarded excellent financial aid packages. The ultimate goal is to have your education paid for, regardless of whether the subsidy is called an "athletic scholarship."

students flunk out midyear. Build a relationship with a financial aid officer, and you could end up paying less for college!

THE COLLEGE COACH

The most important person for you to build a relationship with during the recruiting process is the college coach. You, not your current coach or parents or guardian, should be the one to contact the coach and establish a relationship. Your high school coach can be extremely helpful during the recruiting process; just be sure you are in contact with the college coach as well. The college coach is working hard to determine which athletes will best fit into the program, which good athletes can be developed into better athletes, and which athletes can be admitted to the university.

During his junior year, an athlete had received numerous letters from all the top teams in the country. From this correspondence, he became very excited about one school in particular; however, he allowed his club coach to do the majority of the communicating with the college coaches. When July 1 rolled around, coaches from the other top schools called and set up official visits with the athlete—all but his number one choice. Unfortunately, the athlete's club coach, who happened to have his own opinions of where the athlete should go, had told the college coach the athlete was not interested in that college.

Athletes, if you are interested in a particular school, *you* need to contact the college coach and establish a relationship. Do *not* rely on someone else to convey your desire or level of interest. Remember, college coaches award athletic scholarships, decide who is on the team, and have connections with the admissions department. You will do yourself a great service by personally contacting the coach!

Coaches and Admissions

Coaches know what it takes academically to graduate from the university. The majority of college coaches across the country have connections with their respective admissions offices. Some have more connections and can help just about any eligible athlete get admitted. Other coaches turn in a list of their preferred student athletes, and the admissions committee picks from the list. Keep in mind that coaches do not admit athletes; the admissions committee admits students who happen to be athletes. The coach is the key person for you to be in contact with and for you to build a relationship with to play

> **REMEMBER: THE COACH DOES NOT ADMIT ATHLETES**—the admissions director admits students who happen to be athletes.

college sports, if admitted to the college. The admission representative is the person you need to be in contact with to be admitted. Coaches recruit student athletes hoping that admissions officers like what they see with respect to grades, test scores, and other important pieces of your application.

Coaches and Scholarships

College coaches control the awarding of athletic scholarships, if they are available to the coach. The scholarships are awarded according to the team's needs each year. If the team is graduating a goalie and the team has only one other goalie, the coach will need to replace that graduating goalie. If the team already has three goalies and you are a goalie, chances are that team doesn't need your talents.

NCAA Division III coaches cannot give athletic scholarships, but they do know what the financial aid office has available for prospective students. For example, a soccer player at a Division III college in Texas received the "Be on Time Loan" (worth $4,000 a year). It is a low-interest loan that he will not need to pay back if he graduates on time—in four years. The coach recommended that the athlete ask the financial aid office about it.

Take the Initiative

Building a relationship with the college coach is essential in helping you find your perfect athletic fit. College coaches are trying to determine who will best fit in their program and who has the desire and ability to compete for their school.

Depending on the sport you play, the number of graduating seniors, and the positions the coach needs to fill, the coach may be recruiting five to ten athletes for one spot on the team. Three to five of those athletes may be equally strong athletically and have varying academic credentials. The goal of the coach is to determine which students will say yes. Your goal is to be one of the top five athletes on the

> **TAKE THE INITIATIVE.** If you want to make your decision easier and have more control over the final outcome, take the initiative during your recruiting process. Contact coaches!

coach's list at more than one school. If you do your recruiting homework, you will ultimately find two to three colleges that you know you can compete at, where the coach wants you on the team, and where you are likely to be admitted.

Keep in mind that you are one of many athletes a coach may be recruiting. The more contact you have with the coach, the more information you will gather about the coach, the athletic program, and the school. And don't expect the coach to do all the contacting—to help yourself make a well-informed final decision and have more control over the final outcome, take the initiative and contact prospective coaches yourself.

Most Coaches Have Limited Resources for Recruiting

Remember: Most coaches have limited resources for recruiting. NCAA Division I and II programs usually have more money available to spend on phone calls, mailings, campus visits, home visits, and team travel than do NCAA Division III, NAIA, and NJCAA coaches. Top NCAA Division I and II coaches are hired to coach and win—they'll lose their jobs if their teams are not competitive. Thus, these coaches are usually given more resources than coaches at other levels.

YOUR PARENTS' ROLE

Your relationship with your parent(s) or guardian is an important part of your college search process. Your parents should be and need to be included in your search. They control your family's financial resources, and you will need a parent to complete the FAFSA. A parent can also help with mailing out your initial letter of interest to coaches, videotaping your competitions, and transporting you to a college visit. None of these involves your personal interaction with key people, so having a family member's assistance saves you time and helps you with your search. Keep the adults in your life involved, and you'll be a happier college applicant.

Financial Concerns

Too often, a student gets excited about a university, visits the campus, loves it, gets admitted, and has a coach excited about the student joining his or her team—and then the family discusses finances. Ideally, you and your family should discuss your college financial needs *before* the recruiting process begins. Too many athletes have gotten into the college of their choice but were unable to attend due to the final costs involved, a heartbreaking outcome.

Even athletes on full scholarships must pay for transportation to and from college and for other miscellaneous expenses. For example, a football player in Texas received a full scholarship to attend

KAPLAN

the University of Hawaii. He and his mom were very excited. What he failed to realize was that he would be responsible for his flights there and back.

Athletes who receive partial scholarships need to cover the remaining balance, which is what the majority of student athletes end up having to do. Consider the cost of attending college in your initial search and have the conversation about family finances before the recruiting process begins. Parents, athletes, and coaches will be more informed and won't have to deal with any financial surprises at the end of the process.

Speak for Yourself

Although your parents might want to call a college coach and tell them how great you are, you are the person who should be conversing with the coach. A parent's overly persistent involvement might turn off a coach. Your parents should definitely have a conversation with the coach to feel confident that you will be in good hands during college, but don't let your parents be your spokespeople. Because the coach is trying to determine who will best fit into the team, the coach needs to be able to build a relationship with you. The coach will be working with you over the next four to five years and needs to feel comfortable interacting with you.

An athlete who visited a campus with her dad met with the coach. During the interview, every time the athlete was asked a question, her dad answered. The student barely looked up or made eye contact with the coach and hardly said a word. The coach was recruiting three other swimmers who were equally talented as this student. The following weekend, one of the other athletes visited the coach by herself. Because she met with the coach on her own, she had no choice but to answer the coach's questions, and she arrived with a list of questions for the coach. In the end, the second athlete was offered the scholarship. The first student really liked the school, or at least that's what her dad said when he called, but the coach had very little confidence in the future relationship between athlete and coach.

STEPS TO BUILDING A RELATIONSHIP WITH THE COACH

How can you build a relationship with a coach? The best way is to initiate contact with a personal letter. To get the recruiting process started, send a letter to coaches early in your high school career, introducing yourself and expressing your interest in the athletic and academic programs at the university. Include a copy of your transcript for coaches to evaluate. Next, visit the campus early during your high school years—sophomore or junior year. Be sure to set up an appointment with the coach ahead of time. If the college offers a sports camp and you have the resources and the time, get exposure and show your interest in a school by attending its sports camp on campus.

Contact Coaches Early Sophomore or Junior Year

Coaches love to coach but have to recruit if they want a good team. You can make their job easier by taking the initiative and contacting them first. (Chapter 7 explains contacting coaches in more detail.) Ideally, you should have one to two years of contact with a coach to establish a solid relationship. If your initial contact is during your sophomore year, you will have about two years to develop your athletic ability and build your academic resume. If you contact a coach early in high school, they can let you know exactly what it will take to make the team and what classes you will need to sign up for to build a better academic resume. College coaches want athletes that want to compete for their school. Finding an athlete who can get admitted, help the team win, and in the end will say, "Yes, I accept your offer to attend and compete for your university," can be challenging for coaches. Admissions offices and coaches are looking for those exact words; they are what recruiting is all about.

Share Your Transcript Early in the Recruiting Process

Because the college coach decides who gets to play for the school and has connections with the admissions department, you should share your transcript with the coach early in the recruiting process. The coach will let you know if you have a good chance of getting admitted and can advise you on courses to take in high school. Coaches know their schools' admissions requirements and will recruit athletes they believe can get admitted. Be honest about your academic ability.

An athlete who waited until November of her senior year to share her transcript with coaches found herself in an unfortunate situation. Coaches paid for official visits to four NCAA Division I colleges, and she was offered athletic scholarships. When the signing date came around in November, she called the coach at the school she liked best and said she wanted to attend his university. Unfortunately, he had to tell her she was academically ineligible due to her grades and test scores; thus, he could not sign her. Because she waited until November of her senior year to share her transcript, she had no time to adjust her academic schedule to take required courses or improve her grades, and she was out of a Division I spot.

Another athlete, who made contact with coaches during the spring of her junior year, found out she was academically ineligible, but because she had shared this information with the college coach, the coach was able to suggest adjustments to her course selection for her senior year. She earned the grades she needed and a scholarship at a Big Ten university, and she was a starter on the team all four years. Be sure to begin the process early and share your academic information right off, and the coach will be able to give you some academic advice. Always check with your high school counselor before making any changes to your class schedule; however, you do want to graduate.

Initial Contact

Once you have begun the recruiting process and coaches make contact with you, whether through email, regular mail, campus or home visits, or phone calls, follow up in a timely manner. Some athletes receive a letter from a coach and do not respond. An athlete became excited about receiving a letter and believed the coach was recruiting him, but in the end the athlete never heard back. Well guess what? Early in the recruiting process, many coaches mass-mail athletes. They receive a list of athletes from championship events, then mail questionnaires to any athletes whom they think might fit their program. The coach doesn't personally know the athletes and may not have watched them play, but the coach knows that any athlete at that level is a solid player and might help his team. If an athlete does not respond to this initial letter, that student may end up out in the cold or scrambling to find his or her college opportunity.

Many of these initial letters from college coaches come via your high school or club coach. If you receive a college coach's letter this way, you have likely been mass-mailed and are not really on the coach's recruiting list. To have a shot at being recruited by this coach, you need to follow up. If you receive a letter from a coach and don't respond by sending back the questionnaire, a coach will assume that you must not be interested in the program.

The Athletic Questionnaire and the Follow-Up

Your relationship with a college coach really begins when you return the questionnaire. If you are interested in a college, return the questionnaire. If you are not interested, you don't have to return the questionnaire, but it is helpful to send a note to the coach. Thank them for contacting you but let them know that you are pursuing other opportunities. Be polite and respectful: college coaches are friends, and they share recruiting information with each other. You would not want your behavior with one coach to affect your chances with another, and you never know—you may cross paths with them in the future. Even if you are not interested, there's no point in burning bridges through discourteous behavior.

If coaches start calling and you are not interested in their program, politely say thanks but no thanks. Remember, a coach is trying to determine who is interested in that school and program. So the sooner the coach knows to move on to other athletes, the better. There is an athlete out there who does want to be recruited by that coach.

> **MOST COACHES WILL SEND YOU AN ATHLETIC QUESTIONNAIRE TO FILL OUT AND RETURN.** If you are interested in the college, return the questionnaire promptly. By returning the questionnaire, you help put yourself in the coach's recruiting file.

CAMPUS VISITS

Visiting a college campus can make your final decision easier. Just by visiting, you will get a better feel for the campus as a whole, and after meeting the coach, seeing the facilities, and touring the campus, you can decide whether the school should stay on your list or not. (Chapter 8 has more information on college visits.)

Your relationship with a coach can be greatly impacted by a simple college visit. For example, a female athlete visited a campus in August prior to her junior year. She was given a personal tour that day and then had two years to stay in touch with and get to know the coach. She was able to learn exactly what it would take to make the team, and she fell in love with the campus. Meeting an athlete in person and putting a face with a name personalizes the recruiting process for the athlete and the coach.

You can also get "brownie points" with admissions if you stop by for a campus tour and information session. Students who visit campuses are more likely to attend when admitted than those who do not visit. If you need to, revisit schools during your senior year to help make your final decision.

College Sports Camps

Along with a college visit, one of the best ways to show your interest, establish a relationship with a coach, and be evaluated is to attend a sports camp on campus. Many colleges now offer sports camps sponsored by the athletic department and the coach of each sport. You may even receive an invitation to attend the camp. Coaches use these camps to identify future prospects. You will benefit instructionally from the experience, and you will get a feel for what playing for this coach might be like. Usually, the counselors at the camp are current players from that university, so you can meet some team members and see their skill level as well. Be sure to stop by admissions and the financial aid offices. Coaches cannot actively recruit you during the camp, but you can set up a meeting with the coach before or after the camp. Some camps may have coaches from other colleges working the sessions. If a coach from an NCAA Division III, NAIA, or junior college works at a camp, you can gain some additional exposure by attending the camp. Be sure to follow up with these coaches so they know you might be interested in their programs.

> **WRITING A THANK-YOU NOTE OR CALLING AFTER A VISIT CAN HELP MOVE YOU UP ON A COACH'S RECRUITING LIST,** especially when the coach has provided the campus tour and spent time with you. What coach wouldn't like an athlete who appreciates his or her time?

ARE YOU ON THE "LIST"?

The only person who knows the answer to this question is the coach. Yes, you can ask the coach if you are on his or her recruiting list for admissions and even where you are on the list. The coach may not tell you exactly where you stand but will likely tell you if you are on the list. As mentioned earlier, the coach probably has three to five athletes for one spot, so your job is to be the top choice out of the three to five who are being recruited for the same spot.

Here is where your current coach (club or high school) might be able to help you out. Sometimes when coaches talk to each other, your coach can determine more about your standing than you can. Some college coaches pursue athletes through their club or high school coaches. Often, college coaches have to use your club or high school coach to get your address, especially if you haven't sent them a letter or email with your contact information. (Be sure to read Chapter 7 for more information on the initial letter, videotapes, and college visits.)

Your current coach can help you determine how interested a college coach is in you. Let your coach know what schools you are interested in and give your coach the college coach's phone number. You never know what your high school coach may be able to find out.

CHAPTER SUMMARY

Develop your ability to interact with adults, because as you have read, the college search and your decision will be based largely on your ability to interact with adults (coaches, admissions and financial aid officers, and counselors) and gather information from them. To build these relationships, start early and be yourself.

Contact the coach early during your high school career. Have your current coach help you find opportunities and connect with coaches. Visit the campus and, if you plan on attending summer camps, pick a camp at a college you might like to attend. Most importantly, follow up with the coach. Remember: Follow up, move up!

Be sure to ask lots of questions of both the coach and the athletes playing for that coach. (See Chapter 8 for questions to ask.) You want to be sure the information you get about practice, games, team requirements, team goals, and other important issues is similar from both the athletes and the coach.

Ask your parents to take a backseat in the recruiting process. Coaches want to get to know who you are and what makes you tick. Remember, *you* are your best advocate.

Contacting Coaches

You may imagine that coaches at your top-choice colleges will begin recruiting you without your doing anything; don't be fooled into thinking this. Coaches don't have ESP, and given the number of high school athletes across the country, there is no way college coaches know about every athlete who might be interested in playing on their team. The best way to get recruited is to take initiative and contact coaches yourself. Let them know you want to compete in college. Don't sit back and wait for a coach to find you.

A letter, email, or phone call is all it takes to initiate the process. What to say and when and how to contact coaches will be explained in this chapter. You might want a videotape showing your athletic ability; we will discuss videos in this chapter as well. Coaches might find you, if you are at national or state competitions, but you can definitely find them and show your interest first with a simple letter.

HOW COACHES RECRUIT

Coaches use a variety of avenues to find recruits, including talking with high school and club coaches; observing athletes at large recruiting venues like developmental programs, recruiting camps, and championship tournaments; as well as viewing prospective athletes' videotapes. Another recruiting method that coaches use, and one that you can initiate, is a personal contact letter. Student athletes who send letters to coaches usually receive a response, especially if they are a good match for the college and the athletic program.

Mass Mailings

Coaches mass-mail prospective student athletes. Coaches review tournament rosters, all-regional lists, and national results and rankings, then send letters to any athlete they think could help their program. Often college coaches send letters via your high school or club coach, because they do not have your address. If you received a letter from a coach via your club or high school coach, you were most likely mass-mailed. Remember that until you initiate direct contact with a coach, or respond to a coach's letter and relay your contact information, you are one of many in the recruiting pool.

In addition to a letter from a coach, you may also receive a questionnaire or a request that you complete an online questionnaire. It is up to you to fill in and return the athletic questionnaire if you want to be considered by that college coach. If you do not return the questionnaire, you will probably not be on the recruiting list. Coaches build their recruiting lists from returned questionnaires.

HOW TO GET RECRUITED

Becoming a recruited athlete is easier than most people think. It is as easy as writing a two-paragraph letter introducing yourself to a coach. If you let coaches know you are interested in playing your sport, you can become a recruited athlete. You can do one or all of the following steps listed here to get the recruiting process started: just do something to initiate the process. Not every high school athlete can play college sports, but if you really want to be a part of a team, there is a college out there for you. You just need to go find it.

Send Letters

Once you have followed the college search process (discussed in Chapter 4) to determine which schools you might be interested in, send letters to the coaches. If you already have your list, get your letter sent out. Sending out 20 to 30 letters to a variety of different college programs will enhance your chances of being recruited. You should send out these letters no later than your junior year.

You can have a mix of different levels of athletic and academic options, just like students exploring general college admissions. Identify your "reach" schools—colleges you would love to compete at but where you may not be quite up to their academic or athletic standards. Then, identify your "probable" schools—colleges for which you are qualified academically and athletically and to which you can expect to be admitted. Finally, identify your "safety" schools—colleges you know you can get into. Coaches at these schools may call you often, possibly offer you a scholarship, and communicate that you will be a starter or impact player as a freshman. At your safety schools, you may be more experienced than anyone currently on the team.

You may have your heart set on a specific school, but you should always explore your options. I worked with twin brothers, both baseball players, who loved to play but were not sure if they could compete for a college team. They sent out letters and found that they could play, possible even start, at NCAA Division III colleges and could get fairly decent financial aid packages. They had a number of different Division III coaches calling to recruit them. If they attended a Division I school, they

---

DON'T UNDERESTIMATE YOUR CHANCES

AN ATHLETE CAME INTO MY OFFICE DURING HIS JUNIOR YEAR AND SAID HE DIDN'T THINK HE COULD PLAY COLLEGE BASKETBALL. We looked up a few schools he thought he might like and found that, at 6'5", he would be the tallest player on many of those teams. He sent out letters and heard back from several NCAA Division III colleges right away. He ended up with some wonderful financial aid packages due to his academics and volunteer work. His high school team made it to the third round of the state playoffs in February of his senior year. An NCAA Division II coach from his hometown was at the game. The athlete played well, the coach began recruiting him, and now he plays for a Division II school on an athletic scholarship. And he thought he couldn't play college ball!

---

would have had to try out for the team with no guarantees of making it. By making contact with coaches, the boys had choices and were being recruited. Although they decided to try to walk on at a Division I school, they could have made the team at Division III schools.

Figure 7.1 shows a sample letter. A simple introductory letter will provide enough information for a coach to decide whether you have what they are looking for academically and athletically. Later in this chapter is additional information on what to include in your initial letter.

Possible Responses

If you do your homework, you may find a variety of options at different levels. You may not hear back from every coach, but you should hear from some. In fact, you should get one of four responses from your initial letters.

- *Response one.* You might get a letter saying that the coach is glad to hear from you and requesting that you fill out the enclosed questionnaire. If you are interested in the college, complete and return the questionnaire. By doing that, you will begin to be considered a recruit, and the coach will have your information on file. Even if you think you have already given the coach all the information in your initial letter, fill out the questionnaire and return it. Coaches carry their recruiting folder, filled with completed questionnaires, home to make phone calls. A returned questionnaire can put you in the next round of recruiting.
- *Response two.* The coach might send you a note saying, "Thanks for your letter. At this time, we need to know more about you as a student-athlete. Please fill out the questionnaire and keep us updated on your progress." Send the questionnaire back and be sure

■ Figure 7.1: Sample Letter of Introduction ■

Coach Cool
Boot University Soccer Coach
1000 College Drive
Turf City, NJ 09090

Dear Coach Cool,

I am writing this letter to express my interest in Boot University and your soccer program. I am a junior at Score City High School in Score City, OH. During the past two years, I have been a starter in the midfield for the varsity team. I was selected 1st Team All-State two years in a row and helped lead our team to the state semifinals this fall. I am also a member of the 19 and under travel team, Score City Storm. We will be playing in the Gator Cup in Orlando, Florida, on February 12 to 14. Videotape of my playing ability, including game action and practice sessions, is available at your request.

Academically, I have a 3.4 GPA and my combined Critical Reading and Math score on the PSAT was an 1160. I plan to take the SAT in May. I am interested in pursuing a degree in business. For your review, my transcript has been included.

Please send me information on your soccer program and the business school, as well as any additional information you feel would be important for me to know. If you would like to speak with my high school coach, Pete Moss, he can be reached at (888) 333-1111.

Thank you for your time and consideration. I look forward to receiving information from you.

Sincerely,

Kid Kicker
888 Sidekick Drive
Score City, OH 40404
512-512-51212
kidkicker4@yahoo.com

to update the coach on your athletic improvement through additional letters, emails, or phone calls. Do not expect the coach to follow you closely; because the coach asked you to send updates on your progress, you are currently not what the team needs. Therefore, you need to let the coach know when you have improved.

- *Response three.* A third response, the least favorite, is that the coach says, "Sorry, you are not what we are looking for at this time. Good luck with your college search." This is not what you were hoping for, but at least you know to take this school off your list or work a lot harder and follow up. You can ask about walking on, but if this were an option, the coach would have mentioned it in the letter. You can still attend the college, but you won't be able to compete at the varsity level. There may be a club team or intramural program available, so check out these options as well.
- *Response four.* Some coaches may not respond to your letter. Most students and parents believe that no response means the coach is not interested, and in some cases, that is true. But if a coach does not respond to your letter within two to three weeks, follow up with a phone call or another letter anyway. Don't give up until you have written or verbal confirmation that the coach is not interested in you.

Call the Coach

You, the athlete, should be the one calling the coach. Over and over again, coaches will say, "I want to speak with the athlete. I need to get to know the athlete whom I will be coaching for four or more

---

UPDATE COACHES ON YOUR PROGRESS

A SWIMMER FROM KANSAS WANTED TO COMPETE FOR INDIANA BUT NEEDED A SCHOLARSHIP TO ATTEND. She was not fast enough at the beginning of her senior year for a scholarship but found out exactly how fast she needed to swim to earn financial support. In December, in a championship meet, she swam the times set for her. At that moment in time, she was not on the coach's radar, and in fact, the coach was recruiting three other swimmers who were faster. The Kansas athlete called to let the coach know how well she did and ended up becoming a scholarship athlete who dominated her event over the next four years. The coach would not have known how much the swimmer had improved if she had not followed up with the phone call. The coach was busy coaching the college team and recruiting the athletes who already had the times the team needed. A lot of championship meets were going on across the country in December, including college meets—too many for the coach to pay attention to all of them. It is very important that you call or write coaches and continue to update them on your improvements, or your team's advancement in the playoffs, especially for a college you really like.

> **COLLEGE COACHES LOVE TO COACH. THEY ACCEPTED THEIR JOB BECAUSE THEY LOVE TO COACH.** But if they want to win, they have to recruit! Make their job easier: contact them and keep them updated on your progress.

years." If you decide to call a coach, the best time to reach a coach on the phone is usually in the mornings, Monday through Friday. Most coaches head to their offices in the morning, leave for lunch, and then head to practice. They are likely not in their offices in the afternoon or evening, unless they have said otherwise. If you have a hard time reaching the coach by phone, try calling the athletic department's main number and ask the administrative assistant for the best time to call that coach.

If you leave a message on an answering machine, be aware of the recruiting rules for that coach. In some cases, unless you are a senior, the coach may not be allowed to call you back. Review the rules governing each college's athletic program before assuming that a coach isn't interested because they didn't call you back.

Emails and Text Messaging

Email may seem like the easiest way to contact a coach, but an initial letter that arrives in the post may get more attention than an email. Both email and send a hard copy to the coach. Remember that your email address is a reflection of you. Be sure it is appropriate for the adults with whom you will be interacting: college coaches, admissions, and financial aid directors. Set up a separate email account for your college correspondence. Also, be aware that any individual website you set up, including at MySpace, can be accessed by coaches and college officials. With one easy click, a coach can learn more about you than you may want them to know. Be aware of the image you are conveying on the Internet.

Text messaging had been a new tool in the recruiting game. But as of August 2007, text messaging between coaches and potential athletes is illegal. Coaches are no longer allowed to send text messages. They are allowed to fax and email perspective athletes under current NCAA guidelines.

INCREASE YOUR EXPOSURE

To be seen by NCAA Division I college coaches, most athletes will need to join club teams, especially ones that travel regionally and nationally. Other coaches will rely more heavily on you and your coaches for information on your athletic talents. College coaches rarely attend high school competitions, unless it is a regional- or state-level competition where lots of good athletes are competing. Coaches rarely get to read your local newspaper that has your team's weekly results. If you want to increase your exposure to college coaches, travel outside your local area for competition and get your current coaches involved in helping you with your college search.

High School and Club Coach Involvement

Throughout the initial contact period and the recruiting process, your high school or club coach can be a resource for you. Make sure your coach has good things to say about you if you ask him to call a college coach. No rules prohibit club or high school coaches from making contact. Some college coaches are great about using the high school and club coach; other coaches will never even speak to your current coach. How much contact coaches have depends on the sport and the level at which the college is competing. High school coaches can call college coaches and get feedback for you on where you stand with a coach or if you fit into the program. If you have a hard time getting a college coach on the phone, leave your high school coach's phone number.

Competing in Major Competitions

Depending on how competitive your high school team is, and whether your team travels or makes it to the playoffs, your recruiting exposure can increase. College coaches like to evaluate at venues where they can see the greatest number of prospects at one time. Coaches don't typically spend money traveling to a high school competition unless it is the third or fourth round of the playoffs or a state championship.

Because they have the resources, top NCAA Division I coaches attend national-level competitions, while coaches in other divisions will recruit off the results of these competitions. At national competitions, college coaches can see the best athletes from all over the country at one event, so attending these is cost- and time-efficient. If your sport has a showcase event like soccer's blue-chip tournaments, field hockey's national festival, U.S. swimming's senior nationals, or lacrosse's Memorial Day tournament, college coaches will travel to evaluate athletes at venues like these. These events are *the* recruiting events of the year for many coaches, because they bring the top athletes and the top coaches in the country together.

Send a DVD or Video

Despite the grandeur of national events, many coaches do not travel to recruit. Because the majority of college coaches have limited resources for recruiting, the best way to let coaches observe you at your best is to capture your toughest game or highest level of competition on videotape. More coaches will ask for videos rather than evaluate you in person simply because of budget restraints.

Swimming, track and field, golf, and cross-country are sports where your best results on paper demonstrate your current talent. But even these athletes can produce a video and share it with prospective coaches. By watching a taped meet, a swim coach can determine whether an athlete is fighting for her best time or cruising with room to improve. Coaches have an eye for talent and know their ability to help athletes improve. Usually, the coach wants the "blue-chip" or natural athlete who can make an immediate impact on the team's success. However, some coaches like finding athletes

FIND YOUR SPORT'S MAJOR COMPETITIONS

FOR THE DATES AND LOCATIONS OF YOUR SPORT'S MAJOR COMPETITIONS THROUGHOUT THE YEAR, log on to your sport's national website listed below. Also included in this list are additional websites related to the college application process.

■ **Figure 7.2: National Organization and College-Related Websites** ■

Archery
National Archery Association
www.usarchery.org

Badminton
USA Badminton
www.usabadminton.org

Baseball
John Skilton's Baseball Links
www.baseball-links/link/college_baseball
USA Baseball
www.usabaseball.org

Basketball
USA Basketball
www.usabasketball.com

Bowling
College Bowling
www.collegebowling.com
Young American Bowling Alliance
www.bowl.com

Cross Country
CSTV
www.CSTV.com
USA Track & Field
www.usatf.org

Equestrian
Intercollegiate Horse Show Association
www.ihsa.com

Fencing
US Fencing Association
www.usfencing.org

Field Hockey
Field Hockey Coaches Association
www.eteamz.com/nfhca
United States Field Hockey
www.usfieldhockey.com

Football
American Football Coaches Association
www.afca.com

Golf
Golf Coaches Association
www.collegiategolf.com
Golf Stats
www.golfstat.com

Gymnastics
USAGymnastics
www.usa-gymnastics.org

Ice Hockey
College Hockey
www.collegehockey.com
USA Hockey
www.usahockey.com

Lacrosse
Laxpower
www.laxpower.com
US Lacrosse
www.lacrosse.org
Womens Lacrosse Coaches Association
www.iwlca.org

Rifle
USA Shooting
www.usashooting.org

Rowing
Collegiate Row Coaches Association
www.collegerowcoach.org
US Rowing
www.usrowing.org

Skiing
US Collegiate Ski and Snowboard Association
www.uscsa.com
US Ski and Snowboard Association
www.ussa.org

Soccer
College Soccer
www.collegesoccernews.com
National Soccer Coaches Association
www.nscaa.com
US Soccer
www.ussoccer.com

Softball
Amateur Softball Association
www.softball.org
USA Softball
www.usasoftball.org

Squash
College Squash Association
www.squashtalk.com/collegesquash
US Squash
www.us-squash.org

Swimming and Diving
College Swim Coaches
www.cscaa.org
USA Diving
www.usadiving.org
USA Swimming
www.usa-swimming.org

Synchronized Swimming
US Synchronized Swimming
www.usasynchro.org

Team Handball
US Olympic Committee
www.usoc.org
USA Team Handball
www.usateamhandball.org

Tennis
College Tennis
www.collegetennisonline.com
US Tennis Association
www.usta.com

Track and Field
USA Track & Field
www.usatf.org

Volleyball
College Volleyball Update
www.cvu.com
USA Volleyball
www.usavolleyball.org
Volleyball Coaches Association
www.avca.org

Water Polo
Collegiate Water Polo Association
www.collegiatewaterpolo.com
US Water Polo
www.uswp.org

Wrestling
College Wrestling
www.collegewrestling.iptv.org
Wrestling USA
www.wrestlinguse.com

Additional Websites
College Sports
www.cstv.com
National Association for Girls and Women in Sports
www.aahperd.org
National Collegiate Athletic Association Clearinghouse
www.ncaaclearinghouse.org
National Intramural Recreational Sports Association
www.nirsa.net
Women's Sports Foundation
www.womenssportsfoundation.org

College Athletic Associations
National Collegiate Athletic Association
www.ncaa.org
National Intercollegiate Athletic Association
www.naia.org
National Junior College Athletic Association
www.NJCAA.org

College Resources
ACT
www.act.org
Career Exploration Link
www.uhs.berkeley.edu/careerLibrary/links/occup.cfm
Career Resource Center
www.careers.org
Complete List of American Universities
www.Clas.ufl.edu/clas/American-universities.htlm
Kaplan
www.kaplan.com
SAT
www.Collegeboard.com

Common Applications across the Country
Apply
www.weapply.com
College Link
www.collegelink.com
Private College
www.commonapp.org
Texas State Colleges and Universities
www.applytexas.org

Financial Aid Resources
Fastweb Scholarship Search
www.fastweb.com
FinAid: Financial Aid Information Page
www.finaid.org
Free Application for Federal Student Aid
www.fafsa.ed.gov

Volunteer Resources
Idea List
www.idealist.org
Volunteer Match
www.volunteermatch.org

who they believe are about to blossom. These coaches might take a chance on you but almost always will want to see you compete.

Your Video

The purpose of your videotape is to allow the coach to observe your athletic ability. You can send a DVD or videotape, whichever is convenient for you. Most coaches still have VCRs, but many are up-to-date with the most recent technology and should be able to view a DVD. Your video needs to show you at your best against tough competition. For most sports, action footage from true competition is best, but this is not always possible. If you have to tape a practice, it is still better than nothing. Ask your current coach for assistance. Even a simple video can do the trick.

Football is a sport where coaches want to see the whole game; they want to see you pounding as hard in the fourth quarter as in the first quarter. Other sports' videos can show the whole game but are fine if they show portions of games and highlight clips or drills of specific skills.

Tips for Taping

When it comes to taping, you do not need to have a professional make your tape. A simple home-made tape will do the job. Here are some more tips for making your videotape.

- *Where to put the camera.* Most team sports using a field or court should be filmed at the 50-yard line or at midcourt above ground level. Tennis and volleyball should be filmed from the end of the court and preferably above ground level.
- *Provide context.* Do *not* zoom in on an athlete. Keep three to five other players within sight. Coaches want to see how an athlete moves on and off the ball within the playing area. Are you adjusting and moving to the open space? Are you picking up the defense? Did you set the pick and roll? Did that pass you just made go to another player on your team or the opposing team's player? Did you hit a winner or an unforced error?

  One coach had a soccer recruit who scored 100 goals during his senior year. The video consisted of only the 100 goals—pretty impressive, but not exactly what the coach would have liked to see. A tape of a basketball player running around the court with no other athlete in sight is not an effective tape. The ball comes and goes, but you cannot tell whether the pass or shot was good. The same would hold true for team sports like soccer, lacrosse, hockey, or field hockey. Show more than one athlete in the game.
- *Length.* The tape should be 10 to 15 minutes in length. Coaches are experts at their jobs. They can tell within a matter of five minutes if you are an athlete they believe they can work with or not. Most coaches do not watch more than 15 minutes of tape (unless

it is of a football or basketball player, but even then, the coach will fast-forward to different parts of the tape). If you definitely want a coach to see a certain section of the tape, be sure to include this information in your letter or put a note on the tape telling the coach where to find the specific highlight.

- *No bells or whistles.* Like your letter, keep your videotape simple. Do not add music—you don't want the coach dancing when they should be watching you. It is best if there is no sound, so turn off the sound of your parent's commentary during your game so the audio is not recorded. Don't splice in the same highlight clip over and over again. Making a three-point shot to win the game at the buzzer is exciting and can be included, but unless you do that in every game, you shouldn't repeat a highlight. Also, coaches can rewind; thus, they do not need to see a volleyball player serve the ball 20 times, or a baseball player hit the ball 20 times. Coaches can tell within three to five swings whether they are interested in you or not.

Mailing Your Video

When you send in your tape, include a note to the coach. Tell the coach what is on the tape: highlights, skill drills, and/or a game. If you include a game, it is very important that you include who you are playing against, the date the game was played, the color of your jersey, the position you are playing, and your jersey number.

Make copies of your tape and don't expect it to be returned. If a coach asks for some specific skill demonstration on a tape and you don't currently have it on there, decide whether you are interested in the school. If you are and you haven't already sent a tape, you can always add to the end of the tape and then make a note to the coach. If you already sent the tape, decide how important this school is to you; if it is important, make the changes and resend the tape. Some coaches may be testing you to see how well you take direction. A field hockey player was asked by a coach to add footage of the athlete doing push-ups and chin-ups. The coach wanted to see how strong the athlete

---

LET THE COACH KNOW WHO TO WATCH

A COACH ONCE RECEIVED A TAPE FROM A SOCCER RECRUIT WHO FORGOT TO LET THE COACH KNOW HIS JERSEY COLOR AND NUMBER. The coach watched the tape, saw a wonderful player, and called the high school coach to rave about the athlete. Unfortunately for the athlete who sent the tape, he wasn't the one the coach watched—it was an athlete on the other team. Needless to say, the college coach began recruiting the opponent.

was, or the coach wanted to see if the athlete would do what she requested. If it gets you a scholarship, do the chin-ups!

Attend Summer Camps

During the summers, most colleges run sports camps on their campuses, or you may get invited to a recruiting camp where coaches from around the region or country come to observe. If you can afford it, attend one of these camps. Camps are an important recruiting tool for many coaches. If a college coach has a chance to see you practice (legally, tryouts are not allowed at the NCAA Division I level), both you and the coach can develop a relationship that may make or break the recruiting process.

College coaches run camps to share their knowledge of the game with high school athletes. At a college camp, you will get to experience the coach's personality, philosophy, and knowledge of the game. At some camps, coaches from Division III, NAIA, or junior colleges work with athletes. Check the coaching staff of the camp to see who may be there.

Usually, the camp counselors are current or former athletes, so you will have a chance to get to know the team members as well as the coach. You should make an appointment with the coach for a one-on-one meeting after the camp is over. Because the coach just saw you perform, she should have an idea of whether you might fit into her program. If a coach is not interested in you, don't be afraid to ask if she could recommend another program that might be a better fit. While on campus, make an appointment with the admissions office and the financial aid office and schedule a campus tour.

Recruiting camps are typically invitational camps; you are invited or must be accepted into the camp. These are set up for recruiting purposes and have high school or club coaches as the instructors; college coaches are not allowed to coach at a recruiting camp. College coaches are invited to observe and receive a camp roster with each athlete's bio, including items such as year in school, address, phone number, email, and position played. If you are invited to a recruiting camp, ask for the list of college coaches who attended the previous year and match that list with your list. If colleges in which you are interested are on the list, be sure to send a letter to the coaches ahead of time so they know to watch you.

YOUR INITIAL LETTER

The most important step you can take to initiate the recruiting process is to send a letter introducing yourself and expressing your interest in a college. You do not need anything fancy; just write a simple letter. The following information will help you write your letter and send it off. Sample letters and a sample resume are included to help guide you.

Keep It Simple

Your initial letter should be simple—two paragraphs will do. Coaches need to know two key pieces of information from you: 1) your academic level and 2) your level of athletic ability. Depending on the academic competitiveness of the college, you should include a copy of your transcript with your letter. Coaches at Ivy League colleges will know right away if they can recruit you once they see your transcript. The 50 most competitive academic colleges will require solid grades in advanced placement (AP) classes and high SAT or ACT scores. No matter how strong an athlete you are, grades are important. When the talent levels of two athletes are equal, coaches at most colleges will recruit the athlete with a better academic record. Coaches have more confidence in an athlete who has a better chance of staying academically eligible to play. Also, coaches think that if you work hard in the classroom, you will work hard at practice. So keep up your grades, and you will be helping yourself move up the recruiting list.

What to Include

It is important to include your correct mailing address, email address, and home and cell phone numbers at the top of your letter. A paragraph should include your academic information. Let the coach know your current grade level (freshman, sophomore, junior, or senior). The rest of the paragraph should include your GPA and your SAT or ACT scores (PSAT scores will do if you don't have the other scores yet). If you have taken AP classes, mention them. Have all of your academic information in the first paragraph, especially in a letter for a highly competitive college.

Another paragraph of your letter should include your athletic information. If you are fairly new to the sport (began playing within last two years), you should mention this. If you play a team sport, list your individual accomplishments and your team's highest finish in the most recent season. If you have any personal statistics from the current season, include them. If you play an individual sport, include your best efforts—times, distance, average score, etc. Include your height if you play a sport, like basketball or volleyball, in which height is important.

You should also list your competitive schedule, including any upcoming tournaments or major competitions you might have, and describe your future athletic goals. Mention that you have a videotape available if the coach is interested. You can mass-mail the tape or DVD, but be sure to follow the procedure earlier in this chapter.

Include a third paragraph if you have any special circumstances: parent or relative is an alumnus, you are adopted (tuition is free in most states), you know your major and want information on the program, or a scholarship is a must for you to attend the particular college. Put down your current club or high school coach's name and phone number just in case the college coach wants to contact your coach.

End the letter with a comment like, "I look forward to receiving information on your program. Good luck with your upcoming season. Sincerely . . ." Sign it and make sure to make the appropriate changes within the letter to reflect the correct university or college and coach! Too many letters are sent to coaches with the wrong coach's name or the wrong college's name. Pay attention to these little details.

Your letter can be two paragraphs, but don't make it more than one page. Once you have written your initial letter, it can be sent out to all the college coaches you'd like to contact. Have a coach, counselor, or parent look over your letter before you send it out. It is also a good idea to keep track of each letter you send and the date you send it, so you know who has responded and whom you might need to follow up with.

Attachments

You do not need to send a resume, but if you play a team sport or you play more than one sport, you may want to include highlights of your high school athletic accomplishments (listed by year), which would take more than a paragraph. If you send a resume, remember to fill in and return any questionnaires you receive from coaches, even if you feel you have already given the coach the information they are requesting. See Figure 7.3 for a sample athletic resume.

FOLLOW UP

I cannot stress enough the importance of keeping in touch with a coach once you have begun interacting with them. There is a fine line between overdoing it and not keeping a coach informed, but error on the side of too much contact. Remember, the coach wants to hear from you, the athlete, more than your parents. Follow these guidelines: junior year, once every four to six weeks; senior year, once every two to three weeks until you make your decision.

CHAPTER SUMMARY

Becoming a recruited athlete can be as simple as sending a letter to a coach. You can contact coaches and let them know about your interest in their program. Send your competition schedule and a videotape of your athletic skills. Promote yourself to your top colleges. Follow the suggestions listed in this chapter, and you will discover what athletic opportunities are available to you. Don't wait for coaches to find you; go find them.

■ Figure 7.3: Sample Athletic Resume ■

Mighty Mac
Women's Swim Coach
University of Salt Water
1010 South Street
Minneapolis, MN 52522

Dear Coach Mac,

I am a junior at Water High School and I am interested in attending the University of Salt Water. I was a summer swimmer from the age of five and joined the Reef City Eels Swim Team in the fall of my sophomore year. Since I started training year-round, I have qualified for Junior Nationals in the 50 and 100 free and the 100 and 200 back. I placed 7th in the 100 back at long course Nationals this past summer. I have also been selected to the U. S. Swimming Academic All America Team.

I have enclosed my personal resume providing information on my academic and athletic accomplishments, as well as my personal data. Included is a copy of my transcripts, test scores, and a recommendation letter from my coach. My meet schedule is attached if you are interested in attending a competition. I have a video of my swims at Junior Nationals and I can send it at your request.

My aunt Silly Fish swam at Salt Water. She received a bachelors degree in accounting in 1990 and masters degree in finance in 1993.

Please send me information on your swimming program, any brochures you have on the university and an admissions application. I am interested in visiting your campus this fall. Please be aware that I will need financial assistance to attend college.

Thank you for your time and consideration. I look forward to receiving information from you in the near future.

Sincerely,

Sunny Fish
2 Coral Ridge Road
Reef City, IN 44444
812-333-3333
keeponswimmin@yahoo.com

◼ Figure 7.4: Sample Personal Resume ◼

Sunny Fish
2 Coral Ridge Road
Reef City, IN 44444
812-333-3333
keeponswimmin@yahoo.com

Birthdate:	February 20, 1981		**Height:**	5'8"
Social Security Number:	111-11-1111		**Weight:**	135
Graduation Date:	June 2008		**Best Time to Call:**	After 6:00 PM

GPA:	4.0 on 4.0 Scale	
Class Rank:	2/420	
ACT:	29	
PSAT:	Critical Reading	64
	Math	72
	Writing	68

Scholastic Accomplishments:

National Honor Society – 11	Honor Roll – 9, 10, 11
Student Council – 10, 11	School Newspaper – 10, 11
Science Club President – 10, 11	

Best Events and Times:

50 Yard Freestyle	23.5	100 Yard Freestyle	51.8
200 Yard Freestyle	1:53.3	100 Yard Backstroke	56.9
200 Yard Backstroke	2:05.2	200 Yard IM	2:08.1

Club Swimming:

U.S.S. Team	Reef City Eels Swim Team
U.S.S. Coaches	Skippy Brown: 812-333-3333
	Victoria Black: 812-333-3333

Junior National Champion 400 Medley Relay Long Course 1998
Junior National Qualifier: 50 Free, 100 Free, 100 Back, 200 Back, 400 FR, 400 MR

High School Swimming:

High School	Reef City High School
	210 High School Road
	Reef City, IN 44444
Coach	Debbie Duck: 812-333-3333
State Champion:	50 Free–10, 11
100 Free–11	
100 Back–10	
200 Medley Relay–9, 10, 11	
200 Freestyle Relay–10, 11	
Varsity Letter:	9, 10, 11

KAPLAN

College Visits

There are two different kinds of visits you can take to a college campus: an unofficial visit or an official visit. Any time an athlete visits a campus at his or her own expense, it is called an unofficial visit. An official visit is when the athletic department pays for some part of your visit, other than providing a ticket to an athletic competition.

The type of visit affects the planning and organizing of the visit. We discussed these visits as they relate to recruiting rules in Chapter 3. Now we will look at what it takes to plan for each type of visit and what you should expect from each. Most athletes will make an unofficial visit during their freshman, sophomore, or junior years, and if offered an official (paid) visit, make it during their senior year. Because many schools don't have the resources to pay for a recruit's visit, you will likely make unofficial visits during your senior year. As stated earlier, you absolutely should visit a campus before choosing to attend that college.

PLANNING AN UNOFFICIAL VISIT

Planning a college visit can be a shared project between you and your parent(s) and should begin at least two weeks prior to the visit. Because the unofficial visit is on your dime, you make all the arrangements. A parent or guardian can make all travel and hotel arrangements and set up the meeting with the financial aid office (if needed). However, the athlete, whenever possible, should be the one to communicate directly with the admissions office and the coach to set up meetings. If you can give the coach two weeks notice before a visit, the coach will likely be able to fit you in. You also don't want to plan a visit when the coach is not available, out of town recruiting or at a competition.

If you communicate with the coach first, the coach may be able to help set up the meetings with the admissions representative, financial aid department, and faculty on campus. Do not expect this, but some coaches would be happy to roll out the red carpet and impress you.

If you are making an unofficial visit during your freshman or sophomore years, your parent(s) can set up all meetings, but if you are a junior or senior, you should take charge of your plans. It is more impressive to the adults involved in the decision-making process at the college if you communicate with them directly. Your parents should be encouraging you to interact with adults, which is what the college search process is all about. Some parents want to take care of everything for their child, but you are about to head off to college and need to learn to communicate well with adults.

To get the most out of your college visits, plan ahead and allow at least one full day on each campus. Many students take a long weekend and try to hit as many schools as possible. This approach

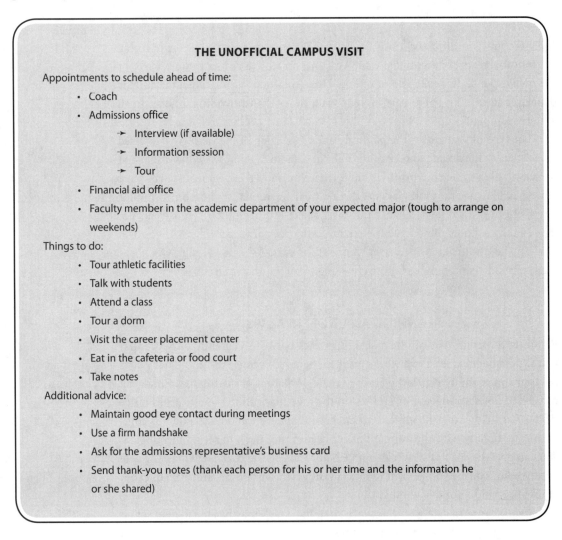

THE UNOFFICIAL CAMPUS VISIT

Appointments to schedule ahead of time:

- Coach
- Admissions office
    - Interview (if available)
    - Information session
    - Tour
- Financial aid office
- Faculty member in the academic department of your expected major (tough to arrange on weekends)

Things to do:

- Tour athletic facilities
- Talk with students
- Attend a class
- Tour a dorm
- Visit the career placement center
- Eat in the cafeteria or food court
- Take notes

Additional advice:

- Maintain good eye contact during meetings
- Use a firm handshake
- Ask for the admissions representative's business card
- Send thank-you notes (thank each person for his or her time and the information he or she shared)

may seem efficient, but it is not very effective and can lead to your feeling overwhelmed or rushed. In Boston, with 50 colleges in a 50-mile radius, you might be able to average two schools a day. But if you have to drive more than an hour between colleges, two visits a day will not give you time to gather the information you need to make your decision. Because you are interested in athletics, you need to fit an appointment with the coach into your schedule. Thus, if you try to do a campus tour, attend an admission information session, meet the coach, and tour the athletic facilities, it will be a challenge to fit two visits into one day. If you absolutely must conduct a short visit, meeting the coach and attending the admissions information session should be the highest priorities.

Meet the Coach

The coach is one of the key people you must meet while on campus. Most coaches will give you a tour of the athletic facilities, and some, depending how important you are to them, will give you the campus tour. Plan to spend at least one hour talking with the coach. Later in this chapter, you will find a list of important questions to ask the coach. Bring these questions with you—and any others you'd like to ask. Try to memorize the most important questions, but if at the end of your conversation, the coach asks if you have any more questions, don't be afraid to look at your list.

If the coach doesn't offer, ask for a tour of the athletic facilities; check out the weight room, practice and competition facilities, and training room. If the training facilities include a campus-wide recreational complex, what access do athletes have to this facility? Some teams may have priority over the others, depending on the priority the athletic department has given them. For example, ask if your team gets to use the same facilities as the football or basketball team. If a coach mentions an academic support staff within the athletic department (Division I and II schools), be sure to meet them. What academic support will you get from the athletic department? Some offer tutors, require mandatory study halls, and give athletes priority course selection. Academic support from the athletic department will vary from college to college, so be sure that you know what your top choices offer.

Attend the Admissions Information Session

When you attend the information session and take a campus tour, your contact information is added to your prospective student file should you apply to that school. While the campus tour is optional, statistics show that those students who visit a campus before they apply tend to matriculate to the school at a higher rate than those who apply and never visit. Once you sign in with the admissions office, you will begin receiving information from the college via postal mail or email.

While on a campus tour of a smaller school (5,000 students or less), the tour guide might take you inside buildings to showcase the small classrooms, thus promoting their low student-to-teacher ratio. Tour guides at large universities (over 10,000 students) typically do a "sidewalk tour," pointing at buildings and answering questions along the way. You can skip the campus tour and drive or walk

QUESTIONS FOR COACHES

WHEN YOU ARE CONSIDERING ATHLETICS IN YOUR COLLEGE SEARCH, you should definitely meet with the coach and ask some important questions. The list that follows can get you started. You will need to be able to trust this person and get along with him or her for four or more years. Your athletic experience will influence what you want in a college. Ask questions and learn more about the competitive opportunities at each college.

- What is your coaching philosophy or strategy?
- What are your goals for this program?
- What are your goals for me?
- Describe a typical practice session.
- What are your expectations academically and athletically for your athletes?
- Hours per week required in training?
- Study hall required, or offered? Is there an academic support office for athletes?
- What weight program would I be involved in?
- Is there an off-season training regiment?
- What is expected of me over the summer?
- What is the procedure for illness or injury?
- How would I earn an increase in my scholarship?
- Have you ever taken scholarships away or asked for scholarship money back?
- Are your athletes allowed to work at a job?
- Are summer jobs available?
- How do you feel about summer work and training?
- How many athletes try out for the team?
- How many athletes do you keep on the team?
- Is there a fitness test to prepare for? What is it?

the campus on your own, but be sure to sign in at the admissions office and attend the information session. When possible, you should return to the campus for an overnight visit during your senior year and tour the campus again.

Other Ways to Meet Admissions Representatives

Admissions representatives travel the country during the fall, visiting high schools and attending college fairs to recruit prospective students. Meet the admissions representatives when they visit your high school campus and attend college fairs. Often, the representative who visits your high school is the person who will read your application and have input into your acceptance. Attending these events can put a gold star into your admissions folder, because the admissions officer will be able to put a face to a name, which might increase your chance of being admitted. Admissions departments keep track of who visits their booth at college fairs by the cards students complete asking for information to be sent to them. Be sure to fill out the card and ask for the representative's business card so you can follow up with an email. The representative is the best connection you can make at the college; the coach is the second-best connection.

Here are some sample questions to prepare you for the admissions interview. If the coach has you on his or her recruiting list, the admissions representative will know you're an athlete, but be prepared to answer questions that are not related to your athletic interests. Review the information packet you've received about a particular college prior to any campus visit or interview so you can speak intelligently about why you are interested in attending that school.

QUESTIONS FROM ADMISSIONS REPRESENTATIVES

THE FOLLOWING IS A LIST OF QUESTIONS YOU MIGHT BE ASKED BY AN ADMISSIONS REPRESENTATIVE. Be prepared to talk about something other than athletics. If you have been recommended by the coach on campus, the admissions person wants to know who you are aside from your athletic talents.

- Why are you interested in going to college?
- What does a college education mean to you?
- If you did not attend college, what would you do?
- What courses interest you at this college?
- Tell me about your high school—its most impressive and least impressive features.
- What has been the most challenging course in high school for you?
- Why do you believe you will be successful here at _____?
- What are your academic goals?
- Describe yourself to me. Include your strengths and weaknesses.
- Tell me about your extracurricular activities.
- Who has been the most inspirational person in your life and why?
- Name a book you have read recently.
- What book has had an effect on your thinking?
- What books do you like reading?
- Do you have a favorite author?
- Where do you see yourself in ten years?
- What are your thoughts on _____ (current events, national or global)?
- Tell me about a recent event that caused you to act, or react. What action did you take?

QUESTIONS FOR ADMISSIONS REPRESENTATIVES

- What are the top five reasons I should attend _____?
- What do you think students like best about _____?
- Are the professors available; office hours?
- Who teaches the lectures? Labs? Discussion groups?
- What percentage of students live on campus?
- What support is available for students needing help?
- What percent of students take online courses? What are the most popular online courses?
- What is unique about this college?
- What are your most common overlaps (other colleges students apply to)?
- In what direction is the college seeking to grow?
- How has the college changed over the past five years?
- What has been the most controversial issue _____ has had to face in the last year?
- Five years?
- Are tutors available for the student body? What is the charge?
- What is the ratio of computers to students on this campus?
- What do you see as the emerging careers of the future?
- How does the college help students with their career choice?
- What are the requirements to get into the program/classes?
- How large are lecture and discussion classes?
- What percent of students graduate in my intended major and receive job offers?
- Is there a job placement office?
- Is there an opportunity to study abroad?
- What are some traditions here?
- One word that best describes this college is _____?

Also be prepared to ask questions related to what you understand the school has to offer: the majors you are interested in and their requirements, meal plans, student organizations, and anything other than athletics.

Stop by the Financial Aid Office

Stop by the financial aid office to obtain information about financing your college education. Each college has its own list of scholarships that it awards, many of which have been endowed by alumni.

There are different qualifications and requirements for each scholarship. There are also scholarships for currently enrolled students, meaning that once you have completed an academic year at the institution as a full-time student, you may be eligible to apply for additional aid. Most of these scholarships are based on your freshman year grades.

Visit the Department That Offers Your Intended Major

Try to set up a meeting with the department head or a professor in the department that offers your planned major. Some college departments have connections with admissions and can request that talented students be admitted, just as coaches request that talented athletes be admitted. You might also find out about academic scholarships specific to that department. A lot of career-specific scholarships are available, and academic departments control some of this money. Ask if the department has a list of scholarships or if it can suggest where you might look for scholarship information.

Talk to Students

While you are on campus, talk to athletes and nonathletes about their experiences at the school. Are they happy and excited about where they are? What are classes like? What do they do with their free time? Hopefully, you will get to meet team members and can ask them about athletics and academics, but it will help you get a better idea of life on campus if you get nonathletes' perspectives as well. Sit in on a class (this can usually be arranged through the academic department). You can get an idea of what college classes are like in terms of size, length, and intensity.

Explore Your Housing Options

Tour a dorm or two so you can see what your options are. Many colleges have built (or are building) new dorms with apartment-like settings, where two to four students, each with their own room, share a common area and kitchenette. Some dorms are more like condominiums with private rooms, bathrooms, and full kitchens. On some campuses, the new dorms are for current students only; freshmen get the old dorms, which tend to be one room with two beds, two desks and a large double door closet and a common bathroom shared by everyone on the hall. Be prepared to ask how you choose your housing and where the freshmen typically live. Talk to students so you know which dorm to request.

Student Life

Another great place to stop on your visit is the student union. Sit in the student union and observe the students who are hanging out between classes. Are they sleeping or studying? Is this an environment

QUESTIONS TO ASK STUDENTS

STUDENT ATHLETES, AS WELL AS NONATHLETES, ARE YOUR BEST RESOURCE ON CAMPUS. They are living the college experience at that institution. Ask students lots and lots of questions and ask more than one student the same question. Here is a sample to get you started. Answers to these questions should help you learn more about life on campus.

- Why did you choose this college?

- What do you like most about this college?

- What do you like least?

- How easy is it to register for the classes you want and need?

- What has been your largest and smallest class?

- How accessible are professors? Which professor do you know the best?

- Who teaches your classes? Your labs? Your discussion groups?

- Do students skip class often?

- What has been your favorite class and why?

- What has been your least favorite class and why?

- What was the most difficult adjustment you had to make in moving from high school to college? How did you handle it?

- If you did not attend this school, where would you have gone?

- What do you miss most about home?

- How many hours a week do you study?

- Where do you like to study?

- What resources are available to help you study and do research?

- Is there an academic support office? Have you used it? What was the result?

- Have you every used a tutor? How did that go?

- Describe the food options here?

- How do you feel about your new team and new program?

- Is the coach approachable? How would you describe your relationship with your coach?

- What is the training like? (Ask specific training questions.)

- Are you being challenged? How?

- What are the coach's strengths? The team's strengths? The athletic department's strengths?

- What are the coach's priorities with respect to academics and athletics?

- How well are your expectations being met?

- What other colleges did you look at?

- Whom do you hang out with the most?

- What do you do on weekends?

- What do you do for fun?

- What team functions has the team had?

- What has surprised you the most about your experience?

KAPLAN

you will be comfortable in? Do you want academics to take a front seat, or are you glad to see that life on campus is not all about academics?

The union is usually where you will find a list of student organizations, clubs, and additional extracurricular activities. As an athlete, depending on the level you choose to compete at, you may not have a lot of extra time on your hands, but then again you may find some off-season time. You may want to join a fraternity/sorority, community service group, or other club. Most campuses have a wide variety of groups to choose from, and the time commitment for each varies.

Eat at the cafeteria or food court so you can check out the food. The food court is also a great place to meet students and ask questions about their experience. If you hang out with the students, you will gain a sense of the type of people who attend the school.

Unofficial Visits: A Summary

- Prospects pay their own expenses.
- College athletics may provide three complimentary tickets, at will-call, to an on-campus athletic event.
- Unofficial visits may be made at any time throughout one's high school career.
- Athlete may make as many unofficial visits as they like.

PLANNING AN OFFICIAL VISIT

Now that you have a better understanding of what an unofficial visit entails, let's take a look at the official visit.

An official visit is when a coach (actually, the athletic department) pays for your travel, meals, or housing expenses while on the visit. Only high school seniors and transfer students who have received a release (explained in Chapter 3) are allowed to make official visits. When a coach invites you to visit and you are unclear as to which type of visit you are making, ask the coach. They will tell you whether they are paying or not, and then you'll know what to expect in the way of expenses.

Due to unequal budgets, two different schools in the same conference may not have the same resources. One may be able to fly you to campus and give you the royal treatment, while another may only be able to pay for the expenses you incur once you arrive on campus. A coach will spend more money on a recruit's transportation if the college is not located near a major metropolitan airport. The coach who is near a major city can talk recruits into providing their own transportation (air, car, or train) and then house and feed them once they are on campus. At a school like Harvard, in the large city of Boston, it is easier for athletes to bring themselves to campus, so quite a few recruits pay their own way for the official visit.

Then there are schools, like Indiana University, where the major airport is an hour away but the school gives coaches the resources to be successful. If a coach needs to bring in 12 athletes, they can bring in 12 athletes. If you might be one of the best athletes on the team, you will probably get the red-carpet treatment: transportation, housing, meals, and entertainment. But if you are one of many athletes being recruited, you may not get anything special.

The NCAA limits seniors to one official visit per campus, and you may not exceed five official visits to Division I and II colleges. A senior may make only one official visit to any one Division III college but has no limits as to the number of different Division III colleges visited. For more

---

OFFICIAL VISIT: SAMPLE ITINERARY

OFFICIAL VISITS ARE 48 HOURS LONG. ACCORDING TO THE NCAA DIVISION I AND II REGULATIONS, the coaching staff and athletes must release you to your parents within 48 hours and have no further contact with you on their campus that day. (However, you do not need to depart the campus.)

A typical itinerary for an official visit might look something like this:

Friday

10:30 AM	Arrive on campus and meet at coach's office for a short meeting
11:15 AM	Meet an athlete to attend Psychology 101 together
12:45 PM	Have lunch with two athletes in the cafeteria
2:30 PM	Walk to practice, watch practice, and tour athletic facilities
6:30 PM	Team dinner
9:00 PM	Movie night at senior house
	Spend night in dorm with a freshman

Saturday

9:00 AM	Team breakfast
11:00 AM	Meet with a faculty member in the psychology department (if possible)
12:30 PM	Watch competition
	Lunch with team members
	Campus tour
	Hang with freshman "roommate"
7:00 PM	Have dinner with coaches
	Spend evening with athletes
	Spend night with sophomore athletes

Sunday

| 9:00 AM | Have breakfast with coach |
| 10:30 AM | Depart campus |

---

information on the rules, review the NCAA's *Guide for the College-Bound Student-Athlete,* available at *www.ncaa.org.*

If the athletic department pays for any part of your visit expenses, transportation (airfare or gas), housing, meals, or entertainment for you or your parents (other than three complimentary tickets to an athletic event), you have been on an official visit. The coach will set up the itinerary (sample shown here), including tours and meetings, for you. You should get a chance to do everything suggested for an unofficial visit described earlier in this chapter. But if there is something you want to be sure you get to do on your visit (like sit in on a class), bring it up with the coach.

Parents and the Official Visit

To experience what life really will be like in college, take your official visits on your own. If your parents do join you, have them take their own tour and eat on their own. Do not stay in a hotel with them; stay with an athlete or student on campus. When you meet with the coach, ask your parents to let you have at little time by yourself with the coach (some coaches may even request this). Again, the coach needs to get to know you—you will be the one playing for them for the next four years, not your parents.

Questions about Financing

While students should meet with the coach alone, parents do deserve time with the coach as well. They can set up a separate meeting while accompanying the student or call to ask questions about the program after the visit. They can (and should) ask the coach about scholarships and what their expected financial contribution will be. Parents should review with their child what questions the student should ask coaches, and parents should feel free to ask the same questions if they feel unclear about the answers. Some important questions parents should ask about financing their child's education include:

- What exactly (tuition, room and board, books) will the scholarship cover?
- Does it cover summer school?
- What happens if my child doesn't start or doesn't perform up to the coach's expectations?
- Can the scholarship be increased or decreased? What would cause either to happen?
- Has an athlete ever not had his or her scholarship renewed?
- Can my child have a job while on scholarship?
- Can my child accept academic or other outside scholarships as well as an athletic scholarship?
- What happens if my child takes more than four years to earn a degree? Who pays for the extra semesters?

WHILE ON YOUR RECRUITING TRIP, THE COACH AND THE TEAM MIGHT ROLL OUT THE RED CARPET FOR YOU and make everything sound and appear wonderful. By asking lots of questions, you should get a better feel for what it really is like to compete at this school. Be sure to ask the team members and coach the same questions. The answers to questions about team goals, training, and academic expectations should be the same or very similar, whether they come from the coach or the athletes. If you hear different stories, then that may be a sign of a problem.

An Athlete's Behavior on Recruiting Trips

It is important for high school students to realize that college athletes do party and they do drink alcohol, even though most college students are underage. However, if you are offered alcohol on your trip, say no thanks. Everything you do will get back to the coach. You are a guest, you are underage, and you do not know the people you are out with. Most coaches do not encourage partying but realize their teams are not immune to it. Some guests at a party you go to with athletes will be people that the athletes don't even know, so be wise and be safe. Stories of recruits sneaking out at night, or getting lost in a fraternity house, or passing out at a party—or the worst, being arrested—while attending a campus party are often told by coaches. Most of those recruits do not end up playing for that college. Behave yourself and use your time wisely while on your visit.

Follow Up

Regardless of whether you are on an official or unofficial visit, be thankful and appreciative of the coaches, faculty members, administrators, and athletes who spend time with you. You should always send thank-you notes to anyone you meet, especially if you really enjoyed your visit and the school is still on your list. If you do so, you will get another gold star in your folder. You are competing against other recruits with similar talent for a spot on the team. A coach is working hard to determine who is most interested in the program, so a short note can make a world of difference and may bump you up on the coach's list. The athlete, not the parent, should call the coach on the Monday following a visit to express appreciation.

Official Visits: A Summary

- College pays part or all of the expenses of the visit.
- Prospect is allowed a maximum of five paid visits senior year.
- One official (paid) visit is allowed per college.

- Visit may last a maximum of 48 hours.
- Requirements for paid visit:
  - NCAA Division I—test scores (SAT, ACT, PLAN) and transcript
  - NCAA Division II—test scores (SAT, ACT, PLAN)

CHAPTER SUMMARY

Choosing your college is a big decision that will affect the next four, or more, years of your life. Make a well-informed decision by visiting college campuses and asking lots of questions. Regardless of whether you are on an official or unofficial visit, meet the coach and team. On your visit, spend a minimum of 12 hours, preferably 24 hours, on each campus. Stop by the admissions office to rack up some brownie points and be prepared to answer questions as well as ask them. Once you walk around a campus and meet the coach, you will feel in your gut whether the school is a good match or not.

Remember, you can always return unofficially during your senior year before making your final decision. And before deciding which college to attend, ask yourself, "If I could never play my sport again, would I choose this college?" It is a good match when your answer to this question is yes.

chapter 9

The Admissions Process

Thus far, you have connected with coaches, visited college campuses, and narrowed your college list down to your final choices. Now it is time to apply. The admissions process has its own set of guidelines and requirements. This chapter will cover each step of the application process and explain the different types of applications (early, regular, and rolling) and how they affect athletes.

THE EVALUATION CRITERIA

The admissions application will vary from school to school. Some only ask for a completed application with your tests scores and transcript, while others require a more elaborate application with short-answer questions, essays, and two or three recommendation letters. The admissions committee or department at each college has different goals for the freshmen class from year to year. At top institutions, an applicant may be admitted one year, while an applicant with identical qualifications is not admitted the next, depending on the desired makeup of the incoming class.

Admissions tends to accept students who match the campus and community needs, and those needs change from year to year. For example, the college may want more engineering majors one year and more chemistry majors the next. Certain criteria are standard, but once the admissions committee gets past your test scores and grade point average, you are evaluated on the individuality presented in your application. Your essay, recommendation letters, and extracurricular activities will give the committee insight into who you are. Advice on completing these sections is included later in this chapter.

THE ADMISSIONS COMMITTEE

Each college determines the athletic department's input into the admissions process. Coaches put together their preferred athlete list (recruiting list). This may be turned over to either an athletic department staff member, who represents the whole department to the admissions committee, or to an admissions representative, or each coach may go directly to admissions. The admissions process a college chooses for its athletic department can affect the outcome for different sports.

The athletic department that sends one athletic representative to the admissions committee to represent the entire athletic department likely has a priority list for its sports. The department tiers its sports, putting a priority on its support for each team. For example, the football and basketball list will probably be the first group of athletes under review for admissions. A college in the Northeast, where ice hockey is very popular, might have ice hockey as a top-tier sport and baseball as a second-tier sport. An ice hockey player with a weak academic record may have a better chance of being admitted than a weak baseball player. However, at a college where coaches work closely with assigned admissions representatives, these same two athletes will have a better chance of being admitted, because admission committee members are working to get them admitted. With this system, all members of the admissions committee have an athletic team or two assigned to them, so the whole committee has a vested interest in athletics and individual athletes.

At a college where athletic scholarships are offered, coaches submit their list of recruited student athletes directly to the admissions committee or director for review. At these colleges, coaches work hard to find talented athletes who will be successful academically. Rarely will an academically eligible scholarship athlete be denied by admissions. Coaches can request admission for a weaker student, but once admitted, if the athlete is not academically successful, the admissions committee will not likely admit a weak student athlete recommended by that coach in the future.

THE APPLICATION

Just about every college allows applicants to apply using an online application. Ask the coach if they would like you to complete the online application; some coaches have an application specially stamped for athletics. College applications typically request your grade point average, class rank, test scores, extracurricular activities, and they may ask for an essay and recommendation letters. Each part of the application serves its purpose in determining your admittance or denial to a college. Each college puts different weight on different parts of your application, but what it is really interested in is the person behind the numbers: GPA, test scores, and class rank. Your essays, recommendation letters, and extracurricular activities can help boost a weaker GPA or test scores. We will take a moment here to explain each piece of the application and recommend ways to improve your application.

GPA and Class Rank

Your GPA is determined by the grades you earn in the courses you take. Students often ask if they should take an advanced placement course or not. The answer: a B in an AP class is better than an A in a regular class, but a C in an AP class might hurt you. Make sure that you are confident that you will do well in an AP class before you take it. AP classes are meant to be challenging and are geared towards college-level work. If you pass an AP class, you are probably well prepared for college and will likely be academically successful.

At most high schools, AP classes are weighted, so if you do well in an AP class, your class rank can actually be higher than a 4.0. Students who receive 90s in all their regular classes but did not take any AP classes, will have a hard time earning a top-fifteen class ranking. The top colleges in the country want students who rank in the top ten and higher. If you are ranked 20th in your class and 10 students ranked above you apply to the same college, the college will need an awfully good reason to pass up the other students and admit you. This is where the other parts of the application come into play.

Extracurricular Activities

"Extracurricular activities" includes athletics. Many college administrators consider athletics to be a tremendous educational experience, and they value the skills learned through playing sports. To be a successful college student, you will need to be hardworking, dedicated, and disciplined and be able to set goals, work as a team, and persevere. The college graduation rates for athletes across the country tend to be higher than for the overall student population. With the coach on the inside pulling for you, your talent and involvement in athletics will help you move up the admissions list.

If you have academic credentials that suggest you can be successful and you have a coach supporting you, you might get admitted ahead of a classmate ranked higher than you in your class. Students who excel in art, dance, music, journalism, science, math, and many other areas get bonus points with admissions committees as well. Colleges want talented students in a variety of areas to enrich their campuses.

Your Essay

Do not, under any circumstances, write about your sport in your personal statement. It will be clear to the admissions representatives that you are an athlete from your extracurricular activities list. Also, they have read more then their share of essays describing the "at-the-buzzer win," and they would rather not have to read another one. Write about any other experience, but not athletics. If you have done any volunteer work, traveled, or started a business or club, you can write about that. Treat your essay as though you are telling a story. Write from your heart. Remember, the admissions representatives have to read a lot of essays. How can you make yours stand out?

Be sure to have someone edit your essay for grammar, but don't let them change your voice. Keep your essay within the guidelines provided on the application. If a college asks for a 200-word essay, don't make it 500 words, and vice versa. Give yourself time to think and write. If you are having a hard time coming up with a topic, ask a friend or family member for ideas. Your essay can come in handy when you apply for scholarships. Scholarship essays tend to ask about an obstacle you have overcome or about a person or event that has impacted your life. You may need to tweak it a bit, but a lot of students can use their application essay for more than one college and more than one scholarship application.

Most of the online applications that require essays will allow you to copy and paste your essay into the online application. Be sure to do this prior to submitting it. You will appear more organized, and the committee always likes to get a completed application rather than sections arriving separately.

RECOMMENDATION LETTERS

If recommendation letters are required, you will need one or two of your core subject teachers and your guidance counselor to write letters for you. Although you may want to, do not ask your coach to write a recommendation letter, unless your coach taught you a core subject. Choose teachers who know you well. Just because you like a teacher is not a reason to ask him for a recommendation. Some students make the mistake of asking a teacher for a recommendation without asking if the teacher can write them a good one or if they have time to do so. Ask for letters in early September or even during the spring of your junior year. Remember, many seniors in your high school class will be asking the same teacher for recommendations at the beginning of the school year. Tell the teacher why you chose her and why you have chosen the colleges on your list. It will also be helpful to the teacher if you provide a resume of all of your extracurricular activities and any awards you may have earned. Give your counselor the same information. Letters with specific information about you are better than general ones.

THE INTERVIEW

Some colleges require an admissions interview. Others offer the opportunity for an informational interview. Required interviews may be conducted on campus with an admissions representative or in your hometown with an alumnus. An informal interview tends to be *informative,* where you interview the college representative to learn more about the school. These can take place at your school or informally at another location (usually in a conference room at a hotel) in your hometown. The off-campus, one-on-one interview tends to be *evaluative,* where you will be the interviewee. An alumnus or admissions representative will gather information from you and then make a recommendation to the admissions committee as to whether they think you are a good match for the college.

Review information about the college prior to your campus visit or interview so you can speak intelligently about why you are interested. Verify your reasons for considering the school by asking questions related to what you know the school has to offer. Know the majors it offers and ask questions that pertain to your specific interest in that major. (In Chapter 8 is a list of sample questions you can have ready for the interview.) The admissions representative will know you're an athlete, so be prepared to answer questions that are not related to your athletic experience.

Regardless of the type of interview, you should plan on being the interviewer. Find out why the alumnus thinks you should choose the school. What do they think is special about it? What would they have changed about their experience? Your goal is to determine whether this college is the right place for you. You don't want too many surprises when you show up on campus as a freshman. A bad interview doesn't usually hurt an applicant, but a good one can lift someone over the fence and gain admission. Take an active part in the interview, and you will probably improve your chances of being admitted.

APPLICATION OPTIONS

There are four types of applications: early decision, early action, rolling admission, and regular admission. Each college chooses its preferred application options. Let's look at the various admission application processes in relation to athletic recruiting.

Early Decision

An early decision application is a binding contract with the school. By applying early decision, you are agreeing that, should you be admitted, you will attend that college. You may only apply to one college early decision. The application deadline is in October or early November. To be considered for early decision admission, you are required to send your completed application postmarked on or before the deadline. You will be notified by early December as to whether you have been accepted, deferred to the spring, or denied admission. You should apply early decision only if that school is your clearly number one choice.

> **IT IS IMPORTANT FOR ALL STUDENTS, INCLUDING ATHLETES, TO KNOW THE DEADLINES FOR EACH COLLEGE'S APPLICATION.** Coaches may encourage you to apply early; if so, you will need to know the requirements and deadlines involved. Colleges that use an early admissions application also have a regular application. Admissions does not waiver on their deadlines; if you miss any of them, you will not be considered.

The drawback to applying early decision is that you will not know what your financial aid package is. This information is not available until after you complete your FAFSA in January and the college awards you the package in the spring. It may be possible to get an early estimate on your financial aid package, but it is just that, an estimate. The estimate is only accurate if you are totally honest about your finances for that year.

The positive to applying early is that the applicant pool is smaller and your chances of being admitted might be greater, especially if a coach is encouraging you to apply early. A coach can often have more influence with an early decision candidate than a regular admission applicant. Colleges want to admit students who want to attend their university. A student who might be considered borderline in the spring would likely have a better chance by applying early admission in November.

Early Action

Early action is very similar to early decision. Early action applications are due in the fall, October or November, and a decision is sent out in December. Applying early action can be advantageous because of the smaller pool of applicants. The main difference between the two is that the early action application is nonbinding; if you get in, you do not have to attend that college but have until May 1 to make your decision. The advantage is that you do have time to get your financial aid package before deciding. And if you get admitted early, you get to enjoy your senior year more than your classmate who has to wait until April for an admittance letter.

Again, if the coach is encouraging you to apply early, it is because they have more pull with admissions at that time. The coach is probably very interested in you if he is encouraging you to apply early. Remember, the admissions office accepts you into the university, not the coach.

Rolling Admission

Rolling admission is usually offered by larger state universities where the application pool tends to be large. When you apply to a college with rolling admissions, you will find out whether or not you are admitted within four to six weeks of applying. You can apply in September and receive an acceptance letter in October. Both athletes and coaches love this option. An athlete will know they are admitted and can enjoy the remainder of their senior year. The coach can focus on other recruits and coaching.

No matter which application method you choose, you need to complete the whole application and send in your application fee before any college will even begin reviewing it. Be sure to take the SAT or ACT during your junior year in case you want to retake it in the fall of your senior year.

KAPLAN

Regular Admission

If you choose not to apply early or the college does not offer early admission, you will be considered a regular admission candidate. Pay attention to the deadlines for regular admissions; rarely will a college waver on these. Some colleges accept students up until August 1, but these are typically less academically competitive schools. Most deadlines fall between January and February. The majority of the acceptance letters go out April 1. You typically have until May 1 to send in a deposit to hold your spot in the class.

If you are a scholarship athlete, you must apply to the college. Do not assume that the college coach or your high school coach is applying for you. *You* must complete the application and be accepted. Remember, your scholarship becomes null and void if you do not apply to a college you have signed with, and you become ineligible within that association if you do not apply to the college that signed you. In other words, you will not be allowed to sign another athletic scholarship within the same association if you did not apply to the first college you signed with.

As a scholarship athlete, if you apply and are denied admission, you are released from the Letter of Intent and may be eligible to apply and sign with another institution in the same association at the same level. Rarely is an athlete denied admission after signing a Letter of Intent. But if you become an academic nonqualifier, you will become ineligible for other institutions within the same level of that association. (The associations' academic rules are explained in Chapter 2.) However, you can be academically ineligible for a NCAA Division I school but be eligible for an NCAA Division II school. You could then apply to that Division II school, be admitted, and sign a Letter of Intent as late as July. (See Chapter 3 for more information on academic eligibility and the rules governing the different associations.)

Note the Application Options for Each School

While you are doing your research on colleges, take note of the type of applications the school offers. A school can offer more than one admissions option and will have another deadline for institutional scholarships. For example, the University of Florida offers early-decision and two different regular admission deadlines: "Regular 1" deadline is November 1 with an early February notification, and "Regular 2" has a January deadline with a late March notification. The University of California system offers a November 1–30 application filing deadline with a March notification date. The University of Texas has an admissions application deadline of February 1 but a scholarship application deadline of December 1.

If you have narrowed down your choices to your top three to five colleges by September 1, you might be ready for an early-decision application. Work with the coach and realize that if you are being encouraged to apply early, you are probably high on the coach's list. If you do get denied by admissions in December, at least you can move on and find another option.

CHAPTER SUMMARY

Take the application seriously. Always review your information to make sure it is correct and accurate. Double-check your Social Security number, because once on campus, you become that number. Proofread for mistakes. Ask your parents or a teacher to check the application; they may think of something you left out.

When possible, try to send your official transcript, essay, and recommendation letters together in one envelope. If everything arrives at the same time, it will be easier for admissions, and you will know that all components of your application have been sent. Remember, admissions will not begin looking at your application until it receives your application fee. So if you submit your application online, which most colleges prefer, have a credit card ready or send a check in the mail the same day you submit the application.

Remember, if you sign a Letter of Intent, you still need to apply and be admitted by the institution for the athletic scholarship to be used.

chapter 10

Choosing Your Best Match

· ·

There are some key areas to take into consideration when deciding where you choose to go to college, such as academic options, athletic expectations, demographic and geographic location of the campus, financial commitments, and the size of the school. You decide what matters to you. Each student-athlete has their own preference about what feels right and where they think they will best reach their goals. Below you will find a list of questions for each area of consideration, which, once answered, will help you in your decision-making process.

KEY AREAS OF CONSIDERATION CHECKLIST

Academic Interests

- ❑ Does this college have your area(s) of academic interest?
- ❑ Is this program respected?
- ❑ What are the requirements to get into the program/classes?
- ❑ What is the average class size?
- ❑ How large are lecture and discussion classes?
- ❑ What percent of students graduate with this major and receive job offers?
- ❑ Are tutors available?
- ❑ Do students have access to computers? Are the computers up-to-date?
- ❑ Is there a job placement office?
- ❑ What is the graduation rate at the college?

Athletic Role

- ❑ Do you like the coach? The team?
- ❑ What is the direction of this program?

❏ What are the coach's goals for the team? What are the athletes' goals for the team? Do they match?

❏ What are the training, practice, and playing facilities like?

❏ How do you fit into this program (big fish/little fish)?

❏ How many current team members are in your position/events? (Does the team need you?)

❏ Is this the right conference for you competitively?

❏ What time demands are there athletically, in season and out of season?

❏ Does the training program fit your expectations?

❏ Is there a weight-training program within the required training time?

❏ Number of allocated scholarships?

❏ Amount of scholarship money available for next year?

❏ What is the history and tradition of the program?

❏ Is the program properly funded? Do you have to cover any expenses?

❏ What is the whole athletic department's financial status?

❏ Is there an athletic academic support center? Computer resource center?

❏ Do athletes get priority registration for classes?

❏ How do the athletes spend their free weekends?

Demographic and Geographic

❏ Size of community (major city, medium-size college town, small town)

❏ Location geographically (north, south, east, west)

❏ Closeness to home—travel expenses

❏ Opportunity to have family members visit and cheer you on!

❏ Weather

❏ The terrain: mountains, hills, plateaus, trees, desolate . . .

Finances

❏ Can you afford this college?

❏ What types of aid are available from the college?

❏ What is the deadline for the financial aid application?

❏ Can you qualify for an athletic scholarship?

❏ Is it possible to earn a scholarship after freshman year?

School Size and College Division

❏ Number of undergraduate and graduate students enrolled?

❏ What percent of the student body commutes?

❏ What are the living arrangements? Are you assured housing? Do you have to live in the dorms? What are the off-campus housing conditions?

❏ What do students do for their social life?

❏ Competitive level: NCAA Division I, II, or III; NAIA; junior college; or community college?

ACADEMICS

Academics are the most important reason for heading to college. The key question you should know the answer to before you choose a college should be, "If I could never play my sport again, would I still choose this school?" The career you want in your future will likely be influenced by the degree you earn in college rather than by the sport that you play. Use the College Board's MyRoad™ career search *(www.collegeboard.com/student/myroad/tour/index.html)* or ACT's Discover˚ *(www.act.org/discover/)* to help locate schools with your major or career interests.

At some schools, you may need to apply to a degree program and be admitted into the program as an incoming freshman, while at others, you are admitted under general studies or as undecided and then choose a degree program after your freshman or sophomore year. Just because you want to major in music at Indiana University doesn't mean you get to; you have to audition and be admitted to the School of Music.

Liberal Arts or Professional Programs

A liberal arts college allows students to take a variety of courses during the first two to three years, and then students choose a major. A college with professional programs places students in their desired degree program freshman year and allows students to gain early exposure to their desired degree choice. If you do not know what you want to study, a liberal arts college will allow you to explore several options. If you switch majors, it may take you five years or more to complete your degree, but it would take the same amount of time if you began a professional program and changed your mind halfway through. This is common; many students, including athletes, take five years to complete a degree.

To help prevent having to pay for five years of college, try to earn college credit by taking AP exams or taking some required college courses at a local community college while you're still in high school. If you choose the second option, be sure to check with the colleges you are interested in attending to be sure they accept community college credits. Many colleges offer assessment tests, such as the College Level Examination Program (CLEP), to incoming freshmen to place them in courses accordingly. You may test out of courses, and earn college credit, by taking these exams. Check on *www.kaptest.com* for information on Kaplan's CLEP review book. Taking these tests can save you hundreds of thousands of dollars in tuition. Another way to earn college credit and graduate on time is to attend summer school between college semesters. Many athletes stay on campus during the summers to take advantage of the great training facilities and to take classes, either to get ahead or to catch up in credits.

Study-Abroad Programs

More and more colleges offer study-abroad programs and encourage students to take part in them. If this is something you are interested in, ask your coach about it. As an NCAA Division I or II athlete on scholarship, it will be challenging for you take off a semester to travel abroad. At this level, you will be required to participate in out-of-season training and deal with high expectations and demands, especially if you are on scholarship. At a NCAA Division III college, NAIA, or non-scholarship Division I colleges like the Ivy League, on the other hand, you may have the freedom to experience these programs. Depending on your major, studying abroad can be a tremendous opportunity for you to gain valuable experience in your field of study.

ATHLETICS

Although you will have already considered this at the beginning of your search, it can't hurt to reevaluate how athletics will fit into your overall college experience. Ask yourself again if you will be able to deal with the following situations:

- Being a big fish in a little pond or a little fish in a big pond
- Being a scholarship athlete, meaning one who is getting paid to play
- Sitting on the bench and not getting a lot of playing time
- Having to attend summer school to take classes because they conflict with practice during the regular school year
- A new freshman coming in and taking over your starting position
- Not being able to spend weekends partying because you have competitions on weekends
- Taking 8:00 AM classes because practice is from 2:00–5:00 PM every day

These are some great questions to ask yourself about how you really feel about the athletic side of your college experience. If more athletes stepped back and looked at the real picture, there would be fewer transfers and more happy athletes on college campuses. Review the questions in Chapter 8 that you should ask coaches, athletes, and students on college campuses to help you gain a better feel for what your college experience will be like.

FINANCIAL COMMITMENTS

A must-have conversation between you and whoever is supporting your education is the conversation about financing your college education. The earlier you talk about money, the better. Before you even begin searching for colleges, you should have a conversation about the costs and what you can afford. Parents should be honest with their student-athletes about their financial situation and the funds that are or are not available for college. Also, parents should be honest and up front with coaches. If you absolutely cannot attend a college without financial support from the college, you should let a coach know. If you want an athletic scholarship to validate your hard work or to repay your parents for all the money they spent on your athletic endeavors thus far, tell the coach that, too.

When you receive your financial aid offer, whether it is an athletic scholarship from the athletic department or an award from the financial aid office, review every word of the offer and know exactly what you will owe. The athletic offer will refer to tuition, room and board, books, and fees. Any of these or portions of these items can be paid for by athletics. More often than not, you will owe some money. Athletes rarely receive full scholarships.

Your award package from the financial aid office may include a list of grants, scholarships, and or loans you can have, *if* you sign and agree to accept. The money will only be available if you return the signed award letter. Grants and scholarships are free money that you do not need to pay back. Loans do need to be paid back. Pay close attention to what the actual cost of attendance is. Do *not* take out a loan for miscellaneous, day-to-day expenses, like shampoo, movies, and notebooks. You can accept a portion of the loan, but do your best to borrow as little as possible. Get a job instead, if allowed by your athletic program.

DEMOGRAPHICS AND LOCATION

You can find similar athletic and academic experiences at a variety of schools in a variety of locations. There are great Division I schools in cities, in the country, or in medium-sized towns all over the country. They are situated in the mountains, hills, and plateaus and on oceans, lakes, and rivers. They are close to home and far away. Some college campuses will experience spring, summer, fall, and winter, while others enjoy over 300 days of sunshine per year. What setting best fits your personality? Do you care if you are near the water? Will you be prepared for a snowstorm? If play a spring sport, do you care if you spend spring practice in a field house?

Once you get an idea of the location of your dream college, realize that there are plenty of options within that location. Look at several schools in the same area of the country. You don't want to end up not getting into that one perfect college in Florida (where you were looking forward to those 300 days of sunshine) and end up in layers of clothing in Minnesota.

How far from home do you want to be? You may not think this is very important, because you are excited to be out on your own. Well, think again. For most athletes, their parents have been their biggest fans throughout their lives. Will you be able to handle everything if your support system is not in the stands? Will you be able to survive if you can't jump in the car and reach a home-cooked meal or your comfy bed? Time and time again, students transfer after their freshman year because they were too far from home. Everyone gets homesick during their first semester away at college. One trip back home in the fall will help you realize that everything is different back home. Give the college a chance and commit one year to it. Athletics will help you feel more connected, and so will joining a club or sorority/fraternity or getting a job. I recommend thinking hard about how far you really want to be from home. If you have rarely spent a night at someone else's house, you should consider this question very seriously.

Student Body Size and Makeup

The size of the student body makes a difference in what a college offers and how connected you may become with the faculty. Size can make a difference in housing options and may make a difference in the overall atmosphere of the campus. Student body size combined with demographic location will lead to completely different atmospheres on two otherwise similar campuses.

Have you ever been in a class of 100? How about 400? How about 15? Which environment allows you to learn better? At larger colleges, where the student body population is over 10,000, many of your basic courses will be held in large lecture halls. The size and makeup of the student body will make a difference in a number of majors offered at the college and class times offered. Smaller colleges may not offer evening classes but will allow you to create your major. Colleges with a larger student body tend to offer evening courses and have a wide selection of majors.

Once you choose a major, depending on what you choose, the class sizes become smaller and you have a great chance of developing relationships with your professors. At a small school, where the student body population is under 4,000 students and the average class size is less than 30, your professor will certainly notice if you are absent from class. A larger college will have more educational and social options. There will be a greater number of majors to choose from and a greater number of sororities, fraternities, and other clubs to join. As discussed in Chapter 8, the best way to get a feel for the campus is to visit during the academic year, preferably when classes are in session.

Diversity

The diversity of a campus may be of interest to you. Large public universities tend to have a lot of in-state students, because tuition is less than for out-of-state students. Private schools usually have a greater variety of students from across the state, the country, and the world. Colleges in large cities likely have a more ethnically diverse population than colleges in small towns.

EACH YEAR, KAPLAN AND *NEWSWEEK* TEAM UP TO COMPILE *THE KAPLAN COLLEGE GUIDE,* which contains a list of America's top colleges. In it, you will find a lot of information on the makeup of different colleges. Items listed include percentages of male and female students, percentages of in-state and out-of-state students, ethnic breakdown, and the most popular majors on the campus. The issue also lists the selectivity of each school; i.e., the percent of applicants admitted.

Housing

Many colleges are currently building new dorms or renovating old ones. Some colleges have increased their enrollment and need additional housing; others have to keep up with the new generation and its demands for single rooms with all the amenities. Will it matter to you whether you have a single or a quad, where you share a room or the main living space of an apartment? Some campuses do not have enough housing for all their students, so on-campus housing is assigned on a first-come, first-served basis while the rest live in off-campus apartments.

If the student body is comprised of 80 percent in-state students, most of them may not even live on campus, instead commuting to campus while living at home. Some may live on campus but go home on the weekends. On some campuses, where the majority of the students are from in-state, if there is no football or basketball game that weekend, the campus becomes deserted. Think about how you would feel if this were the case. If you attend a school in a large city, you won't notice the absence of in-state students on the weekends as much.

CHAPTER SUMMARY

If you have done everything suggested in this book, you will likely have a gut feeling about which college is right for you. This gut feeling will come from your visit and the answers to all the questions you have asked coaches, athlete, students, alumni, and faculty on each campus. You may favor that school because you know the coach is very excited about having you, you enjoyed the team, and it has the academic program you are most interested in pursuing—in other words, everything clicks. The more actively involved you are in your college search process, the more you take control of discovering your options and the easier this decision becomes.

College can be a great experience regardless of athletics, but when you play a sport for a college, you will feel even more connected to it. Statistically, athletes graduate at a higher rate than that of the nonathletic student body, and athletes tend to express greater satisfaction with their college experience. If you liked playing high school sports, you will love competing in college.

Take your time during your search process. Do your research on colleges, coaches, and teams—and also do some soul searching. Be sure to think about what environment will help you become more successful and what type of coach will bring the best out of you. Review the questions in this chapter before and after your college search to make a well-informed decision on where you will spend the next four or more years of your life.

The absolute last question you need to ask yourself before deciding where to go is, "If I could never play my sport again, would I choose this college?" If your answer to this question is yes, then you have found a great match.

Nonathletic Scholarships

Most college athletes are on nonathletic financial aid. They are playing their sport and having their education paid for. The financial resource is not the athletic department but instead the university's financial aid office or an outside organization. Most athletes are competing at the Division III level, where "athletic" scholarships are not allowed. The athletes are getting paid to play, but their performance on the field does not affect their financial aid package. Rather, their performance in the classroom or their involvement in the community, their extra-curricular activities, or their family's need has determined their financial aid.

College coaches may know about their institutional financial aid, but they will not know about the outside scholarships. This chapter will focus on financial resources student athletes can tap into, including institutional, corporate, and community awards, and how to find them.

GRANTS

Before we discuss scholarships, you should understand what a grant is, who awards them, and who can qualify for one. Grants are free money for students with financial need. You do not need to pay them back, and the awards can range from $50 to thousands of dollars. Grant money is money from the government that colleges award based on a family's financial need. Students and their parents or guardian must complete the Federal Application for Federal Student Aid (FAFSA), located at *www.fafsa.ed.gov*. The earliest you can complete the application is January of your senior year. All college-bound students should complete the FAFSA as soon as possible. You must also complete the form each January while attending college to be eligible for aid.

Colleges use your Student Aid Report (SAR), which is determined by the federal government from your FAFSA, to award grants. When you complete the

FAFSA, you will request that your financial information be sent to the colleges to which you have applied. Each college begins awarding its allotment of federal and state grants on a first-come, first-served basis. Thus, it is very important that you complete and send your FAFSA as early in January as you can and be sure to list *all* the colleges to which you have applied. Just because you are qualified does not mean you'll get money; you have to apply for it!

A student who waited until April of her senior year to complete her FAFSA found out that her EFC equaled $0, but because it did not receive her financial information until April, the school she planned on attending had already awarded its allotment of federal aid to incoming freshmen. This woman ended up having to borrow money via student loans. The following year, she completed her FAFSA in January and was awarded over $4,000 in federal grants. That was $4,000 less in loans she had to borrow.

To estimate what your family's EFC might be, go to the College Board's website *(http://www .fafsa.ed.gov)* and use the financial aid calculator there. If you enter accurate information, you should be able to get an idea of what your financial need might be. Also, be aware that even though private schools have larger price tags, they have larger endowments than public schools and tend to offer excellent financial aid packages to their admitted students.

INSTITUTIONAL SCHOLARSHIPS

Colleges offer several institutional merit scholarships, which do not need to be paid back. These awards are connected to your high school resume: your academic performance, community service, and extracurricular activities. These awards usually require you to maintain a certain grade point average and course load for renewal of the award each year.

To locate a list of these awards, log on to the college's website and look under "Financial Aid." You should be able to find a list of scholarships for which you can apply. Be sure to complete each college's scholarship application by the stated deadline. If you miss the deadline, you will not be eligible for the scholarships. To increase your chance of receiving an award, turn in your application as early as possible; be the first person in line rather than the last.

Colleges may offer additional money to students based on the college's needs. These awards are not actual scholarships for which a student applies but financial aid a college chooses to award from its resources. If you are a female interested in engineering, you will find that many schools will offer you nice award package; there is a huge need for women in the field of engineering. Today, more females are entering college than males, so some schools award additional money to attract male students. Just about every college offers aid to underrepresented groups. If a college has added a new undergraduate program, it likely will offer additional money to students interested in that field of study to fill up the classrooms.

More and more colleges are offering free tuition waivers for students who are admitted and have financial need. Harvard is offering aid to students whose family's annual income is below $40,000.

KAPLAN

Other schools have followed with tuition waivers for students with need and students who graduate in four years. Ask each college's financial aid office about these awards.

COMMUNITY, CORPORATE, AND NATIONAL SCHOLARSHIPS

Thousands of scholarships are available to college-bound seniors. Corporations, community organizations, and national organizations offer yearly awards. This book includes a list of scholarships from across the country. These are awarded from sources other than athletic departments, but many are specific to students who have been participating in athletics. It is a great place to begin your search for free financial assistance. If you meet the criteria, apply!

Besides those listed here, scholarships are available for all sorts of students: tall, short, left-handed, diabetic, future lawyers, future doctors, and future mechanics. There are scholarships for asthmatics, triplets, artists, musicians, Native Americans, Hispanics, and African Americans. You will be amazed at the variety of scholarships offered. A great resource for scholarships is Kaplan's *Scholarships 2008,* which contains over 3,000 scholarships. Another great way to locate scholarships is the national search site *http://fastweb.com.* You need to register and answer a long list of questions; then Fastweb matches national scholarships with your personal preferences.

These scholarships are not controlled by colleges but rather by community organizations, foundations, businesses, and national organizations. To win one of these financial awards, you must meet the criteria and apply before the deadline. If you begin reviewing this list as a 9th grader, you will learn more about what you need to do over the next four years to be a candidate for these awards. Unless you happen to be good enough to get a full athletic scholarship (very few athletes are so lucky), you will want to compile a list of nonathletic scholarships to apply for senior year.

Historically Black Colleges and the United Negro College Fund

If you are applying to a historically black college, an extensive list of scholarships exists for those colleges that are members of the United Negro College Fund. These scholarships, from various corporations and foundations, are specifically given to students who plan on attending a United Negro College Fund member institution. Go to *http://uncf.org* for a complete list of colleges that are members and a list of scholarships. Again, these scholarships are usually offered every year and do not need to be paid back.

> **BE AWARE, IF YOU ARE BEING AWARDED AN ATHLETIC SCHOLARSHIP FROM A COLLEGE,** you might not be eligible for any other scholarships. You need to check with the college coach to determine if you can earn additional scholarship money from outside sources.

LOCATING SCHOLARSHIPS

If you are determined to save money on your college education, you can find lots of scholarships from a number of different resources. In additional to this book, Kaplan's *Scholarship 2008,* and Fastweb, see your counselor, check your school district's website, and check with local organizations and clubs. As mentioned earlier, national associations and corporations give away thousands of dollars annually to college-bound students, many of whom are athletes. Some of these are listed on company websites; others come directly through your school counselor.

Most high schools have someone in their building assigned to collect all the local, state, and national scholarship awards available each year. You will most likely find these posted on a website, on a bulletin board, or on a wall in your college counselor's office. Find out who knows about college scholarships in your high school and request that they inform you about any new ones that come up.

Local Scholarships Are Easier to Win

Local businesses, foundations, and community organizations offer college scholarships to graduating seniors. Many are need based and dependent on your FAFSA form, but plenty are based solely on talent or future career interests. A large number of scholarships are awarded based on community service. Begin volunteering freshman year, and you will accumulate more community service hours than the student who starts senior year. Athletes should check with the sports organizations in their hometowns as well as the Kiwanis Club, Knights of Columbus, and local Lodges. Local scholarships are usually easier to win; there are fewer applicants compared to national contests. Most local awards are small amounts, but they do add up. One thing's for sure; if you don't apply, you won't win.

Some school districts post a list of scholarships in order of due date. The list begins in August with applications due through October. Each week, the list is updated with additional applications with due dates in November, then December, and so on. The majority of the scholarships are for graduating high school seniors, but some are available to students in grades 9–12.

> **MANY LOCAL SCHOLARSHIPS ARE ISSUED FOR ONLY ONE YEAR.** If the scholarship application does not state the length of time for the award, be sure to ask for this information once you are awarded it. Scholarships awarded by colleges are often renewable, but they tend to have stipulations such as GPA requirements and credit hours earned.

Employer Matching Funds

One last place to look for financial assistance is with your parent's employer. Have your parent find out if their employer offers any college scholarships or matching funds. Some corporations have a matching funds account where if a child of an employee wins a scholarship, the company will match it. Other companies have their own scholarships for children of employees.

APPLYING FOR SCHOLARSHIPS

Finding college scholarships is the easy part; applying for them is the hard part. Actually, once you complete one application, the rest get easier. If a scholarship requires an essay, as many often do, you can often tweak one essay to fit another application. Many essay topics ask about someone who has influenced you, or why you value your education, or about a hardship you've overcome. Again, if you begin looking in 9th grade, you will have plenty of time to perfect those essays by the time you send them out.

Scholarship Applications

Scholarship applications typically require an essay, your resume, transcript, and two recommendations. Complete the application fully, following the guidelines or rules of each application. If the essay is supposed to be 200 words long, do not send a 500-word essay, and vice versa. If an institution wants the application sent electronically, send it that way. If you need two recommendations, send two. If they ask for a picture, send your school photo. Type your applications and send all parts of the application in the same envelope before the deadline. Make the process easy on the committee, and your chances of winning money for college will increase.

Pay attention to the scholarships with deadlines in the fall of your senior year. There are always fewer applicants at that time. One student turned in an application for a local award that was due October 1, but she forgot to include her essay. Because she was the only applicant, the award committee let her know that she would be receiving the award but that her essay was still needed. She was lucky that no one else applied.

A STUDENT WAS RECENTLY ENCOURAGED TO APPLY FOR A SCHOLARSHIP THAT REQUIRED THREE ESSAYS. She had two that she had written in her senior English class. Yes, she moaned about writing the third, but she was grinning from ear to ear when she won the four-year, $500-per-semester award. At one school, a Hispanic student has been the recipient of a local African American scholarship the past two years because no one else applied. So even if you're not sure you might receive an award, apply anyway! If you don't, someone else who took the time to apply or someone who is not perfectly eligible for it will get that money, and you won't.

Do not miss deadlines, or your application will not be considered. If the directions say that it must be postmarked by midnight on October 15, that means that 12:01 AM on the 16th is too late. If the directions say it must be received by October 15, the application must be in the person's hands on that date. Keep deadlines in mind as you locate scholarships and organize your applications. If anything, turn in your application early, and you might get a few extra points.

YOUR FINANCIAL AWARD PACKAGE

In the spring of your senior year, colleges to which you have been accepted will send you a financial award letter with your financial aid package. Once you receive this from the all the colleges, compare the awards to find out which is the best deal. Go over each *very* carefully. Almost all packages include some type of loan. Even if the FAFSA showed that your EFC is $0, you will likely have to take out loans. Use the worksheet in Figure 11.1 to compare each award. Some colleges include all expenses (tuition, room and board, student fees, books, transportation, and miscellaneous expenses) in their offer, while others may leave out travel, fees, and miscellaneous charges.

Any outside scholarships you are awarded will be sent to the college you request. Money from any loans you take out is sent directly to you. The loan money comes as a lump-sum check in your name. Unfortunately, these checks typically arrive before your college tuition bill. Too many students spend the money before they even arrive on campus. Try not to do this. You do not need to borrow all the money in the award package. Do not borrow money for transportation and miscellaneous expenses; instead, get a job and cover these expenses with money you save over the summer or earn during the school year. Your goal should be to graduate with the least amount of debt possible.

On the FAFSA application, say yes to work-study. Work-study jobs are usually on campus and tend to have a flexible work schedule, so when a conflict comes up for a study session or major exam, you have an easier time adjusting your work hours. In some jobs, you may even be able to study while working (e.g., parking lot attendant) or get free meals (e.g., dining hall or café jobs). Other jobs allow you to work for faculty and establish a network for future jobs or internships after college.

CHAPTER SUMMARY

Financing a college education is expensive, but if you do your research and apply for scholarships, you can reduce your part of the bill. Begin searching early, in your freshman year, and keep a list of possible scholarships to apply for. Remember to complete all applications as directed and do *not* miss deadlines. If anything, apply early.

Complete your FAFSA application as early in January as possible. Colleges award their allotment of federal money on a first-come, first-served basis, and you want to be first in line.

■ Figure 11.1: Financial Aid Comparison Worksheet ■

	College #1	College #2	College #3	College #4
Name				

Your Cost of Attendance

Cost of Attendance	College #1	College #2	College #3	College #4
Tuition and Fees				
Room and Board				
Books and Supplies				
Travel				
Personal Expenses				

Financial Aid Award

Gift in Aid	College #1	College #2	College #3	College #4
Scholarships				
Grants				
Other Gifts				

Self Help/ Loans	College #1	College #2	College #3	College #4
Federal Stafford/ Direct Loan				
Federal Perkins Loan				
Other Student Loans				
Work Study				

Total Cost of Attendance – Total Financial Aid Package =Estimated Family Contribution (EFC)

Cost	College #1	College #2	College #3	College #4
Total Cost to Attend				
Total Financial Aid				
Estimated Family Contribution				

Scholarship
Listings

1 AHEPA DISTRICT SCHOLARSHIP AWARDS

American Hellenic Educational Progressive Association

Attn: AHEPA Educational Foundation

1909 Q Street N.W., Suite 500

Washington, DC 20009

Phone: (202) 232-6300; Fax: (202) 232-2140;

Email: ahepa@ahepa.org

Web: www.ahepa.org

Summary: To provide financial assistance for college to students (particularly student athletes) who apply through district foundations or committees of the American Hellenic Educational Progressive Association (AHEPA)

Eligibility: This program is open to students who are enrolled or planning to enroll in a college or university. Recipients are selected by AHEPA districts that qualify to receive funding from the national foundation. Districts establish their own requirements, but they may follow procedures similar to those of the national organization: applicants must be members in good standing of the Order of Ahepa, Daughters of Penelope, Sons of Pericles, or Maids of Athena or be the children of Order of Ahepa or Daughters of Penelope members in good standing. High school seniors must submit their most recent official transcript as well as SAT or ACT scores; college freshmen and sophomores must submit high school transcripts, SAT or ACT scores, and their most recent college transcript; college juniors and seniors must submit their most recent college transcript. Along with their application, they must also submit a 500-word biographical essay. Selection is based on academic achievement; extracurricular, personal, and volunteer activities; athletic achievements; and work experience. Financial need is not considered.

Financial data: The stipend is $1,000 per year.

Duration: One year

Number awarded: Varies each year; recently, 20 of these scholarships were awarded.

Deadline: Recommendation forms must be submitted to the national office by June of each year.

2 AIA-NJ SCHOLARSHIPS

Association of Indians in America—New Jersey Chapter

c/o Deepa Mehrotra

192 Midland Avenue

Glen Ridge, NJ 07028

Phone: (973) 748-5310; Email: ravim2@verizon.net

Web: www.aianj.org

Summary: To provide financial assistance for college to high school seniors in New Jersey who participate in sports or other activities and are of Asian Indian ancestry

Eligibility: This program is open to seniors graduating from high schools in New Jersey who are of Asian Indian ancestry or origin. Applicants must have a GPA of 3.5 or higher or class standing in the top 10 percent of their class; an excellent SAT or ACT score; and a record of active participation in at least two nonacademic extracurricular activities, such as varsity sports, social service, volunteer work, or cultural activities.

Financial data: The stipend is $1,000.

Duration: One year

Number awarded: Three are awarded each year.

Deadline: February of each year

3 AIR FORCE CLUB MEMBERSHIP SCHOLARSHIP PROGRAM

Air Force Services Agency

Attn: HQ AFSVA/SVICO

10100 Reunion Place, Suite 501

San Antonio, TX 78216-4138

Phone: (210) 652-6312; 800-443-4834;

Fax: (210) 652-7041; Email: svi@agency.afsv.af.mil

Web: www.afsv.af.mil/clubs/cn_scholarship.htm

Summary: To recognize and reward, with college scholarships, Air Force Club members and their families who submit outstanding essays and are involved in sports or other activities

Eligibility: This program is open to Air Force Club members and their spouses, children, and stepchildren who have been accepted by or are enrolled at an accredited college or university. Grandchildren are eligible if they are a dependent of the club member. Applicants may be undergraduate or graduate students enrolled full- or part-time. They must submit an essay of up to 500 words on a topic, which changes annually; a recent topic was "My Hero, and Why." Applicants must also include a one-page summary of their long-term career and life goals and previous accomplishments, including civic, athletic, and academic awards.

Financial data: Awards are scholarships of $6,000 for first place, $5,500 for second place, $4,500 for third place, $3,500 for fourth place, $3,000 for fifth place, and $2,500 for sixth place.

Duration: The competition is held annually.

Number awarded: Six each year

Deadline: Entries must be submitted to the member's base services commander or division chief by July of each year.

4 A.L. "MIKE" MONROE/RALPH D. WILLIAMS III SPORTS SCHOLARSHIP

International Union of Painters and Allied Trades
Attn: IUPAT Scholarship Committee
1750 New York Avenue N.W.
Washington, DC 20006
Phone: (202) 637-0700; Fax: (202) 637-0158
Web: www.ibpat.org/about/scholarships.html
Summary: To provide financial assistance for college to children of members of the International Union of Painters and Allied Trades (IUPAT) who have been active in athletics Eligibility: This program is open to the legal dependents of union members in good standing who are college-bound high school seniors. Applicants must submit a complete history of their athletic participation and sports recognition in high school. They must be registered with the NCAA Clearing House and have declared the athletic program in which they plan to participate in college. A letter of recommendation must be submitted by the coach or athletic director of the institution where they have been accepted and plan to attend.
Financial data: The stipend is $5,000 per year.
Duration: One year; winners must enroll in the college or university of their choice within a year of the award date or forfeit the award.
Number awarded: One in each region of the union each year
Deadline: August of each year

5 ALABAMA JUNIOR AND COMMUNITY COLLEGE ATHLETIC SCHOLARSHIPS

Alabama Commission on Higher Education
Attn: Grants and Scholarships Department
100 N. Union Street
P.O. Box 302000
Montgomery, AL 36130-2000
Phone: (334) 242-2274; Fax: (334) 242-0268;
Email: wwall@ache.state.al.us
Web: www.ache.state.al.us/studentasst/programs.htm
Summary: To provide financial assistance to athletes in Alabama interested in attending a junior or community college
Eligibility: Full-time students enrolled in public junior and community colleges in Alabama. Selection is based on athletic ability as determined through tryouts.
Financial data: Awards cover the cost of tuition and books.
Duration: Scholarships are available as long as the recipient continues to participate in the designated sport or activity.
Number awarded: Varies each year.

6 ARIZONA PTA SCHOLARSHIP PROGRAM

Arizona PTA
Attn: Scholarship Chair
2721 N. Seventh Avenue
Phoenix, AZ 85007-1102
Phone: (602) 279-1811; 800-992-0112 (within AZ);
Fax: (602) 279-1814; Email: az_office@pta.org
Web: www.azpta.org/htm/scholar.htm
Summary: To provide financial assistance for college to high school seniors and current college students in Arizona who have been involved in sports or other activities
Eligibility: Arizona residents who are high school seniors or college students and have earned a GPA of 3.0 or higher. In addition to the completed application form, interested students must submit a letter giving pertinent personal information (school activities, clubs, honors, volunteer service, interscholastic athletics, community organizations, employment), an official transcript, two letters of recommendation, and a brief statement of student goals and how the scholarship will help achieve those goals. Selection is based primarily on financial need.
Financial data: The stipend is $250 per semester up to a lifetime total of $2,000. Funds are paid directly to the recipient's school.
Duration: One semester; may be renewed each semester for up to four years, provided the recipient attends school full time and maintains a GPA of 2.65 or higher.
Number awarded: Varies each year
Deadline: February of each year

7 ARKANSAS STATE FARM SCHOLAR-ATHLETE PROGRAM

Arkansas Activities Association
3920 Richards Road
North Little Rock, AR 72117
Phone: (501) 955-2500; Fax: (501) 955-2600
Web: www.ahsaa.org
Summary: To provide financial assistance for college to high school seniors in Arkansas who have participated in athletics
Eligibility: This program is open to seniors graduating from high schools in Arkansas who have a GPA of 3.5 or higher and scores of at least 21 on the ACT or the equivalent on the SAT. Boys must have participated in the following sports: football, basketball, baseball, track and field, or other sports; girls must have participated in volleyball, basketball, softball, track and field, or other sports. Applicants must submit an essay on why they believe they qualify for this scholarship and why they want to receive it. Selection is based on the

essay, academic achievement, citizenship in school and in the community, leadership traits, and participation in other school activities.

Financial data: The stipend is $500.

Duration: One year, nonrenewable

Number awarded: Ten each year: one boy in each of the five qualifying sports and one girl in each of the five qualifying sports

Deadline: April of each year

---

8 ARTHUR E. COPELAND SCHOLARSHIP FOR MALES

United States Association of Blind Athletes
Attn: Scholarship Committee
33 N. Institute Street
Colorado Springs, CO 80903
Phone: (719) 630-0422; Fax: (719) 630-0616;
Email: usaba@usa.net
Web: www.usaba.org

Summary: To provide financial assistance for undergraduate or graduate study to male members of the United States Association for Blind Athletes (USABA)

Eligibility: This program is open to legally blind males who have participated in USABA activities for the past year and are current members. Applicants must have been admitted to an academic, vocational, technical, professional, or certification program at the postsecondary level. Selection is based on demonstrated academic record, involvement in extracurricular and civic activities, academic goals and objectives, and USABA involvement at various levels.

Financial data: The stipend is $500.

Number awarded: One each year

Deadline: August of each year

---

9 ATHLETIC EXCELLENCE SCHOLARSHIP

Pride Foundation
Attn: Scholarships Manager
PMB 1001
1122 E. Pike Street
Seattle, WA 98122-3934
Phone: (206) 323-3318; 800-735-7287; Fax: (206) 323-1017; Email: scholarships@pridefoundation.org
Web: www.pridefoundation.org/programs_scholarships_main.php

Summary: To provide financial assistance for college to gay, lesbian, bisexual, or transgender (GLBT) students who live in the Northwest and are involved in athletics

Eligibility: This program is open to residents of Alaska, Idaho, Montana, Oregon, or Washington who are at-

tending or planning to attend a college, university, or vocational school. Applicants must be planning to study athletics in college or be athletes planning to pursue national or international sports. Preference is given to students who are self-identified GLBT, members of GLBT families, or allies who have been strongly supportive of the GLBT community. Selection is based on financial need, community involvement, and commitment to civil rights for all people.

Financial data: Stipends average more than $2,000.

Duration: One year; recipients may reapply.

Number awarded: One or more each year

Deadline: January of each year

---

10 BEV AND WES STOCK SCHOLARSHIP

Seattle Mariners Women's Club
P.O. Box 4100
Seattle, WA 98194-0100
Phone: (206) 628-3555

Summary: To provide financial assistance to high school athletes in Washington state who are interested in preparing for an athletic-related career

Eligibility: This program is open to athletes who display good character both on and off the playing field. They must be graduating high school seniors in Washington state who are planning to prepare for an athletic-related career and will be attending a college or university in the coming academic year. There is no application form. Applicants must submit a typewritten essay outlining why they are applying for the scholarship, their extracurricular activities, their goals, and how receiving the scholarship will be an advantage to them. Also required are a transcript and three letters of recommendation. Selection is based on merit, the essay, extracurricular activities, and future goals.

Financial data: The stipend is $1,000.

Duration: One year, nonrenewable

Number awarded: One each year

Deadline: May of each year

---

11 BOB GAINEY HONORARY SCHOLARSHIP

Dallas Stars Foundation
2601 Avenue of the Stars
Frisco, TX 75034
Phone: (214) 387-5526; Fax: (214) 387-5610;
Email: starscommunity@dallasstars.com
Web: www.dallasstars.com/community/education-scholarship.jsp

Summary: To provide financial assistance for college to high school seniors in Texas who have been active in athletics

Eligibility: This program is open to seniors graduating from high schools in Texas who have been an active member of one or more of their school's athletic teams. Applicants must be planning to attend an accredited U.S. two- or four-year college or university as a full-time student. They must have a GPA of 3.0 or higher and a combined critical reading and mathematics SAT score of 1,000 or higher or an ACT score of 24 or higher. Along with their application, they must submit an essay, up to 500 words in length, on the qualities that distinguish them from other applicants and explaining their career plans and goals. Selection is based on academic achievement, community and extracurricular involvement, and financial need. U.S. citizenship is required.

Financial data: The stipend is $1,250 per year. Funds are paid directly to the recipient's institution.

Duration: Four years, provided the recipient maintains full-time enrollment and a GPA of 3.0 or higher

Number awarded: One each year

Deadline: March of each year

---

12 BRIAN PEARSON MEMORIAL SCHOLARSHIPS

Iowa Sports Foundation
Attn: Scholarship
1421 S. Bell Avenue, Suite 104
P.O. Box 2350
Ames, IA 50010
Phone: (888) 777-8881; Email: info@iowagames.org
Web: www.iowagames.org/awards.aspx

Summary: To provide financial assistance for college to high school students who participate in the Iowa Games

Eligibility: This program is open to students currently enrolled as juniors at high schools in Iowa. Applicants must have participated in events sponsored by the Iowa Sports Foundation. Along with the application, they must submit a two-page essay describing their educational goals, examples of good character, citizenship, role modeling, and career aspirations. Males and females are judged separately.

Financial data: The stipend is $1,000. Funds are held in deposit until the recipient graduates from high school and enrolls in college.

Duration: One year

Number awarded: Two each year: one female and one male

Deadline: May of each year

---

13 BURKE FUND TURFGRASS MANAGEMENT STUDY SCHOLARSHIP

Rhode Island Golf Association
Attn: Burke Fund

One Button Hole Drive, Suite 2
Providence, RI 02909-5750
Phone: (401) 272-1350; Fax: (401) 331-3627;
Email: burkefund@rigalinks.org
Web: http://burkefund.org/index.html

Summary: To provide financial assistance to residents of Rhode Island who have worked at a golf course and are interested in studying turf grass and agronomy in college

Eligibility: This program is open to residents of Rhode Island who are graduating high school seniors or current college students. Applicants must have at least two years of successful employment as a caddie or golf shop staff worker or as a cart or bag room operations, practice range, or golf course maintenance staff worker at a member club of the Rhode Island Golf Association (RIGA). They must be attending or planning to attend an accredited college or university to study turf grass and agronomy. Along with their application, they must submit a high school or college transcript; four letters of recommendation (from a high school principal or guidance counselor, an officer or board member of the sponsoring club, a member of the sponsoring club who knows the student, and the golf professional of the sponsoring club); a list of school activities (e.g., academic and athletic interscholastic contests, editorships, entertainments, officer of student organizations, responsible positions in school functions); and documentation of financial need.

Financial data: A stipend is awarded (amount not specified); funds may be used only for tuition, room, board, and other costs billed by postsecondary schools.

Duration: One year; may be renewed for up to three additional years if the recipient maintains a GPA of 2.0 or higher.

Number awarded: One or more each year

Deadline: April of each year

---

14 CBC SPOUSES PERFORMING ARTS SCHOLARSHIP

Congressional Black Caucus Foundation, Inc.
Attn: Director, Educational Programs
1720 Massachusetts Avenue N.W.
Washington, DC 20036
Phone: (202) 263-2836; 800-784-2577;
Fax: (202) 775-0773; Email: spouses@cbcfinc.org
Web: www.cbcfinc.org

Summary: To provide financial assistance to minority and other undergraduate and graduate students who reside in a congressional district represented by an African American, have participated in sports or other school activities, and are interested in studying the performing arts in college

Eligibility: This program is open to minority and other graduating high school seniors planning to attend an accredited institution of higher education and currently enrolled full-time undergraduate, graduate, and doctoral students in good academic standing with a GPA of 2.5 or higher. Applicants must reside or attend school in a congressional district represented by a member of the Congressional Black Caucus (CBC). They must be interested in preparing for a career in the performing arts, music, or a related field in the entertainment industry. Along with their application, they must submit a videotape of their performance and a 500-word personal statement on the field of study they intend to pursue and why they have chosen that field; their interests, involvement in school activities, community and public service, hobbies, special talents, sports, and other highlight areas; and any other experiences, skills, or qualifications they feel should be considered. They must also be able to document financial need.

Financial data: The stipend is $3,000.

Duration: One year

Number awarded: Ten each year

Deadline: April of each year

---

15 CENTRAL COAST SECTION SCHOLAR-ATHLETE SCHOLARSHIP AWARDS PROGRAM

California Interscholastic Federation
Attn: Central Coast Section
6830 Via Del Oro, Suite 103
San Jose, CA 95119
Phone: (408) 224-2994; Fax: (408) 224-0476;
Email: info@cifccs.org
Web: www.cifccs.org/awards/scholarathschship.htm

Summary: To provide funding for college to student-athletes in central California who balance academic achievement, athletic participation, and service to the community

Eligibility: To be eligible for consideration, nominees must be enrolled as a high school senior and graduating from a Central Coast Section member high school (from San Francisco to King City, California), have earned a GPA of 3.5 or higher, have participated in a varsity sport for at least two years, score at least 1,500 on the SAT or 21 on the ACT, be able to verify a record of positive athletic and nonathletic citizenship, and be nominated by their school. They must submit a one-page essay on how they have balanced the demands of attaining high standards of academic achievement and athletic success while maintaining exemplary athletic

citizenship. Females and males compete separately. Selection is based on scholastic achievement (30 percent), athletic achievement (30 percent), school and community service (20 percent), and the essay (20 percent).

Financial data: The stipend is $1,500 or $500. Funds are to be used for tuition, fees, or books.

Duration: One year

Number awarded: Six each year: two at $1,500 (one to a female and one to a male) and four at $500

Deadline: March of each year

---

16 CHEERIOS BRAND HEALTH INITIATIVE SCHOLARSHIP

Congressional Black Caucus Foundation, Inc.
Attn: Director, Educational Programs
1720 Massachusetts Avenue N.W.
Washington, DC 20036
Phone: (202) 263-2836; 800-784-2577;
Fax: (202) 775-0773; Email: spouses@cbcfinc.org
Web: www.cbcfinc.org

Summary: To provide financial assistance to minority and other undergraduate and graduate students who reside in a congressional district represented by an African American, have participated in sports or other activities, and are interested in preparing for a health-related career

Eligibility: This program is open to minority and other graduating high school seniors planning to attend an accredited institution of higher education and currently enrolled full-time undergraduate, graduate, and doctoral students in good academic standing with a GPA of 2.5 or higher. Applicants must reside or attend school in a congressional district represented by a member of the Congressional Black Caucus. They must be interested in preparing for a career in a medical field, food services, or other health-related field, including premedicine, nursing, chemistry, biology, physical education, and engineering. Along with their application, they must submit a 500-word personal statement on the field of study they intend to pursue and why they have chosen that field; their interests, involvement in school activities, community and public service, hobbies, special talents, sports, and other highlight areas; and any other experiences, skills, or qualifications they feel should be considered. They must also be able to document financial need.

Financial data: A stipend is awarded (amount not specified).

Duration: One year

Number awarded: Varies each year

Deadline: April of each year

17 CHRIS GUSTAV RALLIS SCHOLARSHIP

American Hellenic Educational Progressive Association
Attn: AHEPA Educational Foundation
1909 Q Street N.W., Suite 500
Washington, DC 20009
Phone: (202) 232-6300; Fax: (202) 232-2140;
Email: ahepa@ahepa.org
Web: www.ahepa.org

Summary: To provide financial assistance for college to students with a connection to the American Hellenic Educational Progressive Association (AHEPA) who have participated in sports and other activities

Eligibility: This program is open to members in good standing of the Order of Ahepa, Daughters of Penelope, Sons of Pericles, or Maids of Athena and the children of Order of Ahepa or Daughters of Penelope members in good standing. Applicants must be currently enrolled or planning to enroll in a college or university. High school seniors must submit their most recent official transcript as well as SAT or ACT scores; college freshmen and sophomores must submit high school transcripts, SAT or ACT scores, and their most recent college transcript; college juniors and seniors must submit their most recent college transcript. Along with their application, they must also submit a 500-word biographical essay. Selection is based on academic achievement; extracurricular, personal, and volunteer activities; athletic achievements; work experience; and financial need.

Financial data: Stipends range from $500 to $2,000 per year.

Duration: One year

Number awarded: Varies each year; recently, one of these scholarships was awarded.

Deadline: March of each year

18 CHUCK FULGHAM SCHOLARSHIP

Dallas Foundation
Attn: Scholarship Administrator
900 Jackson Street, Suite 150
Dallas, TX 75202
Phone: (214) 741-9898; Fax: (214) 741-9848;
Email: cmcnally@dallasfoundation.org
Web: www.dallasfoundation.org/gs_schfundprofiles.cfm

Summary: To provide financial assistance to adult students and high school seniors in Texas (especially those who have participated in sports) who are interested in studying humanities in college.

Eligibility: This program is open to adult graduates of a literacy program who need financial assistance to attend a regionally accredited college or university and high school seniors who have not been successful in high school by traditional academic standards (must have a GPA below 3.0) but who have a genuine interest in literature and humanities and show promise for achievement in college. Applicants must be Texas residents and demonstrate financial need; preference is given to applicants from the Dallas area and to applicants who have participated in sports activities.

Financial data: The maximum stipend is $2,500. Funds are paid directly to the recipient's school.

Duration: One year, nonrenewable

Number awarded: One or more each year

Deadline: April of each year

19 CIF SCHOLAR-ATHLETE OF THE YEAR

California Interscholastic Federation
Attn: State Office
1320 Harbor Bay Parkway, Suite 140
Alameda, CA 94502-6578
Phone: (510) 521-4447; Fax: (510) 521-4449;
Email: info@cifstate.org
Web: www.cifstate.org

Summary: To provide financial assistance to college-bound high school seniors in California who have participated in athletics

Eligibility: This program is open to high school seniors in California who have an unweighted cumulative GPA of 3.7 or higher and have demonstrated superior athletic ability in at least two years of varsity play within California. Students must submit an application to their principal or counselor and an essay, up to 500 words, on how they display character in their athletic and academic efforts. They may include examples of meaningful behavior in their high school experience; lessons learned about the importance of character in their life; and opportunities that coaches, cheerleaders, athletes, and fans have to promote character in interscholastic athletics. Based on those essays, school officials nominate students for these scholarships. Males and females are judged separately.

Financial data: The stipend is $2,000.

Duration: One year, nonrenewable

Number awarded: Two each year: one for a female and one for a male

Deadline: Students must submit their application and essay to their counselor or principal by mid-February of each year. School officials forward the packets to the state office by the end of March.

20 CLAUDIA DODSON AWARD

Virginia Interscholastic Athletic Administrators Association

c/o Deb Rocke, Scholarship Chair

Norview High School

6501 Chesapeake Boulevard

Norfolk, VA 23513

Phone: (757) 852-4503; Fax: (757) 852-4511

Web: www.viaaa.org

Summary: To provide financial assistance for college to high school seniors in Virginia who have been involved in athletics

Eligibility: This program is open to seniors graduating from high schools in Virginia where the athletic director is a member of the Virginia Interscholastic Athletic Administrators Association. Applicants must have earned at least four varsity athletic letters, be planning to attend an institution of higher learning, have a GPA of 3.0 or higher, have achieved a leadership position in school and community activities, have extensive service to school and community, have received no full athletic scholarship, and be able to demonstrate financial need. Along with their application, they must submit a 100-word essay on how the award would be of special assistance to them and a 200-word essay on how their participation in high school athletics has impacted their life.

Financial data: The stipend is $1,500.

Duration: One year

Number awarded: One each year

Deadline: January of each year

21 CLEVELAND CHAPTER 36 SCHOLARSHIP FUND

American Hellenic Educational Progressive Association—Cleveland Chapter 36

c/o Keith Manos, Scholarship Chair

Richmond Heights High School

447 Richmond Road

Richmond Heights, OH 44143

Phone: (216) 692-0094

Summary: To provide financial assistance for college to high school seniors of Greek descent from northeastern Ohio who have participated in sports and other activities

Eligibility: This program is open to college-bound seniors graduating from high schools in northeastern Ohio. Applicants must be of Greek descent (at least one grandparent must be of 100 percent Greek ethnicity). Along with their application, they must submit an essay (from 200 to 250 words) that expresses their feelings about their Greek ethnicity and its importance to them personally. Selection is based on that essay, two letters of recommendation, an official high school transcript, participation in school and community activities, and participation in varsity sports or athletic teams.

Financial data: A stipend is awarded (amount not specified).

Duration: One year

Number awarded: Varies each year; since the establishment of this program, nearly $320,000 in scholarships has been awarded.

Deadline: April of each year

22 CONGRESSIONAL BLACK CAUCUS SPOUSES EDUCATION SCHOLARSHIP

Congressional Black Caucus Foundation, Inc.

Attn: Director, Educational Programs

1720 Massachusetts Avenue N.W.

Washington, DC 20036

Phone: (202) 263-2836; 800-784-2577;

Fax: (202) 775-0773; Email: spouses@cbcfinc.org

Web: www.cbcfinc.org

Summary: To provide financial assistance to minority and other undergraduate and graduate students who reside in a congressional district represented by an African American and who have participated in sports and other activities

Eligibility: This program is open to minority and other graduating high school seniors planning to attend an accredited institution of higher education and currently enrolled full-time undergraduate, graduate, and doctoral students in good academic standing with a GPA of 2.5 or higher. Applicants must reside or attend school in a congressional district represented by a member of the Congressional Black Caucus. Along with their application, they must submit a 500-word personal statement on the field of study they intend to pursue and why they have chosen that field; their interests, involvement in school activities, community and public service, hobbies, special talents, sports, and other highlight areas; and any other experiences, skills, or qualifications they feel should be considered. They must also be able to document financial need.

Financial data: A stipend is awarded (amount not specified).

Duration: One year

Number awarded: Varies each year

Deadline: April of each year

23 DAN AND LUCILLE WOOD SCHOLARSHIPS

New Mexico Activities Association
Attn: Rudy Aragon
6600 Palomas N.E.
Albuquerque, NM 87109
Phone: (505) 923-3270; 888-820-NMAA;
Fax: (505) 923-3114; Email: raragon@nmact.org
Web: www.nmact.org
Summary: To provide financial assistance for college to high school seniors in New Mexico who have participated in sports
Eligibility: This program is open to seniors graduating from high schools in New Mexico with a GPA of 3.0 or higher. Applicants must have been active in at least two sports sanctioned by the New Mexico Activities Association. They must be planning to attend a college or university in New Mexico. Along with their application, they must submit a personal statement on how being active in high school athletics has helped them during their high school career. Financial need is not considered in the selection process.
Financial data: The stipend is $500.
Duration: One year
Number awarded: Two each year
Deadline: April of each year

24 DAN WHITWORTH MEMORIAL SCHOLARSHIP

Texas Amateur Athletic Federation
P.O. Box 1789
Georgetown, TX 78627-1789
Phone: (512) 863-9400; Fax: (512) 869-2393;
Email: marklord@cox-internet.com
Web: www.taaf.com/pages/schlorship.asp
Summary: To provide financial assistance to undergraduate and graduate students at institutions in Texas who are interested in preparing for a career in the parks and recreation profession and have participated in sports or other activities
Eligibility: This program is open to residents of Texas who are enrolled or planning to enroll full-time at a college or university in an accredited bachelor's, master's, or doctoral degree program for sports sciences or another major relating to the field of parks and recreation. Preference is given to students attending a Texas college or university. Graduating high school seniors must have a class rank in the top quarter, a GPA of 2.5 or higher, an ACT score of 21 or higher (or the equivalent on the SAT). Students already enrolled in college or graduate school must have a GPA of 2.5 or higher. In addition to considering grades and test scores, selection is based on honors and awards from, and participation in, activities, endeavors, volunteerism, and work related to athletics and/or the field of parks and recreation. Financial need is not considered.
Financial data: A stipend is awarded (amount not specified).
Duration: One year
Number awarded: One or more each year
Deadline: April of each year

25 DANIEL CARDILLO CHARITABLE FUND

Maine Community Foundation
Attn: Program Director
245 Main Street
Ellsworth, ME 04605
Phone: (207) 667-9735; 877-700-6800;
Fax: (207) 667-0447; Email: info@mainecf.org
Web: www.mainecf.org/html/scholarships/index.html
Summary: To provide financial assistance to Maine residents who are interested in participating in an athletic or educational program outside of the traditional school environment
Eligibility: This program is open to young residents of Maine who are interested in pursuing their artistic, academic, athletic, and vocational interests or "life's passion" outside of the traditional school environment (e.g., experiential education, summer programs or studies, special athletic instruction). Applicants must have a demonstrated compassion for others (through school and community involvement); clearly demonstrate a commitment to their "passion" (through participation in lessons, performances, competitions, or volunteerism) and a clear vision of their goals; and be able to demonstrate financial need. Along with their application, they must submit an essay (up to 500 words) telling about themselves; their "passion"; where they think it might take them; and how they feel their life exemplifies the qualities, characteristics, and values demonstrated by Dan Cardillo's life.
Financial data: A stipend is paid (amount not specified).
Duration: Recipients must use the funds within 12 months of the grant or forfeit the award.
Number awarded: One or more each year
Deadline: April of each year

26 DANIELLA ALTFIELD-MORENO SCHOLARSHIP

Pride Foundation
Attn: Scholarships Manager
PMB 1001
1122 E. Pike Street
Seattle, WA 98122-3934

Phone: (206) 323-3318; 800-735-7287; Fax: (206) 323-1017; Email: scholarships@pridefoundation.org Web: www.pridefoundation.org/programs_scholarships_main.php

Summary: To provide financial assistance for college to Latino/a residents of the Northwest (particularly those involved in sports) who are gay and lesbian or the children of gay and lesbian parents

Eligibility: This program is open to residents of Alaska, Idaho, Montana, Oregon, or Washington who are Latino/a youth under 25 years of age. Applicants must be self-identified as gay or lesbian or the children of lesbian and gay parents. Preference is given to students who have been involved in athletics. Selection is based on financial need, community involvement, and commitment to civil rights for all people.

Financial data: Stipends average more than $2,000.

Duration: One year; recipients may reapply.

Number awarded: One each year

Deadline: January of each year

27 DINN BROTHERS STUDENT ATHLETE AWARDS

Community Foundation of Western Massachusetts
Attn: Scholarship Department
1500 Main Street, Suite 2300
P.O. Box 15769
Springfield, MA 01115
Phone: (413) 732-2858; Fax: (413) 733-8565; Email: scholar@communityfoundation.org
Web: www.communityfoundation.org

Summary: To provide financial assistance for college to high school seniors in western Massachusetts who have excelled athletically

Eligibility: This program is open to graduating seniors from high schools in western Massachusetts who have been chosen as an Athlete of the Year by the Springfield newspapers. Separate consideration is given to female and male students. Applicants must submit their most recent academic transcript and documentation of financial need.

Financial data: The stipend is $500 per year.

Duration: One year

Number awarded: Two each year: one specifically for a woman and one for a man

Deadline: March of each year

28 DIVISION I DEGREE-COMPLETION AWARD PROGRAM

National Collegiate Athletic Association
Attn: Leadership Advisory Board
700 W. Washington Avenue
P.O. Box 6222
Indianapolis, IN 46206-6222
Phone: (317) 917-6307; Fax: (317) 917-6364; Email: kcooper@ncaa.org
Web: www1.ncaa.org/membership/scholarships/degree-completion/d1/index.html

Summary: To provide financial assistance to student-athletes at Division I colleges and universities who have exhausted their eligibility for aid from the institutions they attend

Eligibility: This program is open to student-athletes who have exhausted their five years of eligibility for institutional aid at a Division I member institution of the National Collegiate Athletic Association (NCAA). Applicants must be entering at least their sixth year of college and be within 30 semester hours of their degree requirements. They must submit documentation of financial need.

Financial data: Full-time students receive grants equal to a full athletics grant at their institution; part-time students receive tuition and a $400 allowance for books. The NCAA foundation contributes $950,000 to this program each year.

Duration: Up to five semesters of part-time study or two semesters of full-time work.

Number awarded: Varies each year

Deadline: September of each year

29 DIVISION II DEGREE-COMPLETION AWARD PROGRAM

National Collegiate Athletic Association
Attn: Leadership Advisory Board
700 W. Washington Avenue
P.O. Box 6222
Indianapolis, IN 46206-6222
Phone: (317) 917-6222; Fax: (317) 917-6364; Email: dstephens@ncaa.org
Web: www1.ncaa.org/membership/scholarships/degree-completion/d2/index.html

Summary: To provide financial assistance to student-athletes at Division II colleges and universities who have exhausted their eligibility for aid from the institutions they attend

Eligibility: This program is open to student-athletes who have exhausted their eligibility for institutional aid at a Division II member institution of the National Collegiate Athletic Association (NCAA). Applicants must be within their first 10 semesters or 15 quarters of full-time college attendance. They must have a GPA of 2.5 or higher and be within 30 semester hours of their first undergraduate degree. Selection is based on financial circumstances, athletic achievement, and involvement in campus and community activities.

Financial data: The award is the lesser of 1) the recipient's athletics aid for the final year of eligibility; 2) tuition for the remaining credits toward completing an undergraduate degree; or 3) $5,000.

Duration: Until completion of an undergraduate degree

Number awarded: Varies each year; 91 of these awards were granted.

Deadline: April of each year

30 DR. JOHN C. YAVIS SCHOLARSHIPS

American Hellenic Educational Progressive Association
Attn: AHEPA Educational Foundation
1909 Q Street N.W., Suite 500
Washington, DC 20009
Phone: (202) 232-6300; Fax: (202) 232-2140;
Email: ahepa@ahepa.org
Web: www.ahepa.org

Summary: To provide financial assistance to undergraduate and graduate students with a connection to the American Hellenic Educational Progressive Association (AHEPA) who have participated in sports and other activities

Eligibility: This program is open to members in good standing of the Order of Ahepa, Daughters of Penelope, Sons of Pericles, or Maids of Athena and the children of Order of Ahepa or Daughters of Penelope members in good standing. Applicants must be currently enrolled or planning to enroll as undergraduate or graduate students. High school seniors must submit their most recent official transcript as well as SAT or ACT scores; college freshmen and sophomores must submit high school transcripts, SAT or ACT scores, and their most recent college transcript; college juniors and seniors must submit their most recent college transcript; graduate students must submit college transcripts, GRE or MCAT scores (if available), and their most recent graduate school transcript. Along with their application, they must also submit a 500-word biographical essay. Selection is based on academic achievement; extracurricular, personal, and volunteer activities; athletic achievements; and work experience. Financial need is not considered.

Financial data: Stipends range from $500 to $2,000 per year.

Duration: One year

Number awarded: Varies each year; recently, two of these scholarships were awarded.

Deadline: March of each year

31 E. WAYNE COOLEY SCHOLARSHIP AWARD

Iowa Girls' High School Athletic Union
Attn: Scholarships
2900 Grand Avenue
P.O. Box 10348
Des Moines, IA 50306-0348
Phone: (515) 288-9741; Fax: (515) 284-1969;
Email: jasoneslinger@ighsau.org
Web: www.ighsau.org/aspx/cooley_award.aspx

Summary: To provide financial assistance to female high school seniors in Iowa who have participated in athletics and plan to attend college in the state

Eligibility: This program is open to females graduating from high schools in Iowa who have a GPA of 3.75 or higher. Applicants must have earned a varsity letter in at least two different sports, be a first team all-conference selection, and/or have participated in a state tournament in at least one sport. They must be planning to attend a college or university in Iowa. Each high school in the state may nominate one student. Selection is based on academic achievements, athletic accomplishments, nonsports extracurricular activities, and community involvement.

Financial data: The stipend is $3,750 per year.

Duration: Four years, provided the recipient maintains at least a 2.5 GPA while enrolled in college

Number awarded: One each year

Deadline: December of each year

32 ELEANOR L. AND JOHN R. HEILMAN NURSING EDUCATION SCHOLARSHIP

Community Foundation for Northeast Michigan
Attn: Scholarships
111 Water Street
P.O. Box 495
Alpena, MI 49707-0495
Phone: (989) 354-6881; 877-354-6881;
Fax: (989) 356-3319; Email: wiesenj@cfnem.org
Web: www.cfnem.org/cfnem/home.nsf/public/scholarships.htm

Summary: To provide financial assistance to residents of northeastern Michigan who have participated in sports or other activities and are interested in studying nursing

Eligibility: This program is open to residents of northeastern Michigan, including Alcona, Alpena, Cheboygan, Crawford, Iosco, Montmorency, Ogemaw, Oscoda, or Presque Isle counties. Applicants must be studying or planning to study nursing. They must have a GPA of 2.8 or higher. Along with their application, they must submit information on their school-based extracurricular activities (e.g., band, National Honor Society, sports, vocal group, theater); nonschool-based involvement (e.g., dance class, church activities, youth groups, volunteer service); family and home responsibilities; paid employment; awards and honors received during high school and/or college; and any unusual family or personal circumstances. Financial need is not considered in the selection process.

Financial data: A stipend is awarded (amount not specified). Funds are paid directly to the school.

Duration: One year

Number awarded: One each year

Deadline: March of each year

---

33 ESERA TUALOLO SCHOLARSHIP FOR ATHLETIC ACHIEVEMENT

Parents, Families and Friends of Lesbians and Gays
Attn: National Scholarships Program
1726 M Street N.W., Suite 400
Washington, DC 20036
Phone: (202) 467-8180, ext. 219; Fax: (202) 467-8194;
Email: schools@pflag.org
Web: www.pflag.org

Summary: To provide financial assistance for college to high school seniors and recent graduates who have a connection to Parents, Families and Friends of Lesbians and Gays (PFLAG)

Eligibility: This program is open to high school seniors and prior-year graduates who have not attended college. Applicants must have applied to an accredited postsecondary institution to work on an associate's degree leading to transfer to complete a bachelor's degree or a bachelor's degree at a four-year college or university. They must self-identify either as a gay, lesbian, bisexual, or transgender (GLBT) person or as a supporter of GLBT people. Along with their application, they must submit a high school transcript showing a GPA of 3.0 or higher, two letters of recommendation, and a two-page essay discussing either their life as an LGBT student or how they have been involved with and supported the LGBT community. Financial need is also considered in the selection process. This scholarship is presented to the applicant who demonstrates outstanding athletic achievement.

Financial data: The stipend is $2,500.

Duration: One year, nonrenewable

Number awarded: One each year

Deadline: February of each year

---

34 EVELYN OLES NURSING SCHOLARSHIP

Community Foundation for Northeast Michigan
Attn: Scholarships

111 Water Street
P.O. Box 495
Alpena, MI 49707-0495
Phone: (989) 354-6881; 877-354-6881;
Fax: (989) 356-3319; Email: wiesenj@cfnem.org
Web: www.cfnem.org/cfnem/home.nsf/public/scholarships.htm

Summary: To provide financial assistance to residents of northeastern Michigan who have participated in sports or other activities and are interested in studying nursing

Eligibility: This program is open to residents of northeastern Michigan, including Alcona, Alpena, Montmorency, or Presque Isle counties. Applicants must be studying or planning to study nursing. They must have a GPA of 2.8 or higher. Along with their application, they must submit information on their school-based extracurricular activities (e.g., band, National Honor Society, sports, vocal group, theater); non-school-based involvement (e.g., dance class, church activities, youth groups, volunteer service); family and home responsibilities; paid employment; awards and honors received during high school and/or college; and any unusual family or personal circumstances. Financial need is not considered in the selection process.

Financial data: A stipend is awarded (amount not specified). Funds are paid directly to the school.

Duration: One year

Number awarded: One each year

Deadline: March of each year

---

35 FAMILY DISTRICT 1 SCHOLARSHIPS

American Hellenic Educational Progressive Association—District 1
Attn: Family District 1 Educational Fund, Inc.
c/o Melva Zinaich, Co-Chair
P.O. Box 1011
Charleston, SC 29402
Web: www.ahepad1.org

Summary: To provide financial assistance for college or graduate school to residents of designated southeastern states who have participated in sports and other activities

Eligibility: This program is open to residents of Alabama, Georgia, Mississippi, South Carolina, and Tennessee who are high school seniors, high school graduates, or current undergraduate or graduate students. Applicants must be attending or planning to attend an accredited college or university as a full-time student. They must submit a 500-word essay on a topic that changes annually; recently, students were invited to write on "What Hellenism Means to Me." High school seniors must also submit an official transcript and SAT or ACT scores. College freshmen and sophomores must submit an official high school transcript, SAT and ACT scores, and their most recent college transcript. College juniors and seniors must submit their most recent college transcript. Graduate students must submit undergraduate and graduate transcripts and GRE scores. Consideration is also given to extracurricular activities, athletic achievements, work, and community service. Students who also demonstrate financial need are considered in a separate selection process.

Financial data: Stipends range from $500 to $1,500.

Duration: One year

Number awarded: Varies each year

Deadline: January of each year

36 FARM BUREAU INSURANCE—VHSL ACHIEVEMENT AWARDS

Virginia High School League
1642 State Farm Boulevard
Charlottesville, VA 22911
Phone: (434) 977-8475; Fax: (434) 977-5943
Web: www.vfbinsurance.com/vhsl/vhslabout.asp

Summary: To provide financial assistance for college to high school seniors who have participated in activities of the Virginia High School League (VHSL)

Eligibility: This program is open to college-bound seniors graduating from high schools that are members of the VHSL. Applicants must have participated in one or more VHSL athletic activities (baseball, basketball, cheer, cross country, field hockey, football, golf, gymnastics, soccer, softball, swimming, tennis, indoor and outdoor track, volleyball, wrestling) and/or academic activities (student publications, creative writing, theater, forensics, debate, scholastic bowl). They must have a GPA of 3.0 or higher. Each school may nominate up to four students: one female athlete, one male athlete, one academic participant, and one courageous achievement candidate. The courageous achievement category is reserved for students who have overcome serious obstacles to make significant contributions to athletic and/or academic activities. The obstacles may include a serious illness, injury, or disability; a challenging social or home situation; or another extraordinary situation where the student has displayed tremendous courage against overwhelming odds. Along with their application, students must submit a 500-word essay describing how extracurricular activities have enhanced their educational experience. Candidates are judged separately in the three VHSL groups (A, AA, and AAA). Selection is based on the essay, involvement in other school-sponsored activities, involvement in activities outside of school, and two letters of support.

Financial data: The stipend is $1,000.

Duration: One year

Number awarded: Ten each year. For each of the three groups (A, AA, and AAA), one female athlete, one male athlete, and one academic participant are selected. In addition, one courageous achievement candidate is selected statewide.

Deadline: March of each year

37 FHSAA ACADEMIC ALL-STATE AWARDS

Florida High School Athletic Association
1801 N.W. 80th Boulevard
Gainesville, FL 32606
Phone: (352) 372-9551; 800-461-7895;
Fax: (352) 373-1528
Web: www.fhsaa.org

Summary: To provide financial assistance for college to student-athletes in Florida who have excelled in academics and athletics

Eligibility: This program is open to college-bound seniors graduating from high schools in Florida. Candidates must have a cumulative unweighted GPA of 3.5 or higher and have earned a varsity letter in at least two different sports during each of their junior and senior years. Boys and girls are judged separately.

Financial data: Each honoree receives a $500 award. From among those honorees, the Scholar-Athletes of the Year receive an additional $2,500 scholarship.

Duration: The awards are presented annually.

Number awarded: Twenty-four honorees (12 males and 12 females) are selected each year. From among those, two Scholar-Athletes of the Year (one male and one female) are selected each year.

38 FIELD SCOVELL SCHOLARSHIPS

Field Scovell Scholarship Foundation
1300 West Mockingbird Lane, Suite 500
P.O. Box 569420
Dallas, TX 75356-9420
Phone: (972) 289-7012; 888-792-BOWL;
Email: field@attcottonbowl.com
Web: www.attcottonbowl.com/ca_field_scovell.asp

Summary: To provide financial assistance for college to high school seniors in north Texas who have been involved in sports

Eligibility: This program is open to seniors graduating from high schools in north Texas who have a connection to sports (e.g., team, band, cheerleader, fan). Applicants must have a C or equivalent grade average and be planning to attend an institution of higher education within Texas, the Big 12 Conference, or the Southeastern Conference. Selection is based on leadership qualities, moral character, and financial need.

Financial data: The stipend is $2,000 per year.

Duration: One year; the E.E. "Buddy" Fogelson Scholarship is awarded to one of the recipients for study beyond the first year of college.

Number awarded: Twelve each year

Deadline: March of each year

39   FINA ALL-STATE SCHOLAR-ATHLETE TEAM SCHOLARSHIPS

FINA Oil and Chemical Company
Attn: Public Affairs Department
P.O. Box 2159
Dallas, TX 75221
Phone: (972) 801-4111; 800-555-FINA, ext. 4

Summary: To provide financial assistance for college to high school athletes in Texas who also excel in academics

Eligibility: Anyone may nominate a candidate on application forms distributed to all Texas high schools. Nominees must be seniors in Texas high schools who earned a varsity letter in an approved sport, have a high school GPA of 90 percent or higher, and are in the top 10 percent of their graduating class. Selection is based on academic achievement and participation and leadership in academic, athletic, church, community, and other worthwhile organizations. No consideration is given to ethnicity, religion, gender, financial need, or athletic ability.

Financial data: Winners receive $4,000 scholarships; runners-up receive $500 scholarships.

Number awarded: Forty each year: 12 winners and 28 runners-up

Deadline: December of each year

40   FUZZY BROWN MEMORIAL SCHOLARSHIPS

Louisiana High School Athletic Association
Attn: Commissioner
8075 Jefferson Highway
Baton Rouge, LA 70809-7675
Phone: (225) 925-0100; Fax: (225) 925-5901;
Email: lhsaa@lhsaa.org
Web: http://lhsaa.org/Scholarships.htm

Summary: To provide financial assistance to student-athletes in Louisiana who plan to attend college in the state

Eligibility: This program is open to student-athletes who are seniors graduating from high schools in Loui-

siana. Applicants must be planning to attend a college or university in Louisiana. They must be nominated by their principal. Along with their application, they must submit information on their sports activities in high school, honors received in high school, and financial need.

Financial data: The stipend is $1,000.

Duration: One year

Number awarded: Two each year

Deadline: April of each year

41   GALLUP ORGANIZATION/CORNHUSKER STATE GAMES SCHOLARSHIP PROGRAM

Cornhusker State Games
Trabert Hall
2202 S. 11th Street
P.O. Box 82411
Lincoln, NE 68501
Phone: (402) 471-2544; 800-30-GAMES (within NE);
Fax: (402) 471-9712;
Email: csg@cornhuskerstategames.com
Web: www.cornhuskerstategames.com

Summary: To provide financial assistance for college to athletes who participate in the Cornhusker State Games in Nebraska

Eligibility: This program is open to athletes who participate in the summer Cornhusker State Games. All residents of Nebraska are eligible to participate in the games if they have resided in Nebraska for at least 30 days prior to the competition and have amateur status in the sport in which they compete. High school athletes must abide by the rules of the Nebraska School Activities Association. College athletes must abide by national collegiate rules. Participants who are high school graduates (including members of the current graduating class) are eligible for these scholarships. Selection is based on academic honors (15 points); athletic achievements (15 points); other activities (10 points); and an essay of 200 words or less in which they outline their educational objectives (20 points), career goals (20 points), and what this scholarship means to them (20 points).

Financial data: The stipend is $1,000.

Duration: One year

Number awarded: Five each year

Deadline: June of each year

42   GATORADE SCHOLARSHIP PROGRAM

Louisiana High School Athletic Association
Attn: Commissioner
8075 Jefferson Highway

Baton Rouge, LA 70809-7675

Phone: (225) 925-0100; Fax: (225) 925-5901;

Email: lhsaa@lhsaa.org

Web: http://lhsaa.org/Scholarships.htm

Summary: To provide financial assistance for college to student-athletes in Louisiana

Eligibility: This program is open to student-athletes who are seniors graduating from high schools in Louisiana. Applicants must be planning to attend a college or university. They must be nominated by their principal. Students in the seven school classifications of the Louisiana High School Athletic Association (LHSAA) are considered separately. Selection is based primarily on financial need.

Financial data: The stipend is $500.

Duration: One year

Number awarded: Seven each year, one in each of the LHSAA school classifications

Deadline: April of each year

---

43 GEF CORPORATE LEADERSHIP SCHOLARSHIPS

Gravure Association of America

Attn: Gravure Education Foundation

1200-A Scottsville Road

Rochester, NY 14624

Phone: (315) 589-8879; Fax: (585) 436-7689;

Email: lwshatch@gaa.org

Web: www.gaa.org/gef/scholarships.htm

Summary: To provide financial assistance to undergraduate and graduate students who have participated in sports and are interested in a career in printing

Eligibility: This program is open to sophomores, juniors, seniors, and graduate students who are enrolled full-time with a major in printing, graphic arts, or graphic communications. Applicants must be attending a designated learning resource center or an educational partner program supported by the Gravure Education Foundation (GEF) of the Gravure Association of America. They must have a GPA of 3.0 or higher. Along with their application, they must submit a 300-word essay on "How I Can Contribute My Leadership Skills to the Print Communications Industry." Selection is based on the essay, academic success, and leadership development efforts through clubs or associations, sports, community participation, or volunteer activity. Financial need is not considered.

Financial data: The stipend is $1,500.

Duration: One year

Number awarded: Six each year

Deadline: May of each year

---

44 GEORGE CHIRGOTIS SCHOLARSHIP

American Hellenic Educational Progressive Association

Attn: AHEPA Educational Foundation

1909 Q Street N.W., Suite 500

Washington, DC 20009

Phone: (202) 232-6300; Fax: (202) 232-2140;

Email: ahepa@ahepa.org

Web: www.ahepa.org

Summary: To provide financial assistance for college to students with a connection to the American Hellenic Educational Progressive Association (AHEPA) who have participated in sports and other activities

Eligibility: This program is open to members in good standing of the Order of Ahepa, Daughters of Penelope, Sons of Pericles, or Maids of Athena and the children of Order of Ahepa or Daughters of Penelope members in good standing. Applicants must be currently enrolled or planning to enroll in a college or university. High school seniors must submit their most recent official transcript as well as SAT or ACT scores; college freshmen and sophomores must submit high school transcripts, SAT or ACT scores, and their most recent college transcript; college juniors and seniors must submit their most recent college transcript. Along with their application, they must also submit a 500-word biographical essay. Selection is based on academic achievement; extracurricular, personal, and volunteer activities; athletic achievements; and work experience. Financial need is not considered.

Financial data: Stipends range from $500 to $2,000 per year.

Duration: One year

Number awarded: Varies each year; recently, one of these scholarships was awarded.

Deadline: March of each year

---

45 GEORGE LEBER SCHOLARSHIP

American Hellenic Educational Progressive Association

Attn: AHEPA Educational Foundation

1909 Q Street N.W., Suite 500

Washington, DC 20009

Phone: (202) 232-6300; Fax: (202) 232-2140;

Email: ahepa@ahepa.org

Web: www.ahepa.org

Summary: To provide financial assistance for college to students with a connection to the American Hellenic Educational Progressive Association (AHEPA), particularly those who have participated in sports and other activities and are interested in majoring in political science or history

Eligibility: This program is open to members in good standing of the Order of Ahepa, Daughters of Penelope, Sons of Pericles, or Maids of Athena and the children of Order of Ahepa or Daughters of Penelope members in good standing. Applicants must be currently enrolled or planning to enroll in a college or university in the following fall. They may major in any area, but preference is given to upper-division students majoring in political science, history, or international relations. Along with their application, they must submit a 500-word biographical essay and their most recent college transcripts. Selection is based on academic achievement; extracurricular, personal, and volunteer activities; athletic achievements; and work experience. Financial need is not considered.

Financial data: The annual stipend ranges from $500 to $2,000.

Duration: One year

Number awarded: Varies each year; recently, two of these scholarships were awarded.

Deadline: March of each year

---

46   HAL CONNOLLY SCHOLAR-ATHLETE AWARD

California Governor's Committee on Employment of People with Disabilities
Employment Development Department
Attn: Scholar-Athlete Awards Program
800 Capitol Mall, MIC 41
Sacramento, CA 95814
Phone: (916) 654-8055; 800-695-0350;
Fax: (916) 654-9821; TTY: (916) 654-9820;
Email: rnagle@edd.ca.gov
Web: www.disabilityemployment.org/yp_hal_con.htm
Summary: To provide financial assistance to disabled high school seniors in California who have participated in athletics

Eligibility: Applicants must be high school seniors with disabilities, no more than 19 years of age on January 1 of the year of application, who have competed in California high school athletics at a varsity or equivalent level and possess academic and athletic records that demonstrate leadership and accomplishment. They must have completed high school with a GPA of 2.8 or better and plan to attend an accredited college or university in California, but they do not have to intend to participate formally in collegiate athletic activities. Selection is based on cumulative GPA (15 percent), cumulative GPA as it relates to the nature of the student's disability (15 percent), athletic accomplishments as they relate to the student's disability (30 percent), an essay on "How Sports Participation Has Affected My Life at School and in the Community as a Person with a Disability" (25 percent), and overall personal achievement (15 percent). The top finalists may be interviewed before selections are made. Male and female students compete separately.

Financial data: The stipend is $1,000, contingent upon the winner's acceptance at an accredited California college or university. Funds may be used for tuition, books, supplies, and other educational expenses. Exceptions are granted to students who choose to attend schools out of state primarily to accommodate their disability.

Duration: Awards are granted annually.

Number awarded: Up to six each year: three to females and three to males

Deadline: January of each year

---

47   HALLMARK GRAPHIC ARTS SCHOLARSHIP

Gravure Association of America
Attn: Gravure Education Foundation
1200-A Scottsville Road
Rochester, NY 14624
Phone: (315) 589-8879; Fax: (585) 436-7689;
Email: lwshatch@gaa.org
Web: www.gaa.org/gef/scholarships.htm
Summary: To provide financial assistance to upper-division students who have participated in sports and other activities and are interested in a career in printing

Eligibility: This program is open to juniors and seniors who are enrolled full-time in a field related to printing at a designated learning resource center supported by the Gravure Education Foundation (GEF) of the Gravure Association of America. Applicants must have a GPA of 3.0 or higher. Along with their application, they must submit a 300-word essay on "Why I Am Interested in a Career in Graphic Arts." Selection is based on the essay, academic success, and leadership development efforts through clubs or associations, sports, community participation, or volunteer activity. Financial need is not considered.

Financial data: The stipend is $1,500.

Duration: One year

Number awarded: One each year

Deadline: May of each year

---

48   HARTLEY LORD SCHOLARSHIP

Senior Center at Lower Village
Attn: Scholarship Committee
175 Port Road
Kennebunk, ME 04043
Phone: (207) 967-8514

Web: www.seniorcenterkennebunk.org/scholarships
.htm

Summary: To provide financial assistance to college students preparing for a career in service to the elderly

Eligibility: This program is open to students working on a degree or certificate in a field that focuses on the well-being and needs of the senior members of society. Those fields include, but are not limited to, community service, elder care, nursing, or medicine. Applicants must submit essays on why their career choice is consistent with the requirements of the scholarship, extracurricular or community activities in which they have participated, and any awards or other recognition they have received for excellence in scholarship, athletics, or community activities. Selection is based on academic standing, future promise, recommendations, and academic major.

Financial data: The stipend is $1,000. Funds are paid directly to the institution.

Duration: One year

Number awarded: One each year

Deadline: April of each year

---

49 HARVEY E. ANDERSON SCHOLARSHIPS

Rochester Area Community Foundation
Attn: Scholarship Manager
500 East Avenue
Rochester, NY 14607-1912
Phone: (585) 271-4100, ext. 4306; Fax: (585) 271-4292;
TTY: (585) 271-4334; Email: brainey@racf.org
Web: www.racf.org/page12217.cfm

Summary: To provide financial assistance for college to high school seniors in western New York who participate in athletics

Eligibility: This program is open to graduating seniors from western New York (Genesee, Livingston, Monroe, Ontario, Orleans, and Wayne counties plus parts of Allegany, Seneca, Steuben, Wyoming, and Yates counties) who participate in Section V interscholastic athletics. Applicants need not be the best natural athletes or scholars, but they should have demonstrated exceptional effort in both their studies and their chosen sports. Women and men compete separately; at each of the approximately 123 schools in the section, a high school guidance counselor selects one male and one female student to submit an application. Financial need may be considered in the selection process.

Financial data: The amount of the stipend varies.

Duration: One year, renewable

Number awarded: Four each year: two specifically for females and two for males

Deadline: November of each year

---

50 HELEN COPELAND SCHOLARSHIP FOR FEMALES

United States Association of Blind Athletes
Attn: Scholarship Committee
33 N. Institute Street
Colorado Springs, CO 80903
Phone: (719) 630-0422; Fax: (719) 630-0616;
Email: usaba@usa.net
Web: www.usaba.org

Summary: To provide financial assistance for undergraduate or graduate study to female members of the United States Association for Blind Athletes (USABA)

Eligibility: This program is open to legally blind females who have participated in USABA activities for the past year and are current members. Applicants must have been admitted to an academic, vocational, technical, professional, or certification program at the postsecondary level. Selection is based on demonstrated academic record, involvement in extracurricular and civic activities, academic goals and objectives, and USABA involvement at various levels.

Financial data: The stipend is $500.

Number awarded: One each year

Deadline: August of each year

---

51 HISPANIC HERITAGE YOUTH AWARDS

Hispanic Heritage Awards Foundation
2600 Virginia Avenue N.W., Suite 406
Washington, DC 20037
Phone: (202) 861-9797; 866-665-2112;
Fax: (202) 861-9799; Email: contact@
hispanicheritageawards.org
Web: http://hispanicheritage.org/youth.php

Summary: To recognize and reward, with college scholarships, Hispanic high school seniors from selected metropolitan areas who have excelled in various activities (including sports)

Eligibility: This program is open to high school seniors who are U.S. citizens or permanent residents and of Hispanic heritage (at least one parent must be able to trace family origins to Spain, Latin America, or the Spanish-speaking Caribbean). Awards were recently presented to students in 12 metropolitan regions: Chicago, Dallas, Houston, Los Angeles, Miami, New York City, Philadelphia/New Jersey, Phoenix, San Antonio, San Diego, San Jose/San Francisco Bay area, and Washington, D.C. Applicants compete for awards in the following nine categories: academic excellence, arts and culture (film, visual, performing, or literary arts), community service, education, engineering and mathematics, health care, journalism, leadership, and sports.

Applicants must have a GPA of 2.75 or higher. Along with their application, they must submit an essay that describes their personal qualities and strengths, dedication to community service and the impact it has had on their life, future career goals, areas of interest, and significance of heritage and/or family in their life. Selection criteria include, but are not limited to, the following: academic achievement, compelling essay responses, meritorious achievements in the applicant's chosen category, contribution to the community, overall character as a role model, and letters of recommendation.
Financial data: In each category and each city, gold regional winners receive $3,000, and silver regional winners receive $2,000. Awards are in the form of educational grants that recipients may use for any aspect of their college career (tuition, books, and room and board). The gold regional winners then advance to a national competition. National winners receive an additional $5,000 educational grant, a state-of-the-art laptop computer, an all-expense-paid trip to Miami for the winner and a parent to attend the award announcement event, and an all-expense-paid trip to Washington, D.C., for the winner and a parent to attend the awards ceremony at the John F. Kennedy Center for the Performing Arts.
Duration: The awards are presented annually.
Number awarded: Recently, 216 regional winners were selected, comprising a gold and a silver winner in each of the nine categories from each of the 12 cities. From those, nine national winners were chosen, one in each of the categories.
Deadline: February of each year

52 ILIO DEPAOLO SCHOLARSHIP FUND
Ilio DePaolo's Restaurant
Attn: Scholarship Fund
3785 S. Park Avenue
Blasdell, NY 14219
Phone: (716) 825-3675; Fax: (716) 825-1054;
888-875-8079; Email: ID3675@aol.com
Web: www.iliodipaolo.com/scholarship.htm
Summary: To provide financial assistance for college to high school seniors in western New York who have been involved in athletics, especially wrestling
Eligibility: This program is open to college-bound seniors graduating from high schools in western New York who have excelled in academics and athletics. Several of the awards are specifically for wrestlers.
Financial data: A stipend is awarded (amount not specified).
Duration: One year

Number awarded: Varies each year; recently, six of these scholarships were awarded.

53 IOWA-ILLINOIS REGIONAL AUTO SHOW SCHOLARSHIP
Community Foundation of the Great River Bend
Attn: Scholarship Programs
111 E. Third Street, Suite 710
Davenport, IA 52801-1524
Phone: (563) 326-2840; Fax: (563) 326-2870;
Email: info@cfgrb.org
Web: www.cfgrb.org
Summary: To provide financial assistance to employees of automobile dealerships in a number of counties in Illinois and Iowa and their families who have participated in sports and other activities and are interested in attending college
Eligibility: This program is open to seniors graduating from high schools in the Illinois counties of Bureau, Carroll, Henderson, Henry, Jo Daviess, Knox, Mercer, Rock Island, Warren, and Whiteside and the Iowa counties of Cedar, Clinton, Des Moines, Henry, Jackson, Louisa, Muscatine, and Scott. Each high school may submit one application for every 500 students enrolled. Applicants must have worked or had a relative work at least one year at a new car dealership located in 1 of those 18 counties. They must be planning to attend either a two-year or four-year college or university or an automotive technical trade school. Along with their application, they must submit a one-page essay on their future aspirations and/or aims. Selection is based on academic achievement, participation in extracurricular activities and athletics, volunteer and work experience, and financial need.
Financial data: Stipends range from $1,000 to $3,000.
Duration: One year
Number awarded: Varies each year. Recently, six of these scholarships were awarded: one at $3,000, two at $2,000, and three at $1,000.
Deadline: Applications must be submitted to high school counselors or principals by January of each year.

54 ISABELLA M. GILLEN MEMORIAL SCHOLARSHIP
Aviation Boatswain's Mates Association
P.O. Box 1106
Lakehurst, NJ 08733
Email: scholarship@abma-usn.org
Web: www.abma-usn.org/scholarship.htm

Summary: To provide financial assistance for college to the dependents of paid-up members of the Aviation Boatswains Mates Association (ABMA) who have participated in sports and other activities

Eligibility: Applicants must be dependents whose sponsor has been an active, dues-paying member of the ABMA for at least two years. They must prepare a statement describing their vocational or professional goals and relating how their past, present, and future activities make the accomplishment of those goals probable. Other submissions include transcripts, SAT or ACT scores, letters of recommendation, and honors received in athletics and other leadership activities. Selection is based on financial need, character, leadership, and academic achievement.

Financial data: The stipend is $2,500 per year.

Duration: One year; may be renewed

Number awarded: Varies each year

Deadline: May of each year

55 ISADORE AND GERTRUDE ISACKSON SCHOLARSHIP

Community Foundation for Northeast Michigan
Attn: Scholarships
111 Water Street
P.O. Box 495
Alpena, MI 49707-0495
Phone: (989) 354-6881; 877-354-6881;
Fax: (989) 356-3319; Email: wiesenj@cfnem.org
Web: www.cfnem.org/cfnem/home.nsf/public/
scholarships.htm

Summary: To provide financial assistance for college to students in northeastern Michigan who have participated in sports or other activities

Eligibility: This program is open to students who have graduated (in any year) from a high school in northeastern Michigan, including Alcona, Alpena. Montmorency, or Presque Isle counties. Applicants must have a GPA of 2.8 or higher. Along with their application, they must submit information on their school-based extracurricular activities (e.g., band, National Honor Society, sports, vocal group, theater); nonschool-based involvement (e.g., dance class, church activities, youth groups, volunteer service); family and home responsibilities; paid employment; awards and honors received during high school and/or college; and any unusual family or personal circumstances. Financial need is not considered in the selection process.

Financial data: A stipend is awarded (amount not specified). Funds are paid directly to the school.

Duration: One year

Number awarded: One each year

Deadline: March of each year

56 JAMES F. MULHOLLAND AMERICAN LEGION SCHOLARSHIP

American Legion
Attn: Department of New York
112 State Street, Suite 1300
Albany, NY 12207
Phone: (518) 463-2215; Fax: (518) 427-8443;
Email: newyork@legion.org
Web: www.ny.legion.org/scholar.htm

Summary: To provide financial assistance for college to children of members of the American Legion in New York who have participated in sports or other activities

Eligibility: Applicants must be high school seniors in New York who are the children or grandchildren of New York State Legionnaires. Applicants must have been accepted at an accredited institution of higher learning. Selection is based on financial need (ten points); academic record and class standing (nine points); Americanism (eight points); participation in projects to aid the elderly, needy, or disabled (seven points); self-help as demonstrated by work record (six points); participation in social, political, religious, or athletic groups or programs (five points); and neatness and correctness of the letter (four points).

Financial data: The stipend is $500, of which half is paid in September and half in February

Duration: One year

Number awarded: Two each year

Deadline: April of each year

57 JAY RAMSDELL SCHOLARSHIPS

Jay Ramsdell Foundation
Attn: Daniel Lay
First National Bank
Trust Department
P.O. Box 258
Bar Harbor, ME 04609
Email: oct60@acadia.net
Web: www.jramsdellfoundation.org

Summary: To provide financial assistance for college to high school seniors in Maine who have been active in athletics

Eligibility: This program is open to residents of Maine who are seniors graduating from a high school in the state. Students must be nominated by the athletic director at their high school; each director may nominate one student. Nominees must have been active in athletics; special attention is given to team managers and statisticians. Financial need must be demonstrated, although need is not the primary consideration in making the award.

Financial data: The stipend is $5,000. Funds are paid to the college or university after the recipient has successfully completed the first semester and is enrolled for the second semester.

Duration: One year; recipients may reapply.

Number awarded: One each year

---

58 JOHN C. YOUNGBLOOD SCHOLARSHIPS

Virginia Interscholastic Athletic Administrators Association
c/o Deb Rocke, Scholarship Chair
Norview High School
6501 Chesapeake Boulevard
Norfolk, VA 23513
Phone: (757) 852-4503; Fax: (757) 852-4511
Web: www.viaaa.org

Summary: To provide financial assistance for college to high school seniors in Virginia who have been involved in athletics

Eligibility: This program is open to seniors graduating from high schools in Virginia where the athletic director is a member of the Virginia Interscholastic Athletic Administrators Association. Students must be nominated by their athletic director. Nominees must have made a significant contribution to athletics (have received at least one varsity monogram during their high school career and have participated in a varsity athletic program for at least two years), be planning to continue on to higher education, and be able to demonstrate financial need. They must submit a 100-word essay on how the award would be of special assistance to them and a 200-word essay on how their participation in high school athletics positively impacted their school and community.

Financial data: The stipend is $1,500.

Duration: One year

Number awarded: Three each year

Deadline: January of each year

---

59 JOHN P. BURKE MEMORIAL FUND SCHOLARSHIPS

Rhode Island Golf Association
Attn: Burke Fund
One Button Hole Drive, Suite 2
Providence, RI 02909-5750
Phone: (401) 272-1350; Fax: (401) 331-3627;
Email: burkefund@rigalinks.org
Web: http://burkefund.org/index.html

Summary: To provide financial assistance for college to residents of Rhode Island who have worked at a golf course

Eligibility: This program is open to residents of Rhode Island who are graduating high school seniors or current college students. Applicants must have at least two years of successful employment as a caddie or golf shop staff worker or as a cart or bag room operations, practice range, or golf course maintenance staff worker at a member club of the Rhode Island Golf Association (RIGA). They must be attending or planning to attend an accredited college or university. Along with their application, they must submit a high school or college transcript; four letters of recommendation (from a high school principal or guidance counselor, an officer or board member of the sponsoring club, a member of the sponsoring club who knows the student, and the golf professional of the sponsoring club); a list of school activities (e.g., academic and athletic interscholastic contests, editorships, entertainments, officer of student organizations, responsible positions in school functions); and documentation of financial need.

Financial data: A stipend is awarded (amount not specified); funds may be used only for tuition, room, board, and other costs billed by postsecondary schools.

Duration: One year; may be renewed for up to three additional years if the recipient maintains a GPA of 2.0 or higher.

Number awarded: Varies each year; recently, 22 of these scholarships were awarded.

Deadline: April of each year

---

60 JOSEPH P. LIPMAN SCHOLARSHIPS

National High School Coaches Association
Attn: Associate Executive Director
3276 Nazareth Road
Easton, PA 18045
Phone: (610) 923-0900; Fax: (610) 923-0800;
Email: nhsca@nhsca.com
Web: http://nhsca.com/scholarship/index.php

Summary: To provide financial assistance for college to high school athletes who have overcome a disability or other adversity to excel in sports

Eligibility: This program is open to graduating high school seniors who have been involved in athletics. Applicants must be planning to attend a college or university. They must submit an application in which they describe the disability or other adversity they have overcome. Judges select the recipients on the basis of the severity of the hardships they have faced.

Financial data: The stipend is $1,000.

Duration: One year
Number awarded: Five each year

---

61 JUDGE WILLIAM F. COOPER SCHOLARSHIP

Center for Scholarship Administration, Inc.
Attn: Wachovia Accounts
4320-G Wade Hampton Boulevard
Taylors, SC 29687
Phone: 866-608-0001;
Email: wachoviascholars@bellsouth.net
Web: www.wachoviascholars.com/wscholarships.php
Summary: To provide financial assistance for college to female high school seniors in Georgia who have participated in sports and other activities
Eligibility: This program is open to female seniors graduating from high schools in Georgia. Preference is given to residents of Chatham County. Applicants must be planning to enroll at an accredited college or university to study any field except law, theology, or medicine. They must be able to demonstrate financial need. Along with their application, they must submit a one-page essay on their strengths and their most important achievements in their school and community; it should cover hobbies, interests, sports, volunteer work, employment, future plans, and career goals. Selection is based on academic achievement, potential to succeed in their chosen educational field, and financial need.
Financial data: A stipend is awarded (amount not specified).
Duration: One year; may be renewed up to three additional years or until completion of a bachelor's degree, whichever is earlier.
Number awarded: One or more each year
Deadline: March of each year

---

62 KIRSTEN R. LORENTZEN AWARD

Association for Women in Science
Attn: AWIS Educational Foundation
1200 New York Avenue N.W., Suite 650
Washington, DC 20005
Phone: (202) 326-8940; 866-657-AWIS;
Fax: (202) 326-8960; Email: awisedfd@awis.org
Web: www.awis.org/careers/edfoundation.html
Summary: To provide financial assistance to women undergraduates majoring in physics or geoscience who have excelled in sports or other activities
Eligibility: This program is open to women who are sophomores or juniors in college and are U.S. citizens. Applicants must be studying physics (including space physics and geophysics) or geoscience. They must demonstrate excellence in their studies as well as outdoor activities, service, sports, music, or other nonacademic

pursuits or have a record of overcoming significant obstacles. Along with their application, they must submit a two- to three-page essay on their academic interests and plans, including class work and any relevant research, teaching, or outreach activities; their career goals; the nonacademic pursuits that are most important to them; and any significant barriers they have faced and how they overcame them. Financial need is not considered.
Financial data: The stipend is $1,000.
Duration: One year
Number awarded: One each year
Deadline: January of each year

---

63 KOHL EXCELLENCE SCHOLARSHIPS

Herb Kohl Educational Foundation, Inc.
Attn: Kim Marggraf
1711 Cardinal Parkway
Sheboygan, WI 53083-1906
Phone: (920) 457-1727; Email: marggraf@excel.net
Web: www.kohleducation.org/students
Summary: To provide financial assistance for college to Wisconsin high school seniors who have participated in sports and other activities
Eligibility: This program is open to college-bound high school seniors in Wisconsin. Applications are available from the Wisconsin Department of Public Instruction (DPI) for public school students, from the Wisconsin Council of Religious and Independent Schools (WCRIS) for religious and independent school students, or from the Wisconsin Parents Association (WPA) for home-schooled students. Along with their application, applicants must submit an essay of 300 to 500 words describing their goals in future education, personal life, community and society service, and career. Selection is based on the essay (35 points); three letters of recommendation (15 points); leadership and participation in music and speech activities (10 points); leadership and participation in athletic activities (10 points); leadership and participation in other school and community activities (10 points); work experience, hobbies, outside interests, and special talents (10 points); and overall quality of application (8 points).
Financial data: The stipend is $1,000. Funds may be used to pay for tuition and fees during the first year of college only and are paid directly to the recipient's postsecondary institution.
Duration: One year (the first year of college), nonrenewable
Number awarded: One hundred each year; awards are distributed proportionally to students in public schools, religious and independent schools, and home schools.
Deadline: November of each year

64 LAJCC COMMUNITY/JUNIOR COLLEGE SCHOLARSHIP PROGRAM

Los Angeles Junior Chamber of Commerce
Attn: LAJCC Foundation
201 S. Figueroa Street, Suite 300
Los Angeles, CA 90012
Phone: (213) 989-2159; Fax: (213) 580-1490;
Email: ntakata@lajcc.org
Web: www.lajcc.org/foundation/scholarships.html
Summary: To provide financial assistance to students at community colleges in southern California who have participated in sports or other activities
Eligibility: This program is open to students who attend a community or junior college in Los Angeles County or who reside in Los Angeles County and commute to a community or junior college in Orange or Ventura counties. Also eligible are students in an associate's degree program at a four-year institution in Los Angeles County and residents of Los Angeles County who commute to a four-year institution in Orange or Ventura counties to work on an associate's degree. Foreign students attending on a student visa, students who have previously earned a bachelor's degree, previous recipients of this scholarship, and high school students attending a community college are not eligible. Applicants must be California residents who attended a California high school for at least two semesters. They must have completed at least 12 college units with a GPA of 2.5 or higher and must be younger than 26 years of age. Along with their application, they must submit a personal statement (up to three pages) on their reasons for attending community or junior college (or for working on an associate's degree) and their future goals. Selection is based primarily on that statement, academic record, and public service. Other considerations include future goals, financial need, leadership, work history, and other activities (such as athletics and the arts).
Financial data: The stipend is $2,000 per year.
Duration: One year
Number awarded: Varies each year; recently, two of these scholarships were awarded.
Deadline: April of each year

65 LAPP-GARBER SCHOLARSHIP

Community Foundation for Northeast Michigan
Attn: Scholarships
111 Water Street
P.O. Box 495
Alpena, MI 49707-0495
Phone: (989) 354-6881; 877-354-6881;
Fax: (989) 356-3319; Email: wiesenj@cfnem.org
Web: www.cfnem.org/cfnem/home.nsf/public/scholarships.htm
Summary: To provide financial assistance for college to students in northeastern Michigan who have participated in sports or other activities
Eligibility: This program is open to students who have graduated (in any year) from a high school in northeastern Michigan, including Alcona, Alpena, Montmorency, or Presque Isle counties. Applicants must have a GPA of 2.8 or higher. Along with their application, they must submit information on their school-based extracurricular activities (e.g., band, National Honor Society, sports, vocal group, theater); nonschool-based involvement (e.g., dance class, church activities, youth groups, volunteer service); family and home responsibilities; paid employment; awards and honors received during high school and/or college; and any unusual family or personal circumstances. Financial need is not considered in the selection process.
Financial data: A stipend is awarded (amount not specified). Funds are paid directly to the school.
Duration: One year
Number awarded: One each year
Deadline: March of each year

66 LINDY CALLAHAN SCHOLAR ATHLETE

Mississippi High School Activities Association
P.O. Box 127
Clinton, MS 39060
Phone: (601) 924-6400; Fax: (601) 924-1725;
Email: mhsaa@netdoor.com
Web: www.misshsaa.com
Summary: To provide financial assistance to graduating high school scholar-athletes in Mississippi
Eligibility: This program is open to seniors graduating from high schools that belong to the Mississippi High School Activities Association. Applicants must be scholar-athletes. Males and females compete separately.
Financial data: The award is $1,000.
Duration: These are one-time awards.
Number awarded: Sixteen each year: one female and one male in each of the association's eight districts
Deadline: February of each year

67 LISA SECHRIST MEMORIAL FOUNDATION SCHOLARSHIP

Lisa Sechrist Memorial Foundation
Attn: Kim Mackmin, Scholarship Selection Committee
Brookfield Homes
8500 Executive Park Avenue, Suite 300
Fairfax, VA 22031
Web: www.lisasechrist.com/scholarship.html

Summary: To provide financial assistance for college to female high school seniors from Virginia who come from disadvantaged backgrounds and have participated in sports or other activities
Eligibility: This program is open to women graduating from high schools in Virginia who come from a disadvantaged background. Applicants should be able to demonstrate membership in honor societies, participation in sports or other extracurricular activities, citizenship and service within the community, and/or leadership skills within the school or community. Selection is based on merit, integrity, academic potential, and financial need.
Financial data: The stipend is $2,500 per year.
Duration: Four years, provided the recipient maintains a GPA of 2.5 or higher
Number awarded: One each year
Deadline: March of each year

68   LOLA M. PENNEY MEMORIAL NURSING SCHOLARSHIP

Community Foundation for Northeast Michigan
Attn: Scholarships
111 Water Street
P.O. Box 495
Alpena, MI 49707-0495
Phone: (989) 354-6881; 877-354-6881;
Fax: (989) 356-3319; Email: wiesenj@cfnem.org
Web: www.cfnem.org/cfnem/home.nsf/public/scholarships.htm
Summary: To provide financial assistance to residents in northeastern Michigan who have participated in sports or other activities and are interested in studying nursing
Eligibility: This program is open to students who have graduated (in any year) from a high school in northeastern Michigan, including Alcona, Alpena, Montmorency, or Presque Isle counties. Applicants must be studying or planning to study nursing. Along with their application, they must submit information on their school-based extracurricular activities (e.g., band, National Honor Society, sports, vocal group, theater); non-school-based involvement (e.g., dance class, church activities, youth groups, volunteer service); family and home responsibilities; paid employment; awards and honors received during high school and/or college; and any unusual family or personal circumstances. Financial need is not considered in the selection process.
Financial data: A stipend is awarded (amount not specified). Funds are paid directly to the school.
Duration: One year

Number awarded: One each year
Deadline: March of each year

69   L'OREAL/FAMILY CIRCLE CUP "PERSONAL BEST" SCHOLARSHIP

Family Circle Cup
c/o Family Circle Tennis Center
161 Seven Farms Drive
Charleston, SC 29492
Phone: (843) 856-7900; 800-677-2293
Web: www.familycirclecup.com
Summary: To provide financial assistance for college to female high school seniors in North Carolina, South Carolina, and Georgia who have distinguished themselves in sports and other activities
Eligibility: This program is open to women graduating from high schools in North Carolina, South Carolina, and Georgia. Applicants must be planning to enroll full-time at an accredited two-year or four-year college or university. They must have a GPA of 2.0 or higher and be able to demonstrate that they have made a difference in the lives of others through role modeling, community involvement and services, volunteer experiences, athletics, and extracurricular activities.
Financial data: The stipend is $2,500.
Duration: One year
Number awarded: Three each year, one from each of the eligible states
Deadline: February of each year

70   MARK R. MCGINLY MEMORIAL SCHOLARSHIP

Mark R. McGinly Scholarship Fund
Attn: Director
2013 Adams Hill Road
Vienna, VA 22182
Phone: (703) 626-8160
Web: www.mcginlyscholarship.org
Summary: To provide financial assistance for college to high school seniors in northern Virginia who have been active in athletics
Eligibility: Each northern Virginia high school athletic director or guidance counselor may nominate one varsity athlete for this scholarship. Letters of nomination must include information on GPA, SAT scores, and participation in varsity sports, school clubs and activities, and community organizations and activities. The nominee must submit a two- to three-paragraph essay on how they exemplify the qualities of Mark McGinly. Financial need is not considered in the selection process. Special awards are presented to an applicant who demonstrates

achievement in the arts and to an applicant who demonstrates commitment to military service education and plans to attend one of the military service academies.

Financial data: The winner's stipend is $10,000, payable directly to the college or university the recipient attends. Additional awards of $5,000 and $1,000 are made if funds are available. Special awards for achievement in the arts and for commitment to military service education are $2,500.

Duration: One year

Number awarded: One winner is selected each year. Recently, nine additional awards were also presented (two at $5,000 and seven at $1,000) to athletes, one at $2,500 for achievement in the arts, and one at $2,500 for commitment to military service education.

Deadline: April of each year

---

71 MHSAA SCHOLAR-ATHLETE AWARDS

Michigan High School Athletic Association
1661 Ramblewood Drive
East Lansing, MI 48823-7392
Phone: (517) 332-5046; Fax: (517) 332-4071;
Email: afrushour@mhsaa.com
Web: www.mhsaa.com/recognition/sahome.htm

Summary: To provide financial assistance for college to seniors who have participated in athletics at high schools that are members of the Michigan High School Athletic Association (MHSAA)

Eligibility: This program is open to seniors graduating from high schools that are members of the MHSAA. Applicants must be planning to attend an accredited college, university, or trade school and have a GPA of 3.5 or higher. They must have won a varsity letter in one of the following sports in which postseason tournaments are sponsored by MHSAA: baseball, boys' and girls' basketball, boys' and girls' bowling, girls' competitive cheer, boys' and girls' cross-country, football, boys' and girls' golf, girls' gymnastics, ice hockey, boys' and girls' lacrosse, boys' and girls' soccer, softball, boys' and girls' skiing, boys' and girls' swimming and diving, boys' and girls' tennis, boys' and girls' track and field, girls' volleyball, and wrestling. Along with their application, they must submit a 500-word essay on the importance of sportsmanship in educational athletics. Selection is based on the essay, involvement in other school-sponsored activities, involvement in activities outside of school, and two letters of recommendation.

Financial data: The stipend is $1,000.

Duration: One year, nonrenewable

Number awarded: Thirty-two each year: 12 from Class A schools (6 boys and 6 girls), 8 from Class B schools (4

boys and 4 girls), 6 from Class C schools (3 boys and 3 girls), 4 from Class D schools (2 boys and 2 girls), and 2 selected at large.

Deadline: Students must submit applications to their school by November of each year. The number of nominations each school may submit depends on the size of the school: Class A schools may nominate 6 boys and 6 girls, Class B schools may nominate 4 boys and 4 girls, Class C schools may nominate 3 boys and 3 girls, and Class D schools may nominate 2 boys and 2 girls.

---

72 MICHAEL AXE/FIRST STATE ORTHOPAEDICS SCHOLARSHIPS

Delaware Women's Alliance for Sport and Fitness
c/o Evelyn Campbell, Scholarship Committee Chair
Howard High School of Technology
401 E. 12th Street
Wilmington, DE 19801
Phone: (302) 571-5422; Email: scholarships@dwasf.org
Web: www.dwasf.org/scholarships.html

Summary: To provide financial assistance to female graduating high school seniors in Delaware who have significantly contributed to sports at the varsity level

Eligibility: This program is open to female high school seniors in Delaware who have a GPA of 3.0 or higher and have participated in at least one varsity sport. Applicants must submit a student profile describing their sports participation, school activities, community activities, and career objectives; a short paragraph describing why they feel they are deserving of this scholarship; and three letters of recommendation. Financial need is not considered in the selection process.

Financial data: The stipend ranges from $500 to $1,000.

Duration: One year

Number awarded: Two each year, one to a student from north of the canal and one to a student from south of the canal

Deadline: April of each year

---

73 MICHAEL WEIDEMANN AWARD

American Association of University Women—Buffalo Branch
Attn: Chamberlin Loan Fund
P.O. Box 397
Amherst, NY 14226-0397
Phone: (716) 885-2486;
Email: chamberlinfund@yahoo.com
Web: www.aauw.buffalo.edu/edu.htm

Summary: To provide financial assistance for college to residents of western New York who have participated in sports or are preparing for a career related to sports

Eligibility: This program is open to residents of western New York, both men and women, who are enrolled in college. Applicants must have participated in sports and/or be planning a career in sports. Selection is based on academic achievement, potential for achieving academic goals, potential for success in chosen field, and financial need. A personal interview is required.

Financial data: A stipend is awarded (amount not specified).

Duration: One year

Number awarded: One each year

Deadline: May or November of each year

74   MINNESOTA STATE HIGH SCHOOL LEAGUE TRIPLE "A" AWARDS

Minnesota State High School League
2100 Freeway Boulevard
Brooklyn Center, MN 55430-1735
Phone: (763) 560-2262
Web: www.mshsl.org/mshsl/recognition.asp?program=5

Summary: To provide financial assistance for college to high school seniors in Minnesota who excel in the Triple "A" activities: academics, arts, and athletics

Eligibility: This program is open to college-bound seniors graduating from high schools in Minnesota. Each school may nominate two students, a female and a male. Selection of state winners is based on academic performance; involvement in athletic programs sponsored by the Minnesota State High School League (badminton, baseball, basketball, cross-country running, football, golf, gymnastics, hockey, lacrosse, skiing, soccer, softball, swimming and diving, synchronized swimming, tennis, track, volleyball, wrestling, and adapted soccer, bowling, floor hockey, and softball); involvement in League-sponsored fine arts activities (state, section, subsection, school, or community-sponsored activities in instrumental or vocal music, drama, debate, or speech); and involvement in other school and community activities. Nominees must have a GPA of 3.0 or higher and be in compliance with the League's Student Code of Conduct. They must submit a 250-word essay on what they plan to do after high school and how their participation in athletics and fine arts activities has prepared them to achieve that goal. Students from Class A and Class AA schools are judged separately, as are females and males.

Financial data: The stipend is $1,000 per year.

Duration: Four years

Number awarded: Four each year, to a female and a male from each of the two classes of schools

Deadline: January of each year

75   MONTANA ATHLETIC FEE WAIVER

Montana Guaranteed Student Loan Program
2500 Broadway
P.O. Box 203101
Helena, MT 59620-3101
Phone: (406) 444-0638; 800-537-7508;
Fax: (406) 444-1869; Email: scholar@mgslp.state.mt.us
Web: www.mgslp.state.mt.us

Summary: To provide financial assistance for undergraduate education to athletes attending universities in Montana

Eligibility: Athletes selected by the staff of branches of the Montana University System are eligible for these fee waivers.

Financial data: Students eligible for this benefit are entitled to attend any unit of the Montana University System without payment of undergraduate registration, incidental, or out-of-state fees.

Duration: Undergraduate students are eligible for continued fee waiver as long as they maintain reasonable academic progress as full-time students.

Number awarded: Varies each year, to the maximum authorized by the National Collegiate Athletic Association, National Association of Intercollegiate Athletics, or appropriate affiliated conferences for officially sanctioned or recognized intercollegiate sports.

76   MUSEMECHE SCHOLARSHIP PROGRAM

Louisiana High School Athletic Association
Attn: Commissioner
8075 Jefferson Highway
Baton Rouge, LA 70809-7675
Phone: (225) 925-0100; Fax: (225) 925-5901;
Email: lhsaa@lhsaa.org
Web: http://lhsaa.org/Scholarships.htm

Summary: To provide financial assistance to student-athletes in Louisiana who plan to attend college in the state

Eligibility: This program is open to student-athletes who are seniors graduating from high schools in Louisiana. Applicants must be planning to attend a college or university in the state. They must be nominated by their principal. Females and males are considered separately. Selection is based primarily on financial need.

Financial data: The stipend is $500.

Duration: One year

Number awarded: Four each year: two for females and two for males

Deadline: April of each year

77 NATIONAL CITY/KHSAA SWEET 16 SCHOLARSHIPS

Kentucky High School Athletic Association
2280 Executive Drive
Lexington, KY 40505
Phone: (859) 299-5472; Fax: (859) 293-5999;
Email: general@khsaa.org
Web: www.khsaa.org

Summary: To provide financial assistance for college to student-athletes in Kentucky high schools

Eligibility: This program is open to high school seniors in Kentucky who have participated in athletics or cheerleading. The awards are presented in conjunction with the state basketball tournament, but all student-athletes, not just basketball players, are eligible. Students must be nominated by a school representative. Letters of nomination must explain why the student is an exemplary leader and should receive the scholarship. Selection is based on academic achievement, leadership, citizenship, and sportsmanship. Men and women are judged separately.

Financial data: The stipend is $1,000.

Duration: One year, nonrenewable

Number awarded: Thirty-two each year: one female and one male in each of 16 regions in Kentucky

Deadline: February of each year

78 NATIONAL EXCHANGE CLUB YOUTH OF THE YEAR AWARD

National Exchange Club
Attn: Awards Program
3050 Central Avenue
Toledo, OH 43606-1700
Phone: (419) 535-3232; 800-XCHANGE;
Fax: (419) 535-1989; Email: nechq@aol.com
Web: www.nationalexchangeclub.com

Summary: To recognize and reward outstanding high school seniors who have participated in sports or other activities

Eligibility: This competition starts at the local level, where Exchange Clubs select their own Youth of the Month and (from them) Youth of the Year winners. Then, clubs nominate their Youth of the Year winners for a district competition. The district winners then compete on the national level. National candidates must be high school seniors who are qualified for graduation from public, parochial, or private schools and who have been selected Youth of the Year winners on both the club and district levels. As part of their application, they must submit an essay (from 800 to 1,200 words) on a topic that changes annually; recently, the topic was "A New Spirit of America in a Changing World." Selection is based on school participation (e.g., student government, newspaper or annual, athletic teams, musical activities, debate activities, stage productions), community service activities, grades, special achievements and awards, the essay, and biographical information.

Financial data: The winner receives $10,000 to be used for educational purposes. Half the award is paid at the sponsor's national convention in the year of the competition, and the second installment when the winner registers for the second year of college.

Duration: The award is presented annually.

Number awarded: One each year

Deadline: May of each year

79 NCAIAW SCHOLARSHIP

North Carolina Alliance for Athletics, Health, Physical Education, Recreation and Dance
Attn: Executive Director
P.O. Box 27751
Raleigh, NC 27611
Phone: 888-840-6500; Fax: (919) 833-7700;
Email: ncaahperd@ncaahperd.org
Web: www.ncaahperd.org/awards/scholarships.htm

Summary: To provide financial assistance to women who are college seniors involved in sports at an institution that is a member of the former North Carolina Association of Intercollegiate Athletics for Women (NCAIAW)

Eligibility: This program is open to women who have been a participant on one or more varsity athletic teams either as a player or in the support role of manager, trainer, etc. Applicants must be attending one of the following former NCAIAW colleges or universities in North Carolina: Appalachian State, Belmont Abbey, Bennett, Campbell, Davidson, Duke, East Carolina, Gardner-Webb, High Point, Mars Hill, Meredith, North Carolina A&T, North Carolina State, Pembroke State, Salem, University of North Carolina at Asheville, University of North Carolina at Chapel Hill, University of North Carolina at Charlotte, University of North Carolina at Wilmington, Wake Forest, or Western Carolina. They must be college seniors at the time of application, be able to demonstrate high standards of scholarship, and show evidence of leadership potential (as indicated by participation in school and community activities).

Financial data: The stipend is $1,000. Funds are sent to the recipient's school.

Duration: One year

Number awarded: One each year

Deadline: June of each year

80 NEBRASKA COACHES ASSOCIATION SCHOLARSHIPS

Nebraska Coaches Association
Attn: Scholarship Committee
2546 S. 48th Street, Suite 5
Lincoln, NE 68506
Phone: (402) 434-5675; Fax: (402) 434-5689;
Email: ncacoach@inetnebr.com
Web: http://ncacoach.inetnebr.com
Summary: To provide financial assistance for college to high school seniors in Nebraska who have participated in sports
Eligibility: This program is open to seniors graduating from high schools in Nebraska in the upper 25 percent of their class. Applicants must have at least a two-year participation in two sports, have earned a varsity letter in two sports, and have a score of at least 24 on the ACT. Along with their application, they must submit brief essays on their contribution to athletics at their school, how athletics and coaches have affected their high school life and their future plans, and what sportsmanship means to them as an individual. Students participating in athletics at NCAA Division I or II schools may not be eligible.
Financial data: The stipend is $500.
Duration: One year
Number awarded: One or more each year
Deadline: March of each year

81 NEVA NELSON SCHOLARSHIP

Community Foundation for Northeast Michigan
Attn: Scholarships
111 Water Street
P.O. Box 495
Alpena, MI 49707-0495
Phone: (989) 354-6881; 877-354-6881;
Fax: (989) 356-3319; Email: wiesenj@cfnem.org
Web: www.cfnem.org/cfnem/home.nsf/public/scholarships.htm
Summary: To provide financial assistance for college to students in northeastern Michigan who have participated in sports or other activities
Eligibility: This program is open to students who have graduated (in any year) from a high school in northeastern Michigan, including Alcona, Alpena. Montmorency, or Presque Isle counties. Applicants must have a GPA of 2.8 or higher. Along with their application, they must submit information on their school-based extracurricular activities (e.g., band, National Honor Society, sports, vocal group, theater); nonschool-based involvement (e.g., dance class, church activities, youth

groups, volunteer service); family and home responsibilities; paid employment; awards and honors received during high school and/or college; and any unusual family or personal circumstances. Financial need is not considered in the selection process.
Financial data: A stipend is awarded (amount not specified). Funds are paid directly to the school.
Duration: One year
Number awarded: One each year
Deadline: March of each year

82 NEW MEXICO ATHLETIC SCHOLARSHIPS

New Mexico Higher Education Department
Attn: Financial Aid Director
1068 Cerrillos Road
P.O. Box 15910
Santa Fe, NM 87506-5910
Phone: (505) 476-6506; 800-279-9777; Fax: (505) 476-6511; Email: ofelia.morales@state.nm.us
Web: http://hed.state.nm.us/collegefinance/athlete.asp
Summary: To provide financial assistance to student-athletes in New Mexico
Eligibility: This program is open to both residents and nonresidents of New Mexico who are accepted by the athletic department of a public postsecondary institution in New Mexico.
Financial data: Awards vary but are applied to tuition and fees.
Duration: One year; may be renewed.
Number awarded: Varies each year.
Deadline: Deadlines are established by the participating institutions.

83 NICK COST SCHOLARSHIPS

American Hellenic Educational Progressive Association
Attn: AHEPA Educational Foundation
1909 Q Street N.W., Suite 500
Washington, DC 20009
Phone: (202) 232-6300; Fax: (202) 232-2140;
Email: ahepa@ahepa.org
Web: www.ahepa.org
Summary: To provide financial assistance to undergraduate and graduate students with a connection to the American Hellenic Educational Progressive Association (AHEPA) who have participated in sports or other activities
Eligibility: This program is open to members in good standing of the Order of Ahepa, Daughters of Penelope, Sons of Pericles, or Maids of Athena and the children of Order of Ahepa or Daughters of Penelope members

in good standing. Applicants must be currently enrolled or planning to enroll as undergraduate or graduate students. High school seniors must submit their most recent official transcript as well as SAT or ACT scores; college freshmen and sophomores must submit high school transcripts, SAT or ACT scores, and their most recent college transcript; college juniors and seniors must submit their most recent college transcript; graduate students must submit college transcripts, GRE or MCAT scores (if available), and their most recent graduate school transcript. Along with their application, they must also submit a 500-word biographical essay. Selection is based on academic achievement; extracurricular, personal, and volunteer activities; athletic achievements; and work experience. Financial need is not considered.

Financial data: Stipends range from $500 to $2,000 per year.

Duration: One year

Number awarded: Varies each year; recently, two of these scholarships were awarded.

Deadline: March of each year

---

84 NORTH COAST SECTION FOUNDATION SCHOLARSHIPS

California Interscholastic Federation
Attn: North Coast Section
12925 Alcosta Boulevard, Suite 8
San Ramon, CA 94583
Phone: (925) 866-8400; Fax: (925) 866-7100;
Email: sphillips@cifncs.org
Web: www.cifncs.org

Summary: To provide financial assistance for college to high school student-athletes in northern California who balance academic achievement, athletic participation, and service to the community

Eligibility: This program is open to seniors graduating from high schools in the North Coast Section of the California Interscholastic Federation who are nominated by a coach, athletic director, or school administrator. Nominees must have a GPA of 3.3 or higher, have participated in a varsity sport during their senior year, have demonstrated a commitment to their school through leadership or service, have demonstrated a commitment to their community through volunteerism, and be planning to enroll at a 2- or 4-year college within one year of graduating from high school.

Financial data: The stipend is $1,000. Funds are to be used for tuition, fees, or books.

Duration: One year.

Number awarded: Six each year: three are set aside for females and three for males.

Deadline: Nominations must be submitted by April of each year.

---

85 NORTHERN VIRGINIA ATHLETIC DIRECTORS, ADMINISTRATORS AND COACHES ASSOCIATION SCHOLARSHIPS

Northern Virginia Athletic Directors, Administrators and Coaches Association
P.O. Box 305
Burke, VA 22009
Phone: (703) 644-1959; Fax: (703) 250-6515;
Email: info@nvadaca.org
Web: www.nvadaca.org/scholarships.htm

Summary: To provide financial assistance for college to high school seniors in northern Virginia who have played sports, been a cheerleader, etc.

Eligibility: This program is open to students graduating from public high schools in northern Virginia where they have served as an athletic player, manager, trainer, or cheerleader. Applications are accepted from six groups of students: 1) female students, 2) male students, 3) students who have served as an athletic trainer and plan to prepare for a career as an athletic trainer or health care professional, 4) students with a physical disability, 5) students planning a career in early childhood education, and 6) male students who have earned a varsity letter in baseball for two years and female students who have earned a varsity letter in softball for two years. Selection is based on academic achievement; participation in athletics, leadership, and service to school and community; recommendations; and financial need.

Financial data: The stipend is $2,000.

Duration: One year

Number awarded: Fourteen each year

Deadline: March of each year

---

86 NOTAY BEGAY III SCHOLARSHIP PROGRAM

Albuquerque Community Foundation
Attn: Scholarship Program
P.O. Box 36960
Albuquerque, NM 87176-6960
Phone: (505) 883-6240; Fax: (505) 883-3629;
Email: foundation@albuquerquefoundation.org
Web: www.albuquerquefoundation.org/scholar/scholar1.htm

Summary: To provide financial assistance for college to Native American high school seniors in New Mexico who have participated in athletics

Eligibility: This program is open to seniors graduating from high schools in New Mexico who are Native

Americans. Applicants must be scholar-athletes with a varsity-level sports background and a GPA of 3.0 or higher. They must be planning to attend a college or university as a full-time student. Along with their application, they must submit a personal statement describing why they are going to college, what they plan to study, their career goals, any unusual challenges they face in continuing their education, and how they plan to give back to their community after college; transcripts; a reference from a current academic teacher or counselor; a reference from an athletic coach; and proof of tribal enrollment or Certificate of Indian Blood (at least 50 percent).

Financial data: The stipend is $2,000 per year.
Duration: One year, nonrenewable
Number awarded: Two each year
Deadline: March of each year

87 P.A. MARGARONIS SCHOLARSHIPS

American Hellenic Educational Progressive Association
Attn: AHEPA Educational Foundation
1909 Q Street N.W., Suite 500
Washington, DC 20009
Phone: (202) 232-6300; Fax: (202) 232-2140;
Email: ahepa@ahepa.org
Web: www.ahepa.org
Summary: To provide financial assistance to undergraduate and graduate students of Hellenic heritage who have participated in sports or other activities
Eligibility: Applicants must be of Hellenic heritage (although their ancestry does not need to be 100 percent Greek) and currently enrolled or planning to enroll as undergraduate or graduate students. High school seniors must submit their most recent official transcript as well as SAT or ACT scores; college freshmen and sophomores must submit high school transcripts, SAT or ACT scores, and their most recent college transcript; college juniors and seniors must submit their most recent college transcript; graduate students must submit college transcripts, GRE or MCAT scores (if available), and their most recent graduate school transcript. Along with their application, they must also submit a 500-word biographical essay. Selection is based on academic achievement; extracurricular, personal, and volunteer activities; athletic achievements; work experience; and financial need.
Financial data: Stipends range from $500 to $2,000 per year.
Duration: One year

Number awarded: Varies each year. Recently, 14 of these scholarships were awarded, 6 to graduate students and 8 to undergraduates.
Deadline: March of each year

88 PAPA JOHN'S SCHOLARSHIPS

Papa John's International, Inc.
Attn: Scholarship Program
2002 Papa John's Boulevard
Louisville, KY 40299
Phone: (502) 261-7272; 800-865-9373;
Email: info@papajohnsscholars.com
Web: www.papajohnsscholars.com
Summary: To provide financial assistance for college to high school seniors at selected U.S. high schools who have participated in sports or other activities
Eligibility: This program is open to graduating high school seniors who have a GPA of 2.5 or higher. Applicants must attend a high school located near a participating Papa John's restaurant. Selection is based on creative ability, community involvement, academic achievement, quality of character, demonstrated leadership, life goals and interests, athletic achievement, and meaningful obstacles the student has overcome.
Financial data: The stipend is $1,000.
Duration: One year
Number awarded: Varies each year; recently, 1,185 of these scholarships were awarded.

89 PIERRE H. GUILLEMETTE SCHOLARSHIP

Rhode Island Society of Professional Land Surveyors
Attn: Scholarship Committee
280 Drybridge Road
North Kingstown, RI 02852-5207
Phone: (401) 294-1262; Email: info@rispls.org
Web: www.rispls.org
Summary: To provide financial assistance to Rhode Island residents who have participated in sports or other activities and are studying surveying
Eligibility: This program is open to residents of Rhode Island who are enrolled in a course of study leading to a certificate or degree in land surveying offered by a qualified institution of higher learning. Applicants must submit brief essays on any special skills or qualifications they have acquired from employment, previous volunteer work, or through other activities, including hobbies or sports; and their previous surveying experience. Financial need is not considered in the selection process.
Financial data: The amount of the award depends on the availability of funds.

Duration: One year
Number awarded: One or more each year
Deadline: October of each year

---

90 RBC DAIN RAUSCHER COLORADO SCHOLARSHIPS

Denver Foundation
Attn: Scholarships and Special Projects
950 S. Cherry Street, Suite 200
Denver, CO 80246
Phone: (303) 300-1790, ext. 141; Fax: (303) 300-6547;
Email: kbellina@denverfoundation.org
Web: www.denverfoundation.org/page17851.cfm
Summary: To provide financial assistance for college to high school seniors from Colorado who can demonstrate exceptional levels of achievement in sports or other areas
Eligibility: This program is open to seniors graduating from high schools in Colorado who can demonstrate exceptional levels of achievement in such areas as arts, athletics, community service, leadership, or academics. Applicants must have a GPA of 3.75 or higher, a rank in the top 5 percent of their class, or an SAT score of 1,200 or higher or an ACT score of 26. They must have received an acceptance letter from an accredited college, university, or technical school. Selection is based on academic excellence, leadership in school and community activities, personal achievements, significant challenges that have been overcome, and financial need. A personal interview may be required.
Financial data: Stipends are at least $3,000.
Duration: One year
Number awarded: Ten or more each year
Deadline: March of each year

---

91 RE/MAX AMERICAN DREAM SCHOLARSHIPS

RE/MAX of Southeastern Michigan
Attn: Scholarship Program
28411 Northwestern Highway, Suite 1130
Southfield, MI 48034
Web: www.manyhouses.com
Summary: To provide financial assistance for college to high school seniors in southeastern Michigan who have participated in sports or other activities
Eligibility: This program is open to seniors graduating from high schools in southeastern Michigan, including Macomb, Monroe, Oakland, and Wayne counties. Applicants must be planning to continue their education after high school. They must submit an essay, up to two pages in length, on what the American Dream means to them and the role higher education can play in helping

them achieve that dream. They may also include up to two additional pages of supporting material, including pictures of art projects they have created, photographs of sports participation, samples of literature or poetry, letters of reference, or proof of involvement in politics, community service, or leadership roles.
Financial data: The stipend is $500.
Duration: One year
Number awarded: Twenty each year
Deadline: January of each year

---

92 REAM'S FOOD STORES SCHOLARSHIPS

Utah Sports Hall of Fame Foundation
Attn: Scholarship Chair
10182 South Cornerstone
South Jordan, UT 84095
Phone: (801) 253-7361
Summary: To recognize and reward outstanding high school seniors in Utah who have been involved in athletics and are interested in attending college in the state
Eligibility: Each high school in Utah may nominate one male and one female who are graduating this year. Nominees must be planning to attend college in the state. Selection is based on academic record, personal character, financial need, leadership qualities, and involvement in athletic activities, including football, basketball, cross-country, volleyball, tennis, track and field, soccer, rodeo, baseball, swimming, wrestling, officiating, community recreation, or intramural sports.
Financial data: The stipend is $2,000. Funds are paid to the recipient's institution.
Duration: One year, nonrenewable
Number awarded: Six each year: three males and three females
Deadline: March of each year

---

93 RICHARD J. PHELPS SCHOLAR-ATHLETE PROGRAM

Boston Globe
135 Morrissey Boulevard
P.O. Box 2378
Boston, MA 02107-2378
Phone: (617) 929-2000
Web: www.boston.com
Summary: To provide financial assistance for college to outstanding scholar-athletes from Massachusetts
Eligibility: This program is open to seniors graduating from high schools in Massachusetts who are nominated by their principals. Selection is based on academic and athletic excellence. Females and males are evaluated separately.

Financial data: The stipend is $2,000 per year.

Duration: One year

Number awarded: Fourteen each year: one female and one male from each district of the Massachusetts Interscholastic Athletic Association (MIAA)

Deadline: April of each year

---

94 ROBERT SMILEY SCHOLARSHIP

Iowa Girls' High School Athletic Union

Attn: Scholarships

2900 Grand Avenue

P.O. Box 10348

Des Moines, IA 50306-0348

Phone: (515) 288-9741; Fax: (515) 284-1969;

Email: lisa@ighsau.org

Web: www.ighsau.org

Summary: To provide financial assistance to female high school seniors in Iowa who have participated in athletics and plan to attend college in the state

Eligibility: This program is open to females graduating from high schools in Iowa who have lettered in one varsity sport sponsored by the Iowa Girls' High School Athletic Union (IGHSAU) each year of high school and have a GPA of 2.5 or higher. Applicants must be planning to attend a college or university in Iowa. Each high school in the state may nominate one student. Selection is based on academic achievements, athletic accomplishments, nonsports extracurricular activities, and community involvement.

Financial data: The stipend is $1,000.

Duration: One year

Number awarded: One each year

Deadline: March of each year

---

95 RON HALL MEMORIAL SCHOLARSHIP

Big 33 Scholarship Foundation

Attn: Scholarship Committee

511 Bridge Street

P.O. Box 213

New Cumberland, PA 17070

Phone: (717) 774-3303; 877-PABIG-33;

Fax: (717) 774-1749; Email: info@big33.org

Web: www.big33.org/scholarships/default.ashx

Summary: To provide financial assistance for college to graduating high school seniors in central Pennsylvania who demonstrate special skills in sports or other areas

Eligibility: This program is open to seniors who are graduating from public and accredited private high schools in central Pennsylvania. Applicants must be able to demonstrate qualities exhibited by the late Ron Hall:

leadership, integrity, athletics, and excellence. Along with their application, they must submit a one-page essay describing why they deserve this scholarship, including their motivation, need (financial and otherwise), leadership, and academic accomplishments.

Financial data: The stipend is $5,500.

Duration: One year, nonrenewable

Number awarded: One each year

Deadline: February of each year

---

96 SAM DAKIS SCHOLARSHIP

American Hellenic Educational Progressive Association

Attn: AHEPA Educational Foundation

1909 Q Street N.W., Suite 500

Washington, DC 20009

Phone: (202) 232-6300; Fax: (202) 232-2140;

Email: ahepa@ahepa.org

Web: www.ahepa.org

Summary: To provide financial assistance for college to students with a connection to the American Hellenic Educational Progressive Association (AHEPA) who have participated in sports or other activities

Eligibility: This program is open to members in good standing of the Order of Ahepa, Daughters of Penelope, Sons of Pericles, or Maids of Athena and the children of Order of Ahepa or Daughters of Penelope members in good standing. Applicants must be currently enrolled or planning to enroll in a college or university. High school seniors must submit their most recent official transcript as well as SAT or ACT scores; college freshmen and sophomores must submit high school transcripts, SAT or ACT scores, and their most recent college transcript; college juniors and seniors must submit their most recent college transcript. Along with their application, applicants must also submit a 500-word biographical essay. Selection is based on academic achievement; extracurricular, personal, and volunteer activities; athletic achievements; and work experience. Financial need is not considered.

Financial data: Stipends range from $500 to $2,000 per year.

Duration: One year

Number awarded: Varies each year; recently, one of these scholarships was awarded.

Deadline: March of each year

---

97 SAMMY AWARDS

Milk Processor Education Program

Attn: Scholar Athlete Milk Mustache of the Year (SAMMY)

1250 H Street N.W., Suite 950
Washington, DC 20005
Phone: (202) 737-0153; 800-WHY-MILK
Web: www.whymilk.com

Summary: To provide financial assistance for college to outstanding high school scholar-athletes

Eligibility: This program is open to residents of the 48 contiguous United States and the District of Columbia who are currently high school seniors and who participate in a high school or club sport. The country is divided into 25 geographic regions, and three finalists are selected from each region. From those, one winner from each region is chosen. Selection is based on academic achievement (35 percent), athletic excellence (35 percent), leadership (15 percent), citizenship/community service (10 percent), and a 75-word essay on how drinking milk is part of their life and training regimen (5 percent).

Financial data: College scholarships of $7,500 each are awarded. In addition, each winner plus two guests are invited to attend the winners' ceremony at Disney World in Orlando, Florida.

Duration: The awards are presented annually.

Number awarded: Twenty-five each year (one from each of 25 geographic districts)

Deadline: March of each year

---

98 SARAH KLENKE MEMORIAL TEACHING SCHOLARSHIP

Sarah Klenke Memorial
c/o Aaron Klenke
3131 Glade Springs
Kingwood, TX 77339
Phone: (281) 358-7933;
Email: dks@dskwebservices.com
Web: www.sarahklenkescholarship.org

Summary: To provide financial assistance to high school seniors and graduates who have participated in JROTC or a team sport and are interested in majoring in education in college

Eligibility: This program is open to high school seniors and graduates or those who are already enrolled in college. Applicants must plan to major in education. They must have a GPA of 2.0 or higher and have participated in a team sport or JROTC. Along with their application, they must submit a handwritten essay on why they are interested in education as a major or career.

Financial data: The stipend is $1,000.

Duration: One year

Number awarded: One or two each year

Deadline: March of each year

---

99 SCHERING/KEY "WILL TO WIN" ASTHMA ATHLETE SCHOLARSHIP

Schering/Key Asthma Athlete Scholarship Program
2000 Galloping Hill Road
Kenilworth, NJ 07033
Phone: 800-558-7305

Summary: To provide financial assistance for college to outstanding high school athletes who have asthma

Eligibility: This program is open to high school seniors with asthma who have achieved both excellence in competitive sports and a superior high school academic record. Applications must be accompanied by an official high school academic transcript, a letter of support from a physical education director or coach, a statement from a physician describing the type of asthma and the treatment for it, and a letter from the applicant describing educational and career goals. Leadership qualities and notable extracurricular activities and accomplishments are also considered in the selection process.

Financial data: The Gold Award is $20,000, Silver Awards are $12,500, and Bronze Awards are $5,000.

Duration: One year, nonrenewable

Number awarded: Eleven each year: one Gold Award, four Silver Awards, and six Bronze Awards

Deadline: March of each year

---

100 SCOTT RODRIGUEZ SCHOLARSHIP

Pride Foundation
Attn: Scholarships Manager
PMB 1001
1122 E. Pike Street
Seattle, WA 98122-3934
Phone: (206) 323-3318; 800-735-7287; Fax: (206) 323-1017; Email: scholarships@pridefoundation.org
Web: www.pridefoundation.org/programs_scholarships_main.php

Summary: To provide financial assistance for college to gay, lesbian, bisexual, or transgender (GLBT) students who live in the Northwest and have a background in leadership activities and/or participatory athletics

Eligibility: This program is open to residents of Alaska, Idaho, Montana, Oregon, or Washington who are attending or planning to attend a college, university, or vocational school. Applicants must be able to demonstrate participation in leadership activities and/or participatory athletics. Preference is given to students who are self-identified GLBT, members of GLBT families, or allies who have been strongly supportive of the GLBT community. Selection is based on financial need, community involvement, and commitment to civil rights for all people.

Financial data: Stipends average more than $2,000.

Duration: One year; recipients may reapply.

Number awarded: One or more each year

Deadline: January of each year

---

101 SKANDALARIS FAMILY FOUNDATION SCHOLARSHIPS

Skandalaris Family Foundation

P.O. Box 2061

Venice, FL 34284

Phone: (941) 544-8659; Fax: (941) 408-9526;

Email: info@skandalaris.com

Web: http://skandalaris.org

Summary: To provide financial assistance for college to high school seniors and current college students (especially those from Michigan) who have participated in sports or other activities

Eligibility: This program is open to graduating high school seniors and students already enrolled in college. The majority of the scholarships are awarded to residents of Michigan. High school seniors must have a GPA of 3.5 or higher, minimum scores of 1,200 on the SAT or 24 on the ACT, and a record of involvement in school, athletic, and community activities. College students must have a cumulative GPA of 3.4 or higher and a record of active involvement in university, athletic, or community services. All applicants must be U.S. citizens and able to demonstrate financial need.

Financial data: The stipend is at least $2,000.

Duration: One year; may be renewed.

Number awarded: Varies each year; recently, 115 of these scholarships were awarded.

Deadline: April of each year

---

102 SONS OF PERICLES UNDERGRADUATE SCHOLARSHIPS

American Hellenic Educational Progressive Association

Attn: AHEPA Educational Foundation

1909 Q Street N.W., Suite 500

Washington, DC 20009

Phone: (202) 232-6300; Fax: (202) 232-2140;

Email: ahepa@ahepa.org

Web: www.ahepa.org

Summary: To provide financial assistance to undergraduate students who are members of the Sons of Pericles and have participated in sports or other activities

Eligibility: This program is open to current undergraduates who are members of the Sons of Pericles. Freshmen and sophomores must submit a complete high school transcript, SAT or ACT scores, and their most recent college transcript. Juniors and seniors must submit their most recent college transcript. Along with their application, they must also submit a 500-word biographical essay. Selection is based on academic achievement; extracurricular, personal, and volunteer activities; athletic achievements; and work experience. Financial need is not considered.

Financial data: Stipends range from $500 to $2,000 per year.

Duration: One year

Number awarded: One each year

Deadline: March of each year

---

103 SPORTQUEST ALL-AMERICAN SCHOLARSHIPS FOR FEMALES

Athletes of Good News

Attn: SportQuest All-American Program

6425 N.W. Cache Road, Suites 217 and 218

P.O. Box 6272

Lawton, OK 73506

Phone: (580) 536-9524; Fax: (580) 536-7495;

Email: allamerican@aogn.org

Web: www.aogn.org

Summary: To provide financial assistance for college to outstanding female Christian high school athletes

Eligibility: This program is open to female high school sophomores, juniors, and seniors who believe in the Lord Jesus Christ as their personal Lord and Savior and attend a church regularly. Nominees must be one of the top three Christian athletes in their school and have an overall GPA of 3.0 or higher. They must be able to demonstrate an active Christian influence in school and community. Selection is based on GPA, athletic accomplishments, church and community involvement, essays, and references.

Financial data: The award is a $1,000 scholarship for the winner and a $500 scholarship for the runner-up.

Duration: One year

Number awarded: Two each year: one winner and one runner-up

Deadline: November of each year

---

104 SPORTQUEST ALL-AMERICAN SCHOLARSHIPS FOR MALES

Athletes of Good News

Attn: SportQuest All-American Program

6425 N.W. Cache Road, Suites 217 and 218

P.O. Box 6272

Lawton, OK 73506

Phone: (580) 536-9524; Fax: (580) 536-7495;

Email: allamerican@aogn.org

Web: www.allamericanaward.org/atp.html

Summary: To provide financial assistance for college to outstanding male Christian high school athletes

Eligibility: This program is open to male high school sophomores, juniors, and seniors who believe in the Lord Jesus Christ as their personal Lord and Savior and attend a church regularly. Nominees must be one of the top three Christian athletes in their school and have an overall GPA of 3.0 or higher. They must be able to demonstrate an active Christian influence in school and community. Selection is based on GPA, athletic accomplishments, church and community involvement, essays, and references.

Financial data: The award is a $1,000 scholarship for the winner and a $500 scholarships for the runner-up.

Duration: One year

Number awarded: Two each year: one winner and one runner-up

Deadline: November of each year

105 SPORTS ACHIEVEMENT AWARD

Indian American Heritage Foundation
3818 Gleneagles Drive
Tarzana, CA 91356
Phone: (818) 708-3885; Email: ashok4u@aol.com
Web: www.la-indiacenter.com

Summary: To recognize and reward high school seniors in southern California who are of Asian Indian descent and have participated in athletics

Eligibility: This award is available to seniors graduating from high schools in southern California (south of Fresno) who have at least one parent of Asian Indian descent. Applicants must have participated in high school sports activities and have a GPA of 2.0 or higher. They must attend a function of the sponsoring organization at which they will take a quiz on India, based on material supplied by the organization. Along with their application, they must submit a two-page essay on how athletics has affected and influenced their life. Selection is based on their quiz score (15 percent), the essay (15 percent), years of athletic training (15 percent), number of teams on which they have participated (15 percent), leadership role or captaincy of a team (15 percent), athletics honors and awards (15 percent), and community involvement (10 percent).

Financial data: The award is $500 or $250.

Duration: One year

Number awarded: One each year

Deadline: April of each year

106 SPORTSMANSHIP RECOGNITION PROGRAM SCHOLARSHIP

Kentucky High School Athletic Association
2280 Executive Drive
Lexington, KY 40505
Phone: (859) 299-5472; Fax: (859) 293-5999;
Email: general@khsaa.org
Web: www.khsaa.org

Summary: To recognize and reward, with college scholarships, outstanding student-athletes (including cheerleaders) in Kentucky high schools

Eligibility: This program is open to high school seniors in Kentucky who have participated in athletics or cheerleading. Applicants must have at least a 2.5 GPA, three letters of recommendation from coaches and administrators illustrating the student's traits of good sportsmanship, demonstrated leadership within the school and the community, and a two-page response to a case study developed for each competition. They must be planning to attend a college or university in Kentucky. A male and a female are recognized from each school in the state. They are chosen on the basis of these traits: playing the game by the rules, treating game officials and others with due respect, shaking hands with opponents, taking victory and defeat without undue emotionalism, controlling their tempers, being positive with officials and others who criticize them, cooperating with officials and others, being positive with opponents, letting student and adult audiences know that inappropriate behavior reflects poorly on the team, and serving as a role model for future student-athletes. These students are awarded a certificate and are entered into a regional competition. Males and females continue to compete separately. The regional winners are given a plaque and are considered for the Sportsmanship Recognition Program Scholarship. Selection is based on GPA, recommendations, leadership roles and honors, and the case study essay.

Financial data: The stipend is $3,000.

Duration: One year

Number awarded: Two each year: one for a female and one for a male

Deadline: Applications must be submitted to the school's athletic director in March.

107 SPORTSTOSCHOOL COLLEGE SCHOLARSHIP

SportsToSchool
P.O. Box 6071
Middletown, RI 02842
Phone: (401) 849-2639; Fax: (401) 679-0308;
Email: info@sportstoschool.com

Web: www.sportstoschool.com/scholarship.html

Summary: To provide financial assistance for college to high school students who participate in athletics

Eligibility: This program is open to students who are currently enrolled as a freshman, sophomore, junior, or senior in high school. Applicants must participate in athletics and be interested in continuing their sports activity in college. Along with their application, they must submit a 150-word essay on how sports play a positive role in their lives. Financial need is not considered.

Financial data: The stipend is $500. Funds are sent directly to the recipient.

Duration: One year

Number awarded: One each year

Deadline: February of each year

---

108 STERGIOS B. MILONAS SCHOLARSHIP

American Hellenic Educational Progressive Association

Attn: AHEPA Educational Foundation

1909 Q Street N.W., Suite 500

Washington, DC 20009

Phone: (202) 232-6300; Fax: (202) 232-2140;

Email: ahepa@ahepa.org

Web: www.ahepa.org

Summary: To provide financial assistance to incoming college freshmen who are members of the Sons of Pericles and have been active in sports and other activities

Eligibility: This program is open to incoming college freshmen who are members of the Sons of Pericles. Applicants must submit their most recent high school transcript as well as SAT or ACT scores. Along with their application, they must also submit a 500-word biographical essay. Selection is based on academic achievement; extracurricular, personal, and volunteer activities; athletic achievements; and work experience. Financial need is not considered.

Financial data: Stipends range from $500 to $2,000 per year.

Duration: One year

Number awarded: One each year

Deadline: March of each year

---

109 SUPERCOLLEGE.COM STUDENT SCHOLARSHIPS

SuperCollege.com

Attn: Scholarship Application Request

4546 B10 El Camino Real, Number 281

Los Altos, CA 94022

Phone: (650) 618-2221;

Email: supercollege@supercollege.com

Web: www.supercollege.com

Summary: To provide financial assistance for undergraduate or graduate study to U.S. citizens and permanent residents who have participated in sports and other activities

Eligibility: This program is open to U.S. citizens and permanent residents who are high school students (grades 9–12), college undergraduates, or graduate students. Applicants must submit an essay, up to 1,000 words, on one of the following three topics: 1) describe a person, place, or issue that is important to you; 2) tell us why you deserve to win this scholarship; or 3) if you could have one superpower, what would it be and why? They must also submit 5 20-word statements on their five most important academic or nonacademic achievements (e.g., projects, honors, awards, leadership positions, athletics, talents). Selection is based on the essay and record of academic and extracurricular achievement.

Financial data: Stipends range from $500 to $2,500 per year. Funds must be used for tuition or tuition-related fees, textbooks, or room and board for undergraduate study at an accredited college or university in the United States.

Duration: One year

Number awarded: One each year

Deadline: July of each year

---

110 TAU BETA PI NATIONAL LAUREATE AWARDS

Tau Beta Pi

c/o University of Tennessee at Knoxville

508 Dougherty Engineering Building

1512 Middle Drive

P.O. Box 2697

Knoxville, TN 37901-2697

Phone: (865) 546-4578; Fax: (865) 546-4579;

Email: fellowships@tbp.org

Web: www.tbp.org/pages/publications/informationbook/programs/laureates.cfm

Summary: To recognize and reward undergraduate members of Tau Beta Pi, the engineering honor society, who demonstrate outstanding contributions in other areas of activity (including sports)

Eligibility: This program is open to undergraduate members of the society who are nominated by their chapters. Nominees must have made outstanding contributions in helping to achieve the society's goal "to foster a spirit of liberal culture in engineering colleges." The areas of "other" activity for which they may be nominated include arts, athletics, diverse achievements, and service. Letters of nomination should include a half-page biographical sketch of the nominee prior to enrollment as an engineering student, a three-page description of the contributions by the nominee to the fostering of liberal culture, a short description of Tau Beta Pi activities, an unofficial transcript, a personal resume, and three reference letters.

Financial data: The award is $2,500.

Duration: Awards are presented annually.

Number awarded: Up to five each year

Deadline: March of each year

111 TEXAS AMATEUR ATHLETIC FEDERATION ATHLETE SCHOLARSHIPS

Texas Amateur Athletic Federation
P.O. Box 1789
Georgetown, TX 78627-1789
Phone: (512) 863-9400; Fax: (512) 869-2393;
Email: marklord@cox-internet.com
Web: www.taaf.com/pages/schlorship.asp

Summary: To provide financial assistance to undergraduate and graduate students who have participated in activities of the Texas Amateur Athletic Federation (TAAF)

Eligibility: This program is open to past and present TAAF athletes who have competed in one or more state-level competitions or tournaments. Applicants must be enrolled or planning to enroll at a college or university, preferably in Texas, in an accredited bachelor's, master's, or doctoral degree program. They must have a GPA of 2.5 or higher. Selection is based on honors and awards from and participation in activities, endeavors, volunteerism, and work related to athletics and/or the field of parks and recreation. Financial need is not considered.

Financial data: A stipend is awarded (amount not specified).

Duration: One year

Number awarded: One or more each year

Deadline: April of each year

112 UTAH SPORTS HALL OF FAME NATIVE AMERICAN SCHOLARSHIPS

Utah Sports Hall of Fame Foundation
Attn: Scholarship Chair
10182 South Cornerstone
South Jordan, UT 84095
Phone: (801) 253-7361

Summary: To recognize and reward outstanding Native American high school seniors in Utah who have been involved in athletics and are interested in attending college in the state

Eligibility: Each high school in Utah may nominate one Native American high school senior. Nominees must be planning to attend college in the state. Selection is based on academic record, personal character, financial need, leadership qualities, and involvement in athletic activities, including football, basketball, cross-country, volleyball, tennis, track and field, soccer, rodeo, baseball, swimming, wrestling, officiating, community recreation, or intramural sports.

Financial data: The stipend is $2,000. Funds are paid to the recipient's institution.

Duration: One year, nonrenewable

Number awarded: Two each year

Deadline: March of each year

113 WACHOVIA CITIZENSHIP AWARDS

Virginia High School League
1642 State Farm Boulevard
Charlottesville, VA 22911
Phone: (434) 977-8475; Fax: (434) 977-5943
Web: www.vhsl.org

Summary: To provide financial assistance for college to high school seniors who have participated in activities of the Virginia High School League (VHSL)

Eligibility: This program is open to college-bound seniors graduating from high schools that are members of the VHSL. Applicants must have participated in one or more of the following VHSL activities: baseball, basketball, cheer, creative writing, cross-country, debate, drama, field hockey, football, forensics, golf, gymnastics, lacrosse, leaders conference, magazines, newspapers/newsmagazines, scholastic bowl, soccer, softball, sportsmanship summit/committee, swimming and diving, tennis, track (indoor and outdoor), volleyball, wrestling, or yearbook. They must submit an essay (from 500 to 1,000 words) on what they have done that meets a definition of citizenship and how others have benefited. Each school may nominate one female and one male. Candidates are judged separately in the three VHSL groups (A, AA, and AAA). Selection is based on the essay; contributions to family, school, and community; promotion of good citizenship and sportsmanship; and two letters of support.

Financial data: The stipend is $1,000.

Duration: One year

Number awarded: Six each year: one female and one male in each of the three VHSL groups

Deadline: March of each year

114 WASHINGTON DENTAL SERVICE FOUNDATION SCHOLARSHIPS

Washington Dental Service Foundation
Attn: Grant Administrator

P.O. Box 75688
Seattle, WA 98125
Phone: (206) 528-2337; 800-572-7835, ext. 2337;
Fax: (206) 528-7373; Email: foundation@
deltadentalwa.com
Web: www.deltadentalwa.com

Summary: To provide financial assistance to members of underrepresented minority groups in Washington who are interested in preparing for a career as a dental hygienist, dental assistant, or laboratory technician and have participated in sports or other activities

Eligibility: This program is open to residents of Washington who are African or Black Americans, Native Americans, Alaskan Natives, Hispanics/Latinos, or Pacific Islanders. Applicants must be planning to enroll in an eligible program in dental hygiene, dental assisting, or laboratory technology at a community or technical college in the state. They must be able to demonstrate financial need. Along with their application, they must submit essays of 100 to 300 words covering these five topics: 1) why they are interested in becoming a dental professional; 2) their career goals, how they decided upon those goals, and how completion of their proposed program will help them reach those goals; 3) how they have prepared themselves academically for those chosen program of study; 4) a leadership experience they have had in school, work, athletics, family, church, community, or other area of their life; and 5) how they help or serve others in their family and/or community.

Financial data: Stipends range from $1,000 to $4,000 per year, depending on the need of the recipient.

Duration: One year

Number awarded: One or more each year

Deadline: September of each year

115 WHO'S WHO AMONG AMERICAN HIGH SCHOOL STUDENTS—SPORTS EDITION SCHOLARSHIPS

Educational Communications Scholarship Foundation
Attn: Scholarship Coordinator
7211 Circle S Road
P.O. Box 149319
Austin, TX 78714-9319
Phone: (512) 440-2300; Fax: (512) 447-1687
Web: www.ecisf.org/sp_main.aspx

Summary: To provide financial assistance to high school honor students who are listed in *Who's Who Among American High School Students—Sports Edition*

Eligibility: This program is open to high school students who are U.S. citizens and have been involved in high school sports activities. Candidates must first be nominated by a school official, youth activity sponsor, or educational organization to have their name appear in *Who's Who Among American High School Students—Sports Edition*. All students listed in that publication automatically receive an application for these scholarships in the mail. Selection is based on GPA, achievement test scores, leadership qualifications, work experience, evaluation of an essay, and some consideration for financial need.

Financial data: The stipend is $1,000; payments are issued directly to the financial aid office at the institution the student attends.

Duration: One year

Number awarded: Ten each year

Deadline: May of each year

116 WOMEN IN SPORTS DAY SCHOLARSHIPS

Delaware Women's Alliance for Sport and Fitness
c/o Evelyn Campbell, Scholarship Committee Chair
Howard High School of Technology
401 E. 12th Street
Wilmington, DE 19801
Phone: (302) 571-5422; Email: scholarships@dwasf.org
Web: www.dwasf.org/scholarships.html

Summary: To provide financial assistance to female graduating high school seniors in Delaware who have significantly contributed to sports at the varsity level

Eligibility: This program is open to female high school seniors in Delaware who have a GPA of 3.0 or higher and have participated in at least one varsity sport. Applicants must submit a student profile describing their sports participation, school activities, community activities, and career objectives; a short paragraph describing why they feel they are deserving of this scholarship; and three letters of recommendation. Financial need is not considered in the selection process.

Financial data: The stipend ranges from $500 to $1,000.

Duration: One year

Number awarded: Several each year

Deadline: April of each year

117 XX OLYMPIAD MEMORIAL AWARD

Jewish War Veterans of the United State of America
1811 R Street N.W.
Washington, DC 20009-1659
Phone: (202) 265-6280; Fax: (202) 234-5662;
Email: jwv@jvw.org
Web: www.jwv.org/program/oma.html

Summary: To recognize and reward outstanding high school athletes

Eligibility: This award is presented to an outstanding senior high school athlete. Selection is based on athletic accomplishment (60 percent), academic achievement (20 percent), community service (10 percent), and leadership (10 percent). The award is presented on a nonsectarian basis.

Financial data: Awards are $500, $150, and $100.

Duration: The awards are presented annually.

Number awarded: Three each year

Deadline: The names of department winners must be submitted to national headquarters by June of each year.

118 YOUNG AMERICAN AWARDS

Boy Scouts of America
Attn: Learning for Life Division, S210
1325 W. Walnut Hill Lane
P.O. Box 152079
Irving, TX 75015-2079
Phone: (972) 580-2418; Fax: (972) 580-2137
Web: www.learning-for-life.org/exploring/
scholarships/index.html

Summary: To recognize and reward college and graduate students who demonstrate exceptional community service and achievement in sports or other areas

Eligibility: This program is open to students younger than 25 years of age who are currently enrolled in college or graduate school. Candidates must be nominated by a Boy Scout troop, Explorer post, Venturing crew, Learning for Life group, individual, or community youth-serving organization that shares the same program objectives. Nominees must have achieved exceptional excellence in one or more fields, such as art, athletics, business, community service, education, government, humanities, literature, mathematics, music, religion, or science; be involved in service in their community, state, or country that adds to the quality of life; and have maintained an above-average GPA. They must submit high school and college transcripts (graduate students need to submit only college transcripts) and at least three letters of recommendation. Nominations must be submitted to a local Boy Scout council, but nominees are not required to be a participant in a council unit or program.

Financial data: The award is $5,000. Local councils may also provide awards to their nominees.

Duration: The awards are presented annually.

Number awarded: Five each year

Deadline: Applications must be submitted to the local council office by November of each year

119 ZOE CAVALARIS OUTSTANDING FEMALE ATHLETE AWARD

Daughters of Penelope
1909 Q Street N.W., Suite 500
Washington, DC 20009-1007
Phone: (202) 234-9741; Fax: (202) 483-6983;
Email: daughters@ahepa.org
Web: www.ahepa.org

Summary: To recognize and reward women of Greek descent who demonstrate excellence in high school or college athletics

Eligibility: This award is presented to a young woman of Hellenic descent who has exceptional athletic ability and a record of accomplishment in any sport or any series of sports. Nominees must be outstanding high school or college amateur female athletes recognized for their accomplishments during their high school and/or college years. Along with a letter of nomination from a sponsoring chapter of Daughters of Penelope, they must submit documentation of their current overall GPA, academic honors, other honors, extracurricular activities (other than sports), church and/or community activities, and special achievements (other than sports).

Financial data: The award includes a $500 college scholarship, an engraved plaque, and public recognition through Daughters of Penelope events and publications.

Duration: The award is presented annually.

Number awarded: One each year

Deadline: May of each year

120 ALBERTA E. CROWE STAR OF TOMORROW AWARD

United States Bowling Congress
Attn: SMART Program
5301 South 76th Street
Greendale, WI 53129-1192
Phone: (414) 423-3343; 800-514-BOWL, ext. 3343;
Fax: (414) 421-3014; Email: smart@bowl.com
Web: www.bowl.com/scholarships/main.aspx

Summary: To provide financial assistance for college to outstanding women bowlers

Eligibility: This program is open to women amateur bowlers who are current members in good standing of the United States Bowling Congress (USBC) or USBC Youth and competitors in events sanctioned by those organizations. Applicants must be high school or college students younger than 22 years of age, have a GPA of 2.5 or higher, and have a bowling average of 175 or greater. They may not have competed in a professional bowling tournament. Along with their application, they must submit an essay, up to 500 words, on how this scholarship will influence their bowling, academic, and personal goals. Selection is based on bowling performances on local, regional, state, and national levels; academic achievement; and extracurricular involvement.

Financial data: The stipend is $1,500 per year.

Duration: One year; may be renewed for three additional years.

Number awarded: One each year

Deadline: September of each year

---

121 AMANDA "BABE" SLATTERY SCHOLARSHIPS

Western Athletic Scholarship Association
Attn: Scholarship Coordinator
13730 Loumont Street
Whittier, CA 90601

Summary: To provide financial assistance for college to outstanding softball players

Eligibility: This program is open to graduating high school seniors who have played an active role in amateur softball. Applicants must be planning to attend an accredited two-year or four-year college or university. They need not have played on a high school team and are not required to play softball in college. Selection is based on academic achievement, community service, participation in softball, and financial need.

Financial data: The stipend is $2,000 per year.

Duration: One year; may be renewed.

Number awarded: Up to ten each year

Deadline: February of each year

---

122 AMERICAN DARTS ORGANIZATION MEMORIAL SCHOLARSHIPS

American Darts Organization
230 N. Crescent Way, Suite K
Anaheim, CA 92801-6707
Phone: (714) 254-0212; Fax: (714) 254-0214;
Email: adodarts1@aol.com
Web: http://adodarts.com

Summary: To provide financial aid for college to players in the American Darts Organization (ADO) Youth Playoff Program

Eligibility: This program is open to ADO members who are area or national winners in the Youth Playoff Program and under 21 years of age. Applicants must be enrolled or accepted at an accredited U.S. college as a full-time student with a GPA of 2.0 or higher. They must be U.S. citizens or have lived in the United States for at least two years.

Financial data: Stipends are $500 for quarterfinalists in the National Championship; $750 for each semifinalist; $1,000 for each runner-up; and $1,500 for each National Champion. Any participant/winner who is eligible to compete in more than one area/national championship may repeat as a scholarship winner, receiving up to $8,000 in prizes. Funds may be used for any legitimate college expense, including fees for parking stickers, library fees, student union fees, tuition, and books.

Duration: The funds are awarded annually.

Number awarded: Eight each year: four quarterfinalists, two semifinalists, one runner-up, and one National Champion

---

123 AMERICAN LEGION BASEBALL SCHOLARSHIP

American Legion Baseball
700 N. Pennsylvania Street
Indianapolis, IN 46204
Phone: (317) 630-1249; Fax: (317) 630-1223;
Email: acy@legion.org
Web: www.baseball.legion.org/awards.htm

Summary: To recognize and reward outstanding participants in the American Legion baseball program

Eligibility: This program is open to participants in the American Legion baseball program who are high school graduates or college freshmen; students still in high school are not eligible. In each of the 50 states and Puerto Rico, candidates may be nominated by a team manager or head coach. The department baseball committee selects a player who demonstrates outstanding leadership, citizenship, character, scholarship, and financial need.

Financial data: The award is a $1,000 scholarship. Funds are disbursed jointly to the winner and the school.

Duration: Students have eight years to use the scholarship funds from the date of the award, excluding any time spent on active military duty.

Additional information: The scholarship may be used at any accredited school above high school level.

Number awarded: Fifty-one each year: one in each state and Puerto Rico

Deadline: July of each year

---

124 AMERICAN LUNG ASSOCIATION OF MAINE GOLF SCHOLARSHIP

American Lung Association of Maine
Attn: Golf Scholarship
122 State Street
Augusta, ME 04330
Phone: (207) 622-6394; 888-241-6566, ext. 112; Fax: (207) 626-2919; Email: kmarkham@mainelung.org

Web: www.mainelung.org/events/golfcard/scholarship_program.asp

Summary: To provide financial assistance to high school seniors in Maine who have been active in golf and are interested in studying a medical or health-related field in college

Eligibility: This program is open to high school seniors in Maine who have been accepted at an accredited college or vocational/technical school to study a medical or health-related field. Applicants must have been involved in the game of golf as players or as employees of a facility. They must be U.S. citizens and nonusers of tobacco. Along with their application, they must submit a letter of intent explaining their goals and objectives and documentation of financial need.

Financial data: The stipend is $500.

Duration: One year

Number awarded: Three each year: one to a graduating high school senior from western Maine, one to a graduating high school senior from eastern Maine, and one to a graduating high school senior from anywhere in Maine

Deadline: March of each year

125 AMHI EDUCATIONAL SCHOLARSHIPS

American Morgan Horse Institute, Inc.
Attn: AMHI Scholarships
P.O. Box 519
Shelburne, VT 05482-0519
Phone: (802) 985-8477; Fax: (802) 985-8430;
Email: info@morganhorse.com
Web: www.morganhorse.com/benefits/kids_scholarships.php

Summary: To provide financial assistance for college to high school seniors and graduates who have experience with and an interest in Morgan horses

Eligibility: This program is open to high school seniors and graduates who have experience with and an interest in registered Morgan horses. Applicants must have completed or be involved in the American Morgan Horse Association (AMHA) horsemastership program; be involved in a four-H or FFA program; have won a USA Equestrian and/or AMHA Medal for equitation; or have placed in the top two in the junior division or the top four in the adult division of an open competition program. Selection is based on ability and aptitude for serious study, community service, leadership, financial need, and achievement with Morgan horses.

Financial data: The stipend is $3,000.

Duration: One year, nonrenewable

Number awarded: Five each year

Deadline: February of each year

126 ANDY STONE SCHOLARSHIP

US Youth Soccer—Region III
c/o Denise Davis
12320 Jacksonville Cato Road
North Little Rock, AR 72120
Phone: (501) 834-1300; Fax: (501) 835-1300;
Email: r3usysa@swbell.net
Web: www.usysregion3.org

Summary: To provide financial assistance for college to high school seniors in selected southern states who have been active in soccer

Eligibility: This program is open to seniors graduating from high schools in states that are part of Region III of U.S. Youth Soccer (Alabama, Arkansas, Florida, Georgia, Louisiana, Mississippi, North Carolina, Oklahoma, South Carolina, Tennessee, and Texas). Applicants must have been an active member of Region III as a player, coach, and/or referee. Selection is based on years and depth of involvement in U.S. Youth Soccer and soccer in general, academic achievement, financial need, citizenship, and extracurricular activities.

Financial data: The stipend is $1,000. The first $500 is issued at the beginning of the school year, and the second $500 is issued upon receipt of proof of a C average overall for the first grading period.

Duration: One year

Number awarded: One each year

Deadline: April of each year

127 ANNA VIOLANTI SCHOLARSHIP

Anthracite Golf Association
617 Keystone Avenue
Peckville, PA 18452
Phone: (570) 383-GOLF; Fax: (570) 383-4654;
Email: palloyd127@cs.com
Web: www.anthracitegolf.org/anthracite_golf_association_scho.htm

Summary: To provide financial assistance for college to high school seniors from northeastern Pennsylvania who have been involved in golf

Eligibility: This program is open to seniors graduating from high schools in northeastern Pennsylvania who have been involved in golf. Applicants must have been accepted by a postsecondary institution. They are not required to be affiliated with a golf club. Along with their application, they must submit a personal statement about their career goals. Selection is based on that statement, academic achievement, leadership and service, golf accomplishments, participation in the Anthracite Golf Association junior tour, and two letters of recommendation.

Financial data: Stipends range from $500 to $3,000. Half the funds are paid at the beginning of the first semester and half at the beginning the second semester, provided recipients earn a GPA of 2.5 or higher for the first semester.

Duration: One year

Number awarded: Varies each year

Deadline: February of each year

---

128 ANNUAL ZEB SCHOLARSHIP

United States Bowling Congress

Attn: SMART Program

5301 S. 76th Street

Greendale, WI 53129-1192

Phone: (414) 423-3223; 800-514-BOWL, ext. 3223;

Fax: (414) 421-3014; Email: smart@bowl.com

Web: www.bowl.com/scholarships/main.aspx

Summary: To recognize and reward, with college scholarships, young bowlers who demonstrate outstanding community service

Eligibility: This award is presented to U.S. Bowling Congress (USBC) Youth members in the junior or senior year of high school. Applicants must have a GPA of 2.0 or higher and not have competed in a professional bowling tournament. Along with their application, they must submit an essay of 500 words on a topic of their choosing. Selection is based on the essay, grades, letters of reference, and academic and community involvement.

Financial data: The award consists of a $2,500 college scholarship.

Duration: The award is presented annually.

Additional information: This award, named in honor or Jim Zebehazy, executive director of the Young American Bowling Alliance prior to its merger with the USBC, is presented at the USBC Junior Gold Championships award ceremony. Travel and hotel expenses for the recipient and a parent or guardian to attend the ceremony are also provided.

Number awarded: One each year

Deadline: March of each year

---

129 ANTHRACITE GOLF ASSOCIATION FOUNDERS SCHOLARSHIP

Anthracite Golf Association

617 Keystone Avenue

Peckville, PA 18452

Phone: (570) 383-GOLF; Fax: (570) 383-4654;

Email: palloyd127@cs.com

Web: www.anthracitegolf.org/anthracite_golf_association_scho.htm

Summary: To provide financial assistance for college to high school seniors from northeastern Pennsylvania who have been involved in golf

Eligibility: This program is open to seniors graduating from high schools in northeastern Pennsylvania who have been involved in golf. Applicants must have been accepted by a postsecondary institution. They are not required to be affiliated with a golf club. Along with their application, they must submit a personal statement about their career goals. Selection is based on that statement, academic achievement, leadership and service, golf accomplishments, participation in the Anthracite Golf Association junior tour, and two letters of recommendation.

Financial data: Stipends range from $500 to $3,000. Half the funds are paid at the beginning of the first semester and half at the beginning the second semester, provided recipient earns a GPA of 2.5 or higher for the first semester.

Duration: One year

Additional information: These scholarships are offered as part of the Anthracite Golf Association Scholarship program.

Number awarded: Varies each year

Deadline: February of each year

---

130 APHA YOUTH DEVELOPMENT FOUNDATION SCHOLARSHIPS

American Paint Horse Association

Attn: Director of Youth Activities

2800 Meacham Boulevard

P.O. Box 961023

Fort Worth, TX 76161-0023

Phone: (817) 834-APHA, ext. 248; Fax: (817) 834-3152;

Email: coordinator@ajpha.com

Web: www.apha.com/foundation/scholarships.html

Summary: To provide financial assistance for college to members of the American Paint Horse Association (APHA)

Eligibility: This program is open to members in good standing (regular or junior) of the association involved in horse activity using a paint horse or contributing actively to a regional club for at least a year prior to and at the time of application. Applicants must be high school seniors or students already enrolled in college and must have never been married. They must have a GPA of 3.0 or higher. Along with their application, they must submit a 500-word essay on their educational plans and goals. Selection is based on that essay (15 percent), participation in APHA club activities (25 percent), participation in APHA horse activities (25 percent), participation in extracurricular activities (20 percent), and three letters of recommendation (15 percent).

Financial data: The stipend is $1,000 per year. Funds are paid directly to the recipient's school.

Duration: One year; may be renewed for up to four additional years if the recipient maintains full-time enrollment and a GPA of 3.0 or higher.

Number awarded: Varies each year; recently, 36 of these scholarships (14 new and 22 renewal) were awarded.

Deadline: February of each year

---

131 APPALOOSA YOUTH EDUCATIONAL SCHOLARSHIPS

Appaloosa Youth Foundation, Inc.
c/o Appaloosa Horse Club
Attn: Youth Coordinator
2720 W. Pullman Road
Moscow, ID 83843-4024
Phone: (208) 882-5578, ext. 264; Fax: (208) 882-8150;
Email: aphc@appaloosa.com
Web: www.appaloosa.com/youth/ycontests.shtm

Summary: To provide financial assistance for college to members or dependents of members of the Appaloosa Horse Club

Eligibility: This program is open to members of the Appaloosa Youth Association or the Appaloosa Horse Club who are attending or planning to attend a college or university. Applicants must submit three letters of recommendation; a high school or college transcript (GPA of 2.5 or higher); copies of SAT or ACT exam scores; and an essay in which they describe what their experience with horses has meant to them, why they desire to continue their education, the personal qualities that qualify them to receive a scholarship, any circumstances regarding financial need, and how receiving this scholarship will enhance their educational experiences. Selection is based on academic aptitude, involvement in the Appaloosa industry, leadership potential, sportsmanship, community and civic responsibility, and general knowledge and accomplishments in horsemanship.

Financial data: The stipend is $1,000.

Duration: One year; may be renewed.

Number awarded: Eight each year, of which six are awarded in each of the six territories of the Appaloosa Horse Club, one is awarded at large, and one is awarded to a previous winner as a continuing scholarship

Deadline: June of each year

---

132 AQHA FOUNDATION YOUTH SCHOLARSHIPS

American Quarter Horse Foundation
Attn: Scholarship Coordinator
2601 I-40 East
Amarillo, TX 79104
Phone: (806) 378-5034; 888-209-8322;
Fax: (806) 376-1005; Email: lowens@aqha.org
Web: www.aqha.com/foundation/scholarships/index .html

Summary: To provide financial assistance for college to members of the American Quarter Horse Youth Association (AQHYA)

Eligibility: Applicants must have been members in good standing for at least three years and be high school seniors or entering college freshmen. They must have ranked in the upper 25 percent of their high school graduating class and be able to demonstrate financial need. All majors in college are eligible.

Financial data: The stipend is $2,000 per year.

Duration: Up to four years

Number awarded: Varies each year; recently, 30 of these scholarships were awarded.

Deadline: January of each year

---

133 ARABIAN HORSE FOUNDATION GENERAL SCHOLARSHIPS

Arabian Horse Foundation
1024 K Street
Lincoln, NE 68508
Phone: (402) 477-2233; Fax: (402) 477-2286
Web: www.arabianhorsefoundation.org/scholarship .html

Summary: To provide financial assistance to undergraduate and graduate students who have a record of equine involvement

Eligibility: This program is open to students who have a record of involvement with horses. Applicants must be enrolled or planning to enroll as a full-time undergraduate or graduate student at an accredited college or university. High school seniors must have a GPA of B or higher; college students must have at least a 3.5 GPA. Along with their application, they must submit information on their financial need, honors or academic awards, extracurricular activities and offices, leadership roles, career goals, and equine involvement for the past two years.

Financial data: A stipend is awarded (amount not specified).

Duration: One year; may be renewed if the recipient maintains a GPA of 2.5 or higher with no grade below a D.

Number awarded: One or more each year

Deadline: January of each year

134 ARABIAN HORSE FOUNDATION REGIONAL SCHOLARSHIPS

Arabian Horse Foundation
1024 K Street
Lincoln, NE 68508
Phone: (402) 477-2233; Fax: (402) 477-2286
Web: www.arabianhorsefoundation.org/scholarship
.html

Summary: To provide financial assistance to undergraduate and graduate students who have a record of equine involvement

Eligibility: This program is open to students who have a record of involvement with horses. Applicants must be enrolled or planning to enroll as a full-time undergraduate or graduate student at an accredited college or university. High school seniors must have a GPA of B or higher; college students must have at least a 3.5 GPA. Along with their application, they must submit information on their financial need, honors or academic awards, extracurricular activities and offices, leadership roles, career goals, and equine involvement for the past two years.

Financial data: A stipend is awarded (amount not specified).

Duration: One year; may be renewed if the recipient maintains of GPA of 2.5 or higher with no grade below a D.

Number awarded: Eighteen each year: one in each region of the Arabian Horse Association

Deadline: January of each year

135 ARIZONA QUARTER HORSE RACING SCHOLARSHIP

American Quarter Horse Foundation
Attn: Scholarship Coordinator
2601 I-40 East
Amarillo, TX 79104
Phone: (806) 378-5034; 888-209-8322;
Fax: (806) 376-1005; Email: lowens@aqha.org
Web: www.aqha.com/foundation/scholarships/index
.html

Summary: To provide financial assistance to members of the American Quarter Horse Association (AQHA) or the American Quarter Horse Youth Association (AQHYA) from Arizona who wish to attend college to prepare for a career in the quarter horse racing industry

Eligibility: Applicants must have been members of either organization for at least one year and be residents of Arizona. They must be graduating high school seniors or already enrolled in college, have a GPA of 2.5 or higher, and be interested in preparing for a career in

the quarter horse racing industry by earning a degree in animal science, veterinary science, track management, or other related field. Financial need is considered in the selection process.

Financial data: The stipend is $500.

Duration: One year

Number awarded: One each year

Deadline: January of each year

136 ARIZONA QUARTER HORSE YOUTH SCHOLARSHIP

American Quarter Horse Foundation
Attn: Scholarship Coordinator
2601 I-40 East
Amarillo, TX 79104
Phone: (806) 378-5034; 888-209-8322;
Fax: (806) 376-1005; Email: lowens@aqha.org
Web: www.aqha.com/foundation/scholarships/index
.html

Summary: To provide financial assistance for college to members of the American Quarter Horse Association (AQHA) or the American Quarter Horse Youth Association (AQHYA) from Arizona

Eligibility: Applicants must be current members of either organization, be current or previous members of the Arizona Quarter Horse Youth Association, and be residents of Arizona. They must be graduating high school seniors or already enrolled in college with a GPA of 2.5 or higher. Financial need is considered in the selection process.

Financial data: The stipend is $500.

Duration: One year

Number awarded: One each year

Deadline: January of each year

137 ARROWCREEK COUNTRY CLUB JUNIOR GOLF SCHOLARSHIPS

ArrowCreek Country Club
Attn: Junior Golf Scholarship Committee
2905 ArrowCreek Parkway
Reno, NV 89522
Phone: (775) 850-4653
Web: www.arrowcreekcc.com/scholarshipProgram
.php

Summary: To provide financial assistance for college to high school seniors in northern Nevada who have been active in golf

Eligibility: This program is open to seniors graduating from high schools in northern Nevada who have been members of their high school golf team. Applicants must be planning to attend a college or university as a full-time student and become a member of their college golf team. Along with their application, they must submit a statement that describes their interest in attending college, career path, community service and school activities, golf history, and previous work experience. Selection is based primarily on golf skills and financial need, although academic performance, school and community involvement, citizenship, and recommendations are also considered. Males and females are considered separately.

Financial data: The stipend is $1,000. Funds are paid directly to the school of the recipient's choice to be used for tuition, course registration, special class or laboratory fees, room and board, textbooks, and class materials.

Duration: One year

Number awarded: Two each year: one male and one female

Deadline: March of each year

138 ART WALL JR. SCHOLARSHIP

Anthracite Golf Association
617 Keystone Avenue
Peckville, PA 18452
Phone: (570) 383-GOLF; Fax: (570) 383-4654;
Email: palloyd127@cs.com
Web: www.anthracitegolf.org/anthracite_golf_
association_scho.htm
Summary: To provide financial assistance for college to high school seniors from northeastern Pennsylvania who have been involved in golf
Eligibility: This program is open to seniors graduating from high schools in northeastern Pennsylvania who have been involved in golf. Applicants must have been accepted by a postsecondary institution. They are not required to be affiliated with a golf club. Along with their application, they must submit a personal statement about their career goals. Selection is based on that statement, academic achievement, leadership and service, golf accomplishments, participation in the Anthracite Golf Association junior tour, and two letters of recommendation.
Financial data: Stipends range from $500 to $3,000. Half the funds are paid at the beginning of the first semester and half at the beginning the second semester, provided recipients earn a GPA of 2.5 or higher for the first semester.
Duration: One year
Number awarded: Varies each year
Deadline: February of each year

139 BABE RUTH LEAGUE SCHOLARSHIPS

Babe Ruth League, Inc.
1770 Brunswick Pike
P.O. Box 5000
Trenton, NJ 08638
Phone: (609) 695-1434; Fax: (609) 695-2505;
Email: info@baberuthleague.org
Web: www.baberuthleague.org/scholarship.html
Summary: To provide financial assistance for college to high school seniors who played Babe Ruth League baseball or softball
Eligibility: This program is open to graduating high school seniors who played Babe Ruth League baseball or softball previously. Applicants must be planning to attend college. Along with their application, they must submit a 100-word essay on how playing Babe Ruth baseball or softball has affected their life. Financial need is not considered in the selection process.
Financial data: The stipend is $1,000.
Duration: One year
Number awarded: Varies each year; recently, ten of these scholarships were awarded.
Deadline: September of each year

140 BARB MILLER MEMORIAL SCHOLARSHIP AWARD

Indiana Water Ski Association
Attn: Scholarship
12266 East Jefferson
Mishawaka, IN 46545
Phone: (574) 255-3572;
Email: rsharkeywaterski@comcast.net
Web: indianawaterski.org/awards/scholar/
babmillerscholarship.htm
Summary: To provide financial assistance for college to residents of Indiana who have been active in water skiing
Eligibility: This program is open to Indiana residents who are full-time students entering their freshman through senior year at an accredited two- or four-year college or university. Applicants must be residents of Indiana and members of USA Water Ski and the Indiana Water Ski Association (IWSA). Along with their application, they must submit a 500-word essay on the changes they feel need to take place to attract new membership into the tournament water ski community and why. Selection is based on the essay, number of years in USA Water Ski and IWSA, academic achievement, leadership, extracurricular involvement, letters of recommendation, and financial need.
Financial data: The stipend is $500.

Duration: One year; may be renewed up to two additional years.

Number awarded: One each year

Deadline: June of each year

---

141 BARBARA BOLDING/JIM GREW SCHOLARSHIP

American Water Ski Educational Foundation

Attn: Director

1251 Holy Cow Road

Polk City, FL 33868-8200

Phone: (863) 324-2472; Fax: (863) 324-3996;

Email: info@waterskihalloffame.com

Web: www.waterskihalloffame.com

Summary: To provide financial assistance to currently enrolled college students who participate in water skiing

Eligibility: This program is open to full-time students at two- or four-year accredited colleges entering their sophomore, junior, or senior year. Applicants must be U.S. citizens and active members of a sport division within USA Water Ski (AWSA, ABC, AKA, WSDA, NSSA, NCWSA, NWSRA, USAWB, and HYD). Along with their application, they must submit a 500-word essay on a topic that changes annually but relates to water skiing; recently, students were asked to assume that they had just acquired the position of marketing director for the American Water Ski Educational Foundation and to describe the creative measures they would implement to increase membership in the foundation. Selection is based on the essay, academic record, leadership, extracurricular involvement, letters of recommendation, AWSA membership activities, and financial need.

Financial data: The stipend is $1,500 per year.

Duration: One year; may be renewed for up to two additional years.

Number awarded: Two each year

Deadline: March of each year

---

142 BARBARA H. DENGLER SCHOLARSHIP

Delaware Community Foundation

Attn: Executive Vice President

100 W. 10th Street, Suite 115

P.O. Box 1636

Wilmington, DE 19899

Phone: (302) 504-5222; Fax: (302) 571-1553;

Email: rgentsch@delcf.org

Web: www.delcf.org

Summary: To provide financial assistance for college to students in Delaware who have been involved with golf

Eligibility: This program is open to active participants in the LPGA Urban Youth Golf Program of Delaware, a subsidiary of McDonald's Kids Charity. Applicants must be working on a college degree or other higher education program.

Financial data: The stipend varies, depending on the number of applicants and awards.

Duration: One year

Number awarded: Varies each year

Deadline: May of each year

---

143 BILL CASS MEMORIAL SCHOLARSHIP

Mississippi Golf Association

Attn: Scholarship Committee

400 Clubhouse Drive

Jackson, MS 39208

Phone: (601) 939-1131; Fax: (601) 939-0773;

Email: missgolf@missgolf.org

Web: www.missgolf.org/mjga/mjga.html

Summary: To provide financial assistance for college to high school seniors in Mississippi who have been involved in golf

Eligibility: This program is open to college-bound seniors graduating from high schools in Mississippi. Applicants must have participated in activities related to golf. Along with their application, they must submit information on their high school GPA, SAT/ACT scores, and participation in extracurricular activities (school-related, interscholastic athletics, nonschool-related clubs and activities, and honors and awards). Financial need is not considered in the selection process.

Financial data: A stipend is awarded (amount not specified).

Duration: One year

Number awarded: One or more each year

Deadline: June of each year

---

144 BILL DICKEY GOLF SCHOLARSHIPS

Bill Dickey Scholarship Association.

Attn: Scholarship Committee

4950 E. Thomas Road

Phoenix, AZ 85018

Phone: (602) 258-7851; Fax: (602) 258-3412;

Email: andrea@nmjgsa.org

Web: www.nmjgsa.org/scholarships.html

Summary: To provide financial assistance to minority high school seniors and undergraduate students who excel at golf

Eligibility: This program is open to graduating high school seniors who are members of minority groups (African American, Asian/Pacific Islander, Hispanic, or American Indian/Alaskan Native). Applicants must submit a 500-word essay on this question: "One of the principal goals of education and golf is fostering ways for people to respect and get along with individuals who think, dress, look, and act differently. How might you make this goal a reality?" Selection is based on academic achievement; personal recommendations; participation in golf, school, and community activities; and financial need.

Financial data: Stipends range from one-time awards of $1,000 to four-year awards of $6,000 per year. Funds are paid directly to the recipient's college.

Duration: One year or longer

Number awarded: Varies; generally 80 or more each year

Deadline: April of each year

145 BILL GOODSON MEMORIAL SCHOLARSHIP

Amarillo Area Foundation
Attn: Scholarship Coordinator
801 S. Fillmore Street, Suite 700
Amarillo, TX 79101
Phone: (806) 376-4521; Fax: (806) 373-3656;
Email: laquita@aaf-hf.org
Web: www.aaf-hf.org/scholarships/content/hand_gunners.htm

Summary: To provide financial assistance for college to high school seniors in northern Texas who are interested in shooting sports

Eligibility: This program is open to residents of the 26 northernmost counties of the Texas panhandle: Dallam, Sherman, Hansford, Ochiltree, Lipscomb, Hartley, Moore, Hutchinson, Roberts, Hemphill, Oldham, Potter, Carson, Gray, Wheeler, Deaf Smith, Randall, Armstrong, Donley, Collingsworth, Parmer, Castro, Swisher, Briscoe, Hall, and Childress. Applicants must be graduating high school seniors who have an interest in a shooting sport or activity, can demonstrate financial need, and have a GPA of 2.0 or higher. They may attend a college or university anywhere in the country and major in any subject.

Financial data: The stipend is $500.

Duration: One year

Number awarded: One or more each year

Deadline: January of each year

146 BILLY ADKINS MEMORIAL SCHOLARSHIP

Dixie Softball, Inc.
Attn: President
1101 Skelton Drive
Birmingham, AL 35224
Phone: (205) 785-2255; Fax: (205) 785-2258;

Email: softball@dixie.org
Web: www.dixie.org

Summary: To provide financial assistance for college to high school senior women who have participated in the Dixie Softball program

Eligibility: This program is open to high school senior women who played in the Dixie Softball program for at least two seasons. Applicants must submit a transcript of grades, letter of recommendation from a high school principal or other school official, verification from a Dixie Softball local official of the number of years the applicant participated in the program, and documentation of financial need. Ability as an athlete is not considered in the selection process.

Financial data: The stipend is $1,500.

Duration: One year

Number awarded: One each year

Deadline: February of each year

147 BILLY WELU SCHOLARSHIP

Professional Bowlers Association
Attn: Billy Welu Bowling Scholarship
719 Second Avenue, Suite 701
Seattle, WA 98104
Phone: (206) 332-9688; Fax: (206) 654-6030
Web: www.pba.com/corporate/scholarships.asp

Summary: To provide financial assistance to college students who are active bowlers

Eligibility: This program is open to currently enrolled college students who compete in the sport of bowling. Applicants must submit a 500-word essay describing how the scholarship will positively affect their bowling, academic, and personal goals. They must have a GPA of 2.5 or higher. Financial need is not considered in the selection process.

Financial data: The stipend is $1,000.

Duration: One year

Number awarded: One each year

Deadline: May of each year

148 BOBBY SOX HIGH SCHOOL SENIOR SCHOLARSHIP PROGRAM

Bobby Sox Softball
Attn: Scholarship
P.O. Box 5880
Buena Park, CA 90622-5880
Phone: (714) 522-1234; Fax: (714) 522-6548
Web: www.bobbysoxsoftball.org/scholar.html

Summary: To provide financial assistance for college to high school seniors who have participated in Bobby Sox Softball

Eligibility: This program is open to females graduating from high school with a GPA of 2.0 or higher. Applicants must have participated in Bobby Sox Softball for at least five seasons. They must submit an essay on "The Value of Participation in Bobby Sox Softball." Selection is based on the essay (60 points); academic excellence (20 points); and three letters of recommendation regarding participation in Bobby Sox Softball, participation in other extracurricular activities, and academic accomplishments (20 points).

Financial data: Stipends range from $100 to $2,500.

Duration: One year

Number awarded: Varies each year; recently, 44 of these scholarships were awarded.

Deadline: April of each year

149 BOOKJAMMIN' SCHOLARSHIPS

Cardinal Basketball Officials Association
Attn: CBOA Scholarship Fund
6425 Nice Place
Alexandria, VA 22310
Phone: (703) 402 1487; Email: cboascholarship@att.net
Web: www.cboa.org/bookjamm.asp

Summary: To provide financial assistance for college to seniors at designated high schools in Maryland, Virginia, and Washington, D.C., who have participated in basketball

Eligibility: This program is open to college-bound seniors at 55 designated high schools in Maryland, Virginia, and Washington, D.C., who have participated in interscholastic basketball as a player, cheerleader, manager, or trainer at the varsity level. Applicants must have a GPA of 3.0 or higher and be able to demonstrate leadership and sportsmanship through participation in extracurricular activities, community service, and/or work experience. They must submit an essay on the impact their participation in basketball has had on their educational and career plans.

Financial data: The stipend is $2,000.

Duration: One year

Number awarded: Varies each year; recently, five of these scholarships were awarded.

Deadline: February of each year

150 BUDDY PELLETIER SURFING FOUNDATION SCHOLARSHIP

Buddy Pelletier Surfing Foundation Fund
5121 Chalk Street
Morehead City, NC 28557
Phone: (252) 727-7917; Fax: (252) 727-7965;
Email: buddy@pelletier.com

Web: www.buddy.pelletier.com

Summary: To provide financial assistance for college to high school senior or college surfers

Eligibility: Applicants must be a surfer, a high school senior or currently enrolled in college, and able to demonstrate both merit and financial need. Official transcripts, two letters of recommendation, and a short statement (250 to 500 words) on future goals are required.

Financial data: The stipend is $1,000.

Duration: One year

Number awarded: Varies each year; recently, four of these scholarships were awarded.

Deadline: April of each year

151 BURKE FUND TURFGRASS MANAGEMENT STUDY SCHOLARSHIP

Summary: To provide financial assistance to residents of Rhode Island who have worked at a golf course and are interested in studying turf grass and agronomy in college

See Listing #13.

152 BYRON NELSON SCHOLARSHIP

Southern Texas PGA Section
Attn: Foundation
21604 Cypresswood Drive
Spring, TX 77373
Phone: (832) 442-2404; Fax: (832) 442-2403;
Email: stexas@pgahq.com
Web: www.stpga.com/index.cfm?menu=2706

Summary: To provide financial assistance for college to residents of southern Texas who have an interest in golf

Eligibility: This program is open to residents of the Southern Texas PGA Section who are enrolled or planning to enroll in college as a full-time student. Applicants must have a GPA of 2.5 or higher and be able to demonstrate financial need. They must have shown an interest in the game of golf, although golfing ability is not considered in the selection process and applicants are not required to be junior golfers. For graduating high school seniors, selection is based on academic record, ACT and/or SAT scores, extracurricular activities, voluntary statements, financial need, and junior golf participation and interest. For current college students, selection is based on cumulative college GPA, financial need, voluntary statements, college extracurricular activities, and golf participation and interest.

Financial data: Stipends range from $1,000 to $3,000.

Duration: One year; recipients may reapply.

Number awarded: Varies each year
Deadline: April of each year

---

153 CALIFORNIA ATHLETIC TRAINERS ASSOCIATION SCHOLARSHIP

Far West Athletic Trainers' Association
c/o Jason Bennett, Scholarship Chair
Chapman University
1 University Drive
Orange, CA 92866
Phone: (714) 997-6567; Email: jbennett@chapman.edu
Web: www.fwata.org/com_scholarships.html
Summary: To provide financial assistance to members of the National Athletic Trainers Association (NATA) who are attending a community college in its District 8
Eligibility: This program is open to students enrolled at a community college in California, Guam, Hawaii, or Nevada who are preparing for a career as an athletic trainer. Applicants must be student members of NATA and a District 8 member of NATA planning to continue academic work to the baccalaureate level as a full-time undergraduate. They must have a GPA of 3.0 or higher and a record of distinction in their athletic training program, academic major, institution, intercollegiate athletics, and higher education. Along with their application, they must submit a statement on their athletic training background, experience, philosophy, and goals. Financial need is not considered in the selection process.
Financial data: The stipend is $1,000.
Duration: One year
Number awarded: One each year
Deadline: February of each year

---

154 CALIFORNIA MARINE SCIENCES SCHOLARSHIP

Central California Council of Diving Clubs
c/o James L. Kaller, Scholarship Director
155 Montgomery Street, Suite 1004
San Francisco, CA 94104
Phone: (415) 362-9134, ext. 12; Fax: (415) 434-1880;
Email: jameskaller@batnet.com
Web: www.cencal.org/scholarship.html
Summary: To provide financial assistance to college students in California engaged in the study of underwater habitats
Eligibility: Eligible to apply are California residents who are enrolled full-time in a California academic institute, are at least 18 years of age, are a certified diver holding current national certification, and have at least a 3.0 GPA. Applicants must be engaged in the study of underwater habitats. Aquatic-related programs in the disciplines of biology, physical sciences, marine education, maritime archaeology, historical and social aspects of marine resources, and the science of diving are considered relevant for this program. Selection is based on college grades, letters of recommendation, honors earned, and professional goals. Financial need is not considered in the selection process.
Financial data: The stipend is $1,000.
Duration: One year
Number awarded: One each year
Deadline: April of each year

---

155 CCCAM SCHOLARSHIPS

Competitive Cheer Coaches Association of Michigan
c/o Tricia Williams, Scholarship Director
47111 Burton Drive
Shelby Township, MI 48317
Web: www.cccam.org/scholarship/index.htm
Summary: To provide financial assistance for college to high school cheerleaders in Michigan who have participated in events sponsored by the Competitive Cheer Coaches Association of Michigan (CCCAM)
Eligibility: This program is open to seniors graduating from high schools in Michigan with a GPA of 3.5 or higher. Applicants must be a member of a Michigan High School Athletic Association (MHSAA) competitive cheer team and have participated in the annual scholarship invitational sponsored by the CCCAM. Their coach must be a CCCAM member. Along with their application, they must submit a short essay on how competitive cheer has affected their life. Financial need is not considered in the selection process.
Financial data: Stipends are $1,000 or $500.
Duration: One year
Number awarded: Fifteen each year: five at $1,000 and ten at $500
Deadline: February of each year

---

156 CHALLENGE SPORTS SOCCER TOURNAMENTS COLLEGE SCHOLARSHIPS

Challenge Sports
Attn: Scholarship
2440 Michigan Street
Melbourne, FL 32904
Phone: (321) 676-1373; Fax: (321) 951-7475;
Email: soccer@challengesports.com
Web: www.challengesports.com/Scholarships/ScholarshipInfo.htm
Summary: To provide financial assistance for college to high school seniors in Florida who have participated in a Challenge Soccer Tournament

Eligibility: This program is open to seniors graduating from high schools in Florida who have participated in a Challenge Soccer Tournament as a player, referee, or volunteer. Applicants must be planning to attend an accredited two- or four-year college or university. Along with their application, they must submit a short essay describing one or more experiences during their Challenge Tournament participation that pertain to sportsmanship and fairness. They must demonstrate a high level of co-operation, sportsmanship, and fairness in athletic competition, academics, and other aspects of their lives.

Financial data: The stipend is around $500.

Duration: One year

Number awarded: Two each year

Deadline: April of each year

157 CHARLES PEREZ JR. WRESTLING SCHOLARSHIPS

Charles Perez, Jr. Wrestling Scholarship Fund
c/o Richard R. Famluaro
24 Winchester Drive
Howell, NJ 07731

Summary: To provide financial assistance for college to high school seniors in central New Jersey who have been on their wrestling team

Eligibility: This program is open to seniors graduating from high schools in Hunterdon, Mercer Middlesex, Monmouth, Ocean, and Somerset counties in New Jersey. Applicants must have participated in their school wresting program and have the endorsement of their varsity wrestling coach. They must be planning to attend a vocational school or a two- or four-year college or university. Along with their application, they must submit two essays on 1) the special qualities or characteristics they think wrestling has instilled in them and 2) their fondest memory that embodies and defines what the sport of wrestling is all about.

Financial data: The stipend is $500.

Duration: One year

Number awarded: Three each year

Deadline: October of each year

158 CHARLIE BURKHART SCHOLARSHIP

Iowa Section PGA of America
1930 Saint Andrews N.E.
Cedar Rapids, IA 52402
Phone: 888-213-8265; Fax: (319) 378-9203
Web: www.iowapga.com/scholarship.html

Summary: To provide financial assistance for college to high school seniors from Iowa and western Illinois who have an affiliation with golf

Eligibility: This program is open to seniors graduating from high schools in Iowa and those portions of western Illinois that are part of the Iowa Section PGA (including the cities of Monmouth, Macomb, Galesburg, Moline, Rock Island, Kewanee, and Galena but not the cities of Freeport, Springfield, or Quincy). Applicants must be the child of a member of a club or course that employs a member of the Professional Golfers Association (PGA) or registered apprentice of the Iowa section. Along with their application, they must submit a statement on their interest in golf, other activities and awards, their educational and vocational plans, and their financial need. They must be planning to attend a college or university as a full-time student. Selection is based primarily on interest and activity in golf and the potential for future contributions, then on academic ability and financial need.

Financial data: The stipend is $1,000 per year.

Duration: Four years

Number awarded: One each year

Deadline: June of each year

159 CHICK EVANS CADDIE SCHOLARSHIPS

Western Golf Association
Attn: Evans Scholars Foundation
1 Briar Road
Golf, IL 60029-0301
Phone: (847) 724-4600; Fax: (847) 724-7133;
Email: evansscholars@wgaesf.com
Web: www.evansscholarsfoundation.com

Summary: To provide financial assistance for college to students who have worked as golf caddies

Eligibility: Candidates for these scholarships must have completed their junior year in high school, rank in the upper quarter of their graduating class, have a GPA of 3.0 or higher, have taken the SAT or ACT test, be able to demonstrate financial need, and have been a full-time caddie on a regular basis for at least two years. Applicants from 12 states (Colorado, Illinois, Indiana, Michigan, Minnesota, Missouri, Ohio, Oregon, Pennsylvania, Virginia, Washington, and Wisconsin) must attend designated universities; applicants from other states must attend their state university, as approved by the scholarship committee. Selection is based on character, integrity, leadership, and financial need.

Financial data: The awards cover tuition and housing at universities approved by the scholarship committee.

Duration: One year; may be renewed for up to three additional years

Number awarded: Varies each year; recently, 820 caddies were receiving support from this program.

Deadline: September of each year

160 CHRISTOPHER LAWRENCE JUNKER MEMORIAL NEBRASKA SCHOLARSHIP

American Quarter Horse Foundation
Attn: Scholarship Coordinator
2601 I-40 East
Amarillo, TX 79104
Phone: (806) 378-5034; 888-209-8322;
Fax: (806) 376-1005; Email: lowens@aqha.org
Web: www.aqha.com/foundation/scholarships/index
.html
Summary: To provide financial assistance for college to members of the American Quarter Horse Association (AQHA) or the American Quarter Horse Youth Association (AQHYA) who are from Nebraska
Eligibility: Applicants must have been members of either organization for at least one year and be residents of Nebraska. They must be graduating high school seniors or already enrolled in college with a GPA of 2.5 or higher. Financial need is considered in the selection process.
Financial data: The stipend is $500.
Duration: One year
Number awarded: One each year
Deadline: January of each year

161 CHUCK BRENKUS SCHOLARSHIP

Southern California Section PGA
Attn: Foundation
36201 Champions Drive
Beaumont, CA 92223
Phone: (951) 845-4653; Fax: (951) 769-6733;
Email: ngatch@pgahq.com
Web: southerncal.pga.com
Summary: To provide financial assistance for college to high school seniors in southern California, especially those who have played golf
Eligibility: This program is open to seniors graduating from high schools in southern California. Applicants must be planning to enroll at an accredited two- or four-year college or university. They must be able to demonstrate academic achievement (rank in the top 30 percent of their class), participation in extracurricular activities, personal character, and leadership ability. Active participation in golf is not mandatory but is preferred.
Financial data: The stipend is $1,000.
Duration: One year
Number awarded: One each year
Deadline: May of each year

162 CHUCK HALL STAR OF TOMORROW AWARD

United States Bowling Congress
Attn: SMART Program

5301 S. 76th Street
Greendale, WI 53129-1192
Phone: (414) 423-3343; 800-514-BOWL, ext. 3343;
Fax: (414) 421-3014; Email: smart@bowl.com
Web: www.bowl.com/scholarships/main.aspx
Summary: To provide financial assistance for college to outstanding male bowlers
Eligibility: This program is open to male amateur bowlers who are current members in good standing of the United States Bowling Congress (USBC) or USBC Youth and competitors in events sanctioned by those organizations. Applicants must be high school or college students younger than 22 years of age, have a GPA of 2.5 or higher, and have a bowling average of 175 or greater. They may not have competed in a professional bowling tournament. Along with their application, they must submit an essay, up to 500 words, on how bowling has influenced their life, academic, and personal goals. Selection is based on bowling performances on local, state, and national levels; academic achievement; and community involvement.
Financial data: The stipend is $1,250 per year.
Duration: One year; may be renewed up to three additional years
Number awarded: One each year
Deadline: November of each year

163 CODY HAYES MEMORIAL GOLF SCHOLARSHIPS

Idaho Golf Association
Attn: Idaho Junior Golf Foundation
4696 Overland Road, Suite 120
P.O. Box 9958
Boise, ID 83707
Phone: (208) 385-7911; Fax: (208) 342-5959;
Email: foundation@idahogolfassn.org
Web: www.idahogolfassn.org
Summary: To provide financial assistance for college to high school seniors in Idaho who have been members of the Idaho Golf Association (IGA) Juniors
Eligibility: This program is open to residents of Idaho who are entering their freshman year of college. Applicants must be or have been a member in good standing of IGA Juniors. They must list the highlights of their high school golf record, the highlights of their amateur record, any contributions that they feel they have made in the area of golf, and any jobs they have held in the field of golf or related areas. They must also submit an essay of approximately 500 words on their most memorable golf experience, what they have gained by playing golf, someone they look up to and why, or

their ambitions and goals. Financial need may also be considered.

Financial data: The stipend is $500.

Duration: One year

Number awarded: Varies each year; recently, ten of these scholarships were awarded.

Deadline: May of each year

---

164 COLUMBIA 300 JOHN JOWDY SCHOLARSHIP

Columbia 300, Inc.
5005 West Avenue
P.O. Box 13430
San Antonio, TX 78213
Phone: (210) 344-9211; 800-531-5920
Web: www.columbia300.com

Summary: To provide financial assistance for college to high school bowlers

Eligibility: Eligible are graduating high school seniors actively involved in the sport of bowling. Selection is based on GPA, academic honors, and bowling background.

Financial data: The stipend is $500 per year.

Duration: One year; will be renewed up to three additional years if the recipient maintains a GPA of 3.0 or higher

Number awarded: One each year

Deadline: March of each year

---

165 CONNECTICUT JUNIOR SOCCER ASSOCIATION SCHOLARSHIPS

Connecticut Junior Soccer Association
Attn: Scholarship Committee
11 Executive Drive
Farmington, CT 06032
Phone: (860) 676-1161; Fax: (860) 676-1162;
Email: cjsacup@bysa.org
Web: www.cjsa.net

Summary: To provide financial assistance for college to high school seniors in Connecticut who have been involved in soccer

Eligibility: This program is open to seniors graduating from high schools in Connecticut who have played soccer with a club affiliated with the Connecticut Junior Soccer Association. Applicants must have a C+ average or higher and plan to attend a school of higher education. Along with their application, they must submit a 250-word essay on "What Soccer Means to Me."

Financial data: The stipend is $1,000.

Duration: One year

Number awarded: Four each year

Deadline: March of each year

---

166 CPHA FOUNDATION SCHOLARSHIPS

California Professional Horsemen's Association
Attn: CPHA Foundation
10153½ Riverside Drive, Suite 391
Toluca Lake, CA 91602
Phone: (818) 955-9500; Fax: (818) 558-5772
Web: www.cpha.org/Foundation/index.htm

Summary: To provide financial assistance for college to members of the California Professional Horsemen's Association (CPHA) and their families

Eligibility: This program is open to CPHA equestrian working students and the children of CPHA professional members (including, but not limited to, trainers, assistant trainers, foremen, grooms, farriers, and other show professionals). Applicants must be attending or planning to attend a college or university. Along with their application, they must submit an essay on why they are seeking financial assistance to attend college and documentation of financial need.

Financial data: The stipend is $2,000.

Duration: One year

Number awarded: One or more each year

Deadline: March of each year

---

167 CROOKED STICK SCHOLARSHIP FUND

Central Indiana Community Foundation
Attn: Scholarship Program
615 N. Alabama Street, Suite 119
Indianapolis, IN 46204-1498
Phone: (317) 634-2423, ext. 139; Fax: (317) 684-0943;
Email: zebbiec@cicf.org
Web: www.cicf.org/page26450.cfm

Summary: To provide financial assistance for college to high school seniors in central Indiana who have been involved in golf

Eligibility: This program is open to seniors graduating from high schools in central Indiana who plan to attend college. Applicants must be able to demonstrate academic achievement, financial need, interest and involvement in golf, and a strong work ethic and dedication. Preference is given to current and former employees of Crooked Stick Golf Club, but all students are encouraged to apply.

Financial data: A stipend is awarded (amount not specified).

Duration: One year

Number awarded: Varies each year; recently, two of these scholarships were awarded.

Deadline: June of each year

168 CURT GREENE MEMORIAL SCHOLARSHIP

Harness Horse Youth Foundation
Attn: Executive Director
16575 Carey Road
Westfield, IN 46074
Phone: (317) 867-5877; Fax: (317) 867-5896;
Email: ellen@hhyf.org
Web: www.hhyf.org/scholarships.html

Summary: To provide financial assistance to undergraduate students in any major who have an interest in harness-horse racing

Eligibility: This program is open to students who are at least high school seniors and preferably younger than 25 years of age. Applicants may be pursuing any course of study, but they must have "a passion for harness racing." Along with their application, they must submit an essay of 1,000–2,000 words on the facet of the harness racing industry in which they plan to participate and how their innate skills and college education will be beneficial. Selection is based on academic achievement, completeness of the application, quality of the essay, and financial need.

Financial data: A stipend is awarded (amount not specified).

Duration: One year

Number awarded: One or more each year

Deadline: April of each year

169 DAVID C. GOODWIN MEMORIAL SCHOLARSHIP

American Legion
Attn: Department of New Jersey
Attn: State Baseball Chairman
135 W. Hanover Street
Trenton, NJ 08618
Phone: (609) 695-5418; Fax: (609) 394-1532;
Email: newjersey@legion.org
Web: www.nj.legion.org

Summary: To provide financial assistance for college to outstanding participants in the New Jersey American Legion Baseball Program

Eligibility: High school juniors who participate in the New Jersey American Legion Baseball Program are eligible to apply for this scholarship. The American Legion Baseball Committee of the Department of New Jersey selects the recipients.

Financial data: Stipends are $1,000 or $500 per year.

Duration: Four years

Number awarded: Two each year: one at $1,000 per year and one at $500 per year

Deadline: August of each year

170 DEAN WEESE SCHOLARSHIP

University Interscholastic League
Attn: Texas Interscholastic League Foundation
1701 Manor Road
P.O. Box 8028
Austin, TX 78713-8028
Phone: (512) 232-4937; Fax: (512) 471-5908;
Email: bbaxendale@mail.utexas.edu
Web: www.uil.utexas.edu/tilf/scholarships.html

Summary: To provide financial assistance to students who participate in programs of the Texas Interscholastic League Foundation (TILF) and have competed in girls' high school varsity basketball

Eligibility: This program is open to students who have competed in girls' high school varsity basketball and meet the five basic requirements of the TILF: 1) graduate from high school during the current year and begin college or university in Texas by the following fall; 2) enroll full-time and maintain a GPA of 2.5 or higher during the first semester; 3) compete in a University Interscholastic League (UIL) academic state meet contest in accounting, calculator applications, computer applications, computer science, current issues and events, debate (cross-examination and Lincoln-Douglas), journalism (editorial writing, feature writing, headline writing, and news writing), literary criticism, mathematics, number sense, one-act play, ready writing, science, social studies, speech (prose interpretation, poetry interpretation, informative speaking, and persuasive speaking), or spelling and vocabulary; 4) submit high school transcripts that include SAT and/or ACT scores; and 5) submit parents' latest income tax returns.

Financial data: The stipend is $1,000 per year.

Duration: One year, nonrenewable

Number awarded: One each year

Deadline: May of each year

171 DELAWARE OPEN CROSS-COUNTRY CHAMPIONSHIP SCHOLARSHIPS

Delaware Higher Education Commission
Carvel State Office Building
820 N. French Street
Wilmington, DE 19801
Phone: (302) 577-3240; 800-292-7935;
Fax: (302) 577-6765; Email: dhec@doe.k12.de.us
Web: www.doe.state.de.us/high-ed/crosscountry.htm

Summary: To provide financial assistance for college to high school seniors in Delaware who participate in cross-country racing

Eligibility: This program is open to seniors who are Delaware residents at high schools in the state that are members of the New Castle County Cross-Country and Track Coaches Association (N5CTA) and have participated in cross-country programs during their junior and senior years. Each member may nominate one male and one female student. Nominees must have a cumulative GPA of 2.5 or higher and be planning to enroll full-time in a two- or four-year program of study at an accredited college or university. Preference is given to students selected as All-State, All-County, and/or All-Catholic. Selection is based on financial need (50 percent), GPA (25 percent), SAT scores (15 percent), and leadership or community activities (10 percent).

Financial data: The stipend is $1,000 per year.

Duration: One year, nonrenewable

Number awarded: Two each year: one for a female and one for a male

Deadline: October of each year

172 DELAWARE STATE GOLF ASSOCIATION SCHOLARSHIPS

Delaware State Golf Association
Attn: DSGA Scholarship Fund, Inc.
7234 Lancaster Pike, Suite 302-B
Hockessin, DE 19707
Phone: (302) 234-3365; Fax: (302) 234-3359;
Email: dsga@usga.org
Web: www.dsga.org/juniors/scholarships.php

Summary: To provide financial assistance for college to residents of Delaware who have been active in golf

Eligibility: This program is open to high school seniors and current college students in Delaware who have been active in golf. Applicants must submit an essay on why they desire this scholarship (including career plans), two letters of reference, transcripts, information on financial need, a list of golf accomplishments, and a list of extracurricular activities.

Financial data: Stipends range from $1,000 to $4,000 per year for four years or $1,000 for one year.

Duration: One year or four years

Number awarded: Varies each year. Recently, the association awarded six four-year scholarships (one at $4,000, one at $2,500, two at $2,000, and two at $1,000) and four one-year scholarships (each at $1,000).

Deadline: March of each year

173 DELMARVA PAINT HORSE CLUB SCHOLARSHIP

Delmarva Paint Horse Club
c/o Jane Griesa
400 Almshouse Road
Wyoming, DE 19934

Web: www.dphconline.com/schol.htm

Summary: To provide financial assistance for college to students who are members of the Delmarva Paint Horse Club (DPHC)

Eligibility: This program is open to high school seniors and college students in the Delmarva region who are members of the DPHC and active in the promotion of paint horses. They may major in any subject in college. Along with their application, they must submit a brief essay on their most memorable experiences with paint horses. Selection is based on merit and financial need.

Financial data: The stipend is $500. Funds are paid directly to the recipient's school.

Duration: One year; may be renewed for three additional years

Number awarded: One or more each year

Deadline: March of each year

174 DELMARVA PENINSULA GOLF ASSOCIATION SCHOLARSHIP

Delmarva Peninsula Golf Association, Inc.
c/o Jack Slayton, Secretary Treasurer
7772 Broad Leaf Drive
Parsonburg, MD 21849
Phone: (410) 749-6685
Web: home.comcast.net/~dpga-golf/scholarships.htm

Summary: To provide financial assistance for college to residents of the Delmarva region who are active golfers

Eligibility: This program is open to residents of the Delmarva Peninsula region of Delaware, Maryland, and Virginia who are graduating high school seniors or current college students. Preference is given to applicants who can demonstrate financial need; are active golfers; and are majoring in, or planning to major in, a field related to golf (e.g., agronomy, agriculture). Applicants must submit two letters of recommendation, including one from a Delmarva Peninsula Golf Association golf professional, representative, or junior golf committee chair.

Financial data: The stipend is $2,000 per year.

Duration: One year; may be renewed, provided the recipient maintains a GPA of 2.0 or higher

Number awarded: Varies each year; recently, ten of these scholarships were awarded.

Deadline: June of each year

175 DIAMONDS AND DREAMS SCHOLARSHIP PROGRAM

Minnesota Twins
Attn: Community Fund
34 Kirby Puckett Place

Minneapolis, MN 55415

Phone: (612) 375-1366; 800-33-TWINS;

Fax: (612) 375-7480

Web: http://minnesota.twins.mlb.com/min/ community/diamonds_dreams.jsp

Summary: To provide financial assistance for college to high school seniors in upper Midwestern states and southwestern Florida who have played baseball or softball

Eligibility: This program is open to seniors graduating from high schools in Minnesota, Iowa, North Dakota, South Dakota, Wisconsin, or southwestern Florida with a GPA of 2.0 or higher. Applicants must have participated, as a player or volunteer, with an organized youth baseball or softball organization. They must be planning to enroll full-time at an accredited two- or four-year college, university, or vocational/technical school. Selection is based on involvement in baseball or softball, participation in community service and/or volunteer work, leadership awards and honors, academic record, and financial need.

Financial data: The stipend is $1,000.

Duration: One year, nonrenewable

Number awarded: Up to 19 each year

Deadline: February of each year

---

176 DINAH SHORE SCHOLARSHIP

Ladies Professional Golf Association

Attn: LPGA Foundation

100 International Golf Drive

Daytona Beach, FL 32124-1092

Phone: (386) 274-6200; Fax: (386) 274-1099;

Email: foundation.scholarships@lpga.com

Web: www.lpga.com/content_1.aspx?mid=6& pid=55

Summary: To provide financial assistance for college to female graduating high school seniors who played golf in high school

Eligibility: This program is open to female high school seniors who have a GPA of 3.2 or higher. Applicants must have played in at least 50 percent of their high school golf team's scheduled events or have played golf "regularly" for the past two years. They must be planning to attend a college or university in the continental United States but not planning to play collegiate golf. Along with their application, they must submit a letter that describes how golf has been an integral part of their lives and includes their personal and professional goals, chosen discipline of study, and how this scholarship will be of assistance. Financial need is not considered in the selection process.

Financial data: The stipend is $3,000.

Duration: One year

Number awarded: One each year

Deadline: June of each year

---

177 DIXIE BOYS BASEBALL SCHOLARSHIPS

Dixie Boys Baseball, Inc.

P.O. Box 1778

Marshall, TX 75671

Phone: (903) 927-1845; Fax: (903) 927-1846;

Email: boys@dixie.org

Web: www.dixie.org

Summary: To provide financial assistance for college to high school senior males who have participated in a Dixie Boys or Dixie Majors franchised baseball program

Eligibility: This program is open to high school senior males who played baseball in a Dixie Boys (for boys 13 and 14 years of age) or Dixie Majors (for boys from 15 through 18 years of age) franchised program. Applicants must submit a 150-word essay on their career objectives, how college relates to those, and how they expect to contribute to society. While the applicants must have participated in the baseball program, ability is not a factor. Selection is based on high school grades and testing, school and community leadership, and financial need.

Financial data: The stipend is $1,500.

Duration: One year

Number awarded: One each year

Deadline: March of each year

---

178 DIXIE YOUTH BASEBALL SCHOLARSHIPS

Dixie Youth Baseball, Inc.

Attn: Scholarship Committee

P.O. Box 877

Marshall, TX 75671-0877

Phone: (903) 927-2255; Fax: (903) 927-1846;

Email: dyb@dixie.org

Web: www.dixie.org

Summary: To provide financial assistance for college to high school senior males who have participated in a Dixie Youth Baseball franchised league

Eligibility: This program is open to high school senior males who played in a Dixie Youth Baseball franchised league when they were 12 years of age or younger. Applicants must submit a transcript of grades, letter of recommendation from a high school principal or other school official, verification from a Dixie Youth local official of participation in a franchised league, and documentation of financial need. Ability as an athlete is not considered in the selection process.

Financial data: The stipend is $2,000.

Duration: One year

Number awarded: Varies each year; recently, 50 of these scholarships were awarded.

Deadline: February of each year

---

179 DON THOMPSON MEMORIAL SCHOLARSHIP

Arabian Horse Foundation
1024 K Street
Lincoln, NE 68508
Phone: (402) 477-2233; Fax: (402) 477-2286
Web: www.arabianhorsefoundation.org/scholarship
.html

Summary: To provide financial assistance to undergraduate and graduate students who have a record of equine involvement

Eligibility: This program is open to students who have a record of involvement with horses. Applicants must be enrolled or planning to enroll as a full-time undergraduate or graduate student at an accredited college or university. Preference is given to students who have a GPA between 2.8 and 3.25, whose financial resources are modest, and who are attending a school with relatively low tuition. Along with their application, they must submit information on their financial need, honors or academic awards, extracurricular activities and offices, leadership role, career goal, and equine involvement for the past two years.

Financial data: A stipend is awarded (amount not specified).

Duration: One year; may be renewed if the recipient maintains a GPA of 2.5 or higher with no grade below a D

Number awarded: One or more each year

Deadline: January of each year

---

180 DOROTHY CAMPBELL MEMORIAL SCHOLARSHIP

Oregon Student Assistance Commission
Attn: Grants and Scholarships Division
1500 Valley River Drive, Suite 100
Eugene, OR 97401-2146
Phone: (541) 687-7395; 800-452-8807, ext. 7395;
Fax: (541) 687-7419; Email: awardinfo@mercury
.osac.state.or.us
Web: www.osac.state.or.us

Summary: To provide financial assistance for college to women in Oregon who are interested in golf

Eligibility: This program is open to residents of Oregon who are U.S. citizens or permanent residents. Applicants must be female high school seniors or graduates with a cumulative GPA of 2.75 or higher and a strong

continuing interest in golf. They must be or planning to become full-time students at an Oregon four-year college. Along with their application, they must submit a one-page essay on the contribution that golf has made to their development. Financial need must be demonstrated.

Financial data: The stipend is at least $1,500.

Duration: One year; may be renewed up to three additional years

Number awarded: Varies each year; recently, two of these scholarships were awarded.

Deadline: February of each year

---

181 DR. GERALD O'CONNOR MICHIGAN QUARTER HORSE YOUTH SCHOLARSHIP

American Quarter Horse Foundation
Attn: Scholarship Coordinator
2601 I-40 East
Amarillo, TX 79104
Phone: (806) 378-5034; 888-209-8322;
Fax: (806) 376-1005; Email: lowens@aqha.org
Web: www.aqha.com/foundation/scholarships/index
.html

Summary: To provide financial assistance for college to members of the American Quarter Horse Association (AQHA) or the American Quarter Horse Youth Association (AQHYA) who are from Michigan

Eligibility: Applicants must have been members of either organization for at least one year and be residents of Michigan. They must be graduating high school seniors or already enrolled in college with a GPA of 2.5 or higher. Financial need is considered in the selection process.

Financial data: The stipend is $500 per year.

Duration: Up to four years, provided the recipient maintains a GPA of 2.5 or higher and full-time enrollment

Number awarded: One every four years (next available in 2008)

Deadline: January of the year of the award

---

182 DR. IRVIN L. "CLICK" COWGER MEMORIAL BASEBALL SCHOLARSHIP

American Legion
Attn: Department of Kansas
1314 S.W. Topeka Boulevard
Topeka, KS 66612-1886
Phone: (785) 232-9315; Fax: (785) 232-1399
Web: www.ksamlegion.org/programs.htm

Summary: To provide financial assistance for college to outstanding American Legion baseball players in Kansas

Eligibility: This program is open to boys who have participated in the Kansas American Legion baseball program. Applicants must be high school seniors or college freshmen or sophomores who are attending or planning to attend an approved Kansas college, university, community college, or trade school. They must have an average or higher academic record.

Financial data: The stipend is $500.

Duration: One year

Number awarded: One each year

Deadline: July of each year

---

183 DWIGHT F. DAVIS MEMORIAL SCHOLARSHIPS

United States Tennis Association
Attn: USTA Tennis & Education Foundation
70 West Road Oak Lane
White Plains, NY 10604
Phone: (914) 696-7223; Email: eliezer@usta.com
Web: www.usta.com/communitytennis/fullstory.sps
?iNewsid=66422

Summary: To provide financial assistance for college to high school seniors who have participated in an organized community tennis program

Eligibility: This program is open to high school seniors who have excelled academically, demonstrated achievements in leadership, and participated extensively in an organized community tennis program. Applicants must be planning to enroll as a full-time undergraduate student at a four-year college or university. They must be able to demonstrate financial need. Along with their application, they must submit an essay about themselves and how their participation in a tennis program has impacted their lives.

Financial data: The stipend is $1,875 per year. Funds are paid directly to the recipient's college or university.

Duration: Four years

Number awarded: Two each year

Deadline: February of each year

---

184 DWIGHT MOSLEY SCHOLARSHIPS

United States Tennis Association
Attn: USTA Tennis & Education Foundation
70 West Road Oak Lane
White Plains, NY 10604
Phone: (914) 696-7223; Email: eliezer@usta.com
Web: www.usta.com/communitytennis/fullstory.sps
?iNewsid=66422

Summary: To provide financial assistance for college to high school seniors from diverse ethnic backgrounds who have participated in an organized community tennis program.

Eligibility: This program is open to high school seniors from diverse ethnic backgrounds who have excelled

academically, demonstrated achievements in leadership, and participated extensively in an organized community tennis program. Applicants must be planning to enroll as a full-time undergraduate student at a four-year college or university. They must have a GPA of 3.0 or higher and be able to demonstrate financial need and sportsmanship. Along with their application, they must submit an essay about themselves and how their participation in a tennis program has impacted their lives. Males and females are considered separately.

Financial data: The stipend is $2,500 per year. Funds are paid directly to the recipient's college or university.

Duration: Four years

Number awarded: Two each year: one male and one female

Deadline: February of each year

---

185 EARL ANTHONY MEMORIAL SCHOLARSHIPS

United States Bowling Congress
Attn: SMART Program
5301 S. 76th Street
Greendale, WI 53129-1192
Phone: (414) 423-3223; 800-514-BOWL, ext. 3223;
Fax: (414) 421-3014; Email: smart@bowl.com
Web: www.bowl.com/scholarships/main.aspx

Summary: To provide financial assistance for college to members of the United States Bowling Congress (USBC) Youth who demonstrate outstanding community service and financial need

Eligibility: This program is open to USBC Youth members who are seniors in high school or current college students. Applicants must have a GPA of 2.5 or higher and not have competed in a professional bowling tournament. Along with their application, they must submit an essay of 500 words on how their bowling, community service, and educational achievements have influenced their life and their goals for the future. Financial need is also considered in the selection process.

Financial data: The stipend is $5,000.

Duration: One year, nonrenewable

Number awarded: Five each year

Deadline: April of each year

---

186 EASTERN PENNSYLVANIA YOUTH SOCCER ASSOCIATION COLLEGE SCHOLARSHIPS

Eastern Pennsylvania Youth Soccer Association
Attn: Scholarship Committee
Two Village Road, Suite 3
Horsham, PA 19044
Phone: (215) 657-7727; Fax: (215) 657-7740;
Email: charmor@epysa.org

Web: www.epysa.org/scholarship.shtml

Summary: To provide financial assistance for college to high school seniors in eastern Pennsylvania who have been involved in soccer

Eligibility: This program is open to college-bound high school seniors who are registered players, coaches, or referees within the Eastern Pennsylvania Youth Soccer Association. Selection is based on academic ability, leadership, and character.

Financial data: The stipend is $1,000 per year.

Duration: One year; may be renewed up to three additional years if the recipient maintains satisfactory academic progress and remains involved in soccer (by volunteering, coaching, refereeing, or playing in a soccer program at college or a local community).

Number awarded: Four each year

Deadline: April of each year

187 EDUCATION OR NURSING SCHOLARSHIP

American Quarter Horse Foundation
Attn: Scholarship Coordinator
2601 I-40 East
Amarillo, TX 79104
Phone: (806) 378-5034; 888-209-8322;
Fax: (806) 376-1005; Email: lowens@aqha.org
Web: www.aqha.com/foundation/scholarships/index
.html

Summary: To provide financial assistance for college to members of the American Quarter Horse Association (AQHA) or the American Quarter Horse Youth Association (AQHYA) who are planning a career in education or nursing

Eligibility: Applicants must have been members of either organization for at least one year and be graduating high school seniors or already enrolled in college. They must have a GPA of 2.5 or higher and be planning to work on a degree in education or nursing. Financial need is considered in the selection process.

Financial data: The maximum stipend is $2,500 per year.

Duration: Up to four years, provided the recipient maintains a GPA of 2.5 or higher and full-time enrollment

Number awarded: One each year

Deadline: January of each year

188 EL RICHARDS SPIRIT SCHOLARSHIPS

New Mexico Activities Association
Attn: Rudy Aragon
6600 Palomas N.E.
Albuquerque, NM 87109
Phone: (505) 923-3270; 888-820-NMAA;
Fax: (505) 923-3114; Email: raragon@nmact.org

Web: www.nmact.org

Summary: To provide financial assistance for college to high school seniors in New Mexico who have participated in cheerleading

Eligibility: This program is open to seniors graduating from high schools in New Mexico with a GPA of 3.0 or higher. Applicants must have been active as a cheer/dance/drill member and in at least one other interscholastic activity. They must be planning to attend a college or university. Along with their application, they must submit a personal statement on how being active in cheer, dance, or drill has helped them during their high school career. Financial need is not considered in the selection process.

Financial data: The stipend is $500.

Duration: One year

Number awarded: Two each year

Deadline: January of each year

189 EQUINE SCHOLARSHIPS

State Fair of West Virginia
P.O. Drawer 986
Lewisburg, WV 24901
Phone: (304) 645-1090; Fax: (304) 645-6660;
Email: wvstatefair@wvstatefair.com
Web: www.wvstatefair.com/sf/scholarships.htm

Summary: To provide financial assistance for college to previous entrants in the West Virginia state fair's open horse show

Eligibility: This program is open to graduating high school seniors or currently enrolled college students who have competed in a previous West Virginia state fair open horse show. Applicants must submit a recommendation from their principal or guidance counselor, a character reference from their community, and a high school transcript. Selection is based on academic achievement, character, leadership, and community service.

Financial data: Stipends average approximately $1,300.

Duration: One year

Number awarded: Varies each year; recently, three of these scholarships were awarded.

Deadline: May of each year

190 EVE KRAFT EDUCATION AND COLLEGE SCHOLARSHIPS

United States Tennis Association
Attn: USTA Tennis & Education Foundation
70 West Road Oak Lane
White Plains, NY 10604
Phone: (914) 696-7223; Email: eliezer@usta.com

Web: www.usta.com/communitytennis/fullstory.sps?iNewsid=66422

Summary: To provide financial assistance for college to high school seniors who have participated in an organized community tennis program

Eligibility: This program is open to high school seniors who have excelled academically, demonstrated achievements in leadership, and participated extensively in an organized community tennis program. Applicants must be planning to enroll as a full-time undergraduate student at a four-year college or university. They must be able to demonstrate financial need. Along with their application, they must submit an essay about themselves and how their participation in a tennis program has impacted their lives. Males and females are considered separately.

Financial data: The stipend is $2,500. Funds are paid directly to the recipient's college or university.

Duration: One year, nonrenewable

Number awarded: Two each year: one male and one female

Deadline: February of each year

---

191 EXCELLENCE IN EQUINE/AGRICULTURAL INVOLVEMENT SCHOLARSHIP

American Quarter Horse Foundation
Attn: Scholarship Coordinator
2601 I-40 East
Amarillo, TX 79104
Phone: (806) 378-5034; 888-209-8322;
Fax: (806) 376-1005; Email: lowens@aqha.org
Web: www.aqha.com/foundation/scholarships/index.html

Summary: To provide financial assistance for college to members of the American Quarter Horse Association (AQHA) or the American Quarter Horse Youth Association (AQHYA) who have been involved in equine or agricultural activities

Eligibility: Applicants must have been members of either organization for at least one year and be graduating high school seniors or already enrolled in college. They must have a GPA of 3.5 or higher and a record of leadership and excellence acquired through participation in equine and/or agriculture activities. Financial need is considered in the selection process.

Financial data: The maximum stipend is $6,250 per year.

Duration: Up to four years, provided the recipient maintains a GPA of 3.5 or higher and full-time enrollment

Number awarded: One each year

Deadline: January of each year

---

192 FAR WEST ATHLETIC TRAINERS' ASSOCIATION UNDERGRADUATE SCHOLARSHIPS

Far West Athletic Trainers' Association
c/o Jason Bennett, Scholarship Chair
Chapman University
1 University Drive
Orange, CA 92866
Phone: (714) 997-6567; Email: jbennett@chapman.edu
Web: www.fwata.org/com_scholarships.html

Summary: To provide financial assistance to members of the National Athletic Trainers Association (NATA) who are working on a bachelor's degree in its District 8

Eligibility: This program is open to students enrolled as undergraduates at colleges and universities in California, Guam, Hawaii, or Nevada who are preparing for a career as an athletic trainer. Applicants must be student members of NATA and a District 8 member of NATA working full-time on a bachelor's degree in athletic training. They must have a GPA of 3.0 or higher and a record of distinction in their athletic training program, academic major, institution, intercollegiate athletics, and higher education. Along with their application, they must submit a statement on their athletic training background, experience, philosophy, and goals. Financial need is not considered in the selection process.

Financial data: The stipend is $1,000.

Duration: One year

Number awarded: Four each year

Deadline: February of each year

---

193 FARM AND RANCH HERITAGE SCHOLARSHIPS

American Quarter Horse Foundation
Attn: Scholarship Coordinator
2601 I-40 East
Amarillo, TX 79104
Phone: (806) 378-5034; 888-209-8322;
Fax: (806) 376-1005; Email: lowens@aqha.org
Web: www.aqha.com/foundation/scholarships/index.html

Summary: To provide financial assistance for college to members of the American Quarter Horse Association (AQHA) or the American Quarter Horse Youth Association (AQHYA) who come from a farming and/or ranching background

Eligibility: Applicants must have been members of either organization for at least one year and be graduating high school seniors or already enrolled in college. They must have a GPA of 3.0 or higher and come from a farming and/or ranching background. Financial need is considered in the selection process.

Financial data: The maximum stipend is $3,125 per year.

Duration: Up to four years, provided the recipient maintains a GPA of 3.0 or higher and full-time enrollment

Number awarded: Varies each year; recently, four of these scholarships were awarded.

Deadline: January of each year

---

194 FLORIDA LEGION SHOOTING SPORTS SCHOLARSHIPS

American Legion
Attn: Department of Florida
1912 Lee Road
P.O. Box 547859
Orlando, FL 32854-7859
Phone: (407) 295-2631; Fax: (407) 299-0901;
Email: fal@fllegion.newsouth.net
Web: www.floridalegion.org/programs/scholarships/schol.html

Summary: To recognize and reward, with college scholarships, winners of the American Legion shooting sports competition in Florida

Eligibility: This competition is open to Florida residents between 14 and 20 years of age who are enrolled in a junior or senior high school or who graduated in the current year. Applicants must participate in the precision air rifle, sporter air rifle, or sporter air rifle team events. Shooters and teams must be active members of a Junior Shooting Club sponsored by a Florida American Legion post.

Financial data: Florida winners receive $500 scholarships.

Duration: The competition is held annually.

Number awarded: One scholarship is presented to the winner of the precision category, the winner of the sporter category, and each member of the winning sporter team.

Deadline: December of each year

---

195 FRANCES WALSH SPIRIT SCHOLARSHIPS

New Mexico Activities Association
Attn: Rudy Aragon
6600 Palomas N.E.
Albuquerque, NM 87109
Phone: (505) 923-3270; 888-820-NMAA;
Fax: (505) 923-3114; Email: raragon@nmact.org
Web: www.nmact.org

Summary: To provide financial assistance for college to high school seniors in New Mexico who have participated in cheerleading

Eligibility: This program is open to seniors graduating from high schools in New Mexico with a GPA of 3.0 or higher. Applicants must have been active as a cheer/dance/drill member and at least one other interscholastic activity. They must be planning to attend a college or university. Along with their application, they must submit a personal statement on how being active in cheer, dance, or drill has helped them during their high school career. Financial need is not considered in the selection process.

Financial data: The stipend is $500.

Duration: One year

Number awarded: Two each year

Deadline: January of each year

---

196 FRANCIS "GUNNER" HAYES SCHOLARSHIP

Anthracite Golf Association
617 Keystone Avenue
Peckville, PA 18452
Phone: (570) 383-GOLF; Fax: (570) 383-4654;
Email: palloyd127@cs.com
Web: www.anthracitegolf.org/junior-golf/scholarships/index.asp

Summary: To provide financial assistance for college to high school seniors from northeastern Pennsylvania who have been involved in golf

Eligibility: This program is open to seniors graduating from high schools in northeastern Pennsylvania who have been involved in golf. Applicants must have been accepted by a postsecondary institution. They are not required to be affiliated with a golf club. Along with their application, they must submit a personal statement about their career goals. Selection is based on that statement, academic achievement, leadership and service, golf accomplishments, participation in the Anthracite Golf Association junior tour, and two letters of recommendation.

Financial data: Stipends range from $500 to $3,000. Half the funds are paid at the beginning of the first semester and half at the beginning the second semester, provided recipients earn a GPA of 2.5 or higher for the first semester.

Duration: One year

Number awarded: Varies each year

Deadline: February of each year

---

197 FRANCIS OUIMET SCHOLARSHIPS

Francis Ouimet Scholarship Fund
c/o William F. Connell Golf House and Museum
300 Arnold Palmer Boulevard
Norton, MA 02766
Phone: (774) 430-9090; Fax: (774) 430-9091;
Email: marionm@ouimet.org
Web: www.ouimet.org

Summary: To provide financial assistance for college to young people in Massachusetts who have worked at a golf course

Eligibility: This program is open to students entering or attending college or technical school in Massachusetts. They must have worked for at least two years at a public, private, semiprivate, resort, or municipal golf club in Massachusetts as caddies, helpers in pro shop operations (including bag room, range, cart storage, and starter's area), or course superintendent operations. Ineligible students include those who have worked at a golf course but in a position not in direct service to golf (e.g., workers in the dining room, office, kitchen, banquet area) and those who have worked in a job related to golf but not actually at a golf course (e.g., driving range, off-course golf stores, miniature golf course). Selection is based on academic achievement and potential, leadership (including school and community activities), interviews, essays, motivation, character, integrity, service to golf, and recommendations. In addition, awards may be either need based or "honorary" with need not considered.

Financial data: Stipends range from $1,500 to $7,500 per year.

Duration: One year; may be renewed for three additional years

Number awarded: Approximately 350 each year

Deadline: November of each year

---

198 FRANK EMMET SCHOLARSHIP

Washington Metropolitan Golf Association
P.O. Box 3189
Gaithersburg, MD 20885
Phone: (301) 869-6020; Email: wmgagolf@earthlink.net
Web: www.wmgagolf.org

Summary: To provide financial assistance for college to high school seniors who have participated in the junior golf program of the Washington Metropolitan Golf Association (WMGA)

Eligibility: This program is open to seniors graduating from high schools in the WMGA service area. Applicants must be planning to attend a college or university. Along with their application, they must submit a letter specifically identifying their interest in receiving a scholarship and why they believe they are a worthy applicant; official transcripts; and letters of recommendation from a teacher or administrator, someone who can attest to their character, and someone who is aware of their participation in the WMGA junior golf program.

Financial data: A stipend is awarded (amount not specified).

Duration: One year; may be renewed
Number awarded: One or more each year
Deadline: July of each year

---

199 FRANK L. BAXTER SCHOLARSHIP

Dixie Softball, Inc.
Attn: President
1101 Skelton Drive
Birmingham, AL 35224
Phone: (205) 785-2255; Fax: (205) 785-2258;
Email: softball@dixie.org
Web: www.dixie.org

Summary: To provide financial assistance for college to high school senior women who have participated in the Dixie Softball program

Eligibility: This program is open to high school senior women who played in the Dixie Softball program for at least two seasons. Applicants must submit a transcript of grades, a letter of recommendation from a high school principal or other school official, verification from a Dixie Softball local official of the number of years the applicant participated in the program, and documentation of financial need. Ability as an athlete is not considered in the selection process.

Financial data: The stipend is $1,500.
Duration: One year
Number awarded: One each year
Deadline: February of each year

---

200 GABE HRAB/CANYON LAKE SCHOLARSHIPS

Southern California Section PGA
Attn: Foundation
36201 Champions Drive
Beaumont, CA 92223
Phone: (951) 845-4653; Fax: (951) 769-6733;
Email: ngatch@pgahq.com
Web: http://southerncal.pga.com

Summary: To provide financial assistance for college to high school seniors in southern California, especially those who have played golf

Eligibility: This program is open to seniors graduating from high schools in southern California. Applicants must be planning to enroll at an accredited two- or four-year college or university. They must be able to demonstrate academic achievement, participation in extracurricular activities, personal character, and leadership ability. Active participation in golf is not mandatory but is preferred. Preference is given to residents of the Canyon Lake area.

Financial data: The stipend is $1,000.
Duration: One year

Number awarded: Two each year
Deadline: May of each year

201 GATORADE LEADERSHIP AWARDS

American Legion Baseball
700 N. Pennsylvania Street
Indianapolis, IN 46204
Phone: (317) 630-1249; Fax: (317) 630-1223;
Email: acy@legion.org
Web: www.baseball.legion.org/awards.htm
Summary: To recognize and reward, with college scholarships, participants in the American Legion baseball program who demonstrate outstanding leadership
Eligibility: This program is open to participants in the American Legion baseball regional tournaments and the American Legion World Series. Candidates must be high school seniors or graduates who will be entering college as a freshman in the fall; students still in high school are not eligible. Selection is based on integrity, mental attitude, cooperation, citizenship, sportsmanship, scholastic aptitude, and general good conduct.
Financial data: The outstanding participants in the regional tournaments receive $1,000 scholarships; the outstanding participant in the American Legion World Series receives an additional $2,000 scholarship.
Duration: The awards are presented annually.
Number awarded: Eight winners in regional tournaments receive $1,000 scholarships; one of those receives an additional scholarship as the George W. Rulon American Legion Player of the Year.

202 GEORGE HANNON SCHOLARSHIP

Southern Texas PGA Section
Attn: Foundation
21604 Cypresswood Drive
Spring, TX 77373
Phone: (832) 442-2404; Fax: (832) 442-2403;
Email: stexas@pgahq.com
Web: www.stpga.com/index.cfm?menu=2706
Summary: To provide financial assistance for college to residents of southern Texas who have an interest in golf
Eligibility: This program is open to residents of the Southern Texas PGA Section who are enrolled or planning to enroll in college as a full-time student. Applicants must have a GPA of 2.5 or higher and be able to demonstrate financial need. They must have shown an interest in the game of golf, although golfing ability is not considered in the selection process and applicants are not required to be junior golfers. For graduating

high school seniors, selection is based on academic record, ACT and/or SAT scores, extracurricular activities, voluntary statements, financial need, and junior golf participation and interest. For current college students, selection is based on cumulative college GPA, financial need, voluntary statements, college extracurricular activities, and golf participation and interest.
Financial data: Stipends range from $1,000 to $3,000.
Duration: One year; recipients may reapply.
Number awarded: Varies each year
Deadline: April of each year

203 GEORGE "SLATS" O'BRIEN SCHOLARSHIPS

Western Athletic Scholarship Association
Attn: Scholarship Coordinator
13730 Loumont Street
Whittier, CA 90601
Summary: To provide financial assistance for college to outstanding volleyball players
Eligibility: This program is open to graduating high school seniors who have played an active role in amateur volleyball. Applicants must be planning to attend an accredited two- or four-year college or university. They need not have played on a high school team and are not required to play volleyball in college. Selection is based on academic achievement, community service, participation in volleyball, and financial need.
Financial data: The stipend is $2,000 per year.
Duration: One year; may be renewed
Number awarded: Up to ten each year
Deadline: February of each year

204 GEORGIA WRESTLING COACHES ASSOCIATION SCHOLARSHIPS

Georgia Wrestling Coaches Association
c/o Cliff Ramos
1119 Mt. Water Lane
Lawrenceville, GA 30043
Web: www.georgiawrestling.net
Summary: To provide financial assistance for college to high school seniors in Georgia who have been involved in wrestling
Eligibility: This program is open to college-bound seniors graduating from high schools in Georgia. Applicants must submit essays on what wrestling has meant to them and how they plan to stay involved in wrestling. Selection is based on the essays, GPA, wrestling accomplishments, and community involvement.
Financial data: The stipend is $500.
Duration: One year
Number awarded: Two each year

205 GIFT FOR LIFE SCHOLARSHIPS

United States Bowling Congress
Attn: SMART Program
5301 S. 76th Street
Greendale, WI 53129-1192
Phone: (414) 423-3343; 800-514-BOWL, ext. 3343;
Fax: (414) 421-3014; Email: smart@bowl.com
Web: www.bowl.com/scholarships/main.aspx
Summary: To provide financial assistance for college to members of the United States Bowling Congress (USBC) who demonstrate a financial hardship
Eligibility: This program is open to USBC members who are high school students (grades 9–12) and who have not yet competed in a professional bowling tournament. Applicants must be able to demonstrate a financial hardship, defined as residing in a household where the number of children, the income level of their parents, and possible extenuating circumstances make obtaining a college education financially unlikely. They must submit an essay, up to 500 words, explaining how their financial situation could hinder or stop them from achieving their educational goals. Other factors considered in the selection process include GPA (2.0 or higher required), scholastic honors, extracurricular activities, and bowling activities. Applications from males and females are evaluated separately. In honor of the heroes of September 11, 2001, two scholarships are reserved for an eligible son and daughter of fire/police/emergency rescue personnel.
Financial data: The stipend is $1,000.
Duration: Scholarships are presented annually. Students may apply each year they are eligible and may win one scholarship each year before their high school graduation.
Number awarded: Twelve each year: six for females and six for males. That includes two awards reserved for children (one female and one male) of fire/police/ emergency rescue department employees.
Deadline: March of each year

206 GOLF ASSOCIATION OF MICHIGAN SCHOLARSHIPS

Golf Association of Michigan
Attn: Junior Golf
24116 Research Drive
Farmington Hills, MI 48335
Phone: (248) 478-9242; Fax: (248) 478-5536
Web: www.gam.org/
Summary: To provide financial assistance to high school seniors in Michigan who have participated in golf activities

Eligibility: This program is open to seniors graduating from high schools in Michigan with a GPA of 3.0 or higher. Applicants must have played in a junior tournament sponsored by the Golf Association of Michigan. They must be planning to attend college in the fall following high school graduation. Along with their application, they must submit an essay on why they deserve the award. Females and males are considered separately.
Financial data: The stipend is $2,000.
Duration: One year
Number awarded: Two each year: one female and one male
Deadline: July of each year

207 GRAHAM BAKER MORIN MEMORIAL SCHOLARSHIP

Scholarship America
Attn: Washington State Wrestling Coaches Association Scholarship
One Scholarship Way
P.O. Box 297
St. Peter, MN 56082
Phone: (507) 931-1682; 800-537-4180;
Fax: (507) 931-9168
Web: www.washingtonwrestling.com/scholarship
Summary: To provide financial assistance for college to high school seniors in Washington who have participated in the state high school wrestling tournament
Eligibility: This program is open to seniors graduating from high schools in Washington with a GPA of 3.0 or higher. Applicants must have participated in the state high school wrestling tournament. They must plan to enroll and wrestle in college. Along with their application, they must submit a two-page essay on their leadership, scholastic, and sportsmanship qualities. Selection is based on that essay, academic record, demonstrated leadership and sportsmanship in school and in wrestling, participation in school and community activities, honors, wrestling experiences, and an outside appraisal.
Financial data: The stipend is $3,000.
Duration: One year
Number awarded: One each year
Deadline: March of each year

208 HANK BARGER SCHOLARSHIP

Southern California Section PGA
Attn: Foundation
36201 Champions Drive
Beaumont, CA 92223
Phone: (951) 845-4653; Fax: (951) 769-6733;
Email: ngatch@pgahq.com

Web: http://southerncal.pga.com

Summary: To provide financial assistance for college to high school seniors in southern California, especially those who have played golf

Eligibility: This program is open to seniors graduating from high schools in southern California. Applicants must be planning to enroll at an accredited two- or four-year college or university. They must be able to demonstrate academic achievement (rank in the top 30 percent of their class), participation in extracurricular activities, personal character, and leadership ability. Active participation in golf is not mandatory but preferred.

Financial data: The stipend is $1,000.

Duration: One year

Number awarded: One each year

Deadline: May of each year

209 HARDY LOUDERMILK SCHOLARSHIP

Southern Texas PGA Section
Attn: Foundation
21604 Cypresswood Drive
Spring, TX 77373
Phone: (832) 442-2404; Fax: (832) 442-2403;
Email: stexas@pgahq.com
Web: www.stpga.com/index.cfm?menu=2706

Summary: To provide financial assistance for college to residents of southern Texas who have an interest in golf

Eligibility: This program is open to residents of the Southern Texas PGA Section who are enrolled or planning to enroll in college as a full-time student. Applicants must have a GPA of 2.5 or higher and be able to demonstrate financial need. They must have shown an interest in the game of golf, although golfing ability is not considered in the selection process and applicants are not required to be junior golfers. For graduating high school seniors, selection is based on academic record, ACT and/or SAT scores, extracurricular activities, voluntary statements, financial need, and junior golf participation and interest. For current college students, selection is based on cumulative college GPA, financial need, voluntary statements, college extracurricular activities, and golf participation and interest.

Financial data: Stipends range from $1,000 to $3,000.

Duration: One year; recipients may reapply.

Number awarded: Varies each year

Deadline: April of each year

210 HARNESS TRACKS OF AMERICA SCHOLARSHIP PROGRAM

Harness Tracks of America
Attn: Sable Downs

4640 E. Sunrise Drive, Suite 200
Tucson, AZ 85718
Phone: (520) 529-2525; Fax: (520) 529-3235;
Email: info@harnesstracks.com
Web: www.harnesstracks.com/scholarships.htm

Summary: To provide financial assistance for college or graduate school to people engaged in the harness racing industry and their children

Eligibility: This program is open to children of licensed drivers, trainers, caretakers, or harness racing management and young people actively engaged in the harness racing industry themselves. Applicants must submit essays on their present and future educational goals, the extent to which they and/or other members of their family are involved in the harness racing industry, and why they believe they are deserving of scholarship support. Selection is based on academic merit, financial need, and active harness racing involvement.

Financial data: The stipend is $10,000 or $7,500 per year.

Duration: One year

Number awarded: Six each year: two at $10,000 and four at $7,500

Deadline: June of each year

211 HARTFORD WHALERS BOOSTER CLUB SCHOLARSHIPS

Hartford Whalers Booster Club
Attn: President
P.O. Box 273
Hartford, CT 06141
Phone: (860) 925-1548; Fax: (860) 926-1196;
Email: hartfordwhalersboosterclub@hotmail.com
Web: www.whalerwatch.com/hartford_whalers_booster_club_sc.htm

Summary: To provide financial assistance to high school seniors from Connecticut who are interested in playing hockey in college

Eligibility: This program is open to Connecticut residents who are graduating high school seniors. Applicants must be interested in attending a four-year college or university with a hockey program. Selection is based on academic achievement, financial need, and hockey ability.

Financial data: A stipend up to $1,000 per year is provided.

Duration: One year

Number awarded: One each year

Deadline: April of each year

212 HENRY E. WILLIAMS JR. MEMORIAL GOLF AWARD

Berks County Community Foundation
501 Washington Street, Suite 801
P.O. Box 212
Reading, PA 19603-0212
Phone: (610) 685-BCCF; Fax: (610) 685-2240;
Email: info@bccf.org
Web: www.bccf.org/scholarships/index.html
Summary: To provide financial assistance for college to high school seniors in Berks County, Pennsylvania, who have played golf
Eligibility: This program is open to seniors graduating from high schools in Berks County, Pennsylvania. Applicants must have participated on their high school golf team. The golf coach of each school nominates one team member's name annually.
Financial data: The stipend is $1,000.
Duration: One year
Number awarded: One each year
Deadline: March of each year

213 HERMAN SANI SCHOLARSHIP

Iowa Golf Association
Attn: Scholarship Selection Committee
8515 Douglas Avenue, Suite 25
Urbandale, IA 50322
Phone: 888-388-4442; Fax: (515) 331-3636
Web: www.iowagolf.org
Summary: To provide financial assistance for college to high school seniors in Iowa who have been active in golf
Eligibility: This program is open to college-bound seniors graduating from high schools in Iowa. Applicants must submit a narrative description of their school experience, including golf, sports, other extracurricular activities, academics, and awards; a statement summarizing their work experience, financial need, and college and career plans; at least two letters of recommendation; and an official school transcript.
Financial data: The stipend is $2,000 per year.
Duration: Four years, provided the recipient is making reasonable academic progress
Number awarded: Varies each year; recently, three of these scholarships were awarded.
Deadline: June of each year

214 HORSE RACING SCHOLARSHIPS

American Quarter Horse Foundation
Attn: Scholarship Coordinator
2601 I-40 East
Amarillo, TX 79104

Phone: (806) 378-5034; 888-209-8322;
Fax: (806) 376-1005; Email: lowens@aqha.org
Web: www.aqha.com/foundation/scholarships/index .html
Summary: To provide financial assistance for college or graduate school to members of the American Quarter Horse Association (AQHA) or the American Quarter Horse Youth Association (AQHYA) who are planning a career in the horse racing industry
Eligibility: This program is open to members of either organization who are graduating high school seniors, already enrolled in college, or working on a graduate degree. Applicants must have a GPA of 2.5 or higher and be planning to prepare for a career in the racing industry or a related field. Financial need is considered in the selection process.
Financial data: The maximum stipend is $2,000 per year.
Duration: Up to four years, provided the recipient maintains a GPA of 2.5 or higher and full-time enrollment
Number awarded: Varies each year; recently, five of these scholarships were awarded.
Deadline: January of each year

215 HORSE SHOW FOUNDATION 4-H SCHOLARSHIP

Ohio 4-H
c/o Ohio State University
Agriculture Administration Building
2120 Fyffe Road, Room 25
Columbus, OH 43210-1084
Phone: (614) 292-4444; Fax: (614) 292-5937;
Email: 4hweb@ag.osu.edu
Web: www.ohio4h.org/youth/awards/index.html
Summary: To provide financial assistance for college to high school seniors in Ohio who have been involved in 4-H horse activities
Eligibility: This program is open to seniors graduating from high schools in Ohio who are 4-H members. Applicants must have been involved in 4-H horse activities. They may be planning to major in any field at any college or university. Along with their application, they must submit a two-page essay on how 4-H contributed to their personal development, leadership skills, and/or career plans. Selection is based on that essay (5 percent), potential for success (10 percent), 4-H leadership activities (40 percent), major 4-H honors (20 percent), 4-H community service and citizenship (15 percent), and financial need (10 percent).
Financial data: The stipend is $1,500.
Duration: One year
Number awarded: One each year
Deadline: January of each year

216 HOWARD TAYLOR AMPUTEE-PRO CLASSIC SCHOLARSHIP

Eastern Amputee Golf Association
Attn: Bob Buck, Executive Director
2015 Amherst Drive
Bethlehem, PA 18015-5606
Phone: 888-868-0992; Fax: (610) 867-9295;
Email: info@eaga.org
Web: www.eaga.org

Summary: To provide financial assistance for college to members of the Eastern Amputee Golf Association (EAGA) and their families

Eligibility: This program is open to students who are residents of and/or currently enrolled or accepted for enrollment at a college or university in designated Eastern states (Connecticut, Delaware, District of Columbia, Maine, Maryland, Massachusetts, New Hampshire, New Jersey, New York, Pennsylvania, Rhode Island, Vermont, Virginia, or West Virginia). Applicants must be amputee members of the association (those who have experienced the loss of one or more extremities at a major joint due to amputation or birth defect) or members of their families. Financial need is considered in the selection process.

Financial data: The stipend is $1,000.

Duration: One year; may be renewed if the recipient maintains a GPA of 2.0 or higher and continues to demonstrate financial need

Number awarded: One or more each year

Deadline: June of each year

217 ILIO DEPAOLO SCHOLARSHIP FUND

Summary: To provide financial assistance for college to high school seniors in western New York who have been involved in athletics, especially wrestling
See Listing #52.

218 ILLINOIS LEGION BASEBALL SCHOLARSHIPS

American Legion
Attn: Department of Illinois
2720 E. Lincoln Street
P.O. Box 2910
Bloomington, IL 61702-2910
Phone: (309) 663-0361; Fax: (309) 663-5783;
Email: hdqs@illegion.org
Web: www.illegion.org/scholarship.html

Summary: To provide financial assistance for college to Illinois residents who participate in American Legion baseball

Eligibility: This program is open to residents of Illinois who have played on a baseball team that is sponsored or affiliated with an American Legion post. Applicants must have graduated from high school or be a college

freshman; students still in high school are not eligible. They must be planning to attend college in the fall. Selection is based on leadership, scholarship, character, citizenship, and financial need.

Financial data: The stipend is $1,000.

Duration: One year

Number awarded: Five each year, one in each division of the Illinois American Legion. The Illinois player of the year also receives a $1,000 scholarship from the national American Legion.

219 IMPROVE YOUR LIFE SCHOLARSHIPS

San Antonio Area Foundation
110 Broadway, Suite 230
San Antonio, TX 78205
Phone: (210) 225-2243; Fax: (210) 225-1980;
Email: info@saafdn.org
Web: www.saafdn.org

Summary: To provide financial assistance for college to high school seniors in Bexar County, Texas, who have played golf

Eligibility: This program is open to seniors graduating from high schools in Bexar County, Texas, in the upper 25 percent of their class. Applicants must have played golf regularly at a local municipal golf course as a teenager. They must submit a letter of recommendation from their high school golf coach, although they are not required to be on the team. Selection is based on moral character, interest in golf, and financial need.

Financial data: The stipend is $2,500 per year.

Duration: One year; may be renewed

Number awarded: Varies each year; recently, five of these scholarships were awarded.

Deadline: October of each year

220 INDIANA GOLF FOUNDATION SCHOLARSHIP

Indiana Golf Association
Attn: Foundation
2625 Hurricane Road
P.O. Box 516
Franklin, IN 46131
Phone: (317) 738-9696, ext. 240; 800-779-7271;
Fax: (317) 738-9436; Email: bhill@indianagolf.org
Web: igf.indianagolf.org

Summary: To provide financial assistance for college to high school seniors in Indiana who have participated in the Indiana Junior Golf Tour

Eligibility: This program is open to seniors graduating from high schools in Indiana with a GPA of 3.0 or higher. Applicants must be nominated by their high school golf coach or PGA of America professional and have participated in the Indiana Junior Golf Tour. They must be planning to enroll full-time at an accredited two- or four-year college or university in the United States. Selection is based on high school GPA, class rank, SAT/ACT score, extracurricular activities, letters of recommendation, and financial need.

Financial data: A stipend is awarded (amount not specified).

Duration: One year, nonrenewable

Number awarded: One or more each year

Deadline: April of each year

---

221 INDIANA QUARTER HORSE YOUTH SCHOLARSHIP

American Quarter Horse Foundation
Attn: Scholarship Coordinator
2601 I-40 East
Amarillo, TX 79104
Phone: (806) 378-5034; 888-209-8322;
Fax: (806) 376-1005; Email: lowens@aqha.org
Web: www.aqha.com/foundation/scholarships/index
.html

Summary: To provide financial assistance for college to members of the American Quarter Horse Association (AQHA) or the American Quarter Horse Youth Association (AQHYA) who are from Indiana

Eligibility: Applicants must have been members of either organization for at least one year, have been members of the Indiana Quarter Horse Association for at least two years, and be residents of Indiana. They must be graduating high school seniors or already enrolled in college with a GPA of 2.5 or higher. Financial need is considered in the selection process.

Financial data: The stipend is $1,000.

Duration: One year

Number awarded: One each year

Deadline: January of each year

---

222 INTERNATIONAL ARABIAN BREEDERS SWEEPSTAKES SCHOLARSHIPS

Arabian Horse Association
Attn: Sweepstakes Scholarships
10805 E. Bethany Drive
Aurora, CO 80014
Phone: (303) 696-4500; Fax: (303) 696-4599
Web: www.arabianhorses.org/education/education_
scholarships_foundation.asp

Summary: To provide financial assistance for college to high school seniors who are members of the Arabian Horse Association (AHA)

Eligibility: This program is open to AHA members who are graduating from high school and planning to attend an accredited college or university as a full-time student. Applicants must have competed at the regional or national level on a sweepstakes-nominated horse. Along with their application, they must submit their most recent high school transcript, a list of sweepstakes horses and the regional or national competitions where they have shown, a description of their extracurricular activities and leadership roles, a list of any honors or academic distinctions they have received, a description of their specific equine involvement over the past two years, and a brief essay on their future career goals. Selection is based on merit.

Financial data: The stipend is $2,500.

Duration: One year

Number awarded: Forty each year

Deadline: June of each year

---

223 IOWA CHEERLEADING COACHES' ASSOCIATION SCHOLARSHIPS

Iowa Cheerleading Coaches' Association
c/o JoEllen Wesselmann
2466 Trailridge Road
Adel, IA 50003
Phone: (515) 834-1345;
Email: jwesselmann@email.adel.k12.ia.us
Web: www.iowacheercoaches.org

Summary: To provide financial assistance for college to cheerleaders in Iowa whose coach is a member of the Iowa Cheerleading Coaches' Association (ICCA)

Eligibility: This program is open to seniors graduating from high schools in Iowa and to students enrolled at colleges in the state. Applicants must be cheerleaders whose coach is an ICCA member. High school seniors must have a GPA of 3.5 or higher; college students must have a GPA of 3.0 or higher. Along with their application, they must submit a one-page essay on what they have gained from cheerleading and how it will help them in the future. Selection is based on that essay; two letters of recommendation; grades; and high school, community, and religious activities. Financial need is not considered.

Financial data: The stipend is $500.

Duration: One year, nonrenewable

Number awarded: Seven each year: six to high school seniors and one to a college student

Deadline: January of each year

---

224 IOWA LEGION FOUNDATION OUTSTANDING SENIOR BASEBALL PLAYER SCHOLARSHIP

American Legion
Attn: Department of Iowa
720 Lyon Street
Des Moines, IA 50309-5481
Phone: (515) 282-5068; Fax: (515) 282-7583;

Email: programs@ialegion.org

Web: www.ialegion.org/baseball.htm

Summary: To provide financial assistance for college to outstanding participants in the Iowa American Legion Senior Baseball Tournament

Eligibility: Males who participate in the Iowa American Legion Senior Baseball Tournament are eligible to receive this scholarship. The State Baseball Committee selects the recipient on the basis of outstanding sportsmanship, team play, athletic ability, and proven academic achievements.

Financial data: The award is $1,500.

Duration: One year

Number awarded: One each year

---

225 ISIA EDUCATION FOUNDATION SCHOLARSHIP

Ice Skating Institute of America

Attn: ISIA Education Foundation

17120 N. Dallas Parkway, Suite 140

Dallas, TX 75248-1187

Phone: (972) 735-8800; Fax: (972) 735-8815;

Email: kchasc@skatcisi.com

Web: www.skateisi.com

Summary: To provide financial assistance to high school seniors and currently enrolled undergraduates who are members of the Ice Skating Institute of America (ISI)

Eligibility: Applicants may be graduating high school seniors or currently enrolled college students. They must have completed at least three years of high school with a GPA of 3.0 or higher, have been an individual member of ISI for at least four years, have participated in ISI group classes or ISI endorsed competitions within the last two years, and have completed 240 hours of verified service (of which 120 must be volunteered) with an ISI administrative member rink or skating school. Along with their application process, they must submit an official transcript, SAT/ACT scores, two evaluation forms, and a statement (up to 500 words) on "Why I Should Receive an ISIA Education Foundation Scholarship." Selection is based on community service, awards and recognition, educational goals, and competitive ice-skating experience.

Financial data: The stipend is at least $4,000 per year.

Duration: One year

Number awarded: Varies each year; recently, four of these scholarships were awarded.

Deadline: February of each year

---

226 JACK AND MARCI MCMICKEN SCHOLARSHIP

Amarillo Area Foundation

Attn: Scholarship Coordinator

801 S. Fillmore Street, Suite 700

Amarillo, TX 79101

Phone: (806) 376-4521; Fax: (806) 373-3656;

Email: laquita@aaf-hf.org

Web: www.aaf-hf.org/scholarships/content/jack_mcmicken.htm

Summary: To provide financial assistance for college to high school seniors in northern Texas who have been involved in bowling

Eligibility: This program is open to seniors who are graduating from high schools in the 26 most northern counties of the Texas Panhandle: Dallam, Sherman, Hansford, Ochiltree, Lipscomb, Hartley, Moore, Hutchinson, Roberts, Hemphill, Oldham, Potter, Carson, Gray, Wheeler, Deaf Smith, Randall, Armstrong, Donley, Collingsworth, Parmer, Castro, Swisher, Briscoe, Hall, and Childress. Applicants must be a member or an immediate family member of the Amarillo Bowling Association, Amarillo Women's Bowling Association, or Amarillo Young American Bowling Alliance. They must have a GPA of 2.0 or higher. Selection is based on academic excellence, financial need, high school attendance, and a recommendation from their high school counselor.

Financial data: The stipend ranges from $750 to $1,000.

Duration: One year, nonrenewable

Number awarded: One or more each year

---

227 JACK BAUMAN SCHOLARSHIP

Eastern New York Youth Soccer Association

Attn: Scholarship Committee

53 Park Avenue, Suite 207

Rockville Centre, NY 11570

Phone: (516) 766-0849; Fax: (516) 678-7411;

888-5-ENYYSA; Email: enyoffice@enysoccer.com

Web: www.enysoccer.com/scholarships.htm

Summary: To provide financial assistance for college to female high school seniors in eastern New York who have been involved in soccer

Eligibility: This program is open to female seniors graduating from high schools in eastern New York with a C+ average or higher. Applicants must have played travel club soccer with a team affiliated with the Eastern New York Youth Soccer Association. They must be planning to attend a school of higher education and play college soccer. Along with their application, they must submit a personal resume, high school transcript, and 250-word essay on why they deserve the scholarship. A personal interview is required.

Financial data: The stipend is $1,000.

Duration: One year

Number awarded: One each year
Deadline: May of each year

---

228 JAIME HORN MEMORIAL SOFTBALL SCHOLARSHIP

Babe Ruth League, Inc.
1770 Brunswick Pike
P.O. Box 5000
Trenton, NJ 08638
Phone: (609) 695-1434; Fax: (609) 695-2505;
Email: info@baberuthleague.org
Web: www.baberuthleague.org/scholarship.html
Summary: To provide financial assistance for college to high school seniors who played Babe Ruth League softball
Eligibility: This program is open to graduating high school seniors who played Babe Ruth League softball previously. Applicants must be planning to attend college. Along with their application, they must submit a 100-word essay on how playing Babe Ruth softball has affected their life. Financial need is not considered in the selection process.
Financial data: The stipend is $1,000.
Duration: One year
Number awarded: One each year
Deadline: June of each year

---

229 JANE RING/SUE RING-JARVI GIRLS'/WOMEN'S HOCKEY SCHOLARSHIP

Saint Paul Foundation
Attn: Program Officer
600 Fifth Street Center
55 Fifth Street East
St. Paul, MN 55101-1797
Phone: (651) 325-4236; 800-875-6167; Fax: (651) 224-8123; Email: trh@saintpaulfoundation.org
Web: www.saintpaulfoundation.org/scholarships
Summary: To provide financial assistance for college to female high school seniors in Minnesota who have played hockey in high school
Eligibility: This program is open to female hockey players graduating from high school in Minnesota. Applicants must have a GPA of 3.0 or higher and be planning to attend an accredited four-year college or university. Along with their application, they must submit a two-page personal statement describing how hockey has affected their life, the contributions they have made to hockey in high school, and what role they expect hockey to play in their future. Selection is based on athletic and academic achievement, character, leadership ability, ambition to succeed, and evidence of present and future useful citizenship.

Financial data: The stipend is $2,000.
Duration: One year, nonrenewable
Number awarded: Two each year
Deadline: April of each year

---

230 JAY WOODWARD SCHOLARSHIPS

Cactus and Pine Golf Course Superintendents Association
Attn: Scholarship Committee
10685 N. 69th Street
Scottsdale, AZ 85254
Phone: (480) 609-6778; Fax: (480) 348-5976;
Email: carmella@cactusandpine.com
Web: www.cactusandpine.com
Summary: To provide financial assistance to undergraduate or graduate students from Arizona who have played golf in school and are preparing for a career in turf grass management
Eligibility: Applicants must have been residents of Arizona for at least one year and either be attending school or working at a golf course in the state. They must have completed the first year of a two-year, four-year, or certificate program in a field related to golf course management or be a graduate student planning a career as a golf course superintendent. Their GPA must be 3.0 or higher. Along with their application, they must submit 100-word essays on why they want to become a golf course superintendent, what they have done to prepare themselves to become a golf course superintendent, and what they expect from a career as a golf course superintendent. They must also identify any academic distinctions and honors they have received, school or college activities in which they have participated (e.g., athletics, clubs, school paper, fine arts), activities outside of school or college, employment experience, and the ways in which they have contributed toward their financial support or some else's support while in high school or college. Selection is based on academic excellence, career preparation, and potential to make an outstanding professional contribution.
Financial data: For students attending a school within Arizona, the stipend is $1,000 in a four-year degree program, $750 in a two-year degree program, or $500 in a certificate program. For students attending a school outside Arizona, the stipend is $750 in a four-year degree program or $500 in a two-year degree program.
Duration: One year
Number awarded: One or more each year
Deadline: June of each year

231 J.B. FERGUSON GOLF SCHOLARSHIP
Nebraska Elks Association
c/o Melvin Nespor, Scholarship Committee
P.O. Box 14
Endicott, NE 68350
Email: mnespor@beatricene.com
Summary: To provide financial assistance for college to high school seniors in Nebraska who have played golf
Eligibility: This program is open to seniors graduating from high schools in Nebraska. Applicants must have been members of their high school golf team and be planning to participate in a college golf program. Financial need is considered in the selection process. Each Nebraska Elks Lodge can submit one application.
Financial data: The stipend is $500.
Duration: One year
Number awarded: One each year
Deadline: January of each year

232 JEAN FITZGERALD SCHOLARSHIP
Hawai'i Community Foundation
Attn: Scholarship Department
1164 Bishop Street, Suite 800
Honolulu, HI 96813
Phone: (808) 566-5570; 888-731-3863; Fax: (808) 521-6286; Email: scholarships@hcf-hawaii.org
Web: www.hawaiicommunityfoundation.org/scholar/scholar.php
Summary: To provide financial assistance to women tennis players in Hawaii who are just beginning college
Eligibility: This program is open to female Hawaiian residents who have been active members of the Hawai'i Pacific Tennis Association for at least four years and are entering their freshman year in college as full-time students. They must be able to demonstrate academic achievement (GPA of 2.7 or higher), good moral character, and financial need. In addition to filling out the standard application form, applicants must write a short statement indicating their reasons for attending college, their planned course of study, and their career goals.
Financial data: The amounts of the awards depend on the availability of funds and the need of the recipient; recently, stipends averaged $2,000.
Duration: One year
Number awarded: Varies each year; recently, five of these scholarships were awarded.
Deadline: February of each year

233 JENNIFER ODOM SCHOLARSHIP
American Water Ski Educational Foundation
Attn: Director

1251 Holy Cow Road
Polk City, FL 33868-8200
Phone: (863) 324-2472; Fax: (863) 324-3996;
Email: info@waterskihalloffame.com
Web: www.waterskihalloffame.com
Summary: To provide financial assistance to currently enrolled college students who participate in water skiing
Eligibility: This program is open to full-time students at two- or four-year accredited colleges entering their sophomore, junior, or senior year. Applicants must be U.S. citizens and active members of a sport division within USA Water Ski (AWSA, ABC, AKA, WSDA, NSSA, NCWSA, NWSRA, USAWB, and HYD). Along with their application, they must submit a 500-word essay on a topic that changes annually but relates to water skiing; recently, students were asked to assume that they had just acquired the position of marketing director for the American Water Ski Educational Foundation and to describe the creative measures they would implement to increase membership in the foundation. Selection is based on the essay, academic record, leadership, extracurricular involvement, letters of recommendation, AWSA membership activities, and financial need.
Financial data: The stipend is $1,500 per year.
Duration: One year; may be renewed for up to two additional years
Number awarded: One each year
Deadline: March of each year

234 JOAN CAIN FLORIDA QUARTER HORSE YOUTH SCHOLARSHIP
American Quarter Horse Foundation
Attn: Scholarship Coordinator
2601 I-40 East
Amarillo, TX 79104
Phone: (806) 378-5034; 888-209-8322;
Fax: (806) 376-1005; Email: lowens@aqha.org
Web: www.aqha.com/foundation/scholarships/index.html
Summary: To provide financial assistance for college to members of the American Quarter Horse Association (AQHA) or the American Quarter Horse Youth Association (AQHYA) who are from Florida
Eligibility: Applicants must have been members of either organization for at least two years, have been members of the Florida Quarter Horse Youth Association for at least two years, and be residents of Florida. They must be graduating high school seniors or already enrolled in college with a GPA of 2.5 or higher. Financial need is considered in the selection process.

Financial data: The stipend is $1,000.
Duration: One year
Number awarded: One each year
Deadline: January of each year

---

235 JOE FINGER SCHOLARSHIPS

Southern Texas PGA Section
Attn: Foundation
21604 Cypresswood Drive
Spring, TX 77373
Phone: (832) 442-2404; Fax: (832) 442-2403;
Email: stexas@pgahq.com
Web: www.stpga.com/index.cfm?menu=2706
Summary: To provide financial assistance for college to residents of southern Texas who have an interest in golf
Eligibility: This program is open to residents of the Southern Texas PGA Section who are enrolled or planning to enroll in college as a full-time student. Applicants must have a GPA of 2.5 or higher and be able to demonstrate financial need. They must have shown an interest in the game of golf, although golfing ability is not considered in the selection process and applicants are not required to be junior golfers. For graduating high school seniors, selection is based on academic record, ACT and/or SAT scores, extracurricular activities, voluntary statements, financial need, and junior golf participation and interest. For current college students, selection is based on cumulative college GPA, financial need, voluntary statements, college extracurricular activities, and golf participation and interest.
Financial data: Stipends range from $1,000 to $3,000.
Duration: One year; recipients may reapply.
Number awarded: Varies each year
Deadline: April of each year

---

236 JOE MOORE SCHOLARSHIP

Southern Texas PGA Section
Attn: Foundation
21604 Cypresswood Drive
Spring, TX 77373
Phone: (832) 442-2404; Fax: (832) 442-2403;
Email: stexas@pgahq.com
Web: www.stpga.com/index.cfm?menu=2706
Summary: To provide financial assistance for college to residents of southern Texas who have an interest in golf
Eligibility: This program is open to residents of the Southern Texas PGA Section who are enrolled or planning to enroll in college as a full-time student. Applicants must have a GPA of 2.5 or higher and be able to demonstrate financial need. They must have shown an

interest in the game of golf, although golfing ability is not considered in the selection process and applicants are not required to be junior golfers. For graduating high school seniors, selection is based on academic record, ACT and/or SAT scores, extracurricular activities, voluntary statements, financial need, and junior golf participation and interest. For current college students, selection is based on cumulative college GPA, financial need, voluntary statements, college extracurricular activities, and golf participation and interest.
Financial data: Stipends range from $1,000 to $3,000.
Duration: One year; recipients may reapply.
Number awarded: Varies each year
Deadline: April of each year

---

237 JOHN P. BURKE MEMORIAL FUND SCHOLARSHIPS

Summary: To provide financial assistance for college to residents of Rhode Island who have worked at a golf course
See Listing #59.

---

238 JOHNNY REVOLTA MEMORIAL SCHOLARSHIP

Southern California Section PGA
Attn: Foundation
36201 Champions Drive
Beaumont, CA 92223
Phone: (951) 845-4653; Fax: (951) 769-6733;
Email: ngatch@pgahq.com
Web: southerncal.pga.com
Summary: To provide financial assistance for college to high school seniors in southern California, especially those who have played golf
Eligibility: This program is open to seniors graduating from high schools in southern California. Applicants must be planning to enroll at an accredited two- or four-year college or university. They must be able to demonstrate academic achievement, participation in extracurricular activities, personal character, and leadership ability. Active participation in golf is not mandatory but is preferred.
Financial data: The stipend is $1,000 per year.
Duration: Four years
Number awarded: One each year
Deadline: May of each year

---

239 JON OOSTERMEYER MEMORIAL SCHOLARSHIP

Arabian Horse Foundation
1024 K Street
Lincoln, NE 68508

Phone: (402) 477-2233; Fax: (402) 477-2286

Web: www.arabianhorsefoundation.org/scholarship.html

Summary: To provide financial assistance to undergraduate and graduate students who have a record of equine involvement

Eligibility: This program is open to students who have a record of involvement with horses. Applicants must be enrolled or planning to enroll as a full-time undergraduate or graduate student at an accredited college or university. High school seniors must have a GPA of B or higher; college students must have at least a 3.5 GPA. Along with their application, they must submit information on their financial need, honors or academic awards, extracurricular activities and offices, leadership roles, career goals, and equine involvement for the past two years.

Financial data: A stipend is awarded (amount not specified).

Duration: One year; may be renewed if the recipient maintains a GPA of 2.5 or higher with no grade below a D

Number awarded: One or more each year

Deadline: January of each year

240 JOURNALISM OR COMMUNICATIONS SCHOLARSHIP

American Quarter Horse Foundation

Attn: Scholarship Coordinator

2601 I-40 East

Amarillo, TX 79104

Phone: (806) 378-5034; 888-209-8322;

Fax: (806) 376-1005; Email: lowens@aqha.org

Web: www.aqha.com/foundation/scholarships/index.html

Summary: To provide financial assistance for college to members of the American Quarter Horse Association (AQHA) or the American Quarter Horse Youth Association (AQHYA) who are planning a career in journalism or communications

Eligibility: Applicants must have been members of either organization for at least one year and be graduating high school seniors or college freshmen. They must have a GPA of 2.5 or higher and be planning to work on a degree in journalism, communications, or a related field. Financial need is considered in the selection process.

Financial data: The maximum stipend is $2,000 per year.

Duration: Up to four years, provided the recipient maintains a GPA of 2.5 or higher and full-time enrollment

Number awarded: One each year

Deadline: January of each year

241 JULIA H. DODDS JUNIOR GIRL'S AWARD

Illinois Women's Golf Association

c/o Marlene Miller

351 Birkdale Road

Lake Bluff, IL 60044

Phone: (847) 234-2154; Email: mememiller@aol.com

Web: www.iwga.org

Summary: To provide financial assistance for college to women in Illinois who have participated in golf

Eligibility: This program is open to female high school seniors in Illinois who have played in the Illinois Women's Golf Association (IWGA) State Junior Tournament. Nominations may be submitted by anyone with knowledge of qualified students. Nominees must arrange for two letters of recommendation, one from their high school golf coach and one from a teacher or principal at their high school. Selection is based on character, scholarship, leadership, sportsmanship, and love for the game of golf.

Financial data: The stipend is $1,000. Funds are paid directly to the recipient's college.

Duration: One year

Number awarded: One each year

Deadline: April of each year

242 JUNIOR AIR RIFLE NATIONAL CHAMPIONSHIP SCHOLARSHIPS

American Legion

Attn: Americanism and Children & Youth Division

P.O. Box 1055

Indianapolis, IN 46206-1055

Phone: (317) 630-1249; Fax: (317) 630-1223;

Email: acy@legion.org

Web: www.legion.org

Summary: To provide college scholarships to the top competitors in the American Legion Junior Position Air Rifle Tournament

Eligibility: This program is open to students ages 14–20 who compete in air rifle tournaments sponsored by local posts of the American Legion. Based on posted scores in the precision and sporter categories, the top 30 competitors and state and regional champions compete in a qualification round and postal tournament. The top 15 shooters then participate in a shoulder-to-shoulder match in August at the Olympic Training Center, Colorado Springs, Colorado.

Financial data: The awards are $1,000 college scholarships.

Duration: The awards are presented annually.

Number awarded: Two each year: one in the precision category and one in the sporter category

243 JUNIOR PLAYER CLARENCE CAMP SCHOLARSHIPS

Florida State Golf Association
Attn: Future of Golf Foundation
8875 Hidden River Parkway, Suite 110
Tampa, FL 33637
Phone: (813) 632-3742; Fax: (813) 910-2129
Web: www.fsga.org/clubservices/scholarship_guidelines.asp

Summary: To provide financial assistance for college to members of the Florida State Golf Association (FSGA) and/or the Florida Junior Tour (FJT)

Eligibility: This program is open to U.S. citizens who have been residents of Florida for at least one year. Applicants must be a current FSGA and/or FJT member who has competed in at least three FSGA and/or FJT events in the past two years They must have a GPA of 3.0 or higher. Along with their application, they must submit a 300-word essay on why they should be selected for this scholarship and a resume of their golf activities. Selection is based on academic achievement and financial need.

Financial data: Stipends range from $500 to $2,000.

Duration: One year

Number awarded: Varies each year; the foundation awards at least $20,000 in scholarships each year.

Deadline: Applications may be submitted at any time.

244 KANSAS JUNIOR GOLF SCHOLARSHIPS

Kansas Golf Association
Attn: Kansas Golf Foundation
3301 Clinton Parkway Court, Suite 4
Lawrence, KS 66047
Phone: (785) 842-4833, ext. 205; Fax: (785) 842-3831;
Email: foundation@kansasgolf.org
Web: www.kansasgolf.org/kgf/scholarships.htm

Summary: To provide financial assistance for college to high school seniors in Kansas who have been active in playing golf

Eligibility: This program is open to seniors graduating from high schools in Kansas who are enrolling as a full-time student at an accredited four-year college or university in the state. Applicants must have participated in each of the two previous seasons in high school golf or junior golf programs sponsored by Kansas organizations. They must submit a two-page essay on why they deserve this scholarship, how they have benefited from the game of golf, and their five- and ten-year goals. Selection is based on the essay, academic record, leadership, letters of recommendation, financial need, and participation in golf (but not playing ability or performance).

Financial data: The stipend is $1,250.

Duration: One year

Number awarded: Five each year

Deadline: March of each year

245 KANSAS JUNIOR SHOOTING SPORTS SCHOLARSHIP

American Legion
Attn: Department of Kansas
1314 S.W. Topeka Boulevard
Topeka, KS 66612-1886
Phone: (785) 232-9315; Fax: (785) 232-1399
Web: www.ksamlegion.org/programs.htm

Summary: To provide financial assistance for college to students in Kansas who participate in American Legion-sponsored shooting sports programs

Eligibility: This program is open to students in Kansas who have participated in an American Legion-sponsored shooting sports program at the state and regional levels. Applicants may be high school juniors or seniors or college-level freshmen. They must be enrolled or planning to enroll at an approved Kansas college, university, junior college, or trade school. Along with their application, they must submit an essay of 125 to 250 words on "What Shooting Sports Means to Me" and an essay of 250 to 500 words on "Why I Want to Go to College." Financial need is not considered in the selection process.

Financial data: The stipend is $500.

Duration: One year

Number awarded: One each year

Deadline: February of each year

246 KEVIN E. REICHARDT FOUNDATION COLLEGE SCHOLARSHIPS

Kevin E. Reichardt Foundation, Inc.
Attn: Scholarship Committee
P.O. Box 6055
Annapolis, MD 21401
Phone: (410) 741-0381; 800-515-8752;
Fax: (410) 741-0383; Email: reichardtfdtn@aol.com
Web: www.reichardtlacrosse.org

Summary: To provide financial assistance for college to high school seniors who have played lacrosse

Eligibility: This program is open to seniors graduating from high school with a GPA of 3.3 or higher. Applicants must have played varsity lacrosse, have participated in at least one other varsity sport, and be planning to play college lacrosse. They must be able to demonstrate outstanding leadership qualities and character. Along with their application, they must submit transcripts, a letter of recommendation, an essay of 250 to 500 words on a significant experience or achievement that has special meaning to them, and documentation of financial need.

Financial data: The stipend is $4,000. Funds are paid directly to the recipient's college or university, half at the beginning of the fall semester and half at the beginning of the spring semester, provided the recipient achieves a GPA of 3.0 or higher for the fall semester.

Duration: One year, nonrenewable

Number awarded: One or two each year

Deadline: March of each year

247 LAURA WOODMAN MEMORIAL SCHOLARSHIP

Coastal Bend Community Foundation
Attn: Edie Hamilton
600 Leopard Street, Suite 1716
Corpus Christi, TX 78473
Phone: (361) 882-9745; Fax: (361) 882-2865;
Email: eh@cbcfoundation.org
Web: www.cbcfoundation.org/page27486.cfm

Summary: To provide financial assistance for college to members of the Texas Youth Rodeo Association

Eligibility: This program is open to high school seniors who are members of the Texas Youth Rodeo Association. Applicants must be planning to enroll full-time in a college or university in the continental United States.

Financial data: The stipend is $1,000.

Duration: One year; may be renewed if the recipient maintains a GPA of 2.5 or higher

Number awarded: One each year

248 LEGACY SOCCER/UNILEVER ENDOWED SCHOLARSHIPS

Legacy Soccer Foundation, Inc.
P.O. Box 3481
Winter Park, FL 32790
Phone: (407) 263-8285; Fax: (407) 898-1837
Web: www.legacysoc.org/scholarships.html

Summary: To provide financial assistance for college to high school seniors in central Florida who have played soccer

Eligibility: This program is open to residents of central Florida (Brevard, Orange, Osceola, Seminole, and Volusia counties) who are U.S. citizens, are high school seniors graduating in the top third of their class, have at least a 2.5 GPA, have played organized soccer for two out of the past five years, can demonstrate financial need, and plan to attend an institution of higher learning in central Florida (including Brevard Community College, Florida Tech, Seminole Community College,

Valencia Community College, or University of Central Florida).

Financial data: A stipend is paid (amount not specified).

Duration: One year

249 LETA ANDREWS SCHOLARSHIP

University Interscholastic League
Attn: Texas Interscholastic League Foundation
1701 Manor Road
P.O. Box 8028
Austin, TX 78713-8028
Phone: (512) 232-4937; Fax: (512) 471-5908;
Email: bbaxendale@mail.utexas.edu
Web: www.uil.utexas.edu/tilf/scholarships.html

Summary: To provide financial assistance to students who participate in programs of the Texas Interscholastic League Foundation (TILF) and have competed in girls' high school varsity basketball

Eligibility: This program is open to students who have competed in girls' high school varsity basketball and meet the five basic requirements of the TILF: 1) graduate from high school during the current year and begin college or university in Texas by the following fall; 2) enroll full-time and maintain a GPA of 2.5 or higher during the first semester; 3) compete in a University Interscholastic League (UIL) academic state meet contest in accounting, calculator applications, computer applications, computer science, current issues and events, debate (cross-examination and Lincoln-Douglas), journalism (editorial writing, feature writing, headline writing, and news writing), literary criticism, mathematics, number sense, one-act play, ready writing, science, social studies, speech (prose interpretation, poetry interpretation, informative speaking, and persuasive speaking), or spelling and vocabulary; 4) submit high school transcripts that include SAT and/or ACT scores; and 5) submit parents' latest income tax returns.

Financial data: The stipend is $1,000 per year.

Duration: One year, nonrenewable

Number awarded: One each year

Deadline: May of each year

250 LIVIO D'ARPINO SCHOLARSHIP

Eastern New York Youth Soccer Association
Attn: Scholarship Committee
53 Park Avenue, Suite 207
Rockville Centre, NY 11570
Phone: (516) 766-0849; Fax: (516) 678-7411;
888-5-ENYYSA; Email: enyoffice@enysoccer.com
Web: www.enysoccer.com/scholarships.htm

Summary: To provide financial assistance for college to male high school seniors in eastern New York who have been involved in soccer

Eligibility: This program is open to male seniors graduating from high schools in eastern New York with a C+ average or higher. Applicants must have played travel club soccer with a team affiliated with the Eastern New York Youth Soccer Association. They must be planning to attend a school of higher education and play college soccer. Along with their application, they must submit a personal resume, high school transcript, and 250-word essay on why they deserve the scholarship. A personal interview is required.

Financial data: The stipend is $1,000.

Duration: One year

Number awarded: One each year

Deadline: May of each year

251 LOUISIANA STATE FARM SCHOLARSHIP PROGRAM

Louisiana High School Athletic Association
Attn: Commissioner
8075 Jefferson Highway
Baton Rouge, LA 70809-7675
Phone: (225) 925-0100; Fax: (225) 925-5901;
Email: lhsaa@lhsaa.org
Web: www.lhsaa.org/Scholarships.htm

Summary: To provide financial assistance for college to student-athletes in Louisiana

Eligibility: This program is open to student-athletes who are seniors graduating from high schools in Louisiana with a GPA of 3.5 or higher for their first seven semesters. Applicants must be planning to attend a college or university and be nominated by their principal. They must have participated in one of the following eight sports: girls' volleyball, girls' basketball, girls' softball, girls' track and field, boys' football, boys' basketball, boys' baseball, or boys' track and field. Selection is based on leadership traits, citizenship in school and community, participation in nonathletic school activities and organizations, and nonathletic school honors.

Financial data: The stipend is $500.

Duration: One year

Number awarded: Eight each year: one for a participant in each of the qualifying sports

Deadline: May of each year

252 MAINE STATE GOLF ASSOCIATION SCHOLARSHIP

Maine State Golf Association
Attn: Scholarship Fund

374 U.S. Route One
Yarmouth, ME 04096
Phone: (207) 846-3800; Fax: (207) 846-4055;
Email: msga@mesga.org
Web: www.mesga.org

Summary: To provide financial assistance for college to high school seniors and graduates in Maine who have participated in golf

Eligibility: This program is open to graduates and prospective graduates of accredited Maine secondary schools. Applicants must have shown an active interest in golf by participating as a player, serving as a caddie, and/or working at a golf shop or course. They must demonstrate outstanding character, integrity, and leadership by participation in extracurricular, civic, and/or community activities. Financial need is also considered.

Financial data: The stipend is $1,100 per year.

Duration: One year; may be renewed until completion of a baccalaureate degree, provided the recipient maintains a satisfactory academic record

Number awarded: One or more each year

Deadline: March of each year

253 MARIAN WOOD BAIRD SCHOLARSHIP

United States Tennis Association
Attn: USTA Tennis & Education Foundation
70 West Road Oak Lane
White Plains, NY 10604
Phone: (914) 696-7223; Email: eliezer@usta.com
Web: www.usta.com/communitytennis/fullstory.sps?iNewsid=66422

Summary: To provide financial assistance for college to high school seniors who have participated in an organized community tennis program

Eligibility: This program is open to high school seniors who have excelled academically, demonstrated achievements in leadership, and participated extensively in an organized community tennis program. Applicants must be planning to enroll as a full-time undergraduate student at a four-year college or university. They must have a GPA of 3.0 or higher and be able to demonstrate financial need and sportsmanship. Along with their application, they must submit an essay about themselves and how their participation in a tennis program has impacted their lives.

Financial data: The stipend is $3,750 per year. Funds are paid directly to the recipient's college or university.

Duration: Four years

Number awarded: One each year

Deadline: February of each year

254 MARILYNN SMITH SCHOLARSHIP

Ladies Professional Golf Association
Attn: LPGA Foundation
100 International Golf Drive
Daytona Beach, FL 32124-1092
Phone: (386) 274-6200; Fax: (386) 274-1099;
Email: foundation.scholarships@lpga.com
Web: www.lpga.com/content_1.aspx?mid=6&pid=55
Summary: To provide financial assistance to female graduating high school seniors who played golf in high school and plan to major in education or business in college
Eligibility: This program is open to female high school seniors who have a GPA of 3.2 or higher. Applicants must have played in at least 50 percent of their high school golf team's scheduled events or have played golf "regularly" for the past two years. They must be planning to attend a college or university in the continental United States, major in business or education, and play collegiate golf. Along with their application, they must submit a letter that describes how golf has been an integral part of their lives and includes their personal and professional goals, chosen discipline of study, and how this scholarship will be of assistance. Financial need is not considered in the selection process.
Financial data: The stipend is $3,000.
Duration: One year
Number awarded: One each year
Deadline: June of each year

255 MARSH SCHOLARSHIP

Eastern Surfing Association
P.O. Box 625
Virginia Beach, VA 23451
Phone: (757) 233-1790; Fax: (757) 233-1396;
Email: info@surfesa.org
Web: www.surfesa.org/scholarships
Summary: To provide financial assistance for college to members of the Eastern Surfing Association
Eligibility: This program is open to current members in good standing. Applicants must submit an essay, up to 500 words, detailing their educational goals and how their choice of educational institutions will help them reach those goals. Selection is based on academic record and U.S. citizenship, not athletic ability.
Financial data: Stipends range from $500 to $1,000.
Number awarded: Varies each year; a total of $8,000 is available for this program each year.
Deadline: May of each year

256 MASSACHUSETTS HOCKEY SCHOLARSHIPS

Massachusetts Hockey
c/o Dan Esdale, President
77 Davidson Street
Hyde Park, MA 02136
Phone: (617) 364-6404; Fax: (617) 364-0227;
Email: danesdale@masshockey.com
Web: www.masshockey.com/Menu
Summary: To provide financial assistance for college to high school seniors who have participated in Massachusetts Youth Hockey
Eligibility: This program is open to current and former Massachusetts Youth Hockey players who are college-bound high school seniors. Selection is based primarily on evidence of good sportsmanship.
Financial data: The stipend is $2,000.
Duration: One year
Number awarded: Three each year
Deadline: April of each year

257 MASSACHUSETTS YOUTH SOCCER STUDENT-ATHLETE SCHOLARSHIPS

Mass Youth Soccer
2444 Old Union Turnpike
Lancaster, MA 01523
Phone: (978) 466-8812; 800-852-8111;
Fax: (978) 466-8817
Web: www.mayouthsoccer.org
Summary: To provide financial assistance for college to high school seniors in Massachusetts who have been involved in soccer
Eligibility: This program is open to college-bound seniors graduating from high schools in Massachusetts who have been registered players with Mass Youth Soccer for at least the past two years. Applicants must submit a 500-word essay on their soccer career thus far and what they have learned that they will be able to apply to their future endeavors. Selection is based on the essay, extracurricular activities, volunteer and community service work, academic awards, and athletic awards. Financial need is not considered. Males and females are considered separately.
Financial data: The stipend is $1,000.
Duration: One year
Number awarded: Two each year: one male and one female
Deadline: March of each year

258 MASSMUTUAL SCHOLARSHIP AWARDS

United States Tennis Association
Attn: USTA Tennis & Education Foundation

70 West Road Oak Lane
White Plains, NY 10604
Phone: (914) 696-7223; Email: eliezer@usta.com
Web: www.usta.com/communitytennis/fullstory.sps
?iNewsid=66422
Summary: To provide financial assistance for college to high school seniors who have participated in an organized community tennis program
Eligibility: This program is open to high school seniors who have excelled academically, demonstrated achievements in leadership, and participated extensively in an organized community tennis program. Applicants must be planning to enroll as a full-time undergraduate student at a four-year college or university. They must have a GPA of 3.0 or higher and be able to demonstrate financial need. Along with their application, they must submit an essay about themselves and how their participation in a tennis program has impacted their lives.
Financial data: The stipend is $5,000. Funds are paid directly to the recipient's college or university.
Duration: One year, nonrenewable
Number awarded: Thirty-five each year: two in each USTA section plus one discretionary scholarship
Deadline: February of each year

259 MATTHEW P. FAYLOR MEMORIAL SCHOLARSHIP

North Central Pennsylvania Golf Association
Attn: Executive Director
199 Gettysberg Estates
Sunbury, PA 17801
Email: ncpga2@uplink.net
Web: www.ncpga.net/junior-golf/golf-scholarships/index.asp
Summary: To provide financial assistance for college to high school seniors in northcentral Pennsylvania who have participated in golfing activities
Eligibility: This program is open to seniors graduating from high schools in northcentral Pennsylvania. Applicants must have played golf and be planning to attend college. Along with their application, they must submit information on their golfing background and an essay on a golfing experience of particular importance, a lesson they have learned from the game of golf, or the role they see golf playing in their future.
Financial data: The stipend is a total of $2,400 ($600 per year).
Duration: Four years
Number awarded: One each year
Deadline: March of each year

260 MAZZIO'S OSA COLLEGE SCHOLARSHIP

Oklahoma Soccer Association
Attn: Scholarship Committee
P.O. Box 35174
Tulsa, OK 74153
Phone: (918) 627-2663; 800-347-3590;
Fax: (918) 627-2693; Email: oksoccer@oksoccer.com
Web: www.oksoccer.com/Programs/grants/86551.html
Summary: To provide financial assistance for college to high school seniors and current college students in Oklahoma who have participated in activities of the Oklahoma Soccer Association (OSA)
Eligibility: Applicants must have participated in the OSA for at least three years of organized league play with a member organization. They must be planning to enroll in a college or university as a freshman, sophomore, junior, or senior. Along with their application, they must submit a 100-word essay on their academic and/or civic community contributions. Selection is based on OSA participation, financial need, and academic achievements.
Financial data: The stipend is $500.
Duration: One year
Number awarded: Two each year
Deadline: November of each year

261 MCCA SCHOLARSHIPS

Missouri Cheerleading Coaches Association
Attn: Scholarship Director
904 Wellington Way
Macon, MO 63552
Email: bhodges@missouricheercoaches.org
Web: www.missouricheercoaches.org
Summary: To provide financial assistance for college to cheerleaders in Missouri whose coach is a member of the Missouri Cheerleading Coaches Association (MCCA)
Eligibility: This program is open to seniors graduating from high schools in Missouri with a GPA of 3.0 or higher. Applicants must be cheerleaders whose coach is a MCCA member. Along with their application, they must submit a short essay on what cheerleading means to them. Selection is based on that essay, three letters of recommendation, transcripts, and community service; financial need is not considered.
Financial data: Stipends are $1,000 or $500.
Duration: One year, nonrenewable
Number awarded: Fourteen each year: six at $1,000 and eight at $500
Deadline: January of each year

262 MICHAEL J. BERKELEY FOUNDATION SCHOLARSHIPS

Michael J. Berkeley Foundation
Attn: Scholarship Committee
28 High Ridge Road
P.O. Box 724
Mt. Kisco, NY 10549
Phone: (914) 244-1668; Email: scholarships@
mikebfoundation.org/scholarships.html
Summary: To provide financial assistance for college to minority students who have been involved in golf
Eligibility: This program is open to full-time under-graduate students of color who are enrolled or planning to enroll at an accredited college or university. Applicants must have been involved in the game of golf. Along with their application, they must submit two essays: one on the aspect of the life and legacy of Michael J. Berkeley that has impacted them the most and one on their choice of other topics related to their involvement in golf. Selection is based on the essays, academic achievement, extracurricular and community involvement, leadership and team skills, commendations, honors, letters of recommendation, financial need, written communication skills, and verbal communication skills as demonstrated in a telephone interview.
Financial data: The stipend is $3,000 per year.
Duration: One year, renewable
Number awarded: Varies each year; recently, nine new and three renewal scholarships were awarded.
Deadline: June of each year

263 MICHAEL "PUGSTER" SILOVICH SCHOLARSHIPS

Western Athletic Scholarship Association
Attn: Scholarship Coordinator
13730 Loumont Street
Whittier, CA 90601
Summary: To provide financial assistance for college to outstanding baseball players
Eligibility: This program is open to graduating high school seniors who have played an active role in amateur baseball. Applicants must be planning to attend an accredited two- or four-year college or university. They need not have played on a high school team and are not required to play baseball in college. Selection is based on academic achievement, community service, participation in baseball, and financial need.
Financial data: The stipend is $2,000 per year.
Duration: One year, renewable
Number awarded: Up to ten each year
Deadline: February of each year

264 MICHIGAN STATE YOUTH SOCCER ASSOCIATION COLLEGE SCHOLARSHIPS

Michigan State Youth Soccer Association
9401 General Drive, Suite 120
Plymouth, MI 48170
Phone: (734) 459-6220; Fax: (734) 459-6242
Web: www.msysa.net/programs/scholarship.html
Summary: To provide financial assistance for college to high school seniors in Michigan who have played soccer
Eligibility: This program is open to high school seniors who have played on an affiliate team of the Michigan State Youth Soccer Association for at least six seasons (three years). Applicants must have a GPA of 2.75 or higher and be planning to attend an accredited college, university, or community college. Along with their application, they must submit an official high school transcript, including ACT and/or SAT scores; a one-page personal biography that includes their athletic achievements, honorary or special interest organizations, community involvement, high school major, course of study they plan to pursue, awards or scholarships they have received, and a description of any way they have given back to soccer; and an essay about how they feel soccer has helped them as an individual.
Financial data: The stipend is $1,000.
Duration: One year
Number awarded: Five each year
Deadline: February of each year

265 MIKE KABANICA SCHOLARSHIPS

Wisconsin Youth Soccer Association
Attn: Scholarships
10201 W. Lincoln Avenue, Suite 207
West Allis, WI 53227
Phone: (414) 328-WYSA; 888-328-WYSA;
Fax: (414) 328-8008; Email: info@wiyouthsoccer.net
Web: www.wiyouthsoccer.com/scholarship.html
Summary: To provide financial assistance for college to high school seniors in Wisconsin who have played soccer
Eligibility: This program is open to college-bound seniors graduating from high schools in Wisconsin who have participated in the Wisconsin Youth Soccer Association and other soccer activities in the state. Applicants must submit a paragraph detailing their team honors (high school and club) and any difficulties they have had with penalties, suspensions, or other challenges; a list of their school activities and organizations; a list of community activities and organizations; a paragraph detailing their involvement in

community service; a brief narrative on their greatest moment in soccer; a brief narrative on a person who has influenced them and how; and a statement of their future career plans. Financial need is not considered in the selection process. Male and female players are considered separately.

Financial data: The stipend is $500.

Duration: One year

Number awarded: Six each year: three females and three males

Deadline: February of each year

---

266 MIKE WARTER COLLEGE SCHOLARSHIP

Minnesota Youth Soccer Association
Attn: Scholarship Fund
11577 Encore Circle
Minnetonka, MN 55343
Phone: (952) 933-2384; Fax: (952) 933-2627;
Email: mysa@mnyouthsoccer.org
Web: www.mnyouthsoccer.org/programs/grants_scholar.cfm

Summary: To provide financial assistance for college to high school seniors in Minnesota who have been active in soccer

Eligibility: This program is open to seniors graduating from high schools in Minnesota who plan to attend an accredited college, university, or community college. Applicants must be registered in a club affiliated with the Minnesota Youth Soccer Association. Males and females are considered separately in the selection process.

Financial data: The stipend is $500.

Duration: One year

Number awarded: Two each year: one male and one female

Deadline: April of each year

---

267 MINE AND GONSAKU ITO SCHOLARSHIP

Far West Athletic Trainers' Association
c/o Jason Bennett, Scholarship Chair
Chapman University
1 University Drive
Orange, CA 92866
Phone: (714) 997-6567; Email: jbennett@chapman.edu
Web: www.fwata.org/com_scholarships.html

Summary: To provide financial assistance to members of the National Athletic Trainers Association (NATA) who are of Asian descent and working on an undergraduate or graduate degree in its District 8

Eligibility: This program is open to students of Asian descent enrolled as undergraduate or graduate students at colleges and universities in California, Guam, Hawaii, or Nevada who are preparing for a career as an athletic trainer. Applicants must be student members of NATA and a District 8 member of NATA working on a bachelor's, master's, or doctoral degree in athletic training. They must have a GPA of 3.0 or higher and a record of distinction in their athletic training program, academic major, institution, intercollegiate athletics, and higher education. Along with their application, they must submit a statement on their athletic training background, experience, philosophy, and goals. Financial need is not considered in the selection process.

Financial data: The stipend is $1,000.

Duration: One year

Number awarded: One each year

Deadline: February of each year

---

268 MINNESOTA HOCKEY SCHOLARSHIPS

Minnesota Hockey
Attn: Scholarship Committee
317 Washington Street
St. Paul, MN 55102
Phone: (651) 602-5727; Fax: (651) 222-1055;
Email: info@minnesotahockey.org
Web: www.minnesotahockey.org

Summary: To provide financial assistance for college to high school seniors who have participated in activities sponsored by Minnesota Hockey

Eligibility: This program is open to high school seniors who have participated on a youth Junior Gold team or girl's 19-and-under team of an association affiliated with Minnesota Hockey. Applicants must be planning to attend a postsecondary institution of their choice. They must have a GPA of 2.0 or higher. Along with their application, they must submit a transcript, three letters of recommendation, and a letter describing their reasons for applying for the scholarship and their academic goals. Financial need is not considered in the selection process.

Financial data: The stipend is $1,000.

Duration: One year

Number awarded: One or more each year

Deadline: March of each year

---

269 MINNESOTA SECTION PGA FOUNDATION JUNIOR GOLF SCHOLARSHIP

Minnesota Section PGA
Attn: Junior Golf Director
12800 Bunker Prairie Road
Coon Rapids, MN 55448
Phone: (763) 754-6641; Email: bbush@pgahq.com
Web: www.minnesotajuniorgolf.com

Summary: To provide financial assistance for college to residents of Minnesota who have been involved in golf
Eligibility: This program is open to seniors graduating from high schools in Minnesota who are members of the Minnesota Section PGA Junior Golf Association or participate in a junior golf program where a Minnesota Section PGA Professional is employed. Applicants must be planning to enroll full-time at an accredited college or university in the United States. They must have a GPA of 3.0 or higher. Along with their application, they must submit a one-page essay on why they feel they deserve a scholarship. Selection is based on that essay, high school grades, class rank, ACT/SAT scores, and extracurricular activities.
Financial data: The stipend depends on the availability of funds.
Duration: One year
Number awarded: One or more each year
Deadline: April of each year

270 MINNESOTA WOMEN'S GOLF ASSOCIATION SCHOLARSHIP

Minnesota Women's Golf Association
Attn: MWGA Charitable Foundation
6550 York Avenue S., Suite 211
Edina, MN 55435-2333
Phone: (952) 927-4643, ext. 11; Fax: (952) 927-9642;
Email: paula@mwga-online.org
Web: www.mwga-online.org/new/foundation.cfm
Summary: To provide financial assistance for college to female high school seniors in Minnesota who are interested in golf
Eligibility: This program is open to women who are graduating seniors at high schools in Minnesota planning to attend a four-year college or university. Applicants must have an interest or involvement in the sport of golf, although skill or excellence in the game is not considered in the selection process. They must have a GPA of 3.0 or higher and be able to demonstrate financial need.
Financial data: The stipend is $2,000 per year.
Duration: One year; may be renewed up to three additional years
Number awarded: Varies each year; recently, three of these scholarships were awarded.
Deadline: March of each year

271 MISS CHEERLEADER OF AMERICA SCHOLARSHIPS

Miss Cheerleader of America
Attn: Program Director
P.O. Box 667
Taylor, MI 48180
Phone: (734) 946-1200; Fax: (734) 946-1204;
Email: misscheerleaderofamerica@yahoo.com
Web: www.misscheerleaderofamerica.com
Summary: To recognize and reward, with college scholarships, women who are high school cheerleaders
Eligibility: This program is open to female high school cheerleaders in grades 9–12. Females who are interested apply to participate in a pageant in their home state. Based on their applications, finalists are invited to their state pageant where they participate in an evening gown demonstration and an interview. The program is not a beauty, bathing suit, cheer skill, or talent competition. Judges attempt to select "the all-American girl, who normally would not even think about being in a pageant."
Financial data: Prizes are generally scholarships of $1,000 for first place, $750 for second, and $500 for third.
Duration: The competition is held annually.
Number awarded: Varies each year; normally, three prizes are awarded in each state in which a pageant is held.

272 MISSOURI WOMEN'S GOLF EDUCATION ASSOCIATION SCHOLARSHIPS

Missouri Women's Golf Association
c/o Virginia Halpern, Membership Director
24 Picardy Hill Drive
Chesterfield, MO 63017
Email: vchalpern@charter.net
Web: www.mowomensga.org/scholarship.html
Summary: To provide financial assistance for college to female high school seniors in Missouri who have been involved in golf
Eligibility: This program is open to females graduating from high schools in Missouri or Johnson County, Kansas. Applicants must submit a copy of their high school transcript and a brief account of their golf achievements. Financial need is not considered in the selection process.
Financial data: A stipend is awarded (amount not specified).
Duration: One year, nonrenewable
Number awarded: Varies each year; recently, five of these scholarships were awarded.

273 MOLLIE BUTLER/J.D. OREAR SCHOLARSHIP

Welsh Pony and Cob Foundation, Inc.
P.O. Box 2977

Winchester, VA 22604

Phone: (540) 667-6195

Web: www.welshpony.org/scholarship.htm

Summary: To provide financial assistance to high school seniors and currently enrolled undergraduate and graduate students who have experience with Welsh ponies or cobs and are studying an equine or related field

Eligibility: This program is open to U.S. citizens who are graduating high school seniors, undergraduate students, or graduate students working on or planning to work on a degree in an equine or related field. Applicants must submit a one-page statement that outlines their need for the scholarship and their experience with or interest in Welsh ponies or cobs. In addition, one letter of reference is required. Selection is based on the student's academic record, extracurricular activities, community-related activities, and equine-related activities. Financial need is not considered.

Financial data: The stipend is $500.

Duration: One year

Number awarded: One or two each year

Deadline: June of each year

---

274 MONTANA STATE WOMEN'S GOLF ASSOCIATION SCHOLARSHIPS

Montana State Women's Golf Association

c/o Carla Berg, Executive Secretary/Director

P.O. Box 52

Sidney, MT 59270

Phone: (406) 488-5135; Email: carla@mswga.org

Web: www.mswga.org/applications.html

Summary: To provide financial assistance for college to women golfers in Montana

Eligibility: This program is open to female residents of Montana who are entering their freshman year of college. Applicants must have been involved with golf sometime (on a high school team or in a junior program), although they are not required to be participating presently. They must submit information on their high school golf playing record, amateur playing record, leadership positions, activities and organizations, community and volunteer service, and honors and awards. They must also submit a brief essay on their career aspirations and how they hope to achieve those life goals. Neither financial need nor skill in golf are considered in the selection process.

Financial data: The stipend is $500.

Duration: One year

Number awarded: One or more each year

Deadline: March of each year

---

275 NANCIE RIDEOUT-ROBERTSON INTERNSHIP SCHOLARSHIP

American Water Ski Educational Foundation

Attn: Director

1251 Holy Cow Road

Polk City, FL 33868-8200

Phone: (863) 324-2472; Fax: (863) 324-3996;

Email: info@waterskihalloffame.com

Web: www.waterskihalloffame.com

Summary: To provide financial assistance and work experience to upper-division and graduate students who are interested in water skiing

Eligibility: This program is open to upper-division and graduate students who are members of the United States Water Ski Association (USWSA) and the American Water Ski Educational Foundation (AWSEF). Applicants must have participated in the sport of water skiing as a skier, official, and/or volunteer worker and be able to demonstrate leadership potential. They must have a GPA of at least B+ overall and an A average in their major field of study. Along with their application, they must submit a 500-word personal statement on why they wish to be awarded this scholarship and serve as an intern at AWSEF and an internship proposal, covering their learning goals and how they want to apply the skills and knowledge related to their program of study in college or graduate school to their internship, the kinds of contributions they think they can make toward the goals of AWSEF, how they would allocate their time toward their internship activities, when they could complete their "onsite" requirement, and the kinds of skills and knowledge of people with whom they might like to work during their internship.

Financial data: The stipend is $2,500.

Duration: One year, including at least four weeks (during semester breaks, spring break, or summer) at AWSEF headquarters in Polk City, Florida

Number awarded: One each year

Deadline: January of each year

---

276 NATA UNDERGRADUATE SCHOLARSHIPS

National Athletic Trainers' Association

Attn: Research and Education Foundation

2952 Stemmons Freeway, Suite 200

Dallas, TX 75247-6103

Phone: (214) 637-6282; 800-TRY-NATA, ext. 121;

Fax: (214) 637-2206; Email: barbaran@nata.org

Web: www.natafoundation.org/scholarship.html

Summary: To provide financial aid to undergraduate student members of the National Athletic Trainers' Association (NATA)

Eligibility: This program is open to members of the association who are sponsored by an NATA-certified athletic trainer, have a GPA of 3.2 or higher, and intend to pursue athletic training as a profession. Applicants must apply during their junior year or immediately prior to their final undergraduate year. They must submit a statement on their athletic training background, experience, philosophy, and goals. Selection is based on that essay; participation in their school's athletic training program, academic major, institution, intercollegiate athletics, and American higher education; and participation in campus activities other than academic and athletic training. Financial need is not considered.

Financial data: The stipend is $2,000 per year.

Duration: One year

Number awarded: Varies each year; recently, 39 of these scholarships were awarded.

Deadline: February of each year

---

277 NATASHA MATSON FIFE SCHOLARSHIP

Kansas Women's Golf Association
c/o Phyllis Fast, Scholarship Chair
3006 S.E. Skylark Drive
Topeka, KS 66605
Phone: (785) 266-8033; Email: phast@networksplus.net
Web: www.kwga.org/scholarship.htm

Summary: To provide financial assistance for college to women in Kansas who have participated in activities of the Kansas Women's Golf Association (KWGA)

Eligibility: This program is open to women in Kansas who are graduating or have graduated from a high school in the state. Applicants must have participated in at least one KWGA Junior Girls Championship or State Amateur Championship. They must be planning to attend an accredited collegiate institution in the following academic year. Eligibility is not limited to junior golfers. Along with their application, they must submit information on the number of years they have played golf, their handicap index, the KWGA amateur and junior championships and years in which they have participated, an essay of more than 100 words on why they play golf and the benefits they have gained from golf, their golf accomplishments, participation in other high school and/or community activities, a copy of their high school transcript (including name of school, year of graduation, and GPA), and three letters of recommendation.

Financial data: A stipend is awarded (amount not specified). Funds are paid directly to the recipient's collegiate institution.

Duration: One year, nonrenewable

Number awarded: One or more each year

Deadline: March of each year

---

278 NATHALIE A. PRICE MEMORIAL SCHOLARSHIP

Ocean State Women's Golf Association
P.O. Box 597
Portsmouth, RI 02871-0597
Phone: (401) 683-6301; Email: oswgari@aol.com
Web: www.oswga.org

Summary: To provide financial assistance for college to women in Rhode Island who have played golf

Eligibility: This program is open to women in Rhode Island who are graduating high school seniors or current college students. Applicants must have been active in golf, as a member of the Ocean State Women's Golf Association (OSWGA), as a member of another association, or on their school golf team. Along with their application, they must submit a transcript, a list of their citizenship and community service activities, and letters of recommendation. Financial need is not considered.

Financial data: A stipend is awarded (amount not specified).

Duration: One year, renewable

Number awarded: Varies each year; recently, eight of these scholarships were awarded.

Deadline: June of each year

---

279 NATIONAL AMATEUR BASEBALL FEDERATION SCHOLARSHIP PROGRAM

National Amateur Baseball Federation, Inc.
Attn: Executive Director
P.O. Box 705
Bowie, MD 20718
Phone: (301) 464-5460; Fax: (301) 352-0214;
Email: nabf1914@aol.com
Web: www.nabf.com/membership/scholarships.htm

Summary: To provide financial assistance for college to students who have participated in National Amateur Baseball Federation (NABF) events

Eligibility: To be eligible for this support, students must be entering or enrolled at an accredited college or university and have participated in NABF events. Applicants must be sponsored by an NABF-member association. Selection is based on academic record and financial need.

Financial data: A stipend is awarded (amount not specified).

Duration: One year

Number awarded: Varies each year; recently, ten of these scholarships were awarded.

280 NATIONAL AMPUTEE GOLF ASSOCIATION SCHOLARSHIP

National Amputee Golf Association
Attn: Scholarship Grant Program
11 Walnut Hill Road
Amherst, NH 03031
Phone: (603) 672-6444; 800-633-NAGA;
Fax: (603) 672-2987; Email: info@nagagolf.org
Web: www.nagagolf.org/scholarship1.shtml
Summary: To provide financial assistance for college to members of the National Amputee Golf Association and their dependents
Eligibility: This program is open to amputee members in good standing in the association and their dependents. Applicants must submit information on their scholastic background (GPA in high school and college, courses of study), type of amputation and cause (if applicable), a cover letter describing their plans for the future, and documentation of financial need. They need not be competitive golfers. Selection is based on academic record, financial need, involvement in extracurricular or community activities, and area of study.
Financial data: The stipend for a four-year bachelor's degree program is $2,000 per year. The stipend for a two-year technical or associate degree is $1,000 per year.
Duration: Up to four years, provided the recipient maintains at least half-time enrollment and a GPA of 2.0 or higher and continues to demonstrate financial need
Number awarded: One or more each year
Deadline: July of each year

281 NATIONAL GYMNASTICS FOUNDATION AND USA GYMNASTICS SCHOLARSHIP PROGRAM

USA Gymnastics
Attn: Men's Scholarship Program
201 S. Capitol Avenue, Suite 300
Indianapolis, IN 46225
Phone: (317) 237-5050, ext. 230; Fax: (317) 237-5069
Web: www.usa-gymnastics.org/men/scholarship.html
Summary: To provide financial assistance for college to elite-level male gymnasts
Eligibility: This program is open to high school seniors and currently enrolled college students who are gymnasts working on a college or postsecondary degree. Applicants must be training at the elite level, with an emphasis on international competition, and enrolled or planning to enroll in an undergraduate educational program with a GPA of 2.0 or higher. Along with their application, they must submit information on their athletic accomplishments, athletic goals for the current year and next five years, academic goals, probable ca-

reer goals, how a scholarship would contribute to their goals, honors and activities, and financial need.
Financial data: The size of the scholarship varies, depending upon the funds raised throughout the year in support of the program. Funds must be used for college or postsecondary educational expenses.
Duration: One year; may be renewed if the recipient maintains a GPA of 2.0 or higher
Number awarded: Varies each year
Deadline: February of each year

282 NATIONAL HIGH SCHOOL RODEO SCHOLARSHIP

National High School Rodeo Association
Attn: NHSR Foundation
4503 Sheila Court
Lilburn, GA 30047
Phone: (678) 417-9911; 800-46-NHSRA; Fax: (678) 417-9979; Email: ray.spence@raymondjames.com
Web: www.nhsra.org/programs_scholarship.shtml
Summary: To provide financial assistance for college to high school students who compete in the National High School Rodeo Association's (NHSRA) national rodeo, which has been called the largest in the world
Eligibility: Applicants must have qualified for the NHSRA finals. They do that by winning in their state or province rodeos and then presenting a scholarship application in person prior to the national rodeo. Along with their application, they must also present a copy of their high school transcript (Canadian and Australian students must present their last grade report) and a 100-word description of why this scholarship would make a difference to them. In addition, applicants must appear before a two-person interview committee during the national rodeo. They are asked to answer questions on estimated school expenses, where they want to be in five years, their need for this scholarship, and other related topics.
Financial data: Stipends range from $500 to $4,000. Checks are made out jointly to the recipient and the recipient's school. Each year, the foundation, along with the association, gives out close to $250,000 in scholarships.
Duration: The scholarships are awarded annually.
Number awarded: Varies each year
Deadline: July of each year

283 NATIONAL HIGH SCHOOL SCHOLAR-ATHLETE AWARDS

National Football Foundation
22 Maple Avenue
Morristown, NJ 07960

Phone: (973) 829-1933; 800-486-1865; Fax: (973) 829-1737; Email: scholarship@footballfoundation.com
Web: www.footballfoundation.com/NHSaward.php
Summary: To recognize and reward high school football players who demonstrate both athletic and academic excellence
Eligibility: These awards are presented to high school football players who combine academic excellence, leadership, and athletic performance. More than 3,000 scholar-athletes are honored each year, and one of those in each of the four regions in the country is selected to receive a college scholarship.
Financial data: The scholarship stipends are $1,500.
Duration: The awards are presented annually.
Number awarded: Four each year

284 NCCCA SCHOLARSHIPS

North Carolina Cheerleading Coaches Association
c/o Nicole Smith, Scholarship Chair
Asheboro High School
1221 S. Park Street
Asheboro, NC 27205
Phone: (336) 625-6185;
Email: nsmith@asheboro.k12.nc.us
Web: www.nccca.net/Scholarship%20Main.htm
Summary: To provide financial assistance for college to cheerleaders in North Carolina whose coach is a member of the North Carolina Cheerleading Coaches Association (NCCCA)
Eligibility: This program is open to seniors graduating from high schools in North Carolina with a GPA of 3.75 or higher. Applicants must have been a cheerleader for at least one full athletic season. Their coach must be an NCCCA member. Selection is based on leadership positions held, community service, extracurricular activities, and academic honors and awards.
Financial data: Stipends are $2,000 or $1,000.
Duration: One year
Number awarded: Varies each year. Recently, five of these scholarships were awarded: two at $2,000 and three at $1,000.
Deadline: March of each year

285 NEBRASKA AMATEUR SOFTBALL FOUNDATION SCHOLARSHIPS

Nebraska Amateur Softball Association
Attn: Foundation
4103 Osborne Drive E.
Hastings, NE 68901
Phone: (402) 462-7100; Fax: (402) 461-3297;
Email: info@nebraskasoftball.org

Web: http://nebraskasoftball.org
Summary: To provide financial assistance for college to Nebraska residents who have participated in activities of the Nebraska Amateur Softball Association
Eligibility: This program is open to residents of Nebraska who have participated in activities of the association as a player, team manager, umpire, or official. Applicants must be high school seniors and enrolled or planning to enroll as a full-time student at a college or university in Nebraska. They must have a GPA of 3.0 or higher. Along with their application, they must submit a statement on why they should be considered for this scholarship. Selection is based on academic ability, officiating activities, personal qualities, community activities, higher education potential, and financial need.
Financial data: The stipend is $500.
Duration: One year, nonrenewable
Number awarded: Several each year
Deadline: November of each year

286 NEBRASKA QUARTER HORSE YOUTH SCHOLARSHIP

American Quarter Horse Foundation
Attn: Scholarship Coordinator
2601 I-40 East
Amarillo, TX 79104
Phone: (806) 378-5034; 888-209-8322;
Fax: (806) 376-1005; Email: lowens@aqha.org
Web: www.aqha.com/foundation/scholarships/index.html
Summary: To provide financial assistance for college to members of the American Quarter Horse Association (AQHA) or the American Quarter Horse Youth Association (AQHYA) who are from Nebraska
Eligibility: Applicants must have been members of either organization for at least one year and be residents of Nebraska. They must be graduating high school seniors or already enrolled in college with a GPA of 2.5 or higher. Financial need is considered in the selection process.
Financial data: The stipend is $500 per year.
Duration: Up to four years, provided the recipient maintains a GPA of 2.5 or higher and full-time enrollment
Number awarded: One every four years (next available in 2010)
Deadline: January of the year of the award

287 NEDA SCHOLARSHIPS

New England Dressage Association
Attn: Sue Edelen, Scholarship Committee Chair
P.O. Box 2301

South Hamilton, MA 01982

Phone: (978) 356-8704; Email: suedelen@comcast.net

Web: www.neda.org/scholarship.html

Summary: To provide funding to members of the New England Dressage Association (NEDA) who are interested in pursuing training (in the United States or abroad) that advances their skills and standing in the dressage community

Eligibility: This program is open to association members in five categories: international, professional, amateur, young rider, and breeder. Applicants must be interested in participating in a program that will improve their equestrian skills and standing in the dressage community. The program must have a stated objective and must have clear beginning and end dates. It may be a seminar, workshop, clinic, or training program offered by a recognized and/or certified instructor. Selection is based on length of NEDA membership, volunteer history, other scholarships received, goal of the program, competition level, previous awards and recognition, benefit to NEDA's membership, timeliness of goal, credibility and reputation of the program, and the effect on professional contribution. U.S. citizenship or permanent resident status is required.

Financial data: Maximum grants are $4,000 for the international category, $2,000 for the professional category, $1,000 for the amateur and young rider categories, $2,000 for international breeders, and $1,000 for national breeders.

Duration: Recipients may reapply every four years.

Number awarded: Varies each year; recently, two of these scholarships were awarded.

Deadline: March or September of each year

---

288 NEUROLOGY ASSOCIATES SCHOLAR-ATHLETE AWARD

South Texas Youth Soccer Association

15209 Highway 290 East

Manor, TX 78653

Phone: (512) 272-4553; Fax: (512) 272-5167

Web: www.stxsoccer.org

Summary: To provide financial assistance for college to participants in the South Texas Youth Soccer Association (STYSA) who demonstrate outstanding sportsmanship

Eligibility: This program is open to players currently registered in the under-17 through under-19 age group of an STYSA member association. Applicants must be enrolled full-time in high school or college with a GPA of 3.5 or higher. They must have demonstrated sportsmanship, defined as observing the laws of the game;

showing enthusiasm for the game; playing to their utmost potential; demonstrating respect for teammates, officials, and opponents; and consistently participating in a sportsmanlike manner.

Financial data: The stipend is $1,000.

Duration: One year

Number awarded: One each year

Deadline: April of each year

---

289 NEW HAMPSHIRE WOMEN'S GOLF ASSOCIATION SCHOLARSHIPS

New Hampshire Women's Golf Association

c/o Pat Pierson

P.O. Box 2201

Dover, NH 03821-2210

Email: nhwga@usga.org

Web: www.nhwga.org

Summary: To provide financial assistance for college to members of the New Hampshire Women's Golf Association (NHWGA) and their families

Eligibility: This program is open to residents of New Hampshire who are enrolled or planning to enroll as a full-time undergraduate student at an accredited college or university. Applicants must be members or relatives of members of the NHWGA. Along with their application, they must submit an essay about their plans for the future and how they intend to use their education. Selection is based on the essay, GPA, and financial need.

Financial data: Stipends are approximately $500.

Duration: One year; may be renewed up to three additional years

Number awarded: Varies each year; recently, 20 of these scholarships were awarded.

Deadline: July of each year

---

290 NICHOLAS BATTLE SCHOLARSHIP

Southern Texas PGA Section

Attn: Foundation

21604 Cypresswood Drive

Spring, TX 77373

Phone: (832) 442-2404; Fax: (832) 442-2403;

Email: stexas@pgahq.com

Web: www.stpga.com/index.cfm?menu=2706

Summary: To provide financial assistance for college to residents of southern Texas who have an interest in golf

Eligibility: This program is open to residents of the Southern Texas PGA Section who are enrolled or planning to enroll in college as a full-time student. Applicants must have a GPA of 2.5 or higher and be able to demonstrate financial need. They must have shown an interest in the game of golf, although golfing ability is not considered in the selection process and applicants are not required to be junior golfers. For graduating high school seniors, selection is based on academic record, ACT and/or SAT scores, extracurricular activities, voluntary statements, financial need, and junior golf participation and interest. For current college students, selection is based on cumulative college GPA, financial need, voluntary statements, college extracurricular activities, and golf participation and interest.

Financial data: Stipends range from $1,000 to $3,000.

Duration: One year; recipients may reapply.

Number awarded: Varies each year

Deadline: April of each year

291 NJCDCA SCHOLARSHIPS

New Jersey Cheerleading & Dance Coaches Association
c/o Penny Jenkins, Scholarship Director
74 Junco Court
Three Bridges, NJ 08887
Phone: (908) 788-0579; Email: pjenkins03@hotmail.com
Web: www.njcheerleading.com

Summary: To provide financial assistance to high school cheerleaders whose school is a member of the New Jersey Cheerleading & Dance Coaches Association (NJCDCA)

Eligibility: This program is open to seniors graduating from high schools in New Jersey that are members of the NJCDCA. Applicants must be planning to attend a college or university. Along with their application, they must submit a 200-word essay on the impact that cheerleading has had in their lives and their greatest challenge as a cheerleader. Financial need is not considered in the selection process.

Financial data: A stipend is awarded (amount not specified).

Duration: One year

Number awarded: Varies each year; recently, eight of these scholarships were awarded.

Deadline: March of each year

292 NKCCA SCHOLARSHIPS

Northern Kentucky Cheerleading Coaches'
Association
c/o Gay Trame
839 Crocus Lane
Taylor Mill, KY 41015
Phone: (859) 431-1335, ext. 36
Web: www.nkycheer.com

Summary: To provide financial assistance to high school cheerleaders whose school is a member of the Northern Kentucky Cheerleading Coaches' Association (NKCCA)

Eligibility: This program is open to seniors graduating from high schools in northern Kentucky that are members of the NKCCA. Applicants must be planning to attend a college or university. Along with their application, they must submit two essays of one page each: 1) what cheerleading has meant to them and 2) why the committee should award them a scholarship. Financial need is also considered in the selection process.

Financial data: Stipends range from $100 to $500.

Duration: One year

Number awarded: Varies each year. Recently, 14 of these scholarships were awarded: 2 at $100, 10 at $250, 1 at $400, and 1 at $500.

Deadline: February of each year

293 NORTH CAROLINA 4-H HORSE SCHOLARSHIPS

North Carolina 4-H Development Fund
c/o North Carolina State University
Department of 4-H Youth Development
202 Ricks Hall
P.O. Box 7606
Raleigh, NC 27695-7606
Phone: (919) 515-8486; Fax: (919) 515-7812
Web: www.nc4h.org

Summary: To provide financial assistance for college to high school seniors in North Carolina who have been active in the 4-H horse program

Eligibility: This program is open to seniors graduating from high schools in North Carolina who have been active in the 4-H horse program. Applicants must be planning to attend a college or university in the state. Along with their application, they must submit an essay on "how 4-H has prepared me for the challenges of the future." Selection is based on accomplishments in 4-H (50 percent), academic achievement as indicated by GPA and class rank (25 percent), and aptitude for college as indicated by grades and SAT or ACT scores (25 percent).

Financial data: The stipend is $1,000 per year. Funds are issued only after the recipient has completed one semester or quarter of college with a GPA of 2.5 or higher.

Duration: One year

Number awarded: Two each year

Deadline: January of each year

294 NORTHEASTERN AMPUTEE CLASS SCHOLARSHIP

Eastern Amputee Golf Association
Attn: Bob Buck, Executive Director
2015 Amherst Drive

Bethlehem, PA 18015-5606
Phone: 888-868-0992; Fax: (610) 867-9295;
Email: info@eaga.org
Web: www.eaga.org
Summary: To provide financial assistance for college to members of the Eastern Amputee Golf Association (EAGA) and their families
Eligibility: This program is open to students who are residents of and/or currently enrolled or accepted for enrollment at a college or university in designated Eastern states (Connecticut, Delaware, District of Columbia, Maine, Maryland, Massachusetts, New Hampshire, New Jersey, New York, Pennsylvania, Rhode Island, Vermont, Virginia, or West Virginia). Applicants must be amputee members of the association (those who have experienced the loss of one or more extremities at a major joint due to amputation or birth defect) or members of their families. Financial need is considered in the selection process.
Financial data: The stipend is $1,000.
Duration: One year; may be renewed if the recipient maintains a GPA of 2.0 or higher and continues to demonstrate financial need
Number awarded: One or more each year
Deadline: June of each year

---

295 NORTHERN VIRGINIA ATHLETIC DIRECTORS, ADMINISTRATORS AND COACHES ASSOCIATION SCHOLARSHIPS

Summary: To provide financial assistance for college to high school seniors in northern Virginia who have played sports, been a cheerleader, etc.
See Listing #85.

---

296 NOVO NORDISK DONNELLY AWARDS

World Team Tennis, Inc.
Attn: Billie Jean King WTT Charities
1776 Broadway, Suite 600
New York, NY 10019
Phone: (212) 586-3444; Fax: (212) 586-6277
Web: www.wtt.com/charities/donnelly.asp
Summary: To recognize and reward young tennis players who have diabetes
Eligibility: This program is open to scholar-athletes between 14 and 21 years of age who play tennis competitively either on a school team or as a ranked tournament player and have type I diabetes. Applicants must submit a 500-word essay on the significance of diabetes in their lives. Selection is based on values, commitment, sportsmanship, community involvement, and financial need.

Financial data: The award is $5,000; funds may be used for education, tennis development, and/or medical care.
Duration: The nonrenewable awards are presented annually.
Number awarded: Two each year
Deadline: April of each year

---

297 NSSA NATIONAL SCHOLARSHIP PROGRAM

National Scholastic Surfing Association
10031 Dana Drive
P.O. Box 495
Huntington Beach, CA 92648
Phone: (714) 378-0899; Fax: (714) 964-5232;
Email: jaragon@nssa.org
Web: www.nssa.org/special_programs.htm
Summary: To provide financial assistance for college to members of the National Scholastic Surfing Association (NSSA)
Eligibility: This program is open to members in good standing of the association who are enrolled or planning to enroll as full-time college students. Applicants must have a GPA of 3.0 or higher. Selection is based on scholastic achievement, leadership, community and/or NSSA service, career goals, transcripts, and letters of recommendation.
Financial data: Stipends range from $100 to $1,000.
Duration: One year
Number awarded: Varies each year
Deadline: May of each year

---

298 OKLAHOMA QUARTER HORSE YOUTH SCHOLARSHIP

American Quarter Horse Foundation
Attn: Scholarship Coordinator
2601 I-40 East
Amarillo, TX 79104
Phone: (806) 378-5034; 888-209-8322;
Fax: (806) 376-1005; Email: lowens@aqha.org
Web: www.aqha.com/foundation/scholarships/index
.html
Summary: To provide financial assistance for college to members of the American Quarter Horse Association (AQHA) or the American Quarter Horse Youth Association (AQHYA) who are from Oklahoma
Eligibility: Applicants must have been members of either organization for at least one year, have been members of the Oklahoma Quarter Horse Youth Association for at least two years, and be residents of Oklahoma. They must be graduating high school seniors or already enrolled in college with a GPA of 2.5 or higher. Financial need is considered in the selection process.

Financial data: The stipend is $500 per year.

Duration: Up to four years, provided the recipient maintains a GPA of 2.5 or higher and full-time enrollment

Number awarded: Three each year

Deadline: January of each year

---

299 OREGON YOUTH SOCCER FOUNDATION COLLEGE SCHOLARSHIPS

Oregon Youth Soccer Association

Attn: Foundation

4840 S.W. Western Avenue, Suite 800

Beaverton, OR 97005

Phone: (503) 626-4625; 800-275-7353; Fax: (503) 520-0302; Email: Kelly@oregonyouthsoccer.org

Web: www.oysf.org

Summary: To provide financial assistance for college to high school seniors in Oregon who have been involved in soccer

Eligibility: This program is open to members of teams affiliated with the Oregon Youth Soccer Association who are college-bound high school seniors. Applicants must have a GPA of 3.0 or higher and a record of leadership, sportsmanship, teamwork, courage, judgment, responsibility, discipline, and perseverance. Along with their application, they must submit two essays describing 1) how soccer has influenced their character, discipline, teamwork, leadership, and self-esteem and 2) their financial need.

Financial data: The stipend is $500.

Duration: One year

Number awarded: Ten each year

Deadline: March of each year

---

300 OSA COLLEGE SCHOLARSHIP

Oklahoma Soccer Association

Attn: Scholarship Committee

P.O. Box 35174

Tulsa, OK 74153

Phone: (918) 627-2663; 800-347-3590;

Fax: (918) 627-2693; Email: oksoccer@oksoccer.com

Web: www.oksoccer.com/Programs/grants/86551.html

Summary: To provide financial assistance for college to high school seniors in Oklahoma who have participated in activities of the Oklahoma Soccer Association (OSA)

Eligibility: Applicants must have participated in the OSA for at least three seasons within the last four years. They must be graduating from high school or have graduated within the past two years and be planning to enroll in an accredited college or university for the first time. Along with their application, they must submit a 500-word essay on what this scholarship would mean

to them. Financial need is not considered in the selection process.

Financial data: The stipend varies each year.

Duration: One year, nonrenewable

Number awarded: Varies each year

Deadline: March of each year

---

301 OUTRIGGER DUKE KAHANAMOKU SCHOLARSHIP GRANTS

Outrigger Duke Kahanamoku Foundation

P.O. Box 2498

Honolulu, HI 96804

Phone: (808) 545-4880; Fax: (808) 532-0560

Web: www.dukefoundation.org

Summary: To provide financial assistance for college to Hawaii residents who are high school seniors and involved in sports

Eligibility: This program is open to seniors graduating from high schools in Hawaii who plan to attend an accredited college or university as a full-time student. Applicants must have participated and intend to continue to participate in competitive sports, preferably in the areas of canoeing, surfing, kayaking, sailing, swimming, water polo, volleyball, and other related athletic activities. They must have a GPA of 3.3 or higher and be able to demonstrate financial need. Along with their application, they must submit a brief essay on how they would give back to the foundation and the community in the future if they receive a scholarship and an athletic resume for the last three years.

Financial data: A stipend is awarded (amount not specified).

Number awarded: Varies each year; recently, 30 of these scholarships, totaling $43,500, were awarded.

Deadline: March of each year

---

302 PALOMINO HORSE BREEDERS OF AMERICA YOUTH SCHOLARSHIP AND EDUCATIONAL FUND

Palomino Horse Breeders of America

Attn: Youth Scholarship and Educational Fund

15253 E. Skelly Drive

Tulsa, OK 74116-2637

Phone: (918) 438-1234; Fax: (918) 438-1232;

Email: yellahrses@aol.com

Web: www.palominohba.com

Summary: To provide financial assistance for college to youth members of the Palomino Horse Breeders of America (PHBA-Y)

Eligibility: This program is open to high school seniors who have been a member in good standing of the

PHBA-Y during the previous two years and either rank in the upper 20 percent of their high school graduating class or achieved a rank above the 80th percentile on a national college entrance examination and full-time students who have completed at least one semester of college and are younger than 21 years of age. Applicants must provide information on their career goals; academic achievements; extracurricular activities; hobbies; PHBA-Y activities and experiences, awards, and honors; and 4-H or FFA projects and achievements. They must also submit a letter on why they desire to continue their education and the personal qualities that qualify them to receive a scholarship. Financial need is not considered in the selection process.

Financial data: The amount of the stipend varies each year.

Duration: One year; may be renewed if the recipient maintains a GPA of 2.5 or higher

Number awarded: Varies each year

Deadline: January of each year

---

303 PATRICIA CREED SCHOLARSHIP

Connecticut Women's Golf Association
c/o Deborah Boynton, Scholarship Committee
52 Mountain Spring Road
Farmington, CT 06032
Phone: (860) 674-1195; Email: scholarships@cwga.org
Web: www.cwga.org/juniors/juniorhome.htm

Summary: To provide financial assistance for college to female high school seniors from Connecticut who are golfers

Eligibility: This program is open to female high school seniors who are residents of Connecticut and are planning to attend a college or university in the state. Applicants must be active golfers with a handicap. Along with their application, they must submit a 200-word essay on how golf has made an impact on their life. Selection is based on character, academic achievement, interest in golf, and financial need.

Financial data: A stipend is awarded (amount not specified).

Duration: One year

Number awarded: Two each year

Deadline: April of each year

---

304 PATRICIA LOUISE MASOTTO AND BRENDA DRISCOLL SCHOLARSHIPS

Eastern New York Youth Soccer Association
Attn: Scholarship Committee
53 Park Avenue, Suite 207
Rockville Centre, NY 11570

Phone: (516) 766-0849; Fax: (516) 678-7411;
888-5-ENYYSA; Email: enyoffice@enysoccer.com
Web: www.enysoccer.com/scholarships.htm

Summary: To provide financial assistance for college to female high school seniors in eastern New York who have been involved in soccer

Eligibility: This program is open to female seniors graduating from high schools in eastern New York with a C+ average or higher. Applicants must have played travel club soccer with a team affiliated with the Eastern New York Youth Soccer Association. They must be planning to attend a school of higher education and play college soccer. Along with their application, they must submit a personal resume, high school transcript, and 250-word essay on why they deserve the scholarship. A personal interview is required.

Financial data: The stipend is $1,000.

Duration: One year

Number awarded: Two each year

Deadline: May of each year

---

305 PATRICK KERR SKATEBOARD SCHOLARSHIP

Patrick Kerr Skateboard Scholarship Fund
P.O. Box 2054
Jenkintown, PA 19046
Fax: (215) 663-5897;
Email: info@skateboardscholarship.org
Web: www.skateboardscholarship.org

Summary: To provide financial assistance for college to high school seniors who are skateboarders

Eligibility: This program is open to graduating high school seniors who are skateboarders planning to enroll full-time at an accredited two- or four-year college or university. Applicants must have a GPA of 2.5 or higher and be able to demonstrate financial need. Along with their application, they must submit a 300-word essay on how skateboarding has been a positive influence in their life. Special consideration is given to applicants who have been actively promoting skateboarding in their community, but skateboarding skill is not considered in the selection process. U.S. citizenship is required.

Financial data: Stipends are $5,000 or $1,000.

Duration: One year

Number awarded: Four each year: one at $5,000 and three at $1,000

Deadline: April of each year

---

306 PAUL DESCHAMPS SCHOLARSHIP AWARD

Eastern Amputee Golf Association
Attn: Bob Buck, Executive Director

2015 Amherst Drive
Bethlehem, PA 18015-5606
Phone: 888-868-0992; Fax: (610) 867-9295;
Email: info@eaga.org
Web: www.eaga.org
Summary: To provide financial assistance for college to members of the Eastern Amputee Golf Association (EAGA) and their families
Eligibility: This program is open to students who are residents of and/or currently enrolled or accepted for enrollment at a college or university in designated Eastern states (Connecticut, Delaware, District of Columbia, Maine, Maryland, Massachusetts, New Hampshire, New Jersey, New York, Pennsylvania, Rhode Island, Vermont, Virginia, or West Virginia). Applicants must be amputee members of the association (those who have experienced the loss of one or more extremities at a major joint due to amputation or birth defect) or members of their families. Financial need is considered in the selection process.
Financial data: The stipend is $1,000.
Duration: One year; may be renewed if the recipient maintains a GPA of 2.0 or higher and continues to demonstrate financial need
Number awarded: One or more each year
Deadline: June of each year

307 PAUL HAUSSER MEMORIAL SCHOLARSHIP

New Jersey Youth Soccer
Attn: Paul Hausser Memorial Fund
569 Abbington Drive, Suite F
East Windsor, NJ 08520
Phone: (609) 490-0725; Fax: (609) 490-0731;
Email: office@njyouthsoccer.com
Web: www.njyouthsoccer.com/awards/hausser.htm
Summary: To provide financial assistance to high school seniors in New Jersey who have been involved in soccer and are interested in attending college to prepare for a career in education
Eligibility: This program is open to seniors graduating from high schools in New Jersey who have played for an affiliated New Jersey Youth Soccer club. Applicants must be interested in enrolling at a college or university to prepare for a career in education. Along with their application, they must submit their school record and an essay on why they believe they deserve the scholarship. Financial need is not considered in the selection process.
Financial data: The stipend is $500.
Duration: One year
Number awarded: Up to two each year
Deadline: November of each year

308 PAUL J. STEPHAN MEMORIAL AWARD

American Morgan Horse Institute, Inc.
Attn: AMHI Scholarships
P.O. Box 519
Shelburne, VT 05482-0519
Phone: (802) 985-8477; Fax: (802) 985-8430;
Email: info@morganhorse.com
Web: www.morganhorse.com/benefits/kids_scholarships.php
Summary: To provide financial assistance for further education to young men interested in working in the Morgan horse industry
Eligibility: This program is open to men under 21 years of age who are interested in working in the Morgan horse industry. Eligibility is not limited to show ring exhibitors but is available to men who have a goal of active professional involvement with the Morgan breed in any capacity. Applicants may be interested in further training in such disciplines as training, judging, equine reproduction, professional grooming, stable management, farrier or specialized shoeing, stable apprenticeship, or equine veterinary studies. Along with their application, they must submit an essay on their background, areas of interest, financial need (if any), goals in equine studies, and plans for utilization of the award.
Financial data: The stipend is $1,000.
Duration: One year; nonrenewable
Number awarded: One each year
Deadline: January of each year

309 PEPSI USBC YOUTH BOWLING CHAMPIONSHIPS

United States Bowling Congress
Attn: Pepsi-Cola Youth Bowling Event Manager
5301 S. 76th Street
Greendale, WI 53129-1192
Phone: (414) 423-3442; 800-514-BOWL, ext. 3442;
Fax: (414) 421-3014; Email: maureen.vicena@bowl.com
Web: www.bowl.com/tournaments/youth/pepsi/main.aspx
Summary: To recognize and reward (with college scholarships) members of the United States Bowling Congress (USBC) who achieve high scores in an international competition
Eligibility: This competition is open to USBC members in the United States, Puerto Rico, U.S. military zones, and Canada. Applicants enter in one of six categories: 11-and-under boys' handicap, 12-and-above boys' handicap, 12-and-above boys' scratch, 11-and-under girls' handicap, 12-and-above girls' handicap, and 12-and-above girls' scratch. Based on their bowling scores

in state and zone competitions, the top bowlers in the 12-and-above boys' and girls' handicap categories advance to the international finals. Also advancing to the international finals are the state and zone winners in the 12-and-above boys' and girls' scratch categories who are also USBC Junior Gold members (boys must have an average of 175 or above, girls must have an average of 165 or above). All selected finalists (more than 200 qualify each year) are then assigned to Division I or Division II for the international competition, held annually at a site in the United States; assignment is based on their adjusted score from year-end averages and state and zone competitions. Bowlers whose scores are in the top half are assigned to Division I, and bowlers whose scores are in the bottom half are assigned to Division II. Scholarships are awarded solely on the basis of bowling performance in the international finals.

Financial data: At the international finals, the top finishers in each division receive scholarships of $2,000, $1,500, $1,000, and $500, respectively.

Duration: The competition is held annually.

Number awarded: Each year, 16 scholarships are awarded: 8 are set aside for females (4 in each division) and 8 for males (4 in each division).

Deadline: Qualifying tournaments are held in bowling centers from October through February of each year. Center and section qualifying takes place in March and April. State and zone competitions take place through the end of May. The national finals are held in July.

310 PONY BASEBALL AND SOFTBALL ALUMNI SCHOLARSHIPS

PONY Baseball and Softball
Attn: Alumni Association
1951 Pony Place
P.O. Box 225
Washington, PA 15301
Phone: (724) 225-1060; Fax: (724) 225-9852;
Email: info@pony.org
Web: www.pony.org/HOME/default.asp?menu_category=Home&menuid=681

Summary: To provide financial assistance for college to high school seniors who have played Pony League baseball or softball

Eligibility: This program is open to high school seniors who have played on a PONY affiliated Pony, Colt, or Palomino team for at least two years. Applicants must be planning to attend a college or university. Along with their application, they must submit a 100-word essay on the value that PONY, an acronym for Protect Our Nation's Youth, has had on their personal growth

and development. Selection is based on that essay; a transcript; and participation in school, community, and PONY activities.

Financial data: The stipend is $1,500.

Duration: One year

Number awarded: Four each year: one in each PONY zone

Deadline: April of each year

311 POP WARNER LITTLE SCHOLARS SCHOLASTIC AWARDS

Pop Warner Little Scholars, Inc.
Attn: Director of Scholastics
586 Middletown Boulevard, Suite C-100
Langhorne, PA 19047-1829
Phone: (215) 752-2691; Fax: (215) 752-2879;
Email: scholastics@popwarner.com
Web: www.popwarner.com/scholastics/pop.asp

Summary: To provide financial assistance for college to Pop Warner football players or cheerleaders

Eligibility: This program is open to Pop Warner players or cheerleaders who are currently in the fifth through eighth grades (or above). Applicants need a 96 percent average or better to be considered and should have been involved in school-affiliated organizations and/or academic clubs. Selection is based on school marks, other academic accomplishments, and club involvements. The top 35 players and 25 cheerleaders in each of four grade categories (fifth through eighth grades or above) are named to the "Pop Warner First Team of All-American Scholars." The Senior First Team of All-American Scholars (those in the eighth grade or above) are considered for this scholarship.

Financial data: Stipends range from $500 to $5,000. The funds are held in escrow until the recipient enters college; at that time, the sponsor sends the scholarship amount directly to the chosen institution.

Duration: The stipends are awarded annually.

Number awarded: Varies each year. Recently, 67 of these scholarships were awarded: two at $5,000, two at $2,500, one at $1,250, thirty-one at $1,000, one at $750, one at $625, and twenty-nine at $500.

Deadline: Regional associations submit nominations in January of each year.

312 PRISCILLA MAXWELL ENDICOTT SCHOLARSHIPS

Connecticut Women's Golf Association
c/o Deborah Boynton, Scholarship Committee
52 Mountain Spring Road
Farmington, CT 06032

Phone: (860) 674-1195; Email: scholarships@cwga.org
Web: www.cwga.org/juniors/juniorhome.htm
Summary: To provide financial assistance for college to women golfers from Connecticut
Eligibility: This program is open to high school seniors and college students who are residents of Connecticut attending or planning to attend a four-year college or university. Applicants must be active women golfers with a handicap. Along with their application, they must submit a 200-word essay on how golf has made an impact on their life. Selection is based on participation in golf programs, academic achievement, and financial need.
Financial data: The maximum stipend is $1,000 per year.
Duration: Up to four years
Number awarded: Five each year
Deadline: April of each year

313 PROFESSIONAL GOLF MANAGEMENT STUDIES SCHOLARSHIP

Rhode Island Golf Association
Attn: Burkc Fund
One Button Hole Drive, Suite 2
Providence, RI 02909-5750
Phone: (401) 272-1350; Fax: (401) 331-3627;
Email: burkefund@rigalinks.org
Web: http://burkefund.org/index.html
Summary: To provide financial assistance to residents of Rhode Island who have worked at a golf course and are interested in attending college to prepare for a career in golf
Eligibility: This program is open to residents of Rhode Island who are graduating high school seniors or current college students. Applicants must have at least two years of successful employment as a caddie, golf shop staff worker, cart or bag room operations, practice range, or golf course maintenance staff at a member club of the Rhode Island Golf Association (RIGA). They must be attending or planning to attend an accredited college or university to prepare for a career in golf business fields. Along with their application, they must submit a high school or college transcript; four letters of recommendation (from a high school principal or guidance counselor, an officer or board member of the sponsoring club, a member of the sponsoring club who knows the student, and the golf professional of the sponsoring club); a list of school activities (e.g., academic and athletic interscholastic contests, editorships, entertainments, officer of student organizations, responsible positions in school functions); and documentation of financial need.

Financial data: A stipend is awarded (amount not specified); funds may be used only for tuition, room, board, and other costs billed by postsecondary schools.
Duration: One year; may be renewed for up to three additional years if the recipient maintains a GPA of 2.0 or higher
Number awarded: One or more each year
Deadline: April of each year

314 RAY FRONCILLO SCHOLARSHIP

Eastern Amputee Golf Association
Attn: Bob Buck, Executive Director
2015 Amherst Drive
Bethlehem, PA 18015-5606
Phone: 888-868-0992; Fax: (610) 867-9295;
Email: info@eaga.org
Web: www.eaga.org
Summary: To provide financial assistance for college to members of the Eastern Amputee Golf Association (EAGA) and their families
Eligibility: This program is open to students who are residents of and/or currently enrolled or accepted for enrollment at a college or university in designated Eastern states (Connecticut, Delaware, District of Columbia, Maine, Maryland, Massachusetts, New Hampshire, New Jersey, New York, Pennsylvania, Rhode Island, Vermont, Virginia, or West Virginia). Applicants must be amputee members of the association (those who have experienced the loss of one or more extremities at a major joint due to amputation or birth defect) or members of their families. Financial need is considered in the selection process.
Financial data: The stipend is $1,000.
Duration: One year; may be renewed if the recipient maintains a GPA of 2.0 or higher and continues to demonstrate financial need
Number awarded: One or more each year
Deadline: June of each year

315 RAY MELTON MEMORIAL VIRGINIA QUARTER HORSE YOUTH SCHOLARSHIP

American Quarter Horse Foundation
Attn: Scholarship Coordinator
2601 I-40 East
Amarillo, TX 79104
Phone: (806) 378-5034; 888-209-8322;
Fax: (806) 376-1005; Email: lowens@aqha.org
Web: www.aqha.com/foundation/scholarships/index.html
Summary: To provide financial assistance for college to members of the American Quarter Horse Associa-

tion (AQHA) or the American Quarter Horse Youth Association (AQHYA) who are from Virginia

Eligibility: Applicants must have been members of either organization for at least one year and be residents of Virginia. They must be graduating high school seniors or already enrolled in college with a GPA of 2.5 or higher. Financial need is considered in the selection process.

Financial data: The stipend is $500.

Duration: One year

Number awarded: One each year

Deadline: January of each year

---

316 REGION 10 SCHOLARSHIPS

Arabian Horse Association—Region 10
c/o Gay Jeanne Bower
P.O. Box 6
Johnson Creek, WI 53038
Phone: (920) 699-3690; Email: gayjbower@yahoo.com
Web: www.region10arabians.com/scholarships.htm

Summary: To provide financial assistance for college or graduate school to members of Region 10 of the Arabian Horse Association (AHA) in Minnesota, Wisconsin, the upper peninsula of Michigan, and the province of Ontario

Eligibility: This program is open to members of an Arabian horse club affiliated with Region 10 of the AHA (Minnesota, Wisconsin, upper peninsula of Michigan, and Ontario). Applicants must have been a club member for at least two of the last five years and a resident of the region within the past five years. They must be high school seniors or high school graduates currently enrolled in an associate's, bachelor's, or graduate degree program. Both youth and adult members are eligible. Selection is based on academic record, financial need, equine background, leadership, and a sense of direction regarding their education.

Financial data: The stipend is $1,000.

Duration: One year

Number awarded: Two each year

Deadline: May of each year

---

317 REGION 3 YOUTH SCHOLARSHIP

Arabian Horse Association—Region 3
c/o Deborah Johnson, Director
2455 Rhodes Road
Reno, NV 89521
Phone: (775) 720-3548; Fax: (775) 853-1385;
Email: deborah@renotahoearabians.com
Web: www.arabianhorses3.org/youth.htm

Summary: To provide financial assistance for college to high school seniors who have participated in activities of Region 3 of the Arabian Horse Association (AHA) in northern Nevada and northern California

Eligibility: This program is open to graduating high school seniors who are members of an Arabian horse club that is affiliated with AHA's Region 3 (northern Nevada and northern California). Applicants must be planning to enroll full-time in an accredited college or university. Along with their application, they must submit an essay (three to four pages) on how an Arabian horse has affected their life. Essays are judged on originality (30 percent); content (30 percent); grammar, punctuation, and spelling (25 percent); and following guidelines (15 percent). Selection is based on that essay, academic ability, extracurricular activities, and involvement in equine activities.

Financial data: The stipend is $1,000 per year. Funds are issued after each semester or quarter, provided the recipient submits a transcript showing successful completion of that academic period.

Duration: Two years

Number awarded: One each year

Deadline: February of each year

---

318 RHODE ISLAND INTERSCHOLASTIC LEAGUE HOCKEY SCHOLARSHIP

Rhode Island Interscholastic League
c/o Reynolds Lillibridge, Scholarship Committee
4 High Street
Smithfield, RI 02917
Email: coach@rihockey.net
Web: www.ids.net/~egan176/Scholar-game.html

Summary: To provide financial assistance for college to high school seniors in Rhode Island who have played hockey

Eligibility: This program is open to graduating seniors who have played hockey in programs of the Rhode Island Interscholastic League. Applicants must be planning to attend college. They must submit a letter of recommendation from their head coach, a transcript of grades, and documentation of financial need.

Financial data: The stipend is $500.

Duration: One year

Number awarded: Varies each year; recently, four of these scholarships were awarded.

---

319 RHODE ISLAND WOMEN'S GOLF ASSOCIATION SCHOLARSHIPS

Rhode Island Women's Golf Association
c/o Pat Davitt
17 Oak Manor Drive
Barrington, RI 02806

Phone: (401) 245-4959;

Email: pdavitt@lincolnschool.org

Web: www.riwga.org/scholarships.htm

Summary: To provide financial assistance for college to women golfers from Rhode Island

Eligibility: This program is open to women who have participated in the program of the Rhode Island Women's Golf Association. Applicants must be high school seniors or current undergraduates. They must submit information on their community service experiences; special recognition received at school (e.g., athletic, academic, clubs); financial need; and involvement with golf.

Financial data: A stipend is awarded (amount not specified).

Duration: One year

Number awarded: Varies each year; recently, 17 of these scholarships, worth $5,300, were awarded.

Deadline: May of each year

---

320 RICHARD D. MCDONOUGH GOLF SCHOLARSHIPS

Richard D. McDonough Golf Scholarship Foundation

c/o Robert A. Povencher, President

243 Campbell Street

Manchester, NH 03104

Phone: (603) 232-2345

Web: mcdonough.memfirstweb.net/club/scripts/ home/home_simple.asp

Summary: To provide financial assistance for college to caddies and other young people who have been employed at a golf course in New Hampshire

Eligibility: This program is open to all student employees, male or female, of a New Hampshire golf course or club. Applicants must be recommended by the golf club where they have been employed for at least two seasons. Along with their application, they must submit a brief essay on why they want to go to college, what they expect of a college education, and why they believe this foundation should grant them a scholarship. Selection is based on promise of academic success and financial need.

Financial data: Stipends vary, depending on the need of the recipient, but average nearly $1,000 per year.

Duration: One year; may be renewed up to three additional years if the recipient maintains academic standards and continued financial need

Number awarded: Varies each year; recently, the program awarded scholarships worth $113,620 to 122 students employed at 49 New Hampshire clubs.

Deadline: May of each year

321 ROBBIN RINIER MEMORIAL SCHOLARSHIP

Morris County Youth Soccer Association

c/o Art Vespignani

31 Rockaway Boulevard

Lake Hiawatha, NJ 07034

Phone: (973) 335-3368; Fax: (973) 402-6350;

Email: art724@aol.com

Web: www.mcysa.org

Summary: To provide financial assistance for college to female high school seniors from Morris County, New Jersey, who have been involved in soccer

Eligibility: This program is open to female high school seniors who have played in the Morris County Youth Soccer Association. Applicants must be planning to attend a college or university. Along with their application, they must submit a brief essay on what soccer has given to them. Selection is based on the essay, academic record, leadership, athletic ability, and attitude on the field.

Financial data: The stipend is $1,000.

Duration: One year

Number awarded: One each year

Deadline: April of each year

---

322 ROBERT G. PARIS MEMORIAL SCHOLARSHIP

Missouri Golf Association

Attn: MGA Foundation

1808-B Southwest Boulevard

P.O. Box 104164

Jefferson City, MO 65110

Phone: (573) 636-8994; Fax: (573) 636-4225;

Email: mogolf@mogolf.org

Web: www.mogolf.org

Summary: To provide financial assistance to students at colleges and universities in Missouri who are involved in golf

Eligibility: This program is open to sophomores, juniors, and seniors attending colleges and universities in Missouri. Applicants must be Missouri residents with a GPA of 2.5 or higher. They must be nominated by their college golf coach. Selection is based on the applicant's contribution to the team, playing skills, and financial need.

Financial data: A stipend is awarded (amount not specified).

Duration: One year

Number awarded: Generally, three each year

---

323 ROY S. BATES SCHOLARSHIPS

Wayne County Community Foundation

517 N. Market Street

P.O. Box 201

Wooster, OH 44691

Phone: (330) 262-3877; Fax: (330) 262-8057;

Email: gwcf@gwcf.net

Web: www.gwcf.net/scholarships.htm

Summary: To provide financial assistance for college to high school seniors in Wayne County, Ohio, who have played baseball or basketball

Eligibility: This program is open to seniors graduating from high schools in Wayne County, Ohio, who plan to attend college. Applicants must have been outstanding baseball or basketball athletes, maintained a GPA of 3.0 or higher, and demonstrated good citizenship.

Financial data: The stipend is $2,000 per year.

Duration: One year, nonrenewable

Number awarded: Eight each year

---

324 R.T. ADAMS SCHOLARSHIP

Dixie Softball, Inc.

Attn: President

1101 Skelton Drive

Birmingham, AL 35224

Phone: (205) 785-2255; Fax: (205) 785-2258;

Email: softball@dixie.org

Web: www.dixie.org

Summary: To provide financial assistance for college to high school senior women who have participated in the Dixie Softball program

Eligibility: This program is open to high school senior women who played in the Dixie Softball program for at least two seasons. Applicants must submit a transcript of grades, letter of recommendation from a high school principal or other school official, verification from a Dixie Softball local official of the number of years the applicant participated in the program, and documentation of financial need. Ability as an athlete is not considered in the selection process.

Financial data: The stipend is $1,500.

Duration: One year

Number awarded: One each year

Deadline: February of each year

---

325 SAGEBRUSH CIRCUIT—LEW & JOANN EKLUND EDUCATIONAL SCHOLARSHIP

Appaloosa Youth Foundation, Inc.

c/o Appaloosa Horse Club

Attn: Youth Coordinator

2720 W. Pullman Road

Moscow, ID 83843-4024

Phone: (208) 882-5578, ext. 264; Fax: (208) 882-8150;

Email: aphc@appaloosa.com

Web: www.appaloosa.com/youth/youth-contests.htm

Summary: To provide financial assistance for undergraduate or graduate study in a field related to the equine industry to members or dependents of members of the Appaloosa Horse Club

Eligibility: This program is open to members and children of members of the Appaloosa Horse Club who are college juniors or seniors or graduate students. Applicants must be majoring in a field closely related to the equine industry and have a GPA of 3.5 or higher. They must submit an essay on what their experience with horses has meant to them, why they desire to continue their education, their career goals, the personal qualities that qualify them to receive a scholarship, any circumstances regarding financial need, and how receiving this scholarship will enhance their educational experiences. Selection is based on the essay, leadership potential, sportsmanship, involvement in the Appaloosa and equine industries, GPA, extracurricular equine activities, extracurricular school and community activities, career goals, and general knowledge and accomplishments in horsemanship.

Financial data: The stipend is $2,000.

Duration: One year

Number awarded: One each year

Deadline: June of each year

---

326 SARAH E. HUNEYCUTT SCHOLARSHIP

Florida Women's State Golf Association

Attn: Executive Director

8875 Hidden River Parkway, Suite 110

Tampa, FL 33637

Phone: (813) 864-2130; Fax: (813) 864-2129;

Email: info@fwsga.org

Web: www.fwsga.org/juniors

Summary: To provide financial assistance for college to women in Florida who have an interest in golf

Eligibility: This program is open to females in Florida who have an interest in golf but are not skilled enough to qualify for an athletic scholarship. Applicants must have a need for financial assistance. They must have a GPA of 3.0 or higher and be attending or planning to attend a junior college, college, university, or technical school in Florida.

Financial data: Stipends range from $1,000 to $2,000. Funds are paid directly to the recipient's school.

Duration: One year

Number awarded: Varies each year; recently, seven of these scholarships were awarded.

Deadline: March of each year

327 SMART PROGRAM SCHOLARSHIPS

United States Bowling Congress
Attn: SMART Program
5301 S. 76th Street
Greendale, WI 53129-1192
Phone: (414) 423-3343; 800-514-BOWL, ext. 3343;
Fax: (414) 421-3014; Email: smart@bowl.com
Web: www.bowl.com/scholarships/main.aspx
Summary: To provide financial assistance for college and other educational activities to young bowlers
Eligibility: These awards are presented to bowlers throughout the United States and Canada. Some scholarships are presented to winners of bowling tournaments, but others require written applications. Some require demonstrations of financial need, but others are based on bowling and/or academic accomplishments. Some are limited to students, but others are open to bowlers at other levels. All scholarships must conform to the standards of the Scholarship Management and Accounting Reports for Tenpins (SMART) program of the United States Bowling Congress (USBC).
Financial data: The awards vary; recently, a total of $2,914,100 was awarded through this program. Some scholarships must be used at accredited colleges and universities for tuition, housing, and books. Other uses that are specified include: bowling camps and lessons; bowling coaching seminars; business, technical, or trade schools; continuing education classes; and educational camps in mathematics, science, art, or computers.
Number awarded: Varies each year; recently, more than 35,000 bowlers received scholarships.

328 SOUTH CAROLINA JUNIOR GOLF FOUNDATION SCHOLARSHIP PROGRAM

Center for Scholarship Administration, Inc.
Attn: South Carolina Junior Golf Foundation Scholarship Program
P.O. Box 1465
Taylors, SC 29687-1465
Phone: (864) 268-3363; Fax: (864) 268-7160;
Email: cfsainc@bellsouth.net
Web: www.scholarshipprograms.org/cscholarships.php
Summary: To provide financial assistance for college to residents of South Carolina who have a competitive or recreational interest in golf
Eligibility: This program is open to residents of South Carolina who are seniors in high school or already attending college in the state. Applicants must have a GPA of 2.75 or higher and a competitive or recreational interest in golf. Along with their application, they must submit a one-page essay describing themselves, including their

strengths and their most important achievements in school and community. Selection is based on academic merit (SAT/ACT scores, rank in class, and GPA), potential to succeed in their chosen educational field, and financial need.
Financial data: The stipend is $2,500 per year. Funds are sent directly to the college, university, or technical college to be used for educational expenses, including tuition, fees, books, room, and board.
Duration: One year; may be renewed up to three additional years or until completion of a bachelor's degree, whichever is earlier, provided the recipient maintains a GPA of 2.75 or higher and remains enrolled at a college or university in South Carolina
Number awarded: One or more each year
Deadline: February of each year

329 SOUTH DAKOTA JUNIOR GOLF FOUNDATION SCHOLARSHIPS

South Dakota Golf Association
Attn: Junior Golf Foundation
307 W. 41st Street, Suite 8
Sioux Falls, SD 57105
Phone: (605) 338-7499; Email: sdga@sdga.org
Web: www.sdga.org/foundation.php
Summary: To provide financial assistance for college to high school seniors in South Dakota who have participated in golf
Eligibility: This program is open to seniors graduating from high schools in South Dakota who plan to attend a four-year college, university, or accredited postsecondary institution in the state. Applicants must have resided in South Dakota for at least the past two years. Along with their application, they must provide a history of their golf participation and accomplishments and their future plans in the game.
Financial data: The stipend is $1,000.
Duration: One year
Number awarded: Four each year
Deadline: June of each year

330 SOUTH JERSEY GOLF ASSOCIATION SCHOLARSHIPS

South Jersey Golf Association
Attn: Executive Director
215 Kings Croft
Cherry Hill, NJ 08034
Phone: (856) 667-2962; Email: sjgolf@verizon.net
Web: www.sjgolf.org
Summary: To provide financial assistance for college to high school seniors in southern New Jersey who have been involved in golf

Eligibility: This program is open to seniors graduating from high schools in the following New Jersey counties: Atlantic, Burlington, Camden, Cape May, Cumberland, Gloucester, Ocean, and Salem. Applicants must be members in good standing of their golf team. They must be planning to enroll full-time at an accredited college or university in the United States.

Financial data: A stipend is awarded (amount not specified).

Duration: One year

Number awarded: Varies each year; recently, three of these scholarships were awarded.

Deadline: April of each year

---

331 SOUTH JERSEY SOCCER LEAGUE SCHOLARSHIPS

South Jersey Soccer League
c/o Tom DiValerio, Treasurer
526 Thomas Avenue
Barrington, NJ 08007
Phone: (856) 547-7246; Email: Treasurer@sjsl.org
Web: www.sjsl.org

Summary: To provide financial assistance for college to high school seniors who have participated in the South Jersey Soccer League (SJSL)

Eligibility: This program is open to graduating high school seniors who participated in the SJSL for at least four years. Applicants must be planning to continue their education in a program approved by the SJSL. Along with their application, they must submit a short essay describing what they have done to enhance and work with the soccer program in their community. Selection is based on academic achievement, school activities, participation in the SJSL, participation in sports, and community service. Soccer ability or achievements in soccer are not considered.

Financial data: The stipend is at least $500. Funds are paid directly to the recipient's college or university.

Duration: One year

Number awarded: One or more each year

Deadline: January of each year

---

332 SOUTHERN MAINE WOMEN'S GOLF ASSOCIATION SCHOLARSHIPS

Southern Maine Women's Golf Association
Attn: Scholarship Fund
128 Warren Avenue
Portland, ME 04103
Phone: (207) 797-2268; Email: smwga@gwi.net
Web: www.smwga.com/scholar.html

Summary: To provide financial assistance for college to women residents of southern Maine who have demonstrated an interest in golf

Eligibility: This program is open to women residents of southern Maine, defined as the counties of Androscoggin, Cumberland, Sagadahoc, and York; a portion of Oxford County, including the town of Bethel and points south; and the towns of Boothbay and Boothbay Harbor in Lincoln County. Applicants must have demonstrated an interest in golf. They must be attending or planning to attend an institution of higher education. Selection is based on academic achievement, participation in community activities, and interest and participation in the sport of golf. Financial need is not considered.

Financial data: A stipend is awarded (amount not specified). Funds are paid directly to the educational institution.

Duration: One year

Number awarded: One or more each year

Deadline: July of each year

---

333 SPIRIT OF A WINNER SCHOLARSHIP

Arabian Horse Foundation
1024 K Street
Lincoln, NE 68508
Phone: (402) 477-2233; Fax: (402) 477-2286
Web: www.arabianhorsefoundation.org/scholarship.html

Summary: To provide financial assistance for college to high school students who have a record of equine involvement

Eligibility: This program is open to students who have a record of involvement with horses. Applicants must be juniors or seniors in high school who have shown at the Youth Nationals of the Arabian Horse Association. They must have a GPA of B or higher. Along with their application, they must submit information on their financial need, honors or academic awards, extracurricular activities and offices, leadership role, career goal, and equine involvement for the past two years.

Financial data: The stipend is $2,000 per year.

Duration: One year

Number awarded: Seven each year

Deadline: January of each year

---

334 SPORTSMANSHIP RECOGNITION PROGRAM SCHOLARSHIP

Summary: To recognize and reward, with college scholarships, outstanding student-athletes (including cheerleaders) in Kentucky high schools

See Listing #106.

KAPLAN

335 STELLA S. GILB SCHOLARSHIPS

Kentucky Association of Pep Organization Sponsors
c/o Lucy Moore, President
483 Skaggs Road
Morehead, KY 40351
Phone: (606) 783-1307;
Email: lucy.moore@rowan.kyschools.us
Web: www.kapos.org

Summary: To provide financial assistance for college to high school cheerleaders who are members of the Kentucky Association of Pep Organization Sponsors (KAPOS)

Eligibility: This program is open to seniors graduating from high schools in Kentucky in the top 15 percent of their class. Applicants must have cheered on a varsity squad for at least two years and be members of KAPOS. They must have an ACT score of at least 22 or an equivalent score on the SAT. Along with their application, they must submit a 200-word essay on the lessons in life they have learned from cheerleading. Selection is based on the essay, academic ability, leadership, and financial need.

Financial data: The stipend is $500.

Duration: One year

Number awarded: Ten each year

Deadline: February of each year

336 STEVE CONNER MEMORIAL SCHOLARSHIPS

Southern California Section PGA
Attn: Foundation
36201 Champions Drive
Beaumont, CA 92223
Phone: (951) 845-4653; Fax: (951) 769-6733;
Email: ngatch@pgahq.com
Web: http://southerncal.pga.com

Summary: To provide financial assistance for college to high school seniors in southern California, especially those who have played golf

Eligibility: This program is open to seniors graduating from high schools in southern California. Applicants must be planning to enroll at an accredited two- or four-year college or university. They must be able to demonstrate academic achievement, participation in extracurricular activities, personal character, and leadership ability. Active participation in golf is not mandatory but is preferred. Preference is given to residents of the Coachella Valley.

Financial data: The stipend is $1,500.

Duration: One year

Number awarded: Two each year

Deadline: May of each year

337 SWAYZE WOODRUFF MEMORIAL MID-SOUTH SCHOLARSHIP

American Quarter Horse Foundation
Attn: Scholarship Coordinator
2601 I-40 East
Amarillo, TX 79104
Phone: (806) 378-5034; 888-209-8322;
Fax: (806) 376-1005; Email: lowens@aqha.org
Web: www.aqha.com/foundation/scholarships/index
.html

Summary: To provide financial assistance for college to members of the American Quarter Horse Association (AQHA) or the American Quarter Horse Youth Association (AQHYA) who are from selected southern states

Eligibility: This program is open to members of either organization (for at least one year) who are residents of Alabama, Arkansas, Louisiana, Mississippi, or Tennessee. Applicants must have competed in AQHA or AQHYA-approved shows. They must be graduating high school seniors or already enrolled in college with a GPA of 2.5 or higher. Financial need is considered in the selection process.

Financial data: The stipend is $2,000 per year.

Duration: Up to four years, provided the recipient maintains a GPA of 2.5 or higher and full-time enrollment

Number awarded: One each year

Deadline: January of each year

338 TERRENCE FOGARTY HOCKEY SCHOLARSHIP

Terrence Fogarty Artist, LLC
c/o Karen Fogarty
P.O. Box 345
Victoria, MN 55386
Phone: (952) 443-0028; Email: fogartyart1@msn.com
Web: www.terrencefogarty.com

Summary: To provide financial assistance for college to high school seniors in Minnesota who have played hockey

Eligibility: This program is open to seniors graduating from high schools in Minnesota who have played hockey. Applicants must be planning to enroll in college. Along with their application, they must submit brief essays on their community involvement, history of their interest and involvement in hockey, how hockey has played a positive role in shaping them as a person, their knowledge of Minnesota's hockey history, and their plans for further education. In the selection process, character, commitment to the community, and love of the game are given greater weight than individual hockey skills. Financial need is not considered.

Financial data: A stipend is awarded (amount not specified).
Duration: One year
Number awarded: One or more each year
Deadline: February of each year

---

339 TEXAS GULF SURFING ASSOCIATION SCHOLARSHIPS

Texas Gulf Surfing Association
P.O. Box 817
Seabrook, TX 77586
Web: www.tgsa.org
Summary: To provide financial assistance for college to members of the Texas Gulf Surfing Association (TGSA)
Eligibility: This program is open to TGSA members who are or will be attending a college or trade school. Applicants must submit a 500-word personal letter describing their need, their future goals, and how their choice of educational institution and field of study will help them reach those goals; official transcripts; and a letter of recommendation.
Financial data: The stipend is $500.
Duration: One year
Number awarded: Three each year
Deadline: June of each year

---

340 TEXAS TENNIS AND EDUCATION FOUNDATION SCHOLARSHIPS

Texas Tennis and Education Foundation
Attn: Executive Director
8105 Exchange Drive
Austin, TX 78754
Phone: (512) 443-1334, ext. 222; Fax: (512) 443-4748;
Email: leichenbaum@texas.usta.com
Web: www.texastennisfoundation.com/scholar.html
Summary: To provide financial assistance for college to students in Texas who have an interest in tennis
Eligibility: This program is open to students who have an interest in tennis, are U.S. citizens, and live in Texas. Applicants must be high school students who will be entering college or college students who are in good standing at their respective colleges or universities. They must submit a completed application, federal income tax returns from the previous two years, an academic transcript, a copy of their SAT or ACT test results, a list of extracurricular activities (including tennis activities), a personal statement (on their educational goals, tennis activities, and volunteer work), and a letter of recommendation. Selection is based on merit and financial need.
Financial data: The stipend is $1,000.

Duration: One year, renewable
Number awarded: Varies each year
Deadline: April of each year

---

341 TIM NEELY SCHOLARSHIP

Dixie Softball, Inc.
Attn: President
1101 Skelton Drive
Birmingham, AL 35224
Phone: (205) 785-2255; Fax: (205) 785-2258;
Email: softball@dixie.org
Web: www.dixie.org
Summary: To provide financial assistance for college to high school senior women who have participated in the Dixie Softball program
Eligibility: This program is open to high school senior women who played in the Dixie Softball program for at least two seasons. Applicants must submit a transcript of grades, letter of recommendation from a high school principal or other school official, verification from a Dixie Softball local official of the number of years the applicant participated in the program, and documentation of financial need. Ability as an athlete is not considered in the selection process.
Financial data: The stipend is $1,500.
Duration: One year
Number awarded: One each year
Deadline: February of each year

---

342 TIM OLSON MEMORIAL SCHOLARSHIP

American Water Ski Educational Foundation
Attn: Director
1251 Holy Cow Road
Polk City, FL 33868-8200
Phone: (863) 324-2472; Fax: (863) 324-3996;
Email: info@waterskihalloffame.com
Web: www.waterskihalloffame.com
Summary: To provide financial assistance to currently enrolled college students who participate in water skiing
Eligibility: This program is open to full-time students at two- or four-year accredited colleges entering their sophomore, junior, or senior year. Applicants must be U.S. citizens and active members of a sport division within USA Water Ski (AWSA, ABC, AKA, WSDA, NSSA, NCWSA, NWSRA, USAWB, and HYD). Along with their application, they must submit a 500-word essay on a topic that changes annually but relates to water skiing; recently, students were asked to assume that they had just acquired the position of marketing director for the American Water Ski Educational

Foundation and to describe the creative measure they would implement to increase membership in the foundation. Selection is based on the essay, academic record, leadership, extracurricular involvement, letters of recommendation, AWSA membership activities, and financial need.

Financial data: The stipend is $1,500 per year.

Duration: One year; may be renewed for up to two additional years

Number awarded: Two each year

Deadline: March of each year

---

343 TIM & TOM GULLIKSON FOUNDATION COLLEGE SCHOLARSHIPS

Tim & Tom Gullikson Foundation
Attn: Executive Director
175 N. Main Street
Branford, CT 06405
Phone: 888-GULLIKSON
Web: www.gullikson.com

Summary: To provide financial assistance for college to patients or survivors and/or children of patients or survivors of brain tumors, particularly those with ties to tennis

Eligibility: This program is open to high school seniors, high school graduates, and currently enrolled or returning college students. Applicants must be brain tumor patients/survivors and/or children of brain tumor patients/survivors. Special consideration is given to applicants who have a connection to the tennis community. Financial need is considered in the selection process.

Financial data: The maximum stipend is $5,000 per year. Funds are paid directly to the recipient's school and may be used for tuition, fees, books, room, and board.

Duration: One year. Recipients may reapply up to three additional years; however, the total money awarded to each recipient cannot exceed $20,000.

Number awarded: Varies each year; a maximum of $25,000 is available for these scholarships each year.

Deadline: March of each year

---

344 TODD E. CLARK MEMORIAL SCHOLARSHIP

North Central Pennsylvania Golf Association
Attn: Executive Director
199 Gettysberg Estates
Sunbury, PA 17801
Email: ncpga2@uplink.net
Web: www.ncpga.net/junior-golf/golf-scholarships/index.asp

Summary: To provide financial assistance for college to high school seniors in northcentral Pennsylvania who have participated in golfing activities

Eligibility: This program is open to seniors graduating from high schools in northcentral Pennsylvania. Applicants must have played golf and be planning to attend college. Along with their application, they must submit information on their golfing background and an essay on a golfing experience of particular importance, a lesson they have learned from the game of golf, or the role they see golf playing in their future.

Financial data: The stipend is a total of $2,400 ($600 per year).

Duration: Four years

Number awarded: One each year

Deadline: March of each year

---

345 TODD MENEFEE SCHOLARSHIP

Southern Texas PGA Section
Attn: Foundation
21604 Cypresswood Drive
Spring, TX 77373
Phone: (832) 442-2404; Fax: (832) 442-2403;
Email: stexas@pgahq.com
Web: www.stpga.com/index.cfm?menu=2706

Summary: To provide financial assistance for college to residents of southern Texas who have an interest in golf

Eligibility: This program is open to residents of the Southern Texas PGA Section who are enrolled or planning to enroll in college as a full-time student. Applicants must have a GPA of 2.5 or higher and be able to demonstrate financial need. They must have shown an interest in the game of golf, although golfing ability is not considered in the selection process and applicants are not required to be junior golfers. For graduating high school seniors, selection is based on academic record, ACT and/or SAT scores, extracurricular activities, voluntary statements, financial need, and junior golf participation and interest. For current college students, selection is based on cumulative college GPA, financial need, voluntary statements, college extracurricular activities, and golf participation and interest.

Financial data: Stipends range from $1,000 to $3,000.

Duration: One year; recipients may reapply.

Number awarded: Varies each year

Deadline: April of each year

---

346 TOM REED SCHOLARSHIP

Eastern Amputee Golf Association
Attn: Bob Buck, Executive Director
2015 Amherst Drive

Bethlehem, PA 18015-5606
Phone: 888-868-0992; Fax: (610) 867-9295;
Email: info@eaga.org
Web: www.eaga.org
Summary: To provide financial assistance for college to members of the Eastern Amputee Golf Association (EAGA) and their families
Eligibility: This program is open to students who are residents of and/or currently enrolled or accepted for enrollment at a college or university in designated Eastern states (Connecticut, Delaware, District of Columbia, Maine, Maryland, Massachusetts, New Hampshire, New Jersey, New York, Pennsylvania, Rhode Island, Vermont, Virginia, or West Virginia). Applicants must be amputee members of the association (those who have experienced the loss of one or more extremities at a major joint due to amputation or birth defect) or members of their families. Financial need is considered in the selection process.
Financial data: The stipend is $1,000.
Duration: One year; may be renewed if the recipient maintains a GPA of 2.0 or higher and continues to demonstrate financial need
Number awarded: One or more each year
Deadline: June of each year

---

347 TOMMY AYCOCK SCHOLARSHIP

Southern Texas PGA Section
Attn: Foundation
21604 Cypresswood Drive
Spring, TX 77373
Phone: (832) 442-2404; Fax: (832) 442-2403;
Email: stexas@pgahq.com
Web: www.stpga.com/index.cfm?menu=2706
Summary: To provide financial assistance for college to residents of southern Texas who have an interest in golf
Eligibility: This program is open to residents of the Southern Texas PGA Section who are enrolled or planning to enroll in college as a full-time student. Applicants must have a GPA of 2.5 or higher and be able to demonstrate financial need. They must have shown an interest in the game of golf, although golfing ability is not considered in the selection process and applicants are not required to be junior golfers. For graduating high school seniors, selection is based on academic record, ACT and/or SAT scores, extracurricular activities, voluntary statements, financial need, and junior golf participation and interest. For current college students, selection is based on cumulative college GPA, financial need, voluntary statements, college extracurricular activities, and golf participation and interest.
Financial data: Stipends range from $1,000 to $3,000.

Duration: One year; recipients may reapply.
Number awarded: Varies each year
Deadline: April of each year

---

348 TONY MARLOWE JUNIOR SCHOLARSHIP

Middle Atlantic Section PGA of America
Attn: MAPGA Scholarship Foundation
2680 Jefferson Davis Highway
Stafford, VA 22554
Phone: (540) 720-7420, ext. 28; Fax: (540) 720-7076;
Email: midatl@pgahq.com
Web: http://mapga.com/index.cfm?menu=278 &openitem=278
Summary: To provide financial assistance for college to high school juniors and seniors who have participated in the Junior Tour of the Middle Atlantic Section PGA of America (MAPGA)
Eligibility: This program is open to members of the MAPGA Junior Tour who are completing their junior or senior year of high school. Anyone may become members of the tour. Also eligible are the children and grandchildren of PGA members and apprentices seeking their PGA membership. Applicants must submit an essay of 100–300 words describing what it means to gain a college education and what they want to study in college; a list of extracurricular activities; and an essay on their interest in the game of golf, including (but not limited to) playing, working, watching, history, or family involvement in golf. Selection is based on on-course etiquette and academic performance, but consideration is also given to extracurricular activities, financial need, the essays, references, and off-course behavior.
Financial data: A stipend is awarded (amount not specified).
Duration: One year; recipients may reapply.
Number awarded: Varies each year
Deadline: August of each year

---

349 TRAMPOLINE AND TUMBLING SCHOLARSHIP PROGRAM

USA Gymnastics
Attn: Trampoline and Tumbling Program
1309 Tahoka Road
P.O. Box 306
Brownfield, TX 79316
Phone: (806) 637-8670; Fax: (806) 637-9046;
Email: ktyler@usa-gumnastics.org
Web: www.usa-gymnastics.org/tt/about-tt.html
Summary: To provide financial assistance for college to gymnasts who participate in trampoline and tumbling activities

Eligibility: This program is open to high school seniors and currently-enrolled college students who are registered athletes training and competing with USA Gymnastics trampoline and tumbling. Applicants must be enrolled or planning to enroll full or part time at an accredited college or university. They must have a GPA of 2.5 or higher. Along with their application, they must submit information on their athletic accomplishments, athletic goals for the current and next 5 years, academic goals, probable career goals, how a scholarship would contribute to their goals, honors and activities, and financial need.

Financial data: The size of the scholarship varies, depending upon the funds raised throughout the year in support of the program. Funds must be used for college or postsecondary educational expenses.

Duration: One year

Number awarded: Varies each year; recently, 11 of these scholarships, with a value of $23,000, were awarded.

Deadline: May of each year

---

350 USA RACQUETBALL SCHOLARSHIP PROGRAM

USA Racquetball
Attn: Scholarship Program
1685 West Uintah
Colorado Springs, CO 80904-2921
Phone: (719) 635-5396, ext. 123; Fax: (719) 635-0685
Web: www.usra.org

Summary: To provide financial assistance for college to members of the United States Racquetball Association

Eligibility: This program is aimed at members of the association who are high school seniors, although students already in college are also eligible. Applicants must be currently enrolled or accepted in a full-time program at an accredited college, university, vocational, or technical school. They must submit a 200-word autobiography, three teacher's reports, high school or college transcripts, a 200-word essay on their pick of the most influential person in the world of sport, and additional information (such as award certificates, academic awards, racquetball accomplishments, press clippings, volunteer work, and other high school sports or clubs). If they wish to be considered on the basis of financial need, they must also submit a separate letter and financial information.

Financial data: The stipend is generally $500. Funds are paid directly to the recipient (must be cosigned by the recipient and the recipient's school) and are to be used to pay for tuition, textbooks, instructional materials, room and board, and other miscellaneous fees.

Duration: One year; recipients may reapply.

Number awarded: Varies each year; recently, six of these scholarships were awarded.

Deadline: June of each year

---

351 USBC JUNIOR GOLD CHAMPIONSHIPS

United States Bowling Congress
Attn: Junior Gold Program
5301 S. 76th Street
Greendale, WI 53129-1192
Phone: (414) 423-3171; 800-514-BOWL, ext. 3171;
Fax: (414) 421-3014; Email: usbcjuniorgold@bowl.com
Web: www.bowl.com/bowl/yaba

Summary: To recognize and reward, with college scholarships, United States Bowling Congress (USBC) Junior Gold program members who achieve high scores in a national competition

Eligibility: This program is open to USBC members who qualify for the Junior Gold program by maintaining a bowling average score of 165 for girls or 175 for boys, based on at least 21 games. Competitions for Junior Gold members are held throughout the season at bowling centers and in bowling leagues in the United States. Each approved competition may enter its top 10 percent of scorers in the Junior Gold Championships, held annually at a site in the United States. In addition, USBC Junior Gold members who participate in the Pepsi USBC Youth Bowling Championship in the girls' and boys' 12-and-over scratch categories and achieve high scores in state and zone competitions are eligible to advance to the national tournament of this program. They compete in separate divisions for boys and girls. Scholarships are awarded solely on the basis of bowling performance in the national tournament.

Financial data: Scholarships depend on the availability of funding provided by sponsors. Recently, more than $50,000 in scholarships was awarded. Another $15,000 in scholarships was awarded to Junior Gold participants who qualified for the national tournament through the Pepsi competition. That includes $3,000 for first, $2,000 for second, $1,500 for third, and $1,000 for fourth for boys and girls.

Duration: The competition is held annually.

Number awarded: Varies each year. Recently, a total of 1,458 spots were available at the national tournament, and scholarships were provided to approximately 10 percent of the competitors. For bowlers from the Pepsi competition, four girls and four boys win scholarships.

Deadline: Applications must by submitted by May of each year. The national finals are held in July.

352 USBC YOUTH LEADERS OF THE YEAR AWARDS

United States Bowling Congress
Attn: SMART Program
5301 S. 76th Street
Greendale, WI 53129-1192
Phone: (414) 423-3223; 800-514-BOWL, ext. 3223;
Fax: (414) 421-3014; Email: smart@bowl.com
Web: www.bowl.com/scholarships/main.aspx
Summary: To recognize and reward, with college scholarships, outstanding young bowlers
Eligibility: These awards are presented to participants in the Youth Leader program of the United States Bowling Congress (USBC) who are 18 years of age or older. Males and females are considered in separate competitions. Selection is based on exemplary Youth Leader activities and contributions to the sport of bowling.
Financial data: The awards consist of $1,500 college scholarships.
Duration: The awards are presented annually.
Number awarded: Two each year: one for a female and one for a male
Deadline: Nominations must be submitted by January of each year.

353 USSA TUITION ASSISTANCE

United States Ski and Snowboard Association
Attn: U.S. Ski and Snowboard Team Foundation
1500 Kearns Boulevard
P.O. Box 100
Park City, UT 84060
Phone: (435) 647-2074; Fax: (435) 647-2656;
Email: info@ussa.org
Web: www.ussa.org/PublishingFolder/6302_6419.htm
Summary: To provide financial assistance for college to U.S. Ski Team and U S. Snowboarding athletes
Eligibility: This program is open to A, B, and C team members of the U.S. Ski Team and U.S. Snowboarding Team (alpine, cross-country, disabled, freestyle, jumping/nordic combined, snowboard). Alumni are eligible for one year after retirement. Applicants must be in good standing with the United States Ski and Snowboard Association (USSA) and earn less than $50,000 per year. They must be enrolled at an accredited college or university with a GPA of 2.0 or higher. Athletes must first apply for assistance from the USOC Special Assistance/Tuition Program. All qualified applicants receive assistance.
Financial data: The amount awarded varies each year, depending upon the number of eligible recipients. Funds may be used for tuition only and are awarded as reimbursement for completed terms.

Duration: One year
Number awarded: Varies; in recent years, up to 17 have been awarded annually.
Deadline: May of each year

354 USTA TENNIS & EDUCATION FOUNDATION COLLEGE EDUCATION SCHOLARSHIPS

United States Tennis Association
Attn: USTA Tennis & Education Foundation
70 West Road Oak Lane
White Plains, NY 10604
Phone: (914) 696-7223; Email: eliezer@usta.com
Web: www.usta.com/communitytennis/fullstory.sps?iNewsid=66422
Summary: To provide financial assistance for college to high school seniors who have participated in an organized community tennis program
Eligibility: This program is open to high school seniors who have excelled academically, demonstrated achievements in leadership, and participated extensively in an organized community tennis program. Applicants must be planning to enroll as a full-time undergraduate student at a two- or four-year college or university. They must be able to demonstrate financial need. Along with their application, they must submit an essay about themselves and how their participation in a tennis program has impacted their lives.
Financial data: The stipend is $1,500 per year. Funds are paid directly to the recipient's college or university.
Duration: Two years for students at community colleges; four years for students at four-year colleges and universities
Number awarded: Twenty-four each year
Deadline: February of each year

355 USTA TENNIS & EDUCATION FOUNDATION COLLEGE TEXTBOOK SCHOLARSHIPS

United States Tennis Association
Attn: USTA Tennis & Education Foundation
70 West Road Oak Lane
White Plains, NY 10604
Phone: (914) 696-7223; Email: eliezer@usta.com
Web: www.usta.com/communitytennis/fullstory.sps?iNewsid=66422
Summary: To provide financial assistance for the purchase of college textbooks and supplies to high school seniors who have participated in an organized community tennis program
Eligibility: This program is open to high school seniors who have excelled academically, demonstrated achievements in leadership, and participated extensively in an

organized community tennis program. Applicants must be planning to enroll as a full-time undergraduate student at a two- or four-year college or university. Along with their application, they must submit an essay about themselves and how their participation in a tennis program has impacted their lives.

Financial data: The stipend is $500. Funds are paid directly to the recipient's college or university bookstore to assist students in purchasing textbooks or supplies.

Duration: One year, nonrenewable

Number awarded: Ten each year

Deadline: February of each year

---

356 UTAH GOLF ASSOCIATION SCHOLARSHIPS

Utah Golf Association
Attn: Scholarship Committee
9121 S. 150 W., Suite D
P.O. Box 5601
Sandy, UT 84091-5601
Phone: (801) 563-0400; Fax: (801) 563-0632
Web: www.uga.org/awards/scholarship/index.html

Summary: To provide financial assistance for college or graduate school to students in Utah who have been active in golf

Eligibility: This program is open to students enrolled or planning to enroll at a postsecondary institution in Utah. Preference is given to applicants already in college or working on an advanced degree. At least one scholarship is reserved for a student interested in preparing for a career in agronomy, turf grass management, or as a golf course superintendent. Applicants must have been involved in golf, but skill is not considered. They must describe their long-range educational and occupational goals and objectives; what they like about golf; and their background, interests, and future plans in golf. Selection is based on educational experience, achievements, GPA, test scores, goals, and objectives (25 percent); leadership, extracurricular activities, work experience, volunteerism, and character (25 percent); golf affiliation and interest (25 percent); and financial need (25 percent).

Financial data: The stipend is $1,200.

Duration: One year

Number awarded: At least three each year

Deadline: April of each year

---

357 VERMONT GOLF ASSOCIATION SCHOLARSHIP

Vermont Golf Association
P.O. Box 1612, Station A
Rutland, VT 08701-1612
Phone: (802) 773-7180; 800-924-0418;
Email: vga@vtga.org
Web: www.vtga.org/Templates/archive_dump/
scholarship.htm

Summary: To provide financial assistance for college to high school seniors in Vermont who have a connection to golf

Eligibility: This program is open to residents of Vermont who are in the top 40 percent of their graduating class and are enrolled in or accepted as a full-time student at a college or university of their choice. Applicants must submit a high school transcript, at least one letter of recommendation, a letter attesting to their connection with golf, and a copy of their SAR. Finalists are interviewed. Selection is based on academic record, connection to golf, and financial need.

Financial data: The stipend is at least $800 per year.

Duration: Up to four years

Number awarded: Ten each year

Deadline: April of each year

---

358 VINCE SCARPETTA SR. SCHOLARSHIP

Anthracite Golf Association
617 Keystone Avenue
Peckville, PA 18452
Phone: (570) 383-GOLF; Fax: (570) 383-4654;
Email: palloyd127@cs.com
Web: www.ncpga.net/junior-golf/golf-scholarships/
index.asp

Summary: To provide financial assistance for college to high school seniors from northeastern Pennsylvania who have been involved in golf

Eligibility: This program is open to seniors graduating from high schools in northeastern Pennsylvania who have been involved in golf. Applicants must have been accepted by a postsecondary institution. They are not required to be affiliated with a golf club. Along with their application, they must submit a personal statement about their career goals. Selection is based on that statement, academic achievement, leadership and service, golf accomplishments, participation in the Anthracite Golf Association junior tour, and two letters of recommendation.

Financial data: Stipends range from $500 to $3,000. Half the funds are paid at the beginning of the first semester and half at the beginning the second semester, provided recipients earn a GPA of 2.5 or higher for the first semester.

Duration: One year

Number awarded: Varies each year

Deadline: February of each year

359 VIRGINIA ATHLETIC TRAINERS ASSOCIATION SCHOLARSHIP AWARD

Virginia Athletic Trainers Association
c/o Terry Zablocki, Scholarship Committee Chair
Maury High School
322 Shirley Avenue
Norfolk, VA 23517
Phone: (757) 628-9189; Email: tzablocki@nps.k12.va.us
Web: www.vata.us/scholarship/index.htm
Summary: To provide financial assistance to high school seniors in Virginia who are interested in preparing for a career as an athletic trainer
Eligibility: This program is open to seniors graduating from high schools in Virginia who intend to study athletic training in college. Applicants must provide evidence of interest in athletic training through experience as a high school student athletic trainer and/or attendance at an athletic training seminar or workshop. Along with their application, they must submit an essay of 250 to 500 words on their interest in a career in the allied health profession of athletic training. Selection is based on academic ability, leadership ability, responsible citizenship, and dedication and interest in athletic training.
Financial data: Stipends are $1,000 or $500.
Duration: One year
Number awarded: Two each year: one at $1,000 and one at $500
Deadline: March of each year

360 VIRGINIA GOLF FOUNDATION SCHOLARSHIP PROGRAM

Virginia State Golf Association
Attn: Virginia Golf Foundation, Inc.
600 Founders Bridge Boulevard
Midlothian, VA 23113
Phone: (804) 378-2300, ext. 11; Fax: (804) 378-8216;
Email: info@vsga.org
Web: www.vsga.org/article.asp?ID=4857
Summary: To provide financial assistance for college to young Virginians who have an interest in golf
Eligibility: This program is open to high school seniors in Virginia who are interested in golf and wish to attend a college or university in the state. Applicants must submit an essay of 500 words or less on how golf has influenced their life, the role it will play in their future plans, why they are applying for this scholarship, and their career plans following graduation. Selection is based on the essay, interest in golf (excellence and ability are not considered), academic achievement, citizenship, character, and financial need. Applications must be made on behalf of the candidate by a member club of the Virginia State Golf Association (VSGA). Some scholarships are reserved for students working on degrees in turf grass management at Virginia Polytechnic Institute and State University.
Financial data: Stipends range from $750 to $5,000. Funds may be used only for tuition, room, and other approved educational expenses.
Duration: The program includes four-year scholarships and one-year merit awards.
Number awarded: Varies each year. Recently, 30 of these scholarships were awarded: two at $5,000 (the Spencer-Wilkinson Award for a woman and the C. Dan Keffer Award for a man), five at $3,500, three at $3,000, two at $2,500, three at $2,000 (including the David A. King Merit Award and the Red Speigle Award reserved for a golfer from the Peninsula area), eleven at $1,000, and four at $750 for turf grass management students at Virginia Tech. The 26 golf scholarships included 13 for four years and 13 merit awards for one year.
Deadline: February of each year

361 VIRGINIA LORBEER SPIRIT LEADER SCHOLARSHIP

Colorado Spirit Coaches Association
c/o Angela Ottmann, President
10324 Tracery Court
P.O. Box 248
Parker, CO 80134
Phone: (303) 840-4287; 877-840-4287;
Fax: (303) 805-5071; Email: csca@comcast.net
Web: www.cscaonline.org/prog-scholarship.html
Summary: To provide financial assistance for college to high school seniors in college who have performed on their school's cheer and/or dance squad
Eligibility: This program is open to seniors graduating from high schools in Colorado who have cheered and/or danced for at least two years. Applicants must be planning to attend an accredited two- or four-year college. They must have a GPA of 3.0 or higher. Selection is based on participation in school and community activities, number of years in the spirit program, two letters of recommendation, and academic record.
Financial data: The stipend is $500.
Duration: One year
Number awarded: One each year
Deadline: March of each year

362 WARREN SMITH SCHOLARSHIP

Southern Texas PGA Section
Attn: Foundation
21604 Cypresswood Drive

Spring, TX 77373

Phone: (832) 442-2404; Fax: (832) 442-2403;

Email: stexas@pgahq.com

Web: www.stpga.com/index.cfm?menu=2706

Summary: To provide financial assistance for college to residents of southern Texas who have an interest in golf

Eligibility: This program is open to residents of the Southern Texas PGA Section who are enrolled or planning to enroll in college as a full-time student. Applicants must have a GPA of 2.5 or higher and be able to demonstrate financial need. They must have shown an interest in the game of golf, although golfing ability is not considered in the selection process and applicants are not required to be junior golfers. For graduating high school seniors, selection is based on academic record, ACT and/or SAT scores, extracurricular activities, voluntary statements, financial need, and junior golf participation and interest. For current college students, selection is based on cumulative college GPA, financial need, voluntary statements, college extracurricular activities, and golf participation and interest.

Financial data: Stipends range from $1,000 to $3,000.

Duration: One year; recipients may reapply.

Number awarded: Varies each year

Deadline: April of each year

---

363 WEST END SOCCER ASSOCIATION CITIZEN SCHOLARSHIP

West End Soccer Association

Attn: Bruce Angebranndt, President

P.O. Box 7093

Ewing, NJ 08628

Phone: (609) 883-2932;

Email: bangebranndt@westendsoccer.com

Web: www.westendsoccer.com/scholarship.html

Summary: To provide financial assistance for college to high school seniors in central and southern New Jersey who have participated in the West End Soccer Association in a role other than as a player

Eligibility: This program is open to graduating high school seniors who have participated in the West End soccer program in central and southern New Jersey for at least five years prior to reaching 16 years of age. Their participation must have been in a capacity other than as a player (e.g., referee, trainer). Applicants must be planning to enroll full-time at a postsecondary educational institution. Along with their application, they must submit an essay on the values they have gained from their community service and citizenship in the West End Soccer Association and how those values will help them in the future. Selection is based on that

essay, academic record, and participation in West End activities.

Financial data: The stipend is $1,000.

Duration: One year

Number awarded: One each year

Deadline: April of each year

---

364 WEST END SOCCER ASSOCIATION SCHOLAR-ATHLETE SCHOLARSHIP

West End Soccer Association

Attn: Bruce Angebranndt, President

P.O. Box 7093

Ewing, NJ 08628

Phone: (609) 883-2932;

Email: bangebranndt@westendsoccer.com

Web: www.westendsoccer.com/scholarship.html

Summary: To provide financial assistance for college to high school seniors in central and southern New Jersey who have participated in the West End Soccer Association

Eligibility: This program is open to graduating high school seniors who have participated in the West End soccer program in central and southern New Jersey for at least five years prior to reaching 16 years of age. Applicants must be planning to enroll full-time at a postsecondary educational institution. Along with their application, they must submit an essay on the values they have gained from their participation in the West End Soccer Association and how those have help them during their high school years. Selection is based on that essay, academic record, and participation in community and/or school activities.

Financial data: The stipend is $1,000.

Duration: One year

Number awarded: One each year

Deadline: April of each year

---

365 WEST VIRGINIA GOLF ASSOCIATION FUND SCHOLARSHIPS

Greater Kanawha Valley Foundation

Attn: Scholarship Coordinator

1600 Huntington Square

900 Lee Street E.

P.O. Box 3041

Charleston, WV 25331-3041

Phone: (304) 346-3620; Fax: (304) 346-3640;

Email: tgkvf@tgkvf.com

Web: www.tgkvf.com/scholar.html

Summary: To provide financial assistance for college to residents of West Virginia who have been involved in golf

Eligibility: This program is open to residents of West Virginia who are students at a college or university anywhere in the country. Applicants must have played golf in West Virginia as an amateur for recreation or competition or have been or are presently employed in West Virginia as a caddie, groundsreeper, bag boy, or other golf-related job. Along with their application, they must include an essay explaining how the game of golf has made an impact on their life. They must have an ACT score of 20 or higher, be able to demonstrate good moral character, and have a GPA of 2.5 or higher. Selection is based on academic accomplishments, volunteer service, character, and level of exposure to the game of golf; skill level is not a major requirement.

Financial data: The stipend is $1,000 per year.

Duration: One year, renewable

Number awarded: Varies each year; recently, two of these scholarships were awarded.

Deadline: February of each year

366 WESTERN PENNSYLVANIA GOLF ASSOCIATION SCHOLARSHIPS

Western Pennsylvania Golf Association
Attn: Scholarship Fund
524 Fourth Street
Pittsburgh, PA 15238
Phone: (412) 826-2180; Fax: (412) 826-2183;
Email: westpennga@usga.org
Web: www.wpga.org/scholarship/wpga_scholarship_index.htm

Summary: To provide financial assistance for college to high school seniors and college undergraduates in western Pennsylvania who have worked at a golf course

Eligibility: This program is open to graduating high school seniors and college freshmen and sophomores who have been employed for at least two years at a golf club that is a member of the Western Pennsylvania Golf Association (WPGA). Applicants must be attending or planning to attend a college or university. Along with their application, they must submit a 500-word essay on their career plans and why they can benefit from this scholarship. Selection is based on academic qualifications, service to their employer, extracurricular and community activities, and financial need. The program includes the Fred Brand Jr. Scholarship (which also considers sportsmanship in golf in the selection process), the Stan Wiel Scholarship (for students interested in becoming a golf professional), the James Malone Jr. Scholarship, and the C.K. Robinson Scholarship.

Financial data: A stipend is awarded (amount not specified).

Duration: One year; may be renewed up to three additional years if the recipient maintains a GPA of 2.8 or higher

Number awarded: Varies each year; recently, three new scholarships and nine renewals were awarded.

Deadline: December of each year

367 WHO'S WHO SPORTS EDITION ALL-ACADEMIC BOWLING TEAM SCHOLARSHIPS

United States Bowling Congress
Attn: SMART Program
5301 S. 76th Street
Greendale, WI 53129-1192
Phone: (414) 423-3223; 800-514-BOWL, ext. 3223;
Fax: (414) 421-3014; Email: smart@bowl.com
Web: www.bowl.com/scholarships/main.aspx

Summary: To provide financial assistance for college to members of the United States Bowling Congress (USBC) Youth who are also recognized in *Who's Who Among American High School Students—Sports Edition*

Eligibility: This program is open to USBC Youth members who are juniors or seniors in high school. Applicants must have a GPA of 2.5 or higher and not have competed in a professional bowling tournament. They must be listed in the current edition of *Who's Who Among American High School Students—Sports Edition*. Along with their application, they must submit an essay of 500 words on how their involvement in bowling has influenced their life, academic, and personal goals. Financial need is not considered in the selection process.

Financial data: The stipend is $1,000.

Duration: One year, nonrenewable

Number awarded: Up to 20 each year

Deadline: March of each year

368 WILLIAM D. CLIFFORD SCHOLARSHIP

American Water Ski Educational Foundation
Attn: Director
1251 Holy Cow Road
Polk City, FL 33868-8200
Phone: (863) 324-2472; Fax: (863) 324-3996;
Email: info@waterskihalloffame.com
Web: www.waterskihalloffame.com

Summary: To provide financial assistance to currently enrolled college students who participate in water skiing

Eligibility: This program is open to full-time students at two- or four-year accredited colleges entering their sophomore, junior, or senior year. Applicants must be U.S. citizens and active members of a sport division within USA Water Ski (AWSA, ABC, AKA, WSDA, NSSA, NCWSA, NWSRA, USAWB, and HYD). Along with their application, they must submit a 500-word essay on a topic that changes annually but relates to water skiing; recently, students were asked to assume that they had just acquired the position of marketing director for the American Water Ski Educational Foundation and to describe the creative measures they would implement to increase membership in the foundation. Selection is based on the essay, academic record, leadership, extracurricular involvement, letters of recommendation, AWSA membership activities, and financial need.

Financial data: The stipend is $1,500 per year.

Duration: One year; may be renewed for up to two additional years.

Number awarded: One each year

Deadline: March of each year

---

369 WILLIAM (WIDDY) NEALE SCHOLARSHIPS

Connecticut State Golf Association
Attn: Scholarship Committee
35 Cold Spring Road, Suite 212
Rocky Hill, CT 06067
Phone: (860) 257-4171; Fax: (860) 257-8355;
Email: ctstategolf@asga.org
Web: www.csgalinks.org/widdyneale.htm

Summary: To provide financial assistance for college to high school seniors who have worked at a golf club that is a member of the Connecticut State Golf Association (CSGA)

Eligibility: This program is open to seniors graduating from high schools in Connecticut who have worked as a caddie or in another position (in the pro shop or with the maintenance crew or in the clubhouse, locker room, or dining room) at a CSGA member golf club for one full golf season. Applicants must be recommended by the CSGA club representative, golf professional, course superintendent, or other official; each club may recommend only one student. Selection is based on grades, character, citizenship, community service, and financial need.

Financial data: Stipends range from $1,000 to $2,000.

Duration: One year; may be renewed up to three additional years provided the recipient maintains satisfactory academic standing and continues to demonstrate financial need

Number awarded: Ten to 13 each year

Deadline: May of each year

---

370 WISCONSIN AMATEUR HOCKEY ASSOCIATION SCHOLARSHIPS

Wisconsin Amateur Hockey Association
c/o Don Kohlman, Secretary-Treasurer

P.O. Box 1509
Eagle River, WI 54521
Phone: (715) 479-3955; Fax: (715) 479-8717;
Email: dkohlman@wahahockey.com
Web: www.waha-hockey.com/scholarships.html

Summary: To provide financial assistance for college to high school seniors who have participated in activities of the Wisconsin Amateur Hockey Association (WAHA)

Eligibility: This program is open to graduating high school seniors who are among the top 20 players in their high school WAHA sectional. Applicants must be planning to enroll full-time at an accredited college, university, or technical school. Qualifying seniors are invited to complete an application that includes a list of their school and community activities and an essay on why they deserve the scholarship. Financial need is not considered in the selection process.

Financial data: The stipend is $1,000.

Duration: One year

Number awarded: Five each year

Deadline: April of each year

---

371 WISCONSIN AMERICAN LEGION BASEBALL SCHOLARSHIP

American Legion
Department of Wisconsin
Attn: Scholarship Chairperson
2930 American Legion Drive
P.O. Box 388
Portage, WI 53901-0388
Phone: (608) 745-1090; Fax: (608) 745-0179;
Email: info@wilegion.org
Web: www.wilegion.org/programs/legion_baseball_body.htm

Summary: To provide financial assistance for college to outstanding participants in the American Legion baseball program in Wisconsin

Eligibility: This program is open to Wisconsin residents who are in their final season of eligibility for American Legion baseball. Applicants must be planning to attend a four-year college or university, technical school, or two-year college. They must be a good citizen whose conduct on and off the field reflects credit on themselves, their family, their community, and the American Legion baseball program. Financial need is also considered.

Financial data: The stipend is $500.

Duration: One year

Number awarded: One each year

372 WISCONSIN AMERICAN LEGION SHOOTING SPORTS SCHOLARSHIP

American Legion
Department of Wisconsin
Attn: Scholarship Chairperson
2930 American Legion Drive
P.O. Box 388
Portage, WI 53901-0388
Phone: (608) 745-1090; Fax: (608) 745-0179;
Email: info@wilegion.org
Web: www.wilegion.org/scholarships/shooting_sports_body.htm
Summary: To provide financial assistance for college to outstanding participants in the American Legion air rifle program in Wisconsin
Eligibility: Candidates must have participated in the current American Legion regional or Wisconsin state championship junior position air rifle tournament.
Financial data: The award is a $1,000 scholarship.
Number awarded: One each year
Deadline: May of each year

373 WOMEN'S ALABAMA GOLF ASSOCIATION SCHOLARSHIPS

Women's Alabama Golf Association
1025 Montgomery Highway, Suite 210
Birmingham, AL 35216
Email: info@womensalabamagolf.com
Web: http://womensalabamagolf.com/Scholarships.asp
Summary: To provide financial assistance for college to women in Alabama who demonstrate an interest in golf
Eligibility: This program is open to women graduating from high schools in Alabama who are planning to attend a college or university in the state. Applicants must be able to demonstrate an interest in the game of golf and financial need. They must have an ACT score of 22 or higher. Along with their application, they must submit a 200-word statement on why a college education is important to them. Selection is based on academic excellence, citizenship, sportsmanship, community involvement, and financial need.
Financial data: The stipend is $2,000 per year.
Duration: One year; may be renewed if the recipient maintains a GPA of 2.4 or higher during her freshman year and 2.8 or higher during subsequent years
Number awarded: One each year
Deadline: March of each year

374 WOMEN'S BASKETBALL COACHES ASSOCIATION SCHOLARSHIP AWARDS

Women's Basketball Coaches Association
Attn: Manager of Awards
4646 Lawrenceville Highway
Lilburn, GA 30047-3620
Phone: (770) 279-8027, ext. 102; Fax: (770) 279-6290;
Email: alowe@wbca.org
Web: www.wbca.org/wbcascholaraward.asp
Summary: To provide financial assistance for undergraduate or graduate study to women's basketball players
Eligibility: This program is open to women's basketball players who are competing in any of the four intercollegiate divisions (NCAA Divisions I, II, and III and NAIA). Applicants must be interested in completing an undergraduate degree or beginning work on an advanced degree. They must be nominated by a member of the Women's Basketball Coaches Association (WBCA). Selection is based on sportsmanship, commitment to excellence as a student-athlete, honesty, ethical behavior, courage, and dedication to purpose.
Financial data: The stipend is $1,000 per year.
Duration: One year
Number awarded: Two each year

375 WOMEN'S GOLF ASSOCIATION OF MASSACHUSETTS JUNIOR SCHOLAR PROGRAM

Women's Golf Association of Massachusetts, Inc.
Attn: WGAM Junior Scholarship Fund, Inc.
William F. Connell Golf House & Museum
300 Arnold Palmer Boulevard
Norton, MA 02766
Phone: (774) 430-9010; Fax: (774) 430-9011;
Email: info@wgam.org
Web: www.wgam.org/Junior/jrschol.htm
Summary: To provide financial assistance for college to female golfers from Massachusetts
Eligibility: This program is open to junior female golfers who have participated in the Women's Golf Association of Massachusetts (WGAM) junior golf program. Applicants must be attending or planning to attend a college or university. Selection is based on high school academic record and performance, leadership qualities, community and civic involvement, character, personality, and extent of participation in the WGAM junior golf program. Financial need may determine the size of the stipend, but it is not considered in the selection process. An interview is required.
Financial data: A stipend is awarded (amount not specified).
Duration: One year, renewable
Number awarded: Varies each year; recently, eight of these scholarships were awarded.
Deadline: May of each year

376 WOMEN'S SOUTHERN GOLF ASSOCIATION SCHOLARSHIP

Women's Southern Golf Association
c/o Martha Lang
2075 Knollwood Place
Birmingham, AL 34242
Phone: (205) 995-6671; Email: scholarship@
womens-southerngolfassociation.org
Web: www.womens-southerngolfassociation.org/
scholar.htm

Summary: To provide financial assistance for college to women golfers in the southern states

Eligibility: This program is open to amateur female golfers who are residents of one of the 15 Southern states (Alabama, Arkansas, Florida, Georgia, Kentucky, Louisiana, Maryland, Mississippi, North Carolina, Oklahoma, South Carolina, Tennessee, Texas, Virginia, and West Virginia) or the District of Columbia. Applicants must be graduating high school seniors planning to work on an undergraduate degree at an accredited institution of higher learning. Along with their application, they must submit a 200-word essay on why a college education is important to them. Selection is based on academic excellence, citizenship, sportsmanship, and financial need.

Financial data: The stipend is $3,000 per year. Funds are paid directly to the recipient's college.

Duration: One year; may be renewed up to three additional years if the recipient maintains a GPA of 3.0 or higher

Number awarded: One each year

Deadline: May of each year

377 WOMEN'S WESTERN GOLF FOUNDATION SCHOLARSHIP

Women's Western Golf Foundation
c/o Mrs. Richard Willis
393 Ramsay Road
Deerfield, IL 60015
Web: www.wwga.org/scholarship_info.htm

Summary: To provide undergraduate scholarships to high school senior girls who are interested in the sport of golf

Eligibility: Applicants must be high school senior girls who intend to graduate in the year they submit their application. They must meet entrance requirements of, and plan to enroll at, an accredited college or university. Selection is based on academic achievement, financial need, excellence of character, and involvement with the sport of golf. Skill or excellence in the game is not a criterion.

Financial data: The stipend is $2,000 per year. The funds are to be used to pay for room, board, tuition, and other university fees or charges.

Duration: One year; may be renewed up to three additional years if the recipient maintains a GPA of 3.0 or higher

Number awarded: Fifteen each year

Deadline: February of each year

378 WSCCA SCHOLARSHIPS

Washington State Cheerleading Coaches Association
c/o Kathy Crowley, Scholarship Committee
3419 107th Street N.W.
Gig Harbor, WA 98332
Phone: (253) 851-8960; Email: djcrow46@comcast.net
Web: www.wscca.com

Summary: To provide financial assistance for college to cheerleaders in Washington whose coach is a member of the Washington State Cheerleading Coaches Association (WSCCA)

Eligibility: This program is open to seniors graduating from high schools in Washington with a GPA of 3.0 or higher. Applicants must be cheerleaders whose coach is a WSCCA member. Along with their application, they must submit a 500-word essay on any life skills they learned through cheerleading that will be helpful in the future. Selection is based on that essay, three letters of recommendation, transcripts, and community service; financial need is not considered.

Financial data: A stipend is awarded (amount not specified).

Duration: One year

Number awarded: Varies; a total of $15,000 is available for this program each year.

Deadline: February of each year

379 YOUTH EDUCATION SUMMIT SCHOLARSHIPS

National Rifle Association of America
Attn: Field Operations Division, Event Services Coordinator
11250 Waples Mill Road
Fairfax, VA 22030
Phone: (703) 267-1354; 800-423-6894;
Fax: (703) 267-3743; Email: nraf@nrahq.org
Web: www.nrafoundation.org/yes/scholarship_info.asp

Summary: To provide financial assistance for college to high school students who participate in the Youth Education Summit (Y.E.S.) of the National Rifle Association (NRA)

Eligibility: This program is open to high school sophomores and juniors who have a GPA of 3.0 or higher.

Applicants must submit transcripts, information on their extracurricular and shooting sports activities, essays of two to three pages on the second amendment and gun control, recommendations, and a personal statement on why they are a good candidate for this program. Based on their applications, approximately 40 students each year are chosen to visit the Washington, D.C., area in June to spend 7 days touring the city and learning about American government and history, the U.S. Constitution, the Bill of Rights, and the role and mission of the association. The participants in the program judged as most outstanding, based on their original applications and their work in Washington, are selected to receive these scholarships.

Financial data: The stipends are $1,500 or $1,000. Funds are paid directly to the accredited college or technical school of the student's choice.

Duration: These scholarships are presented annually.

Number awarded: Ten each year: five at $1,500 and five at $1,000

Deadline: February of each year

380 YOUTH MEMBER OF THE YEAR

American Paint Horse Association
Attn: Director of Youth Activities
2800 Meacham Boulevard
P.O. Box 961023
Fort Worth, TX 76161-0023
Phone: (817) 834-APHA, ext. 248; Fax: (817) 834-3152;
Email: coordinator@ajpha.com
Web: www.ajpha.com/contest.html

Summary: To recognize and reward outstanding members of the American Junior Paint Horse Association (AJPHA)

Eligibility: This program is open to current AJPHA members who are 18 years of age or younger. Candidates must be nominated by an American Paint Horse Association (APHA) or AJPHA regional club. Selection is based on local, regional, and national AJPHA activities; additional horse-related activities; volunteer work in the community that is horse-related; additional community activities, jobs, or volunteer work; special efforts and accomplishments in promoting the paint horse (other than showing in an APHA-approved show); and school activities.

Financial data: The winner receives a $500 savings bond and a custom-designed belt buckle.

Duration: The award is presented annually.

Number awarded: One each year

Deadline: May of each year

SCHOLARSHIP INDEX

SPORTS INDEX

Use this index when you want to identify funding programs by a specific sports area. In addition to looking for terms that represent your specific sports interests, be sure to check the "Any Sport" entries; programs listed there provide funding to students who have participated in sports but do not require participation in a specific sport. Remember: The numbers cited in this index refer to book entry numbers, not to page numbers in the book.

RESIDENCY INDEX

Some programs listed in this book are restricted to residents of a particular city, county, state, or region. The Residency Index will help you pinpoint programs available only to residents in your area as well as programs that have no residency restrictions (these are listed under "United States"). To use this index, look up the geographic areas that apply to you (always check the listings under "United States"), jot down the entry numbers listed, and use those numbers to find the program descriptions in the directory. The scholarships are categorized as either General Scholar-Athlete scholarships or Sport-Specific scholarships. To help you in your search, we've provided some "see also" references in each index entry. Remember: The numbers cited here refer to program entry numbers, not to page numbers in the book.

TENABILITY INDEX

Some programs listed in this book can be used only in specific cities, counties, states, or regions. Others may be used anywhere in the United States (or even abroad). The Tenability Index will help you locate funding that is restricted to a specific area as well as funding that has no tenability restrictions (these are listed under "United States"). To use this index, look up the geographic areas where you'd like to go (always check the listings under "United States"), jot down the entry numbers listed there, and use those numbers to find the program descriptions in the directory. The scholarships are categorized as either General Scholar-Athlete scholarships or Sport-Specific scholarships. To help you in your search, we've provided some "see also" references in each index entry. Remember: The numbers cited here refer to program entry numbers, not to page numbers in the book.

SPONSORING ORGANIZATION INDEX

The Sponsoring Organization Index makes it easy to identify agencies that offer college funding to students who have participated in sports. In this index, sponsoring organizations are listed alphabetically, word by word. In addition, we've used a code (within parentheses) to help you determine if the funding is restricted to specific athletic activities or not. Here's how the codes work: if an organization's name is followed by (G) 41, the program sponsored by that organization is described in entry 41 and is categorized as a General Scholar-Athlete scholarship. If that sponsoring organization's name is followed by another entry number—for example: (S) 275—the same or a different program is described in entry 275 and is categorized as a Sport-Specific scholarship. Remember: the numbers cited here refer to program entry numbers, not to page numbers in the book.